QUALITY IN HEALTH CARE

Theory, Application, and Evolution

Edited by

Nancy O. Graham, DrPH, RN

Vice President
Nursing /Total Quality Management
Lawrence Hospital
Bronxville, New York

AN ASPEN PUBLICATION®
Aspen Publishers, Inc.
Gaithersburg, Maryland
1995

η-95

Library of Congress Cataloging-in-Publication Data

Quality in health care : theory, application, and evolution / edited
by Nancy O. Graham.
p.   cm.
Includes bibliographical references and index.
ISBN 0-8342-0625-0
1. Medical care—Quality control. 2 Medical care—Quality
control—History—United States. I. Graham, Nancy O.
[DNLM: 1. Quality of Health Care—trends—United States.
2. Total Quality Management. 3. Organizational Innovation. W 84 AA1 Q225
1995]
RA399.A1Q345   1995
362.1'068'5—dc20
DNLM/DLC
For Library of Congress
94-44355
CIP

Editorial Resources: Ruth Bloom

Library of Congress Catalog Card Number: 94-44355
ISBN: 0-8342-0625-0

Printed in the United States of America

1 2 3 4 5

To Irving Abrahams,
my Husband and Friend

To Pamela Jertson and Jill Jertson,
my Daughters
and
Paul Schumacher,
my Son in Law
With Much Love

To Grace Graham,
my Mother
With Special Appreciation

To Julia, Michael, Eve, John, and Charles
With Affection

and

In Memory of Donald Graham,
my Father
Very Special Thanks

Table of Contents

Foreword

The rapidly changing social and economic environment, and rapidly changing technologies, are challenging our perceptions of quality as it relates to health care. All of our old boundaries are being challenged. Many of our concepts of quality have been based upon medical and surgical care in hospitals, using traditional quality assurance or quality control concepts. By looking at care and recovery settings beyond the inpatient setting, how is quality measured? By looking at the long-term outcomes of care, the efficacy and appropriateness of care will be challenged. Are the six-month, one-year, and five-year outcomes significantly altered by different treatments? This introduces a whole new dimension to the quality of care. Now with technology, we have the capacity to keep people alive beyond any reasonable quality of life. So we must now consider not just quality of care, but quality of life. With technology offering genetic changes, what does quality mean? At the other end of the scale, if we really focus on maintaining and improving health, our old measures of quality are meaningless. Maintenance of quality of life, as defined by the person may be more important. Many of these changes challenge our goals and ethics. From whose perspective should quality be measured—the patient's or the health care professional's?

Nancy Graham's previous publications, *Quality Assurance in Hospitals* (1982, 1990) have established her as one of the authorities in quality assurance. In this book, she has integrated the works of several authors, and provided thoughtful bridges to take a much broader look at quality yesterday, today, and tomorrow. She has assembled a set of landmark papers that address a wide range of meaningful topics related to quality. Dr. Graham and the other authors take us far beyond the roots of quality assurance to the new paradigms of the future.

Beginning with the history of quality establishes an excellent context for discussions of current and future issues. The presentation of the history of quality starts much earlier than most of us acknowledge—as early as 2000 B.C. The landmark works of Dr. Avedis Donabedian on quality, and Dr. John Wennberg on variation of care, set the stage for Dr. Don Berwick's work on continuous improvement that changed the way we look at quality.

A wide range of important current topics related to quality are presented, including Total Quality Management, improvement thinking, critical paths, practice guidelines, outcomes measurement, benchmarking, and learning organizations. Practical methods, examples, and case studies are presented, in addition to the concepts and models. The perspectives of patients, physicians, and staff are addressed to present their views and avoid barriers to implementation.

As we look into the future, all of our concepts about health care, and the professionals and organizations that address health care, will be challenged. These authors offer views of the future that can help us consider our options and set our directions. In the future, there will almost certainly be more focus on maintaining health. This will be a vitally important, but difficult, transition for an industry that has been dominantly focused on caring for the sick in hospitals. To make this transition, health care leaders, health care professionals, government agencies, employers, and especially the people within this country will have to address issues like:

- What is health, and how will we measure quality of health?
- What is quality of life, and who has the right to determine this?
- How will quality of health and health care services be measured and judged?
- Who has the right to make judgments about quality—the patient, the family, the health care professional, the employer, the insurer, or the public?
- Will patients become full partners in their health and health care?
- How widely will data be shared about the community, employers, health care institutions, health care providers, and individual patients?

These questions, and many others regarding quality of life and quality of care, cannot be answered in the absence of values and ethics. But, as many of the authors in this book point out, it is in answering these questions that we will redefine quality in health care for today and tomorrow.

As a start, we can all benefit by understanding the works in this book.

—Richard J. Coffey, Ph.D.
Director of Program and Operations Analysis
University of Michigan Hospitals
Ann Arbor, Michigan

Preface

Nancy O. Graham

Times are changing! There have been more changes in the 1990s than at any other time in the history of health care. In fact, the pressure for change is growing stronger.[1] Since the first two editions of my book, *Quality Assurance in Hospitals* (1982, 1990), the quality movement has gone from evolution to revolution. Sweeping changes in the industry no longer permit us just to look at "assuring" quality in hospitals, but mandate that we take a broader approach to continuously improve quality in health care. Thus, the new title—*Quality in Health Care*. It is not business as usual.

The purpose of this book is to examine health care quality from a historical perspective—pragmatic in approach, but with a theoretical basis. It reflects where we came from, where we are today, where we will be tomorrow; and it makes some predictions, or at least asks some questions, about the day after tomorrow. It is hoped that the reading will help provoke the "knowledge"[2] that Deming spoke about and will encourage us all to gain an understanding of the underlying processes of our work.

The future will belong to those who embrace the potential of wider opportunities while recognizing this reality: That more constrained resources compel us to find new situations that permit doing more with less.[3] Barker defines three keys to the success of organization in the future:

> excellence, innovation, and anticipation. Excellence is at the base of the list because it is at the base of the twenty-first century. Many . . . justify the importance of excellence in Total Quality Management (TQM) because they believe it will give them a competitive edge in the twenty-first century. I don't believe that. I say it will give them a competitive edge only until the end of the decade. After that, it becomes the price of entry. If you do not have the component of excellence—statistics process control, continuous improvement, benchmarking and the constant pursuit of excellence—the capability

of knowing how to do the right thing the first time—then you don't even get to play the game.[4]

This book is written for students, practitioners, health care executives, quality improvement professionals, health planners, and other professionals, but first and foremost, for individuals who are continuously learning and have the capacity to change.

This book is divided into three parts: "Yesterday," "Today," and "Tomorrow." At the end of each part introduction questions are presented for thought, discussion, and research. The appendices at the end of this book provide additional information. Appendix A, a case study about the implementation of Total Quality Management in a community hospital, gives a snap shot of some of the trials faced and successes enjoyed on the journey of continuous improvement. Appendix B is an article about the peer review organization and its new approach to improving care for Medicare beneficiaries. In Appendix C, the Joint Commission on Accreditation of Healthcare Organizations defines clinical performance standards and shifts the main focus from the performance of individuals to the organization's system or processes. Appendix D provides a glossary of terms used throughout this book.

Future successes, both individual and organizational, depend on the ability for continuous improvement. The journey to quality begins one step at a time; it is often arduous, but is a matter of survival, demanding superior clinical quality, superb service, and innovation. To paraphrase Tolstoy in *Anna Karenina:* Quality health care organizations are all alike; every poor quality organization is dysfunctional each in it's own way.[5]

NOTES

1. E. Gaucher and R. Coffey, *Total Quality in Healthcare* (Gaithersburg, Md: Aspen Publishers, Inc., 1993), xxi.

2. P. Batalden, Building Knowledge for Quality Improvement in Health-Care: An Individual Glossary, *Journal of Quality Assurance* 13, no. 5 (1991): 8.

3. R. Kanter, *When Giants Learn to Dance* (New York: Simon & Schuster, 1989), 18.

4. J. Barker, *Future Edge: Discovering the New Paradigms of Success* (New York: William Morrow, 1992), 12.

5. L. Tolstoy, *Anna Karenina* (New York: The Heritage Press, 1952), 1.

Acknowledgments

I want to acknowledge a number of people. First, John Racine, PhD, University of Hawaii, for his inspiration, creativity, and enthusiasm to get started. Dr. Stephen Rosenberg, Clinical Professor, School of Public Health, Columbia University, was never too busy over the years to help clarify direction and put things in perspective. His continual help is appreciated. To Dr. Aron Ron, Senior Vice President of Medical Affairs and Medical Education, New York Downtown Hospital; Dr. David Nash, Director of Health Policy, Thomas Jefferson University Hospital, Philadelphia; Ms. Peggy Sawyer, Manager, Peat Marwick; Dee Roberts, CPQI Coordinator, Maine Medical Center; and Dr. Jamsetta A. Halley-Boyce, Assistant Vice President and Director of Nursing Services, University Hospital of Brooklyn—a special thanks.

I also wish to acknowledge additional friends and colleagues for their insight, support, and help: Roger Dvorak, Rita DiPippo, Steven Schoener, Mary Villeneuve, Virgil Larkin, Elizabeth Walsh, and Maureen Connolly. Additionally there is the Lawrence Hospital team, which contributed to my learning and embraced the theory to make it work.

PART I.

YESTERDAY

Part I, "Yesterday", is intended to establish the historical basis of quality in health care in the U.S. The field of quality assurance and quality improvement is dynamic and we need to understand its beginnings and current trends in order to be open to the possibilities of the future. In Chapter 1, Dr. Graham puts quality of care activities into a historical perspective in the twentieth century in the United States. She discusses some of the key studies and the shift from quality assessment, to quality assurance, to quality improvement. In Chapter 2, Dr. Racine discusses quality in health care throughout recorded time, and speculates on the future of quality in health care. In addition to reviewing quality issues from the distant past to tomorrow, he also discusses the rich sources of innovation for the future that lie in the international experience or are now in use in other industries. These unexplored frontiers deserve a "double take." Chapters 1 and 2 set the stage for Chapters 3, 4, and 5, which are classics in the field.

In Chapter 3, Dr. Donabedian elaborates on the issues raised in Chapter 1. Before assessment can begin, however, quality must first be defined. The following topics are therefore discussed in this chapter:

- Does one assess only the performance of a practitioner or also the contribution of patients and of the health care system?
- Is monetary cost a consideration?
- What are the causal linkages among structure, process, and outcome?
- How does one specify the components of care to be sampled?
- What is the source of the information?

1

In Chapter 4, Dr. Wennberg, who pioneered the study of small market area variation in practice patterns, reviews the effects of differences in structure and process (which may or may not result in variations in outcome) on costs for individual hospitals and area-wide systems. In Chapter 5, Dr. Berwick states that the time is ripe for new directions in the quality measurement field in health care. The theory of continuous improvement, which he espouses, holds some badly needed answers for American health care.

QUESTIONS FOR THOUGHT, DISCUSSION, AND RESEARCH

1. What is quality?
2. How can it be measured?
3. What are the key organizational issues?
4. Can we afford quality?
5. Can we afford not to have quality?
6. Can the Total Quality Managment (TQM) method successfully applied to other industries be applied to health care?
7. What is the link between structure, process, and outcome?
8. What are the best methods of feedback to change practice patterns?
9. Are the institutional and professional cultures ready for TQM?
10. If Quality Improvement (QI) is accepted, where is the best place to put it in the organization and with what level of support?
11. What type of information is required by purchasers, providers, and patients to assess quality?
12. What is the effect of regulation on quality?

1. Quality Trends in Health Care

Nancy O. Graham

Let the reader be reminded at the start of this journey of continuous quality improvement that the three major issues facing health care today are: cost, quality, and access. Just one month after his inauguration, President Clinton delivered his State of the Union address to the U.S. Congress in which he stated, "In 1992, Americans spent eight hundred and forty billion dollars on health care or fourteen percent of the GDP, compared to nine percent of GDP only a dozen years ago. At this rate, health spending will reach an astonishing eighteen percent of GDP by the year 2000".[1]

A report of the National Academy of Science, Institute of Medicine, confirms what few policy makers acknowledge, that "poor quality health care is a major problem in the United States."[2] The Institute of Medicine cited widespread overuse of expensive, invasive technology; underuse of inexpensive caring services; and error-prone implementation of care that harms patients and wastes money.[3,4] Poor quality often increases the cost of care in the long run—through waste, rework, and duplication. By implication then, quality improvement is a key ingredient of a reformed health care system. And—as is well known—37 million Americans have no health insurance.

This book is being published at a critical time. Our nation is searching for new ways to design and implement a high quality but a cost-effective health care system. It is a time of transformation—a time of revolution.

THREE MODELS FOR DELIVERING HEALTH CARE

In this century, three conceptual models for organizing health care have emerged—the professional, bureaucratic, and industrial models.[5] All deal in different ways with the issues of control, responsibility, production, and financing. The professional model exists primarily as a means for physicians to

3

organize and control their work. Professional standards are evaluated by peers. The primary mechanism for quality control is the personal responsibility and integrity of each physician. There are also external mechanisms for promoting quality such as specialty boards, the Joint Commission on Accreditation of Healthcare Organizations (Joint Commission), and state licensing departments.

By the 1960s, the pace of change in medical sciences and health care was moving so rapidly that changes in organizational design would become inevitable. As more effective health care technologies emerged, the variety and complexity of service expanded: intensive care units, large multi-specialty group practices, Health Maintenance Organizations (HMOs), and an increase in other types of professionals (i.e., technicians, therapists, etc.). With so many types of personnel working together, communication and coordination became a key to quality of care. "The participants in health care are seen differently in the bureaucratic model as opposed to the professional model. Those who are cared for are not patients but beneficiaries; individual physicians are seen as providers or even as "vendors", terms that also apply to hospital group practices.[6] To minimize the clash between the professional and bureaucratic cultures, hospitals and HMOs usually have separate hierarchies for professionals such as one for physicians and nurses and one for general administration. Each administers its own rules, but none has the authority to change the rules of the other hierarchy. Thus, changing procedures to improve quality is difficult.

In the 1970s, the strategy for quality in the bureaucratic model was enforced through two channels. The first, accreditation by the Joint Commission, had virtually become mandatory as the means for a hospital to be certified as a Medicare provider. In 1974, the Joint Commission mandated the internal quality audit. The second form of mandatory quality assurance was federal legislation that set up the Professional Standards Review Organization (PSRO) program for Medicare and Medicaid. The PSRO conducted utilization review, profile analysis, and medical care evaluation.

Both internal and external quality review were resisted by physicians, who saw them as an attack on professional autonomy. Professional resistance to quality assurance increased because quality assurance, when implemented within bureaucratic institutions, had little impact on quality.

During the 1980s, the industrial model was introduced to health care where job performance is judged not by conformance to rules, but by externally valued criteria—profitability and market share. In this model, patients become customers or consumers rather than beneficiaries. Physicians are either employees or partners (hospital/HMO). In the industrial model, the stimuli for quality comes from the need to survive in a competitive environment.

During the 1980s and 1990s, American corporations began to revise and expand their approach to quality in health care. Quality assurance activities were absorbed into a more comprehensive strategy for quality improvement. Quality must be the preoccupation of top leaders, linked to profitability and defined from the customer perspective. Corporations compete on the basis of quality.[7] Quality is a way to delight your customers and to exceed their expectations.

HISTORICAL PERSPECTIVE

It is key at the macro level to understand these models—professional, bureaucratic, and industrial—so that we can interpret our successes and failures in our efforts to improve quality. It is also important at the micro level to understand Donabedian's classification of the three data types: *structure* (attributes of the setting in which care occurs), *process* (what is actually done in giving or receiving care), and *outcome* (effects of care on the health of patients or of populations).[8] "It is truly awesome to recognize the richness of our historical heritage in quality assessment and to discover that so many others have struggled with the same problems and tried so many of the same solutions we naively consider original today."[9] Understanding the past, while anticipating the future, is our challenge and opportunity. In a world of rapid change, we must do the right things, the right way, the first time.

Laying the Foundation

In the 1860s, Florence Nightingale helped to lay the foundation for quality assurance programs by advocating a uniform system for collecting and evaluating hospital statistics. Her statistics showed that mortality rates varied significantly from hospital to hospital.

In 1910, a report by Dr. Abraham Flexner revealed the poor quality of medical education in the United States. This report was instrumental in closing 60 of 155 U.S. medical schools by 1920. It was also influential in introducing more stringent admission requirements and effecting changes in the curriculum. History has shown that this report aided the education of minorities, who previously had not been admitted to medical schools.[10]

One of the key pioneers in assessing quality was Dr. E. A. Codman, who, in 1914, studied the end results of care. His famous study emphasized the same issues that are being discussed today when examining the quality of care, including: (1) the importance of licensure or certification of providers; (2) the accreditation of institutions; (3) the necessity of taking into consideration the severity or stage of the disease; (4) the issue of comorbidity (two or more illnesses present at one time); (5) the health and illness behavior of the patient; and (6) economic barriers to receiving care.[11]

When the American College of Surgeons was established in 1913, one of its explicit goals was the improvement of patient care in hospitals. Thus, in 1918 it inaugurated the Hospital Standardization Program that established the concept of hospital accreditation as a formal means of assuring good hospital care. The results of the first survey conducted under this program pointed out the severe problems facing hospitals. Of the 692 hospitals surveyed, only 90 (12.9 percent) were approved. By 1950, however, 94.6 percent qualified for approval.[12]

From the 1920s to the 1940s, few advances were made in the area of quality assessment. One might speculate that the public was engrossed in recovering from World War I and coping with the Great Depression.[13]

Quality Becomes Institutional Concern

In the next two decades (1940s to 1960s), the public developed increasing interest in the organization, planning, and evaluation of health care service and demands for accessibility. With the growth of the nonsurgical specialties after World War II, and with the general recognition of the success of the American College of Surgeons' program of accreditation, it soon became clear that the approval programs should be supported by the entire medical and hospital fields. Accordingly, in 1952, the Joint Commission on Accreditation of Hospitals (currently known as the Joint Commission on Accreditation of Healthcare Organizations) was established to assume responsibility for the accreditation program. The purpose of the Joint Commission was to encourage voluntary attainment of uniformly high standards of institutional care in all health care areas (i.e. nursing, x-ray, pharmacy).[14] The emphasis was on structural standards. It was assumed that if you had the capability to give good care, good care would follow. Also during the 1960s, three important process studies were published, each using a different method. Dr. O. L. Peterson observed the quality of care delivered by general practitioners. Dr. M. A. Morehead studied the quality of ambulatory care provided by the Health Insurance Plan. She scored their practice on the basis of adequacy of the history, physical examination, therapy, and follow-up. Dr. B. C. Payne studied the care given in a select group of short-term hospitals by comparing the information in the medical record against a set of disease-specific criteria established by a group of physicians. All three found major problems with the quality of care.[15]

In the 1960s, the public developed greater expectations about health care. The decade was marked by concern for consumer protection, human rights, and the concept of health care as a right. In the courts, major precedents that directly relate to quality of care were established. In the *Darling v. Charleston Community Memorial Hospital* (1965) and in the *Gonzales v. Nork and Mercy Hospital* (1966) cases, it was held that hospitals and their medical staffs have the right and obligation to oversee the quality of professional services rendered by individual staff members. In the *Darling* case, under the theory of corporate liability, the Charleston Community Memorial Hospital was held independently liable for its own negligence in connection with the negligence of a physician practicing in the hospital. The ruling was that a hospital, because it has the authority to regulate the practice of medicine, has a legal duty to do so. A breach of this duty can constitute negligence independent of that of a physician who practices in the hospital. Quality of care has thus become an institutional concern, with a focus expanding beyond the physician/patient interaction.[16] It was also in the 1960s that the federal government became involved in a financing of health care with the passage of Medicare and Medicaid legislation. This brought increased government regulations, particularly structural standards to nursing homes and acute-care organizations. In the nursing sector, the primary focus was on process studies. Leaders in the field were Maria Phaneuf and Eleanor Lambertson. In the medical sector, Donabedian described the difference between structure, process, and outcome and urged the development of criteria for evaluating care. These studies set the stage for a mixed focus in the decade to follow.[17]

The 1970s were plagued with the rising cost of care, inflation, and a rising interest in professional accountability. In 1972, Congress passed PL 92-603, creating the PSRO. The Professional Standard Review Organization (PSRO) program was enacted into law on October 30, 1972 as part of the 1972 amendments to the Social Security Act. This law created a nationwide system of medical peer review. The PSRO law was intended to assure that services provided under Medicare, Medicaid, and the Maternal and Child Health Act were: (1) medically necessary, (2) of a quality that meets professional standards, and (3) provided at the most economical level consistent with quality care.[18] A high degree of variability in its performance led to the program's general ineffectiveness. A number of established interests felt threatened. Many physicians viewed the PSRO as an attempt to control their livelihood. Hospital administrations assumed the role of bystanders since they were not guaranteed a seat at the PSRO table, even though hospitals were responsible for absorbing the economic impact of PSRO.

Focus Shifts to Quality Assessment

Interest in quality assessment accelerated, however, during the 1970s. The traditional method of assessing due process of care through the review of the health care record utilized a list of explicit criteria that left no room for individual variations. The alternative—loose, unwritten, implicit criteria—lacked objectivity and reliability.[19] A modification of the traditional process assessment was criteria mapping. Criteria mapping uses a branching format that enables application of only those criteria items that are relevant to a given patient.[20] Rutstein suggested monitoring of "sentinel events"—truly egregious but rare events such as a maternal death—that imply a failure in quality of care.[21]

The tracer approach to quality assessment was developed by Kessner, et al., to evaluate care provided by a neighborhood health care center. Kessner believed that one could judge the functioning of an entire health care system by studying certain "tracer" health problems, such as essential elements of history and physical examination and necessary lab tests for a particular diagnosis.[22]

A health accounting system of quality assurance was developed by Dr. J. Williamson and his staff at Johns Hopkins in collaboration with 23 hospitals and clinics. It is a five-stage, clinical process in which priorities are set, desired outcomes are stipulated, and actual outcomes are measured. If desired and actual outcomes differ, a definitive assessment is carried out to determine the reason or reasons for this difference; corrective actions are then taken and outcomes are reassessed. The cycle continues until actual outcomes reach an acceptable level. The method is extremely flexible and combines measures of outcome with whatever method of "definitive assessment" is relevant in each situation: chart audit for process review, assessment of structure, evaluation of patient knowledge or satisfaction, etc. By including corrective actions and reevaluations, health accounting becomes not just a method of quality assessment but a model for a "quality assurance" approach to quality assurance. It was a forerunner, in many ways, to the industrial model of quality improvement.[23]

The staging methodology developed by Gonnella, et al., is an outcome-based system for assessing and assuring the quality of ambulatory care. Staging involves defining levels of severity for specific medical or surgical problems. The method calls for the separation of a medical problem into three stages: (stage one) a condition with no complications or with problems of minimal severity; (stage two) a condition with local complications or with problems of moderate severity; and (stage three) a condition with systemic complications or with problems of maximal severity. The basic assumption in staging is that a patient's condition at a specific point is a reliable yardstick for determining the outcome of previous parts of the process.[24]

The Performance Evaluation Procedure (PEP), developed by the Joint Commission, is a retrospective outcome-based approach to audit that uses patient records to identify possible problems in the delivery of patient care.[25] Concurrent Quality Assurance (CQA) was part of the PSRO program, which tested a method of CQA that monitored the technical quality of care given Medicare and Medicaid patients while they were hospitalized.[26]

Linking Costs to Outcomes

Cost containment efforts dominated the 1980s and 1990s. In the mid-1980s, however, there was a growing concern relating to the quality of health care. In 1983, an amendment to Social Security mandated a prospective reimbursement system based on Diagnosis-Related Groups (DRGs) for Medicare recipients. Under this system, hospitals are paid a predetermined rate for each DRG, regardless of the length of stay.[27] In 1982, Congress repealed the PSRO program and replaced it with a new initiative called the Utilization and Quality Control Peer Review Program (PRO).[28] The PRO program arose from the failure of the PSRO program to reduce costs. The PROs reviewed claims for Medicare services to determine reasonableness, medical necessity, and quality of care as well as appropriateness. The PROs had greater authority in recommending sanctions against hospitals, physicians, and nurses than the PSRO. In addition to flagging cases for retrospective review, PROs were required to conduct concurrent preadmission reviews for specific diagnosis and preprocedure reviews. Denial of payment for substandard care, as well as notification of beneficiaries of such decisions, was required by the third phase of the PRO. The fourth phase of work went into effect in 1993, with greater emphasis on education, population, and trend analysis (see Appendix B).

Two interesting studies on quality in the 1980s are those of Knaus and Wennberg. Knaus, et al.,[29] combined structure, process, and outcome in evaluating intensive care units in 13 hospitals. By examining all three aspects of care, they were able to identify the specific aspects of structure and process that affect patient mortality. Wennberg,[30] who pioneered the study of small market area variation in practice patterns, studied the effects of differences in structure and process, which may or may not result in variation in outcomes or costs for individual hospitals and area-wide systems.

In the mid-to-late 1980s, the industrial model or TQM as espoused by Deming, Juran, and Crosby[31] was receiving increased attention. Their strategies for quality improvement were based on the assumption that an organization's quality problems reside predominately in the system, not in its people. Quality improvement necessitated an organizational culture committed to high quality.

The focus on outcomes continues in the 1990s with the emphasis on relating costs to outcomes. The 1990s have also seen a resurgence of interest in health services research. The Joint Commission is responding to this social mandate for measurement. In 1994, the Joint Commission launched the Indicator Measurement System (IM System), a national data base of process and outcome measures.[32] With the demand for performance measurement at the forefront of the national health care agenda, the IM System represents a national source for health care data. The public is demanding accountability at every level of health care. Major decisions by health care organizations, patients, and purchasers will increasingly be based on the results of outcome measures and the subsequent evaluation of the process of care. It is imperative that the data used are valid, reliable, and meaningful. An example with the use of indicators from one of the pilot sites showed that faulty operating room table equipment was found after further analysis of the rate of post-anesthesia peripheral neurological defects.

Exhibit 1-1 Twentieth Century Quality Trends in Health Care

YEAR: DATA TYPE:	1920	1920–1940	1940–1960	1960	1970	1980	1990
	Structure Outcome	Process Structure	Process Structure	Process Structure	Process Structure	Process Structure Outcome	Process Structure Outcome
MODEL:	Professional			Bureaucratic / Increased regulations		Industrial	

MEASUREMENT TYPE:	Implicit criteria, peer review.			Explicit criteria, focused case review, sentinel event, technical aspects versus art of care.	Profile and pattern analysis	Patient satisfaction
						- Indicator rate, population based, adjusted for case mix and severity.
						Quality of life, practice guidelines
						  - benchmarking
						  - improving systems
						  - performance measure, value added, statistical outcome.	

PEOPLE DEFINITION:	Physicians are: Physicians Patients are: Patients			Physicians are: vendors or providers Patients are: beneficiaries		Physicians are: employees/partners Patients are: customers	

	Minimum Standard Capability	Requirement	Expectation
DEFINITION OF QUALITY:	Absence of defect. / Structural standards, capacity to give good care.	Optimal achievable results, medical necessity, negative indices, unnecessary disease and death or disability. / Degree of adherence to generally recognized contemporary standards of good practice and anticipated outcomes.	Performance measurement, meeting customers' expectations, the idea of mutliple customers, not just patients, doing the right thing well. - availability - timeliness - effective- ness - continuity - safety - efficiency - respect - care Services that are clinically efficient, clinically effective, affordable, patient satisfaction.
PUBLIC EXPECTATION:	Concern with other political and economic issues. / Increased interest in organizational planning and evaluation of health care.	Increased public expectations, consumer protection human rights, health care as a right / Costs - inflation - rising costs - increased interest in professional accountability	Quality - cost + value - access - accountability - performance

In 1994, all hospitals are required to participate actively in some comparative information data base such as the IM System, the Maryland Hospital Association Quality Indicator Project, or others. The purpose is twofold: (1) to serve as a basis for improvement, and (2) to serve as a basis for decisions for payers as well as the public.

The transition to a completely reorganized accreditation manual for hospitals began in 1994 when the Standards emphasized organization performance rather than structural standards.[33] By 1995, the Joint Commission is expected to be reorganized into three sectors:

1. Patient care functions including patient assessment, patient, and family education
2. Organizational functions including leadership, prevention, and control of infection
3. Essential structural components including the governing body, management and administration, medical staff and nursing, and medication use

CONCLUSION

Quality assurance activity during the twentieth century showed uneven progress. Exhibit 1–1 provides a snapshot of U.S. quality activities during this time period. "Data Type" indicates whether emphasis was placed on structure, process, or outcome. "Model" stresses the main focus at a particular point in time (today all three models—professional, bureaucratic, industrial—are interacting). The "People Definition" provides insight into how our perception of the roles of physicians and patients has changed over time. In a like manner, the "Definition of Quality" indicates that our standards for care have evolved from the capability to give good care (i.e., MD is certified), to the need to ensure that customer expectations are met. As this exhibit shows, "Public Expectations" have changed dramatically over time, with demands for patient satisfaction greatly increasing in recent years. "We can sum up the experience with quality assurance in the 1970s and 1980s by saying much was learned about quality measurement but dramatic gain in quality of care did not result. Physicians, especially, clung to the professional model."[34] A distaste for quality assurance seemed justified when implemented within bureaucratic health care institutions—it had little effect. Japanese companies made astonishing gains in quality by introducing the industrial model as espoused by Deming, Juran, Crosby, etc. and American industry also began restructuring itself along the same lines. This movement towards TQM or Continuous Quality Improvement (CQI) has now begun to energize the quality movement in health care.

NOTES

1. W.J. Clinton, *A Vision of Change for America*. A report accompanying an address to Joint Session of Congress, February 17, 1993. (Washington, D.C.).

2. K.N. Lohr, *Medicare: A Strategy for Quality Assurance. Vol. 1*. (Washington, DC: National Academy Press, 1990).

3. Lohr, *Medicare*.

4. R.H. Palmer, Confronting Special Implementation Issue: The Epidemiology of Quality Problems, in *Medicare: New Directions in Quality Assurance*, eds. M.S. Donaldson, J. Harris-Wehling, and K.N. Lohr (Washington, DC: National Academy Press, 1991), 96–104.

5. R.H. Palmer, Quality Improvement/Quality Assurance Taxonomy: A Framework, in *Putting Research to Work in Quality Improvement and Quality Assurance*, eds. M. Grady, J. Bernstein, S. Robinson (Washington, DC: U.S. Department of Health and Human Resources, Public Health Service, Agency for Health Care Policy and Research, 1993), 13–37.

6. Palmer, Quality Improvement/Quality Assurance Taxonomy.

7. Ibid.

8. A. Donabedian, The Quality of Care: How Can It Be Assessed?, *Journal of American Medical Association* 260, no. 12 (1988): 1743–1748.

9. J.W. Williamson, Future Policy Directions for Quality Assurance: Lessons from the Health Accounting Experience, *Inquiry* 25 (1988): 67–77.

10. A. Flexner, *Medical Education in the United States and Canada*, A Report to the Carnegie Foundation for the Advancement of Teaching (New York: Carnegie Foundation Bulletin, 1910).

11. E.A. Codman, The Product of the Hospital, *Surgical Gynecology and Obstetrics* 18 (1914): 491–496.

12. R.H. Egdahl and P.M. Gertman, *Quality Assurance in Health Care* (Gaithersburg, Md: Aspen Publishers, Inc., 1976), 65.

13. C.G. Meisenheimer, *Improving Quality: A Guide to Effective Programs* (Gaithersburg, Md: Aspen Publishers, Inc., 1992).

14. Egdahl and Gertman, *Quality Assurance in Health Care*.

15. Meisenheimer, *Improving Quality*.

16. Egdahl and Gertman, *Quality Assurance*.

17. Meisenheimer, *Improving Quality*.

18. M.J. Goran, The Evolution of the PSRO Hospital Review System, *Medical Care Supplement* (1979): 1–47.

19. S.N. Rosenberg, Methods of Assessment and Monitoring, in *Quality Assurance in Hospitals*, ed. N. Graham (Gaithersburg, Md: Aspen Publishers, Inc., 1990), 133–134.

20. S. Greenfield, et al., Peer Review by Criteria Mapping: Criteria for Diabetes Mellitus, *Annals of Internal Medicine* 83 (1975): 761–770.

21. D. Rutstein, et al., Measuring the Quality of Medical Care: A Clinical? Method, *New England Journal of Medicine* 294 (1976): 582–584.

22. D. Kessner, et al., Assessing Health Quality: The Case for Tracers, *New England Journal of Medicine* 288 (1973): 189–194.

23. J.W. Williamson, et al., Health Accounting: An Outcome-Based System of Quality Assurance: Illustrative Application to Hypertension, *Bulletin of New York Academy of Medicine* 51 (1975): 727–738.

24. J. Gonnella, D. Louis, J. McCord, The Staging Concept—An Approach to the Assessment of Outcome of Ambulatory Care, *Medical Care* 14 (1976): 13–21.

25. *The PEP Primer*, (Chicago, Ill.: The Joint Commission on Accreditation of Hospitals, 1974).

26. P.J. Sanazaro and R.M. Worth, Concurrent Quality Assurance in Hospital Care: Report of a Study by Private Initiative in PSRO, *New England Journal of Medicine* 298 (1978): 1171–1177.

27. Meisenheimer, *Improving Quality*.

28. M. Orsolits and F. Abbey, Impact of Peer Review Organization on Hospitals, in *Quality Assurance in Hospitals*, ed. N. Graham (Gaithersburg, Md: Aspen Publishers, Inc., 1990).

29. W.A. Knaus, et al., Academia and Clinic: An Evaluation of Outcome from Intensive Care in Major Medical Centers, *Annals of Internal Medicine* 104 (1986): 410–418.

30. J.E. Wennberg, Variation in Medical Practice and Hospital Costs, *Connecticut Medicine* 49 (1985): 444–453.

31. E. Gaucher and R. Coffey, *Transforming Healthcare Organizations* (San Francisco, Calif.: Jossey-Bass, Inc., Publishers, 1992), 83.

32. D.S. O'Leary, IM System. (Oakbrook Terrace, Ill.: 1994).

33. K. Ciccone and O. Munshi, Quality Initiative Update, *Quality Times* 6, no. 1 (1993): 1–5.

34. Palmer, Quality Improvement/Quality Assurance.

2. A Double Take on the History of Quality in Health Care

John F. Racine

INTRODUCTION

My original idea for this article was to write a chronicle of quality in health care. After researching a great deal of literature, I found that this story had already been told several times, in different ways, and for a variety of purposes. It seemed much more interesting and valuable to review the major perspectives taken and points made in the history that had already been told. This approach differs from a historical account in that its objective is to sharpen our vision of the present, not the past.[1] For those readers interested in a selected chronology of significant events in health care quality and pioneers in the field, please refer to the two appendices at the end of this article. (Appendices 2–A and 2–B.)

My work follows the chronological format of this book: yesterday, today, and tomorrow. While some historians of health care quality begin at the early part of this century[2] or even later, during the 1960s[3] a few articles remind us that quality is as old as medical care itself.[4,5] The perspective of historians who use a longer time span as well as those who consider only the more recent past are included in my discussion of "yesterday."

There have been two traditions of quality assurance in world history, according to Ellis and Whittington: the tradition of quality in industry and the tradition of quality in health care.[6] With the widespread adoption of Total Quality Management (TQM)/Continuous Quality Improvement (CQI), they believe that health care is being assimilated by the industrial tradition, and that is the focus of the section on "today." Because of this convergence, I discuss in the "tomorrow" section how trends in industrial quality as well as current health care reform proposals can help us forecast the future of health care quality.

Besides helping us to predict where we will be going and how to prepare for the future, the past provides insight, lessons, and techniques for current research and practice. Both Donabedian[7] and Wyszewianski[8] have chided the field for repetitious and redundant work in the past, particularly, on the definition, measurement, and assessment of inpatient quality. Researchers during the last 20 years, they say, were not aware or did not acknowledge what had already been done. As a result, they invite us to search out actively and to build upon what we already know in order to substantially advance, rather than merely refine, the accumulated knowledge of the ages. In addition to these reasons for doing a "double take" on the story of quality in health care, I would like to show that the industrial tradition and international experience are also resources for innovative ideas.

YESTERDAY

There are discrepancies in the literature about when the development of quality in health care began. The time spans used by historians range from 30 years[9] to 3000 years.[10] While historical literature about the industrial tradition acknowledges that quality activities are as old as the human race, only a few of the articles in health care recognize that quality can at least be dated to the beginning of recorded medical history.

The reason for the difference between the two traditions and within the health care tradition may be because most historians in health care define quality assurance as the formal and systematic evaluation of health care, which they associate with the activities of the last half of the twentieth century. Fine and Meyer say that "quality assurance activities in health care are often accorded no history beyond the life breathed into these programs by the Joint Commission on Accreditation of Hospitals in the last two decades."[11]

The Distant Past

Quality of care, however, has a longer history that goes beyond even this century. Ellis and Whittington discuss quality activities in ancient Egypt, Assyria, China, Greece, and Rome, which they refer to as the "embryonic" stage of quality assurance.[12] "Embryonic" is defined as the time when techniques were implicit and not specifically referred to as quality. In presenting industrial quality efforts during these same times, though, Banks cites the pyramids, classical Greek works, and Roman structures as evidence of very conscious and formal, albeit embryonic, methods to control quality.[13] Perhaps, it is the scarcity of documentation about these previous efforts, "the temptation in our technocratic age to ascribe most innovation to the near-term past" or even arrogance that has made us slight the distant past.[14] As Harry Truman expressed it, "There is nothing new in the world except the history you do not know."[15]

Besides demonstrating the continuity of organized quality systems, Fine and Meyer also point out that the issues we presently face in assessing and improving quality have existed throughout ancient times.[16] They provide examples of written codes of professional conduct from Hippocrates in the fifth century B.C., practice guidelines on Egyptian papyri, outcomes management in the Chou Dynasty (1122–221 B.C.), and quality assessment and improvement in Persia from A.D. 200. Similar quality activities and issues are also reported during the Middle Ages, the Renaissance, and every succeeding historical era. Although Bull does not go this far back in her history, her statement that "the concept of systematic evaluation of health care is not new" is similarly valid.[17]

The Recent Past

A few historians, usually nurses, start their accounts of quality with Florence Nightingale, the founder of modern professional nursing. Ahead of her time, she used death rates to improve hospital care in the late nineteenth century and encountered medical staff resistance. Quality review, interpreted as an attack on professional autonomy, has been and continues to be opposed by some physicians.[18] In Nightingale's early professional clash, she appealed for and received government support to continue her assessment and improvement activities. Ellis and Whittington refer to her explicit and systematic use of method as the "emergence" of quality assurance in health care.[19]

Many historians, however, start their chronicles with Ernest Avery Codman in the early twentieth century, perhaps because of his current popularity. As a result of today's trend toward outcomes measurement and management, he has become well known and regarded as an early exponent of emphasizing what he called the "end result" of medical care. Patients were recalled a year after discharge to evaluate treatment benefits and side effects. Ellis and Whittington[20] call Codman the first advocate of the regular review of medical practice as well as a premature proponent of the idea that professional competence is not the only determinant of quality. After being dismissed from the medical staff for his traitorous views, he established his own facility which he marketed as "The End Result Hospital."

Almost all the literature recognizes, during the next decade, the publication of the Flexner report, which proposed standards for medical schools, and the development of the Hospital Standardization Program, as pivotal events marking "the consolidation of authority" by the medical profession.[21] Palmer and Adams in their conceptual analysis of historical events in the development of quality in health care, refer to these activities that were intended to demonstrate public accountability as the "professional" stage of quality assurance.[22] The Hospital Standardization Program, the precursor of the Joint Commission on Accreditation of Hospitals in 1952, and today's Joint Commission on Accreditation of Healthcare Organizations, which is still physician-dominated, represents the pinnacle achievement of this period. Ruiz, et al., identified this model as the dominant one in Spain and other European countries until recently.[23]

Bull reports that little of substance occurred from 1920 to 1940, possibly because of the recovery from World War I during the 1920s and the depression in the 1930s.[24] Donabedian, however, says that "by 1964 the foundations of almost all the major approaches to quality assessment had been laid down" and clearly states that this period was very productive. In particular, he singles out the study by Lee and Jones in 1933 on "The Fundamentals of Good Medical Care" which he praises as an "awe-inspiring landmark."[25]

The 1960s and 1970s are considered the beginning of formal quality assurance. Ellis and Whittington refer to this interval as the "mandatory stage" of quality assurance, when quality is no longer an issue only for professionals but becomes important to government and other third-party payors as a means to reduce costs and improve quality.[26] During this time, the federal government required Joint Commission accreditation for certification as a Medicare provider and contracts with Professional Review Organizations to monitor utilization regarding admissions and length of stay. In the early 1970s, the Joint Commission added internal quality assurance as an accreditation standard.

Palmer and Adams call these activities a "radical departure from the professional model of physician autonomy" and describe the new approach as "bureaucratic" in which professionals make decisions within a hierarchy and according to organizational rules.[27] This is the beginning of what has been criticized as external intrusion or "the hassle factor" in medicine. Vladeck poses the question of whether these external controls might have been avoided if professionals had done a better job in policing themselves.[28] Starr argues that "the rise of bureaucracy has been taken as an inexorable necessity in modern life, but in America the medical profession escaped, or as least postponed its capitulation."[29]

During this period, the focus changed from the review, or inspection, of individual cases to the statistical analysis of patterns of care. In industry, the transition from inspection to statistical quality control occurred in the 1930s, but Ellis and Whittington say that health care was arrested at the inspection stage.[30] Starr attributes the reason for this to the parochial interests of the medical profession which, he says, also kept health care organizations at an earlier stage of industrial development.[31]

This bureaucratic approach to quality assurance, however, had little impact on quality.[32] The reason for this is that quality assurance was academic and research-oriented during this period. Donabedian has reviewed the proliferation of studies from 1954–1984 and documented these attempts to define and measure "sound structures, good processes, and suitable outcomes."[33] Berwick, et al., however, had said that this literature was unsuitable for day-to-day use because it lacked applied technology and bore little connection to the work of quality assurance committees.[34] Laffel and Blumenthal catalogue the limitations of the traditional approach to quality: a too-narrow definition of quality to meet the needs of modern providers; a static approach with the goal of conformance to standards; and, an emphasis on physician performance and disregard for the contributions of other participants in complex health care organizations today.[35] Donabedian concluded in his research review that "we must pay much more attention than we have done in the past to the determinants of clinically relevant behaviors in the health care system, and to the means of bringing about desired changes in behavior."[36]

TODAY

The contemporary period in health care quality, in the literature, corresponds with the application of TQM/CQI to health care. According to Ellis and Whittington, health care quality assurance had been proceeding along its own tradition with little reference to the development of industrial ideas and techniques.[37] Problems with traditional quality assurance, however, led to experimentation with the industrial approach of TQM/CQI. This method, a management strategy, is described as "a continuous effort by all members of an organization to meet the needs and expectations of the customer."[38]

Although it has been disputed by some historians,[39,40] the adoption of the industrial model brought the health care tradition to a crossroads[41] resulting in a new direction, or a paradigm shift, in quality assurance.[42,43] "During the transition to QI (quality improvement), quality assurance professionals will be challenged to learn new skills, new approaches, and new vocabularies."[44] The retitling of the quality assurance section in the Joint Commission's 1992 Accreditation Manual to quality assessment and improvement canonizes this approach. The requirement that senior executives be educated in TQM/CQI marks the official beginning of a new era in which managers, not researchers, assume responsibility for quality in health care.

Despite criticism that TQM/CQI is a short-lived fad in health care, more than 4,000 hospitals in the U.S. have reported implementing programs and spending more than a billion dollars to do it.[45] Findings from a national survey on quality improvement activities suggested that TQM/CQI hospitals are more satisfied with their quality improvement efforts, take more governing board actions to improve quality, perceive a more positive impact on human resource development issues and financial outcomes, and are more likely to have improvements in certain patient outcomes and to show cost savings than hospitals not using TQM/CQI.[46] This survey, however, also indicates that health care organizations lag in applying TQM/CQI to clinical care and involving physicians, possibly because of inadequate information systems.

Government and other external agencies, however, perhaps because of their access to large health insurance claims data bases, have been looking at the practice of medicine and the outcomes associated with it. Federal efforts include the research of the Agency for Health Care Policy and Research on medical treatment effectiveness, clinical outcomes, and the development of clinical practice guidelines. It has been estimated that approximately 1,100 practice guidelines are currently available and several hundred more are under development by at least 80 professional societies.[47] Nationwide, there are 30 health data commissions collecting, analyzing and, in some cases, releasing hospital- and physician-specific consumer guides to the public. In addition, the Joint Commission is facilitating clinical quality improvement through its clinical indicators program which collects and feeds back clinical outcomes data so hospitals can benchmark those facilities that score the best performance currently achievable.[48] Managed care organizations and third-party administrators are also using adjusted outcomes data to profile physician practice for peer comparisons.

TQM/CQI is a growing trend in other industrialized countries. The European member nations of the World Health Organization (WHO) decided in 1983 that quality assurance would be introduced into their national health systems by 1990. The field of quality assurance, however, is generally in its early days of development outside the U.S.[49] Ellis and Whittington, in their historical review of quality in the United Kingdom, found no references to the field before 1980.[50] Even Japan, a leader in industrial quality management, is only at the beginning of its efforts to apply it to health care.

Explaining why modern quality assurance in health care was an innovation of the U.S., DuVerlie points out that quality assurance activities among health care systems reflect structural differences that influence how quality needs arise and how they are met. As a result of the high incidence of malpractice and the presence of the Joint Commission—unique phenomena in the U.S.—she says quality assurance is more advanced in this country and, as a result, continues to evolve.[51] Another reason is given by Vladeck who blames the decentralized nature of our health care system that he says has led to external controls to ensure quality of care that are "more extensive, more intrusive, and more complex than anywhere else in the world".[52]

Despite our sophistication, DuVerlie suggests that we may still have something to learn about defining, measuring, and managing quality by watching the evolution of activities in other countries.[53] Ellis and Whittington suggest, in particular, that we study the implementation by the U.K. of formal quality assurance in health care. It begins with the industrial tradition and does not have the heavy baggage of tradition that the U.S. carries and which has created an orthodoxy and dogma difficult to overcome. As a result, they believe that the

U.K. may permit a more complete adoption of industrial models than the U.S. has been able to achieve.[54] Anderson, et al., also call our attention to the International Quality Study, in which the U.S. is participating along with Germany, Japan, and Canada. This study attempts to gain a better understanding of the best management practices in these countries across four industries— health care, banking, automobiles, and computers. The study intends to create a data base of those practices that have achieved quality objectives to serve as a worldwide benchmark for quality progress.[55]

TOMORROW

The field of quality assurance in health care continues to evolve and is rapidly expanding.[56] This growth and development is the result of a current obsession with the quality of care by the public and private sectors, called the third revolution in health care, a fascination which is expected to continue. "For the future," according to Jeffer, "the watch words of medicine are quality, documentation, and accountability."[57] By examining the quality provisions of current health reform proposals and reviewing industrial quality trends, we can foretell what these terms will mean in the future.

According to the Physician Payment Review Commission, health care reform presents an opportunity to improve health care and to advance the state of the art of what we know about quality and how we evaluate and manage it.[58] Jost reviewed the quality components of the major reform plans and found radical changes proposed.[59] These changes reflect the managed competition approach in which health plans would compete for subscribers on the basis of cost and quality. Quality, therefore, would be assured primarily through the marketplace. As a result, quality efforts in the proposals focus on consumer choice by means of quality report cards, outcomes research disseminated through practice guidelines, and provider education.

Comparing the major competing proposals, Oberman concluded that only President Clinton's Health Security Act offered a detailed plan for enhancing quality. Her analysis showed that reform proposals reflected different assessments on the need for improvement. "On the right are plans that assume everything's all right with the quality of care, it's just the financing that needs to be fixed." Others, she says, fear that the flaws are profound and pervasive.[60] Consistent with the President's belief that the health care system is broken and a major overhaul is necessary, the current prescriptive quality assurance system will be transformed into a quality management system focused on performance measures and continuous improvement.[61]

Specifically, the President's plan would establish a National Quality Management Program to be administered by a National Quality Management Council, the creation of which reflects the central role of quality under health reform.[62] This group, supported by a National Quality Consortium, would develop a core set of national measures on quality and performance measures, as well as conduct consumer surveys and feed back data to plans, providers, consumers, and states. The council is also responsible for recommending studies and establishing priorities for research about quality, appropriateness, and effectiveness, as well as working with the Agency for Health Care Policy and Research to develop and update practice guidelines. In addition, regional professional foundations would be created to provide programs of "lifetime learning" for health professionals, through which guidelines, innovations, and research findings would be disseminated and patient education systems would be developed to enhance consumer involvement in treatment decisions. Even more important than these quality components, though, according to Oberman's broader perspective, is that the Clinton plan and other comprehensive managed competition proposals aim "to correct the fundamental flaws in the current system that undermine quality, notably financial incentives that encourage overuse and fragmented care."[63]

Quite unbelievably, given our history of health care quality efforts in which external controls were fought tooth and nail and vehemently criticized when implemented, there have been complaints about the lack of regulatory oversight in the managed competition proposals. Concern is expressed that the incentives in this approach will result in undertreatment and discrimination against consumers with costly medical problems.[64] Skepticism is also voiced about the industry's current ability to produce meaningful data for consumers to understand and to use to make choices in a competitive health care marketplace. As a result, vested interests see a continuing role for the accreditation of health care organizations,[65] which is replaced by the Presidents's plan with state certification of health plans, and PROs which are to be substituted by the purely educational Regional Professional Foundations.[66]

The Physician Payment Review Commission[67] has also expressed concern about the limitations and uncertainties of quality performance reporting. As a result, they have proposed efforts that go beyond quality performance reports and quality improvement programs to external quality monitoring, which they believe would guarantee a minimum threshold of quality for all competitive health plans. A transition strategy, at the least, has been recommended by O'Kane, until quality report cards have reached maturity.[68]

Hillman, et al., however, remind us that the purpose of quality management is "to improve the processes to achieve quality, not react to poor outcomes, and it relies on self-motivated improvements in quality and the use of incentives rather than on inspections and sanctions." They support quality performance reporting and continuous improvement because this approach, they argue, "decreases the reliance of the health care system on regulation, which poses the risk of stifling innovation in managed competition, and allows for more decentralized quality assurance.[69]

The debate over quality components proposed in managed competition health reform plans mirrors, at the systems-wide level, the resistance and hesitancy demonstrated by individual organizations on their implementation of TQM/CQI. The Government Accounting Office (GAO), in fact, estimated that it took between one and five years—and an average of one and a half years—for service companies to realize benefits from TQM/CQI, due to the difficulties involved in winning hearts and minds on putting it into place.[70] As with any paradigmatic shift, part of the problem is understanding what the new model is about and how it differs from what it replaces. TQM/CQI does not eliminate traditional quality assurance functions that protect the public; it internalizes them. Janov urges us to give up the old paradigm of control and caretaking of the many by the few through external controls, and to create organizations that are self-regulating.[71] Past experiences with professional self-regulation in health care showed it did not work because it was so narrow and only involved physicians. Successful experiences, however, in health care organizations and in other industries that have empowered employees and listened to customers suggest that TQM/CQI may eventually, but reluctantly, be accepted and self-regulation achievable on a system-wide basis.

Schmele however, cautions us that in an age of rapid health care reform, "forecasting the future of quality endeavors is somewhat presumptuous or very elusive at best." She does recommend extrapolating from current trends as a safe method.[72] Based on the convergence of health care with and assimilation by the industrial quality tradition, I suggest we examine current ideas and practices in industry to predict the future of quality in health care beyond the resolution of current disputes.

The current literature on quality management in general industry shows that TQM/CQI continues to evolve and expand. Beckham discusses the proliferation of management approaches that TQM/CQI has spun off.[73] Shiba, et al., believe that the most important aspects to TQM/CQI are the development of individuals and the encouragement of human learning by a variety of approaches.[74]

In an attempt to philosophically integrate all of the management developments that have been inspired by it such as reengineering, empowerment, visionary leadership, etc., they define TQM/CQI as a learning system and a model for improving not only organizations but also the personal lives of individuals. Quality, then, will have evolved from external, command and control, punitive methods of inspection to internal, self-regulatory, supportive approaches for personal growth and development. As Roberts and Sergesketter state it, quality is personal and the foundation for TQM/CQI.[75]

CONCLUSION

The twenty-first century is being called the "Century of Quality."[76] The most important trend in health care during this century will be accountability.[77] The history of quality in health care teaches us that new approaches to accountability in health care, particularly as we emulate industry, will continue to be developed. The past, international experience, and other industries are rich sources of innovation for the future and unexplored frontiers that deserve a "double take."

NOTES

1. A.M. Kantrow, Why History Matters to Managers, *Harvard Business Review*, January/February (1986).

2. M.J. Bull, Quality Assurance: Professional Accountability via Continuous Quality Improvement, in *Improving Quality: A Guide to Effective Programs*, ed, C.G. Meisenheimer (Gaithersburg, Md.: Aspen Publishers, Inc., 1992).

3. M.R. Maatson, Quality Assurance: A Literature Review of a Changing Field, *Hospitals and Community Psychiatry* 35, no.6 (1984): 605–616.

4. D.J. Fine and E.R. Meyer, Quality Assurance in Historical Perspective, *Hospital and Health Services Administration* November/December (1983): 94–121.

5. R. Ellis and D.Whittington, *Quality Assurance in Health Care: A Handbook* (London, England: Edward Arnold, 1993).

6. Ellis and Whittington, *Quality Assurance.*

7. A. Donabedian, Twenty Years of Research on the Quality of Medical Care, *Evaluation and the Health Professions* 8, no. 3 (1985): 243–265.

8. L. Wysewianski, Quality of Care: Past Achievements and Future Challenges, *Inquiry* 25 (1988): 13–22.

9. Maatson, Quality Assurance: A Literature Review.

10. Ellis and Whittington, *Quality Assurance.*

11. Fine and Meyer, Quality Assurance in Historical Perspective, 94.

12. Ellis and Whittington, *Quality Assurance.*

13. J. Banks, *Principles of Quality Control* (New York: John Wiley & Sons, Inc., 1989).

14. Fine and Meyer, Quality Assurance in Historical Perspective, 94.

15. O. Renick, The Search for Value: A Quality Improvement Cycle Linking Process, Outcome, and Patient Satisfaction, *The Journal of Health Administration Education* 12, no.1 (1994): 29–38.

16. Fine and Meyer, Quality Assurance in Historical Perspective.

17. Bull, Quality Assurance: Professional Accountability, 3.

18. R.H. Palmer and M.M.E. Adams, Quality Improvement/Quality Assurance Taxonomy: A Framework, in *Putting Research to Work in Quality Improvement and Quality Assurance* (Summary Report) (Washington, D.C.: U.S. Department of Health and Human Services, Public Health Service, Agency for Health Policy and Research, 1993), 13–38.

19. Ellis and Whittington, Quality Assurance.

20. Ibid.

21. P. Starr, *The Social Transformation of American Medicine* (New York: Basic Books, Inc., 1982).

22. Palmer and Adams, Quality Improvement/Quality Assurance.

23. U. Ruiz, et al., Implementing Total Quality Management in the Spanish Health Care System, *Quality Assurance in Health Care* 4, no.1 (1992): 43–59.

24. Bull, Quality Assurance: Professional Accountability.

25. Donabedian, Twenty Years of Research, 220.

26. Ellis and Whittington, *Quality Assurance*.

27. Palmer and Adams, Quality Improvement/Quality Assurance, 17.

28. B.C. Vladeck, Quality Assurance Through External Controls, *Inquiry* 25 (1988): 100–107.

29. Starr, *Social Transformation*, 179.

30. Ellis and Whittington, *Quality Assurance*.

31. Starr, Social Transformation.

32. Palmer and Adams, Quality Improvement/Quality Assurance.

33. Donabedian, Twenty Years of Research.

34. D.M. Berwick, A.B. Godfrey, and J. Roesnner, *Curing Health Care* (San Francisco: Jossey-Bass, Inc., Publishers, 1990).

35. G. Laffel and D. Blumenthal, The Case for Using Industrial Quality Management Science in Health Care Organizations, *Journal of the American Medical Association* 262, no. 20 (1989): 2869–2873.

36. Donabedian, Twenty Years of Research, 226.

37. Ellis and Whittington, *Quality Assurance*.

38. Laffel and Blumenthal, The Case, 2871.

39. E. Ziacik, An Evolutionary Process: Applying CQI Techniques of Quality Assurance Issues, *Journal of Healthcare Quality* 14, no. 2 (1992): 8–18.

40. E. Rooney, TQM/CQI in Business and Health Care: An Overview, *AAOHN Journal* 40, no. 7 (1992): 319–325.

41. E.K. Jeffer, Quality Assurance and Quality Improvement: The 1990s and Beyond, *Journal of Healthcare Quality* 14, no. 3 (1992): 36–40.

42. Palmer and Adams, Quality Improvement/Quality Assurance.

43. Berwick, *Curing Health Care*.

44. Jeffer, Quality Assurance, 36.

45. R.G. Carey and R.C. Lloyd, Measuring the Success of CQI, *Healthcare Executive* March/April (1994): 9–11.

46. The Quality March: Part Three of a National Survey of Quality Improvement Activities, *Hospitals* 20 December 1993, 40–41.

47. W.B. Stason, Implementation of Practice Guidelines: The Next Frontier, *The Internist* October (1991): 9–12.

48. Palmer and Adams, Quality Improvement/Quality Assurance.

49. J. Lomas, Editorial: Quality Assurance and Effectiveness in Health Care, *Quality Assurance in Health Care* 2, no.1 (1990): 5–12.

50. Ellis and Whittington, *Quality* Assurance.

51. E. DuVerlie, Trends in Quality Assurance Activities in France, *Quality Review Bulletin* June (1988): 258–263.

52. Vladeck, Quality Assurance, 100.

53. DuVerlie, Trends.

54. Ellis and Whittington, *Quality Assurance*.

55. C.A. Anderson, B. Cassidy, and P. Rivenburgh, Implementing Continuous Quality Improvement (CQI) in Hospitals: Lessons Learned from the International Quality Study, *Quality Assurance in Health Care* 3 no. 3 (1991): 141–146.

56. Physician Payment Review Commission, *Annual Review to Congress* (Washington, D.C.: Physician Payment Review Commission, 1994).

57. Jeffer, Quality Assurance, 38.

58. Physician Payment Review.

59. J.S. Jost, Health System Reform: Forward or Backward with Quality Oversight?, *Journal of the American Medical Association* 271, no.19 (1994): 150–154.

60. L. Oberman, Main Quality Question: Are We Risking the Best?, *American Medical News* 6 December 1993, 3 and 35.

61. The White House Domestic Policy Council, *The President's Health Security Plan: The Clinton Blueprint* (New York: Times Books, 1993).

62. H.L. Smits, Quality Management and Consumer Protection Under the President's Health Reform Plan, *The Quality Letter* December/January (1993–94): 2–6.

63. Oberman, Main Quality Question, 3.

64. A.L. Hillman, W.R. Greer, and N. Goldfarb, Safeguarding Quality in Managed Competition, *Health Affairs* Supplement (1993): 110–122.

65. D.S. O'Leary, and P.M. Schyve, The Role of Accreditation in Quality Oversight and Improvement of Healthcare Reform, *Quality Letter for Healthcare Leaders* (1993–1994): 11–14.

66. A. Webber, Health Reform and the Quality Assurance Imperative, *The Quality Letter* December/January (1993–94): 15–18.

67. Physician Payment Review Commission.

68. R. Bergman, Making the Grade, *Hospitals & Health Networks* 5 January 1994, 34–36.

69. Hillman, Safeguarding Quality.

70. GAO, *Management Practices: U.S. Companies Improve Performance Through Quality Efforts* (Washington, D.C.: U.S. Government Accounting Office, 1991).

71. J. Janov, *The Innovative Organization: Hope and Daring at Work* (San Francisco: Jossey-Bass, Inc., Publishers, 1994).

72. J.A. Schmele, Research and Total Quality, in *The Textbook of Total Quality in Healthcare*, eds. A.F. A.F. Al-Assaf and J.A. Schmele (Delray Beach, Fla: St. Lucie Press, 1993): 239–257.

73. J.D. Beckham, The Longest Wave, *Healthcare Forum Journal* November/December (1993): 78–82.

74. S. Shiba, A. Graham, and D. Walden, *A New American TQM: Four Practical Revolutions in Management* (Portland, Or: Productivity Services, 1993).

75. H.V. Roberts and B.F. Sergesketter, *Quality Is Personal: A Foundation for Total Quality Management* (New York: The Free Press, 1993).

76. J. Juran, Made in U.S.A.: A Renaissance in Quality, *Harvard Business Review* July/August (1993): 42–50.

77. R.C. Coile, Transformation of American Healthcare in the Post-Reform Era," *Healthcare Executive* July/August (1994): 9–12.

Appendix 2–A. Selected Health Care Quality Milestones

ERA	DEVELOPMENT
2000 B.C.	Egyptian papyri document state-of-the-art medical standards for practice.
1100 B.C.	Chou Dynasty requires physicians to pass a state examination before entering practice and determines physician competence and payment on the basis of patient outcomes.
A.D. 100	Roman Emperor Antoninus Pius issues an edict that requires credentialing by physicians, uniform standards of practice, and uniform geographical distribution.
A.D. 1000	Caliph al-Muqtadir of Persia requires, for the first time, that all medical practitioners have their knowledge examined.
1500s	Royal College of Physicians in England establishes itself for medical licensing and professional self-regulation.
1760s	New York State enacts the first exclusive licensure act which provides that no one practice medicine or surgery without being examined or licensed by a government-appointed board of examiners.
1850s	Medical Care Act in England promulgates government standards for the training and registration of medical practitioners.
1910s	American College of Surgeons develops the Hospital Standardization Program and promotes standards, on-site surveys, and evaluation for accreditation of hospital academic programs.
1950s	Joint Commission for the Accreditation of Hospitals (JCAH) establishes itself to improve and promote the voluntary accreditation of hospitals.

1960s   Social Security amendments to Medicare and Medicaid require accredited hospitals to establish utilization review committees to examine admission criteria, length of stay, and treatment prescribed.

               Darling v. Charleston Community Memorial Hospital legal ruling establishes corporate liability and requires health care organizations to monitor and evaluate professional delivery of care.

1970s   Professional Standard Review Organizations (PSROs) legislation establishes government-sponsored agencies to monitor cost, quality, and utilization of hospital care for Medicare, Medicaid, and Maternal and Child Health Program patients.

               The Joint Commission creates the Performance Evaluation Procedure for Auditing and Improving Patient Care and establishes an audit requirement with a specified number of audits to be performed.

               American Hospital Association (AHA) approves "A Patient's Bill of Rights" which includes rights to informed consent and to considerate and respectful care.

               The Joint Commission replaces diagnosis-specific medical audits with a new quality assurance standard that creates a comprehensive program of problem-focused reviews.

1980s   Peer Review Organizations (PROs) replace PSROs to monitor quality of hospital care and appropriateness of admission.

               The Joint Commission replaces problem-focused approach with the requirement for systematic monitoring and evaluation of important aspects of patient care.

               The Joint Commission expands its mission and changes its name to the Joint Commission on the Accreditation of Healthcare Organizations.

               The Joint Commission announces its agenda for change to emphasize outcomes over structure and process, and to develop a national comparative data base.

               Release of hospital mortality statistics by the Health Care Financing Administration (HCFA).

               John Hartford Foundation and the Harvard Community Health Plan sponsor national demonstration project on quality improvement in health care to determine if industrial TQM could be applied to health care.

Agency for Health Policy and Research (AHPR) initiates Medical Treatment Effectiveness Program to examine effects of variations in health care practices on patient outcomes and to develop and disseminate clinical guidelines.

Pennsylvania and New York state release performance data on individual hospitals and physicians and other states establish data commissions to collect patient-care data.

1990s   The Joint Commission replaces quality assurance with quality assessment and improvement.

AHPR issues the first government-sponsored medical practice guidelines.

Health reform bills propose performance reporting and the managed competition of health plans on the basis of cost and quality.

Appendix 2-B. Selected Health Care Quality Pioneers

PIONEER	CONTRIBUTION
Hammurabi of Babylon	Promulgates code in 2000 B.C. that included physician payment methods and penalties for incompetent practice.
Hippocrates of Cos	Publishes legal and ethical obligations for physicians in 500 B.C.
Galen of Pergamos	Publishes medical treaties in A.D. 200 that report his observations and anatomical studies in an effort to standardize medical knowledge.
Vesalius of Belgium	Publishes an encyclopedia of human anatomy in A.D. 1600 to promote the scientific study of medicine.
Florence Nightingale	Publishes "Notes on Matters Affecting the Health, Efficiency, and Hospital Administration of the British Army" in 1858, and evaluates quality of hospital care using mortality rates.
Abraham Flexner	Publishes "Medical Education in the United States and Canada," a Report to the Carnegie Foundation, in 1910.
Ernest A. Codman	Publishes "A Study of Hospital Efficiency" in 1916 and advocates tracking "end results" of hospital patients after discharge.

Roger I. Lee, Lewis W. Jones, and Barbara Jones	Publish "The Fundamentals of Good Medical Care" (1933) for the Committee on the Costs of Medical Care using professional norms as the standards of assessment.
Avedis Donabedian	Publishes "Evaluating the Quality of Medical Care" in 1966 to define quality in health and present the major approaches to its assessment; a seminal contribution, earning him the distinction of "father of quality assurance."
Paul A. Lembcke	Publishes "Evolution of the Medical Audit" in 1967 that calls for the use of "explicit criteria" in assessment.
John Wennberg	Publishes "Small Area Variations in Health Care Delivery" (with A. Gittelsohn) in 1973.
Jon Williamson	Publishes "Assessing and Improving Health Care Outcomes: The Health Accounting Approach to Quality Assurance" in 1978.
Paul Ellwood	Publishes "Outcomes Mmanagement: A Technology of Patient Experience" in 1988 that calls for a national program of using patient outcomes as the basis for clinical standards and guidelines.
Donald Berwick	Publishes "Continuous Improvement As an Ideal in Health Care" in 1989 to promote the use of industrial quality techniques in health care.

3. The Quality of Care: How Can It Be Assessed?

Avedis Donabedian

There was a time, not too long ago, when this question could not have been asked. The quality of care was considered to be something of a mystery: real, capable of being perceived and appreciated, but not subject to measurement. The very attempt to define and measure quality seemed, then, to denature and belittle it. Now, we may have moved too far in the opposite direction. Those who have not experienced the intricacies of clinical practice demand measures that are easy, precise, and complete—as if a sack of potatoes was being weighed. True, some elements in the quality of care are easy to define and measure, but there are also profundities that still elude us. We must not allow anyone to belittle or ignore them; they are the secret and glory of our art. Therefore, we should avoid claiming for our capacity to assess quality either too little or too much. I shall try to steer this middle course.

SPECIFYING WHAT QUALITY IS

Level and Scope of Concern

Before we attempt to assess the quality of care, either in general terms or in any particular site or situation, it is necessary to come to an agreement on what the elements that constitute it are. To proceed to measurement without a firm foundation of prior agreement on what quality consists in is to court disaster.[1]

As we seek to define quality, we soon become aware of the fact that several formulations are both possible and legitimate, depending on where we are located in the system of care and on what the nature and extent of our

Source: Reprinted from *Journal of the American Medical Association,* Vol. 260, No. 12, pp. 1743–1748, with permission of the American Medical Association, © 1988.

responsibilities are. These several formulations can be envisaged as a progression, for example, as steps in a ladder or as successive circles surrounding the bull's-eye of a target. Our power, our responsibility, and our vulnerability all flow from the fact that we are the foundation for that ladder, the focal point for that family of concentric circles. We must begin, therefore, with the performance of physicians and other health care practitioners.

As shown in Figure 3–1, there are two elements in the performance of practitioners: one technical and the other interpersonal. Technical performance depends on the knowledge and judgment used in arriving at the appropriate strategies of care and on skill in implementing those strategies. The goodness of technical performance is judged in comparison with the best in practice. The best in practice, in its turn, has earned that distinction because, on the average, it is known or believed to produce the greatest improvement in health. This means that the goodness of technical care is proportional to its expected ability to achieve those improvements in health status that the current science and technology of health care have made possible. If the realized fraction of what is achievable is called *effectiveness*, the quality of technical care becomes proportionate to its effectiveness (Figure 3–2).

Here, two points deserve emphasis. First, judgments on technical quality are contingent on the best in current knowledge and technology; they cannot go beyond that limit. Second, the judgment is based on future expectations, not on

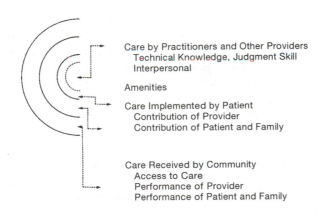

Care by Practitioners and Other Providers
  Technical Knowledge, Judgment Skill
  Interpersonal

Amenities

Care Implemented by Patient
  Contribution of Provider
  Contribution of Patient and Family

Care Received by Community
  Access to Care
  Performance of Provider
  Performance of Patient and Family

Figure 3–1 Levels at Which Quality May Be Assessed

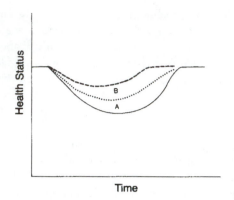

Figure 3–2 Graphical Presentation of Effectiveness (in a Self-Limiting Disease). Solid line indicates course of illness without care; dotted line, course of illness with care to be assessed; and dashed line, course of illness with "best" care. Effectiveness equals A/(A + B).

events already transpired. Even if the actual consequences of care in any given instance prove to be disastrous, quality must be judged as good if care, at the time it was given, conformed to the practice that could have been expected to achieve the best results.

The management of the interpersonal relationship is the second component in the practitioner's performance. It is a vitally important element. Through the interpersonal exchange, the patient communicates information necessary for arriving at a diagnosis, as well as preferences necessary for selecting the most appropriate methods of care. Through this exchange, the physician provides information about the nature of the illness and its management and motivates the patient to active collaboration in care. Clearly, the interpersonal process is the vehicle by which technical care is implemented and on which its success depends. Therefore, the management of the interpersonal process is to a large degree tailored to the achievement of success in technical care.

But the conduct of the interpersonal process must also meet individual and social expectations and standards, whether these aid or hamper technical performance. Privacy, confidentiality, informed choice, concern, empathy, honesty, tact, sensitivity—all these and more are virtues that the interpersonal relationship is expected to have.

If the management of the interpersonal process is so important, why is it so often ignored in assessments of the quality of care? There are many reasons. Information about the interpersonal process is not easily available. For example, in the medical record, special effort is needed to obtain it. Second, the criteria and standards that permit precise measurement of the attributes of the interpersonal process are not well developed or have not been sufficiently called upon to undertake the task. Partly, it may be because the management of the interpersonal process must adapt to so many variations in the preferences and expectations of individual patients that general guidelines do not serve us sufficiently well.

Much of what we call the *art of medicine* consists in almost intuitive adaptions to individual requirements in technical care as well as in the management of the interpersonal process. Another element in the art of medicine is the way, still poorly understood, in which practitioners process information to arrive at a correct diagnosis and an appropriate strategy of care.[2] As our understanding of each of these areas of performance improves, we can expect the realm of our science to expand and that of our art to shrink. Yet I hope that some of the mystery in practice will always remain, since it affirms and celebrates the uniqueness of each individual.

The science and art of health care, as they apply to both technical care and the management of the interpersonal process, are at the heart of the metaphorical family of concentric circles depicted in Figure 3–1. Immediately surrounding the center we can place the amenities of care, these being the desirable attributes of the settings within which care is provided. They include convenience, comfort, quiet, privacy, and so on. In private practice, these are the responsibility of the practitioner to provide. In institutional practice, the responsibility for providing them devolves on the owners and managers of the institution.

By moving to the next circle away from the center of our metaphorical target, we include in assessments of quality the contributions to care of the patients themselves as well as of members of their families. By doing so we cross an important boundary. So far, our concern was primarily with the performance of the providers of care. Now, we are concerned with judging the care as it actually was. The responsibility, now, is shared by provider and consumer. As already described, the management of the interpersonal process by the practitioner influences the implementation of care by and for the patient. Yet, the patient and family must, themselves, also carry some of the responsibility for the success or failure of care. Accordingly, the practitioner may be judged blameless in some situations in which the care, as implemented by the patient, is found to be inferior.

We have one more circle to visit, another watershed to cross. Now, we are concerned with care received by the community as a whole. We must now judge the social distribution of levels of quality in the community.[3] This depends, in turn, on who has greater or lesser access to care and who, after gaining access, receives greater or lesser qualities of care. Obviously, the performance of individual practitioners and health care institutions has much to do with this. But, the quality of care in a community is also influenced by many factors over which the providers have no control, although these are factors they should try to understand and be concerned about.

I have tried, so far, to show that the definition of quality acquires added elements as we move outward from the performance of the practitioners, to the care received by patients, and to the care received by communities. The definition of quality also becomes narrower or more expansive, depending on how narrowly or broadly we define the concept of health and our responsibility for it. It makes a difference in the assessment of our performance whether we see ourselves as responsible for bringing about improvements only in specific aspects of physical or physiological function or whether we include psychological and social function as well.

Valuation of the Consequences of Care

Still another modification in the assessment of performance depends on who is to value the improvements in health that care is expected to produce. If it is our purpose to serve the best interest of our patients, we need to inform them of the alternatives available to them, so they can make the choice most appropriate to their preferences and circumstances. The introduction of patient preferences, though necessary to the assessment of quality, is another source of difficulty in implementing assessment. It means that no preconceived notion of what the objectives and accomplishments of care should be will precisely fit any given patient. All we can hope for is a reasonable approximation, one that must then be subject to individual adjustment.[4-6]

Monetary Cost As a Consideration

Finally, we come to the perplexing question of whether the monetary cost of care should enter the definition of quality and its assessment.[7,8] In theory, it is possible to separate quality from inefficiency. Technical quality is judged by the degree to which achievable improvements in health can be expected to be attained. Inefficiency is judged by the degree to which expected improvements in health are achieved in an unnecessarily costly manner. In practice, lower quality and inefficiency coexist because wasteful care is either directly harmful to health or is harmful by displacing more useful care.

Cost and quality are also confounded because, as shown in Figure 3–3, it is believed that as one adds to care, the corresponding improvements in health become progressively smaller while costs continue to rise unabated. If this is true, there will be a point beyond which additions to care will bring about improvements that are too small to be worth the added cost. Now, we have a choice. We can ignore cost and say that the highest quality is represented by care that can be expected to achieve the greatest improvement in health; this is a "maximalist" specification of quality. Alternatively, if we believe that cost is important, we would say that care must stop short of including elements that are disproportionately costly compared with the improvements in health that they produce. This is an "optimalist" specification of quality. A graphical representation of these alternatives is shown in Figure 3–3.

Health care practitioners tend to prefer a maximalist standard because they only have to decide whether each added element of care is likely to be useful. By contrast, the practice of optimal care requires added knowledge of costs, and also some method of weighing each added bit of expected usefulness against its corresponding cost.[9] Yet, the practice of optimal care is traditional, legitimate, even necessary, as long as costs and benefits are weighed jointly by the practitioner and the fully informed patient. A difficult, perhaps insoluble, problem arises when a third party (for example, a private insurer or a governmental agency) specifies what the optimum that defines quality is.[10]

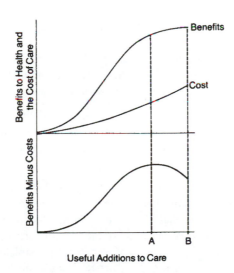

Figure 3–3 Hypothetical Relations Between Health Benefits and Cost of Care as Useful Additions Are Made to Care. **A** indicates optimally effective care; and **B**, maximally effective care.

Preliminaries to Quality Assessment

Before we set out to assess quality, we will have to choose whether we will adopt a maximal or optimal specification of quality and, if the latter, whether we shall accept what is the optimum for each patient or what has been defined as socially optimal. Similarly, we should have decided: (1) how health and our responsibility for it is to be defined; (2) whether the assessment is to be of the performance of practitioners only or also include that of patients and the health care system; and (3) whether the amenities and the management of the interpersonal process are to be included in addition to technical care. In a more practical vein, we need to answer certain questions: Who is being assessed? What are the activities being assessed? How are these activities supposed to be conducted? What are they meant to accomplish? When we agree on the answers to these questions we are ready to look for the measures that will give us the necessary information about quality.

Approaches to Assessment

The information from which inferences can be drawn about the quality of care can be classified under three categories: "structure," "process," and "outcome."[11,12]

Structure. Structure denotes the attributes of the settings in which care occurs. This includes the attributes of material resources (such as facilities, equipment, and money), of human resources (such as the number and qualifications of personnel), and of organizational structure (such as medical staff organization, methods of peer review, and methods of reimbursement).

Process. Process denotes what is actually done in giving and receiving care. It includes the patient's activities in seeking care and carrying it out as well as the practitioner's activities in making a diagnosis and recommending or implementing treatment.

Outcome. Outcome denotes the effects of care on the health status of patients and populations. Improvements in the patient's knowledge and salutary changes in the patient's behavior are included under a broad definition of health status, and so is the degree of the patient's satisfaction with care.

This three-part approach to quality assessment is possible only because good structure increases the likelihood of good process, and good process increases the likelihood of a good outcome. It is necessary, therefore, to have established such a relationship before any particular component of structure, process, or outcome can be used to assess quality. The activity of quality assessment is not itself designed to establish the presence of these relationships. There must be preexisting knowledge of the linkage between structure and process, and between process and outcome, before quality assessment can be undertaken.

Knowledge about the relationship between structure and process (or between structure and outcome) proceeds from the organizational sciences. These sciences are still relatively young, so our knowledge of the effects of structure is rather scanty.[13,14] Furthermore, what we do know suggests that the relationship between structural characteristics and the process of care is rather weak. From these characteristics, we can only infer that conditions are either inimical or conducive to good care. We cannot assert that care, in fact, has been good or bad. Structural characteristics should be a major preoccupation in system design; they are a rather blunt instrument in quality assessment.

As I have already mentioned, knowledge about the relationship between attributes of the interpersonal process and the outcome of care should derive from the behavioral sciences. But so far, these sciences have contributed relatively little to quality assessment. I cannot say whether this is because of a deficiency in these sciences or a narrowness in those who assess quality.

Knowledge about the relationship between technical care and outcome derives, of course, from the health care sciences. Some of that knowledge, as we know, is pretty detailed and firm, deriving from well-conducted trials or extensive, controlled observations. Some of it is of dubious validity and open to question. Our assessments of the quality of technical process of care vary accordingly in their certainty and persuasiveness. If we are confident that a certain strategy of care produces the best outcomes in a given category of patients, we can be equally confident that its practice represents the highest quality of care, barring concern for cost. If we are uncertain of the relationship, then our assessment of quality is correspondingly uncertain. It cannot be emphasized too strongly that our ability to assess the quality of technical care is bounded by the strengths and weaknesses of our clinical science.

There are those who believe that direct assessment of the outcome of care can free us from the limitations imposed by the imperfections of the clinical sciences. I do not believe so. Because a multitude of factors influence outcome, it is not possible to know for certain, even after extensive adjustments for differences in case mix are made, the extent to which an observed outcome is attributable to an antecedent process of care. Confirmation is needed by a direct assessment of the process itself, which brings us to the position we started from.

The assessment of outcomes, under rigorously controlled circumstances, is, of course, the method by which the goodness of alternative strategies of care is established. But, quality assessment is neither clinical research or technology assessment. It is almost never carried out under the rigorous controls that research requires. It is, primarily, an administrative device used to monitor performance to determine whether it continues to remain within acceptable bounds. Quality assessment can, however, make a contribution to research if, in the course of assessment, associations are noted between process and outcome that seem inexplicable by current knowledge. Such discrepancies would call for elucidation through research.

If I am correct in my analysis, we cannot claim either for the measurement of process or the measurement of outcomes an inherently superior validity compared with the other, since the validity of either flows to an equal degree from the validity of the science that postulates a linkage between the two. But, process and outcome do have, on the whole, some different properties that make them more or less suitable objects of measurement for given purposes. Information about technical care is readily available in the medical record, and it is available in a timely manner, so that prompt action to correct deficiencies can be taken. By contrast, many outcomes, by their nature, are delayed, and if they occur after care is completed, information about them is not easy to obtain. Outcomes do have, however, the advantage of reflecting all contributions to care, including those of the patient. But this advantage is also a handicap, since it is not possible to say precisely what went wrong unless the antecedent process is scrutinized.

This brief exposition of strengths and weaknesses should lead to the conclusion that in selecting an approach to assessment one needs to be guided by the precise characteristics of the elements chosen. Beyond causal validity, which is the essential requirement, one is guided by attributes such as relevance to the objectives of care, sensitivity, specificity, timeliness, and costliness.[15] As a general rule, it is best to include in any system of assessment, elements of structure, process, and outcome. This allows supplementation of weakness in one approach by strength in another; it helps one interpret the findings; and if the findings do not seem to make sense, it leads to a reassessment of study design and a questioning of the accuracy of the data themselves.

Before we leave the subject of approaches to assessment, it may be useful to say a few words about patient satisfaction as a measure of the quality of care. Patient satisfaction may be considered to be one of the desired outcomes of care, even an element in health status itself. An expression of satisfaction or dissatisfaction is also the patient's judgment on the quality of care in all its aspects, but particularly as concerns the interpersonal process. By questioning patients, one can obtain information about overall satisfaction and also about satisfaction with specific attributes of the interpersonal relationship, specific components of technical care, and the outcomes of care. In doing so, it should be remembered that, unless special precautions are taken, patients may be reluctant to reveal their opinions for fear of alienating their medical attendants. Therefore, to add to the evidence at hand, information can also be sought about behaviors that indirectly suggest dissatisfaction. These include, in addition to complaints registered, premature termination of care, other forms of noncompliance, termination of membership in a health plan, and seeking care outside the plan.

It is futile to argue about the validity of patient satisfaction as a measure of quality. Whatever its strengths and limitations as an indicator of quality, information about patient satisfaction should be as indispensable to assessments of quality as to the design and management of health care systems.

SAMPLING

If one wishes to obtain a true view of care as it is actually provided, it is necessary to draw a proportionally representative sample of cases, using either simple or stratified random sampling. Because cases are primarily classified by diagnosis, this is the most frequently used attribute for stratification. But one could use other attributes as well: site of care, specialty, demographic and socioeconomic characteristics of patients, and so on.

There is some argument as to whether patients are to be classified by discharge diagnosis, admission diagnosis, or presenting complaint. Classification by presenting complaint (for example, headache or abdominal pain) offers an opportunity to assess both success and failure in diagnosis. If discharge diagnoses are used, one can tell if the diagnosis is justified by the evidence; the failure to diagnose is revealed only if one has an opportunity to find cases misclassified under other diagnostic headings.

A step below strictly proportionate sampling, one finds methods designed to provide an illustrative rather than a representative view of quality. For example, patients may be first classified according to some scheme that represents important subdivisions of the realm of health care in general, or important components in the activities and responsibilities of a clinical department or program in particular. Then, one purposively selects, within each class, one or more categories of patients, identified by diagnosis or otherwise, whose management can be assumed to typify clinical performance for that class.

This is the "tracer method" proposed by Kessner and coworkers.[16,17] The validity of the assumption that the cases selected for assessment represent all cases in their class has not been established.

Most often, those who assess quality are not interested in obtaining a representative, or even an illustrative picture of care as a whole. Their purposes are more managerial, namely, to identify and correct the most serious failures in care and, by doing so, to create an environment of watchful concern that motivates everyone to perform better. Consequently, diagnostic categories are selected according to importance, perhaps using Williamson's[18] principle of "maximum achievable benefit," meaning that the diagnosis is frequent, deficiencies in care are common and serious, and the deficiencies are correctable.

Still another approach to sampling for managerial or reformist purposes is to begin with cases that have suffered an adverse outcome and study the process of care that has led to it. If the outcome is infrequent and disastrous (a maternal or perinatal death, for example), every case might be reviewed. Otherwise, a sample of adverse outcomes, with or without prior stratification, could be studied.[19-21] There is some evidence that, under certain circumstances, this approach will identify a very high proportion of serious deficiencies in the process of care, but not of deficiencies that are less serious.[22]

MEASUREMENT

The progression of steps in quality assessment that I have described so far brings us, at last, to the critical issue of measurement. To measure quality, our concepts of what quality consists in must be translated to more concrete representations that are capable of some degree of quantification—at least on an ordinal scale, but one hopes better. These representations are the criteria and standards of structure, process, and outcome.[23,24]

Ideally, the criteria and standards should derive, as I have already implied, from a sound, scientifically validated fund of knowledge. Failing that, they should represent the best informed, most authoritative opinion available on any particular subject. Criteria and standards can also be inferred from the practice of eminent practitioners in a community. Accordingly, the criteria and standards vary in validity, authoritativeness, and rigor.

The criteria and standards of assessment can also be either implicit or explicit. Implicit, unspoken criteria are used when an expert practitioner is given information about a case and asked to use personal knowledge and experience to judge the goodness of the process of care or of its outcome. By contrast, explicit criteria and standards for each category of cases are developed and specified in advance, often in considerable detail, usually by a panel of experts, before the assessment of individual cases begins. These are the two extremes in specification; there are intermediate variants and combinations as well.

The advantage in using implicit criteria is that they allow assessment of representative samples of cases and are adaptable to the precise characteristics of each case, making possible the highly individualized assessments that the conceptual formulation of quality envisaged. The method is, however, extremely costly and rather imprecise, the imprecision arising from inattentiveness or limitations in knowledge on the part of the reviewer and the lack of precise guidelines for quantification.

By comparison, explicit criteria are costly to develop, but they can be used subsequently to produce precise assessments at low cost, although only cases for which explicit criteria are available can be used in assessment. Moreover, explicit criteria are usually developed for categories of cases and, therefore, cannot be adapted readily to the variability among cases within a category. Still another problem is the difficulty in developing a scoring system that represents the degree to which the deficiencies in care revealed by the criteria influence the outcome of care.

Taking into account the strengths and limitations of implicit and explicit criteria, it may be best to use both in sequence or in combination. One frequently used procedure is to begin with rather abridged explicit criteria to separate cases into those likely to have received good care and those not. All the latter, as well as a sample of the former, are then assessed in greater detail using implicit criteria, perhaps supplemented by more detailed explicit criteria.

At the same time, explicit criteria themselves are being improved. As their use expands, more diagnostic categories have been included. Algorithmic criteria have been developed that are much more adaptable to the clinical characteristics of individual patients than are the more usual criteria lists.[25,26] Methods for weighting the criteria have also been proposed, although we still do not have a method of weighting that is demonstrably related to degree of impact on health status.[27]

When outcomes are used to assess the quality of antecedent care, there is the corresponding problem of specifying the several states of dysfunction and of weighting them in importance relative to each other using some system of preferences. It is possible, of course, to identify specific outcomes, for example, reductions in fatality or blood pressure, and to measure the likelihood of attaining them. It is also possible to construct hierarchical scales of physical function so that any position on the scale tells us what functions can be performed and what functions are lost.[28] The greatest difficulty arises when one attempts to represent as a single quantity various aspects of functional capacity over a life span. Though several methods of valuation and aggregation are available, there is still much controversy about the validity of the values and, in fact, about their ethical implications.[29,30] Nevertheless, such measures, sometimes called *measures of quality-adjusted life*, are being used to assess technological innovations in health care and, as a consequence, play a role in defining what good technical care is.[31,32]

INFORMATION

All the activities of assessment that I have described depend, of course, on the availability of suitable, accurate information.

The key source of information about the process of care and its immediate outcome is, no doubt, the medical record. But we know that the medical record is often incomplete in what it documents, frequently omitting significant elements of technical care and including next to nothing about the interpersonal process. Furthermore, some of the information recorded is inaccurate because of errors in diagnostic testing, in clinical observation, in clinical assessment, in recording, and in coding. Another handicap is that any given set of records usually covers only a limited segment of care, that in the hospital, for example, providing no information about what comes before or after. Appropriate and accurate recording, supplemented by an ability to collate records from various sites, is a fundamental necessity to accurate, complete quality assessment.

The current weakness of the record can be rectified to some extent by independent verification of the accuracy of some of the data it contains, for example, by reexamination of pathological specimens, x-ray films, and electro-cardiographic tracings and by recording diagnostic categorization. The information in the record can also be supplemented by interviews with, or questionnaires to, practitioners and patients, information from patients being indispensable if compliance, satisfaction, and some long-term outcomes are to be assessed. Sometimes, if more precise information on outcomes is needed, patients may have to be called back for reexamination. And for some purposes, especially when medical records are very deficient, videotaping or direct observation by a colleague have been used, even though being observed might itself elicit an improvement in practice.[33,34]

CONCLUSION

In the preceding account, I have detailed, although rather sketchily, the steps to be taken in endeavoring to assess the quality of medical care. I hope it is clear that there is a way, a path worn rather smooth by many who have gone before us. I trust it is equally clear that we have, as yet, much more to learn. We need to know a great deal more about the course of illness with and without alternative methods of care. To compare the consequences of these methods, we need to have more precise measures of the quantity and quality of life. We need to understand more profoundly the nature of the interpersonal exchange between patient and practitioner, to learn how to identify and quantify its attributes, and to determine in what ways these contribute to the patient's health and welfare. Our information about the process and outcome of care needs to be more complete and more accurate. Our criteria and standards need to be more flexibly adaptable to the finer clinical peculiarities of each case. In particular, we need to learn how to accurately elicit the preferences of patients to arrive at truly individualized assessments of quality. All this has to go on against the background of the most profound analysis of the responsibilities of the health care professions to the individual and to society.

NOTES

1. A. Donabedian, *Exploration in Quality Assessment and Monitoring: The Definition of Quality and Approaches to Its Management*. Vol. 1. (Ann Arbor, Mich.: Health Administration Press, 1980).

2. S. Eraker and P. Politser, How Decisions Are Reached: Physician and Patient, *Ann Intern Med* 97 (1982): 262–268.

3. A. Donabedian, Models for Organizing the Delivery of Health Services and Criteria for Evaluating Them, *Milbank Q* 50 (1972): 103–154.

4. B.J. McNeil, R. Weichselbaum, and S.G. Pauker, Fallacy of the Five-Year Survival in Lung Cancer, *N Engl J Med* 299 (1978): 1397–1401.

5. B.J. McNeil, R. Weichselbaum, and S.G. Pauker, Tradeoffs Between Quality and Quantity of Life in Laryngeal Cancer, *N Engl J Med* 305 (1981): 982–987.

6. B.J. McNeil, et al., On the Elicitation of Preferences for Alternative Therapies, *N Engl J Med* 306 (1982): 1259–1262.

7. Donabedian, *Explorations in Quality Assessment*, Vol. 1.

8. A. Donabedian, J.R.C. Wheeler, and L. Wyszewianski, Quality, Cost, and Health: An Integrative Model, *Med Care* 20 (1982): 975–992.

9. G.W. Torrance, Measurement of Health Status Utilities for Economic Appraisal: A Review, *J Health Econ* 5 (1986): 1–30.

10. A. Donabedian, Quality, Cost, and Clinical Decisions, *Ann Am Acad Polit Soc Sci* 468 (1983): 196–204.

11. Donabedian, *Explorations in Quality Assessment*, Vol. 1.

12. A. Donabedian, Evaluating the Quality of Medical Care, *Milbank Q* 44 (1966): 166–203.

13. R.H. Palmer and M.C. Reilly, Individual and Institutional Variables Which May Serve as Indicators of Quality of Medical Care, *Med Care* 17 (1979): 693–717.

14. A. Donabedian, The Epidemiology of Quality, *Inquiry* 22 (1985): 282–292.

15. Donabedian, *Explorations in Quality Assessment*, Vol. 1, 100–118.

16. D.M. Kessner, C.E. Kalk, and S. James, Assessing Health Quality—The Case for Tracers, *N Engl J Med* 288 (1973): 189–194.

17. K.J. Rhee, A. Donabedian, and R.E. Burney, Assessing the Quality of Care in a Hospital Emergency Unit: A Framework and Its Application, *Quality Rev Bull* 13 (1987): 4–16.

18. J.W. Williamson, Formulating Priorities for Quality Assurance Activity: Description of a Method and Its Application, *JAMA* 239 (1978): 631–637.

19. New York Academy of Medicine, Committee on Public Health Relations, *Maternal Mortality in New York City: A Study of All Puerperal Deaths 1930–1932* (New York: Oxford University Press Inc, 1933).

20. S.G. Kohl, *Perinatal Mortality in New York City: Responsible Factors* (Cambridge, Mass.: Harvard University Press, 1955).

21. D.B. Rutstein, et al., Measuring Quality of Medical Care: A Clinical Method, *N Engl J Med* 294 (1976): 582–588.

22. A.I. Mushlin and F.A. Appel, Testing an Outcome-Based Quality Assurance Strategy in Primary Care, *Med Care* 18 (1980): 1–100.

23. A. Donabedian, *Explorations in Quality Assessment and Monitoring: The Criteria and Standards of Quality*, Vol. 2. (Ann Arbor, Mich.: Health Administration Press, 1982).

24. A. Donabedian, Criteria and Standards for Quality Assessment and Monitoring, *Quality Rev Bull* 12 (1986): 99–108.

25. S. Greenfield, et al., Peer Review by Criteria Mapping: Criteria for Diabetes Mellitus: The Use of Decision-Making in Chart Audit, *Ann Intern Med* 83 (1975): 761–770.

26. S. Greenfield, et al., Comparison of a Criteria Map to a Criteria List in Quality-of-Care Assessment for Patients with Chest Pain: The Relation of Each to Outcome, *Med Care* 19 (1981): 255–272.

27. T.F. Lyons and B.C. Payne, The Use of Item Weights in Assessing Physician Performance with Predetermined Criteria Indices, *Med Care* 13 (1975): 432–439.

28. A.L. Stewart, J.E. Ware, Jr., and R.H. Brook, Advances in the Measurement of Functional States: Construction of Aggregate Indexes, *Med Care* 19 (1981): 473–488.

29. S. Fanshel and J.W. Bush, A Health Status Index and Its Application to Health Service Outcomes, *Operations Res* 18 (1970): 1021–1060.

30. D.I. Patrick, J.W. Bush, and M.M. Chen, Methods for Measuring Levels of Well-Being for a Health Status Index, *Health Serv Res* 8 (1973): 228–245.

31. M.C. Weinstein and W.B. Stason, Foundations of Cost-Effectiveness Analysis for Health and Medical Practices, *N Engl J Med* 296 (1977): 716–721.

32. J.S. Willems, et al., Cost-Effectiveness of Vaccination Against Pneumococcal Pneumonia, *N Engl J Med* 303 (1980): 553–559.

33. O.L. Peterson, et al., An Analytical Study of North Carolina General Practice, 1953-1954, *J Med Educ* 31 (1956): 1–165.

34. *What Sort of Doctor? Assessing Quality of Care in General Practice* (London: Royal College of General Practitioners, 1985).

4. Variations in Medical Practice and Hospital Costs

John E. Wennberg

I am very pleased to be asked to testify on the topic of variations in medical practice. My research into geographic patterns of health care delivery reveals extensive variation in the use of hospital services from one community to another. The extent of variation in reimbursements to hospitals under the Medicare program is such that if the low cost patterns of care were the norm, we would not be faced with the pending bankruptcy of the Medicare Trust Fund nor would we be now concerned with the specter that medical care must be rationed. For many medical or surgical conditions, the variations suggest opportunities to reduce expenditures under the Medicare and Medicaid programs without reducing the benefits of medical care. For other conditions, the variations reveal a critical need to evaluate the outcomes of different approaches to treatment, so that patients and physicians may better understand the significance of their choices in using medical care. Before concluding my testimony, I will describe a plan to address the cost containment and outcome assessment imperatives revealed by the variations and make some specific suggestions as to how the Department of Health and Human Services can contribute.

THE PRACTICE VARIATION PHENOMENON

The practice variation phenomenon first came to my attention some 15 years ago, when my colleagues and I implemented a system for monitoring health care delivery among hospital markets in Vermont. A unique feature of our approach is that we can identify the amount of care consumed by individuals in a specific

Source: Reprinted from *Connecticut Medicine,* Vol. 49, No. 7, pp. 444–453, with permission of Connecticut State Medical Society, © July 1985.

population and are thus able to calculate rates per capita. We noticed that the per capita expenditures for hospitalization in some areas were more than double those of others, even though studies of the populations of Vermont communities showed that the patients were quite similar and differed little in terms of medical need. We repeated these studies throughout New England and found similar patterns of variation in each state. These variations are not explained by differences in population characteristics and there seems to be no clear association between the factors that one ordinarily thinks should contribute to high costs, such as a greater percentage of the elderly in the population or the presence of a teaching hospital. However, differences in hospital costs do closely follow the distribution of hospital beds and numbers of persons employed in the hospital industry. (See Table 4–1.)

Table 4-1 The Quantity of Hospital Resources Expended on the Populations of New Haven, Connecticut, and Boston, Massachusetts, by Hospitals Providing Resources (1978)

Hospital	Percent of Admissions from the Local Pop.	Beds Allocated to Local Population	Market Share	Per Capita Rates†		
				Beds	Expend.*	Personnel
New Haven, Connecticut (pop. est. 372,900)						
Yale-New Haven Univ. Hosp	68.3	541.6	54.8	1.5	124	5.5
St. Raphael	86.4	416.6	38.1	1.1	82	3.5
Out-of-area hospital	—	65.0	7.1	0.1	9	0.5
All hospitals	—	1023.2	100.0	2.7	215	9.5
Boston, Massachusetts (pop. est. 732,400)						
Boston teaching hospital (N = 7)	42.6	1,828.0	59.0	2.5	322	13.1
Boston community hospital (N = 11)	50.6	843.0	23.3	1.2	84	3.3
Out-of-area hospital	—	524.4	16.7	.7	42	1.8
All hospitals	—	3195.4	100.0	4.4	448	18.2

Note: The estimates for the resources allocated to the New Haven and the Boston populations are made by multiplying the amount of resources provided by each hospital by the percent of admissions that are from the local population (column 2). For example, 542 of the Yale-New Haven University Hospital's total complement of 793 beds are used by the residents of New Haven. The estimate for the total numbers of beds is obtained by summing column 3 which, it will be noted, includes beds from out-of-area hospitals that provided services to the population of New Haven. For comparative purposes, we are particularly interested in per capita rates. The exhibit shows these for beds, numbers of personnel, and inpatient expenditures. All rates are corrected for boundary crossing.
   *For inpatient services.
   †Beds and personnel per 1,000 population, expenditures per person.

Let me give some examples. We found that hospital costs in Boston are about twice those of New Haven, even though most resident hospitalizations in each of these communities is to a teaching hospital and the percent of the population over 65 is about equal. Boston had about 4.4 beds and, in 1978, about 18.2 employees per 1,000 residents, while New Haven had about 2.7 beds and 9.5 employees. For 1982, we found that reimbursements for hospitalization of the elderly were 74 percent higher in Boston than in New Haven. If hospital insurance reimbursements for 78,000 Medicare enrollees living in Boston were the same as in New Haven, the outlays from the trust fund would have been $85 million rather than the actual $148 million, a savings to the trust fund of $63 million.

Figure 4–1 summarizes the extent of variation in expenditures and hospital bed allocations we have observed in our New England studies.

These differences in the per capita rates of use of resources are not intuitively known by the doctors or the patients on the scene. They become apparent only when they are measured directly. For example, I have asked clinicians who practice in both Yale and Harvard teaching hospitals to estimate the per capita expenditures for hospitals in each market. Their answers indicate they have no awareness of the magnitude of the difference; what is more surprising, many do not accurately guess which of the two markets is more expensive.

In my research, I have been very interested in how hospital resources are used—the specific services the dollars, facilities, and manpower produce. Here the findings are clear and consistent. Some causes of hospitalization show very little variation in admission rates among hospital markets, no matter what the level of resource investment. Examples of low variation admissions include hospitalizations for fractures of the hip, acute myocardial infarction (heart attack), strokes, appendectomy, and inguinal hernia repair. But these are the exceptions. Most causes of admission are highly variable, including many common surgical procedures. For example, we have found that the rates for tonsillectomy have varied as much as eightfold: nearly 70 percent of children had their tonsils removed by age 15 in one area, while in the low-rate community fewer than 8 percent experienced the operation. The probability of having a hysterectomy has varied from less than 15 percent to well over 60 percent of women by age 75, depending on place of residence. And the chances that a male will have a prostatectomy by age 75 have ranged from a low of about 15 percent to well over 50 percent in different hospital market areas.

Figure 4–2 shows the typical patterns of variation seen for common surgical procedures.

The variation phenomenon has been similarly documented in Europe and is not limited to health delivery systems based on fee-for-service financing. I have found the pattern of variation for common surgical procedures consistent among fee-for-service hospital markets in Iowa, Maine, Massachusetts, Rhode Island,

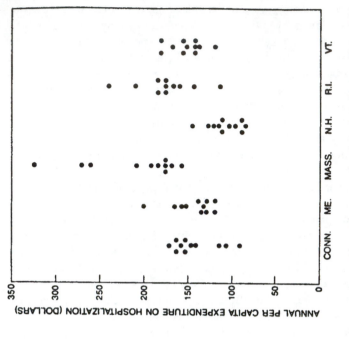

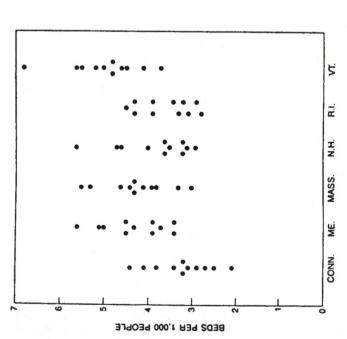

Figure 4–1 Number of Hospital Beds per Capita and the Annual Amount Spent per Capita on Hospital Treatment also Show the Influence of Geographic Variations in Medical Care. The data are for the 11 most populous hospital areas in each of the six New England states. The number of hospital beds per 1,000 people (adjusted for the number of people who leave their hospital area for treatment) ranges from about two to more than six. The ratios thus range from well below to well above the four beds per 1,000 established by the Federal Health Planning Program as a standard. Furthermore, the variation in each state is so great that the number of beds per capita in the state or county as a whole (a measure often employed by health planning agencies) bears little relation to the conditions prevailing in each community. The average amount spent on treatment in hospitals in 1975 ranged from less than $100 per capita to more than $300 in the 66 areas.

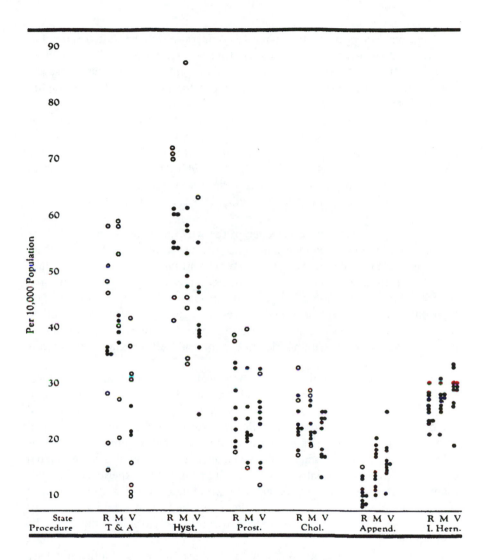

Note: Rates of surgical procedures vary greatly among hospital areas. The rates shown are for the six most common surgical procedures for the repair or removal of an organ in the 11 most populous hospital areas of Maine, Rhode Island, and Vermont (1975). The rate of tonsillectomy varies about sixfold among the 33 areas, the rates of hysterectomy and prostatectomy vary about fourfold. Moreover, many of the extreme rates for these procedures differ from the average rate for the state by an amount that is statistically significant (open circles). There is much disagreement among physicians on the value of the high-variation procedures. Similar patterns of variation for these procedures have been observed in Iowa, England, and Norway. R = Rhode Island, M = Maine, V = Vermont.

Figure 4–2 Age-Adjusted Rate of Procedure for Six Common Surgical Procedures in Rhode Island, Maine, and Vermont (1975)

and Vermont; among health maintenance organizations in the United States and among health care regions in Canada, England, and Norway, even though obvious differences exist in the supply of hospital beds and surgeons, the organization and financing of services, and in the cultural and demographic characteristics of the residents.

Our more recent studies have been concerned with variations in hospitalization rates among medical as well as surgical admissions. We have found that *most* causes of admission as classified by Diagnosis Related Groups (DRGs) have highly variable admission rates. Indeed, nearly 90 percent of all nonobstetrical cases admitted to hospital have greater variation than hysterectomy.

The pattern of variation typical for medical DRGs is shown in Figure 4–3 and Table 4–2.

Why is it that such differences exist in the way medicine is practiced? One reason is that for many common conditions, the necessary scientific studies that allow physicians to define the optimum treatment have not been done. Rather than consensus, there is controversy and disagreement among clinicians on what constitutes the best treatment for a particular problem. This is often the case when the clinical choice involves a medical versus a surgical approach to a given illness. The controversies arise because the natural history of the untreated or conservatively treated case is poorly understood and well-designed clinical trials are notably absent.

Examples include surgical versus nonsurgical treatment for menopausal symptoms, for moderate urinary tract obstruction due to benign hyperplasia of the prostrate, for recurrent sore throats related to hypertrophy of the tonsil, and for coronary bypass surgery following myocardial infarction. Well-defined scientific norms simply do not exist to delimit the practice options physicians select to treat these maladies. As a consequence, the opinions of individual doctors can vary substantially, based upon their subjective experience. Because many of the conditions are extremely common, eventually affecting most if not all people to some degree, the candidates that could qualify for operative intervention sometimes appear upwardly limited only by the size of the population.

Examples of such conditions that are particularly important for the Medicare program include prostatic hypertrophy, cataracts, and coronary artery disease. The public interest would be served by better understanding the implications of the variations, particularly the quality of life gains that follow the use of surgical approaches as compared to more conservative treatments. This should be a compelling priority for operations that carry a high surgical mortality rate. One such operation is prostatectomy, where the postoperative mortality rate during hospitalization is about 1 percent or slightly higher. We calculated that if the conservative or low rate practice style seen in our New England studies were the national norm, one should expect about 1,900 deaths per annum in the United

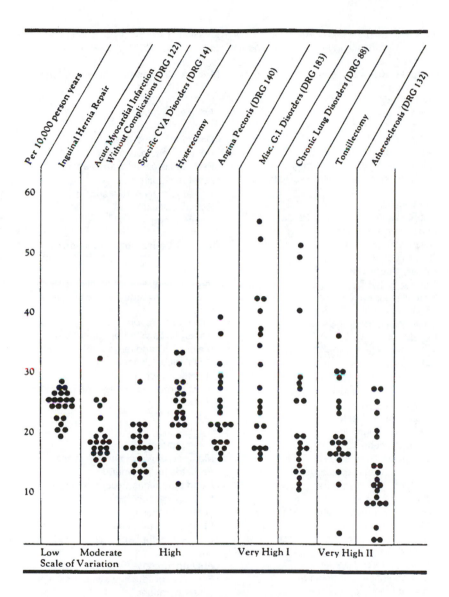

Note: The DRGs with similar statewide rates were selected to demonstrate the spectrum of variation in the incidence of DRG-specific hospitalizations among Maine hospital markets. Each circle represents a hospital market area. The graph is limited to markets with 45,000 person years or greater. The incidence of hospitalization for most DRGs is more variable than for hysterectomy.

Figure 4–3 Age-Adjusted Incidence of Hospitalization (1980–82) for Selected Medical DRGs and Three Common Surgical Procedures for Maine Hospital Markets

Table 4–2 Medical and Surgical Causes of Admissions Ranked in Ascending Order of Variation in Incidence of Hospitalization (1980–1982)*

Medical Causes of Admission

Low Variation
  None

Moderate Variation
  Acute myocardial infarction
  Gastrointestinal hemorrhage
  Specific cerebrovascular disorders

High Variation
  Nutritional and metabolic diseases
  Syncope and collapse
  Respiratory neoplasms
  Cellulitis
  Urinary tract stones
  Cardiac arrhythmias
  Miscellaneous injuries to extremities
  Angina pectoris
  Toxic effects of drugs
  Psychosis
  Heart failure and shock
  Seizures and headaches
  Adult simple pneumonias
  Respiratory signs and symptoms
  Depressive neurosis
  Medical back problems
  Digestive malignancy
  G.I. obstruction
  Adult gastroenteritis
  Peripheral vascular disorders
  Red blood cell disorders
  Adult diabetes
  Circulatory disorders etc., A.M.I. with
    card. cath.

Very High Variation
  Deep vein thrombophlebitis
  Adult bronchitis and asthma
  Organic mental syndromes
  Chest pain
  Transient ischemic attacks
  Kidney and urinary tract infections
  Acute adjustment reaction
  Minor skin disorders
  Trauma to skin, subcut. tiss., and breast
  Chronic obstructive lung disease

Medical Causes of Admission (cont.)

Hypertension
Adult otitis media and URI
Peptic ulcer
Disorders of the biliary tract
Pediatric gastroenteritis
Pediatric bronchitis and asthma
Atherosclerosis
Pediatric otitis media and URI
Pediatric pneumonia
Chemotherapy

Surgical Causes of Admission

Low Variation
  Inguinal and femoral hernia repair
  Hip repair, except joint replacement

Moderate Variation
  Appendicitis with appendectomy
  Major small and large bowel surgery
  Gallbladder disease with
    cholecystectomy
  Adult hernia repairs except inguinal and
    femoral

High Variation
  Hysterectomy
  Major cardiovascular operations
  Pediatric hernia operations
  Hand operations except ganglion
  Foot operations
  Lens operations
  Major joint operations
  Stomach, esophageal, and duodenal
    operations
  Anal operations
  Female reproductive system reconstruc-
    tive operations
  Back and neck operations
  Soft tissue operations

Very High Variation
  Knee operations
  Transurethral operations
  Uterus and andenexa operations

Table 4–2 continued

Surgical Causes of Admission

Very High Variation
Extra-ocular operations
Misc. ear, nose, and throat operations
Breast biopsy and local excision for
  nonmalignancy
D & C, conization except for malignancy
T & A operations except for tonsillectomy

Very High Variation
Tonsillectomy
Female laparoscopic operations, except
  for sterilization
Dental extractions and restorations
Laparoscopic tubal interruptions
Tubal interruption for nonmalignancy

*Causes of hospitalizations are taken from Diagnostic-Related Disease Classification System, but cases have been grouped without regard to presence or absence of significant complication. Obstetrical and neonatal causes of hospitalization are excluded. Ranking is according to the Systematic Component of Variation. Variations are measured across thirty hospital markets: The exhibit lists individually only those with more than 1,500 cases. More than 50 percent of hospitalizations are represented in the exhibit. Classes of variation are defined such that the variation associated with the first entry in a class is significantly more variable than the first entry in the previous class. For additional information see K. McPherson, J.E. Wennberg, O.B. Hovind, and P. Clifford. *The New England Journal of Medicine* 307 (1982): 1310–4.

States following this operation. But if the national norm were the high rate, the number would be about 6,800. The responsibility for further research into the outcome implications for this procedure seems to rest at least in part with the federal government since many of its activities promote the public's use of care and, for this procedure, most of the operations done in the United States are financed by the Medicare program.

There are other important reasons for variations that do not rest on scientific controversies and these provide the best opportunities for immediate savings on the cost of hospitalization. Physicians in some hospital markets practice medicine in ways that have extremely adverse implications for cost because they use the hospital for treating relatively minor illnesses or for performing minor surgery much more often than do most of their colleagues. The professional reasons that lead to a particular practice style are likely to be complex and idiosyncratic—involving matters of professional or patient convenience, inexperience or insecurity on the part of clinicians, individualistic interpretations of the requirement for "defensive medicine," and unexamined viewpoints about the relative risks associated with ambulatory versus inpatient treatment. To one degree or another, most of the medical causes of admission appear to fall into this class as do most minor surgical procedures. Common examples include admissions for virtually all pediatric medical diagnoses, and minor surgery such as a cystoscopy, teeth extractions, sterilization, or breast biopsy. These examples typically exhibit more than a tenfold variation in admission rates among hospital markets. Among the Medicare populations, the common examples include gastroenteritis, chronic obstructive lung disease, atherosclerosis, bronchitis and asthma, and simple pneumonias.

The consequences for costs of practice styles that favor inpatient over ambulatory settings are large, indeed. Take as the first example the differences in pediatric medical hospitalization rates, which are reflective of the variations that may be expected under Medicaid's program for dependent children. In Maine, a state with about one million residents, the largest hospital market area had utilization rates only 55 percent of the state average over the three-year period of our study. Based on an estimated cost per case of $1,300, we can project a net saving of about $2.5 million in this hospital market over average costs. If the practice styles seen in this area were emulated throughout the state, the costs of pediatric medical hospitalizations in Maine during the first three years of this decade would have been about $15.5 million, rather than the estimated $28.3 million—a saving of $12.8 million.

As a second example, consider medical admissions for the population over age 65, that is, those eligible for Medicare. One of the three most populous hospital markets in Iowa hospitalizes the elderly for medical admissions at a rate that is only 66 percent of the state average. Assuming an average cost per case of $2,000, we can estimate a net saving there of $2.2 million for Medicare medical admissions in 1980. If the hospitalization rate for this area were the norm for the state, the bill for medical admissions for the 190,000 persons over 65 years of age in our study would have been $72 million rather than the estimated $109 million—a saving of $37 million in one year alone.

Let me place these estimates of potential savings in a slightly different context. One hears a lot these days about how the cost crisis is leading to the need to ration medical services. This fear seems to me to be misplaced. The problem is that we are uninformed about the opportunities for reallocating existing resources. If the more conservative, ambulatory-oriented practice styles were to become the norm—and if hospital administrators and trustees translated the decrease in demand for specific services into a reduction in the capacity of the hospital system—then substantial cost savings would follow. Indeed, the resources that can be saved through the more judicious use of hospitals should more than meet the demands for investment in effective new technologies, such as liver transplants, for some time to come.

A PLAN FOR ACTION

What Needs To Be Done?

Let me state at the outset that the goal is emphatically *not* to obliterate all variations in the practice of medicine nor to reduce the practice of medicine to a cookbook. Obviously, physicians must have freedom to apply their skills as they and their patients see fit. Medicine is as much art as it is science and will always be so. An enterprise as large as medical care will always produce variations in approach. Rather, the goal should be to reduce variations that are highly aberrant, that reflect supply factors rather than scientific knowledge, or that reflect idiosyncrasies of physicians rather than the values, needs, or wants of their patients.

In the summer 1984 edition of *Health Affairs,* I suggested a three-part plan for dealing with the practice variation phenomenon in a way that improves health care outcomes and promotes cost-containment. I would like to review the outline of this plan and suggest steps the federal government can take to ameliorate the problems.

Monitoring Performances in Hospital Markets

The first part calls for a closer monitoring of medical practice in local markets, using epidemiologic techniques to create reports giving the numbers per capita of hospital beds, employees, and expenditures, as well as the rates of use of services and their outcomes. These reports provide an objective means for identifying variations, for assessing practice patterns, and for planning corrective actions. Without them, people are simply unaware of what is going on. The reports should be made available routinely to practicing physicians, to state and county medical associations, to Professional Review Organizations (PROs), to hospital administrators, and to others with interest in the measurement of hospital performance.

The data necessary to create the reports are, for the most part, generated already as part of the routine management of health insurance or regulatory programs and are contained in Medicare, Medicaid, and Blue Cross/Blue Shield claims systems and in hospital discharge abstracts similar to those used in the DRG program. Because of its national coverage and the richness of its data base, the Medicare program offers the best immediate opportunity to implement feedback in all parts of the country. The federal government now requires each hospital to record uniform information on the costs, reasons for hospitalization, and treatments for each hospitalization paid for under the Medicare program. When this information is linked to claims data under the Medicare part B program and to patient registration files, a registry is created of the medical care events and certain outcomes for virtually the entire population of the United States who are 65 years and older. The many problems for public policy concerning the equity and outcome of care that are illustrated by the variation phenomena, as well as the federal government's own need for effective cost containment, lead me to recommend that this very important national resource be used for this purpose.

Dealing with the Cost-Containment Problem

The second aspect of my plan calls for the use of the reports in a strategy to reduce the use of hospitals for highly variable medical admissions and minor surgery which can be treated effectively and safely in the ambulatory setting. The feedback reports give the information necessary for action: they identify the hospital market areas with costly practice styles for specific discretionary admissions and costly administrative practices with regard to hospital expenditure, bed, and personnel rates. The shift of such patients to the ambulatory setting will neither disrupt the patient-physician relationship nor have a significant negative effect on professional income. If widely implemented, this shift will create the opportunity for an extensive reduction in the resources allocated to hospitals.

Given the current imperatives to contain the costs of medical care and to reallocate resources to more productive ends, it is in everybody's best interest to reduce the use of marginally effective or unnecessary hospitalizations. In some respects, this is already happening. Over the past two years, we have witnessed an important change in practice patterns in the United States as evidenced by a reduction in the long-term trend of increasing hospital utilization. This diminution is the result of pressures from many sources, but the pivotal factor is that physicians are changing their attitudes about how medicine should be practiced. Our data suggest that the changes that have occurred to date should be viewed as just a beginning. We need to create and sustain an environment where cost-effective medical practice is the norm.

For this to happen, practicing physicians must take the lead by examining the pattern of utilization in their own communities and, when necessary, adapting their own practice styles and influencing their colleagues to adapt theirs to the more cost-effective practice patterns. A virtue of this approach is the recognition that decisions on cutbacks in service must be highly selective and specific, and that success depends on an informed and cooperative medical staff. It takes into account the nature of uncertainty concerning the value of most medical services and recognizes the need to make clinical choices that reduce demand for hospitalizations that are not worth the costs. It decentralizes the effort to the sites where clinical decisions are made and provides objective information on variations. Most important, the strategy offers a model for cost containment in which the profession can take a leading, not a defensive, role.

Will practicing physicians participate in such efforts? The evidence I have, based on my experiences in Iowa and New England, is that they will indeed respond. Given information on practice patterns in their local and regional markets, a consensus will emerge that it is safe and in the public interest to reduce hospitalization rates for many of the high variation cases I have listed in Table 4–2. Government officials, managers of benefit plans, and representatives of public or private interest groups have exercised important, sometimes decisive influences in persuading the medical profession of the need to respond to the challenge. But lacking as they must a detailed understanding of the nature of medical choices or the particular circumstances of a specific decision, they are in no position to deal with such issues as the necessity for hospitalization for a given patient.

The federal government can make two very specific contributions to promote market reforms based on feedback and review of high variation causes of admission. First, as indicated above, it can assure that the Medicare data base is available for the construction of market-area-specific reports. Second, it can promote population-based utilization review in hospital markets as part of the strategy for implementing the PRO program.

There are important reasons why the federal government should act. With the adoption of the DRG system, new controls on unit costs are now in place. But the level of variation for utilization rates is generally much greater than for unit prices (Figure 4–4). Since the DRG payments for services in any given hospital market depend upon diagnosis-specific admission rates, per capita reimbursements for most DRGs will typically show a three- and four- and often as much as a tenfold difference among neighboring areas. Many of these DRGs are highly variable because in some communities patients are cared for in the hospital while in others they are treated outside of the hospital.

Some of the variation in the medical DRGs may represent misclassification of patients, so I am reluctant to extrapolate from the variations seen for specific DRGs to predict the savings that might accrue to the Medicare Trust Fund if the PRO program were able to mobilize the physician community to adopt the more conservative practice styles. However, since hospital reimbursements for all causes vary by more than twofold, adoption of the conservative practice styles could easily result in savings that amount to more than 40 percent of the current outlay for hospitals.

Is there danger here of withholding necessary care or decreasing quality? Some expensive procedures are clearly necessary and costs for these will remain high. I am convinced, however, that it is both safe and in the public's best interest to reduce the use of hospitals for most high-variation medical and surgical admissions. Many communities with first-class medical care systems have low hospitalization rates. We find many examples of low-cost markets where most hospitalizations occur within teaching hospitals. I mentioned already the case of the New Haven market area served by Yale teaching hospitals. Others include the local market area of the University of Wisconsin's teaching hospital in Madison where Medicare reimbursements for hospitalizations in 1982 were $876 per enrollee compared to $1,515 in Milwaukee and the University of Iowa's area where reimbursements were $734 compared to $1,320 in Des Moines.

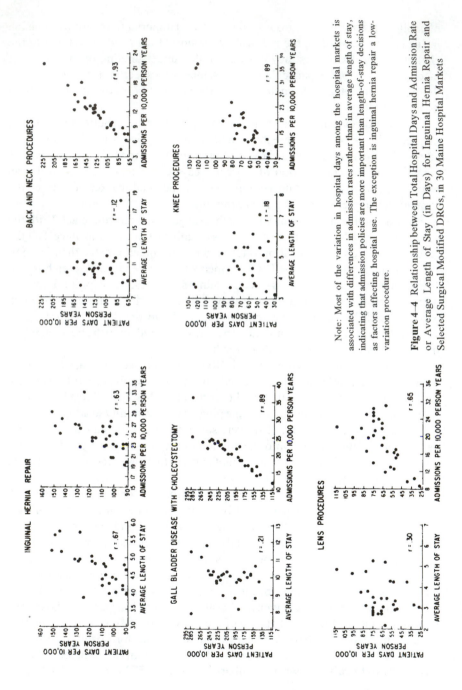

Note: Most of the variation in hospital days among the hospital markets is associated with differences in admission rates rather than in average length of stay, indicating that admission policies are more important than length-of-stay decisions as factors affecting hospital use. The exception is inguinal hernia repair a low-variation procedure.

Figure 4-4 Relationship between Total Hospital Days and Admission Rate or Average Length of Stay (in Days) for Inguinal Hernia Repair and Selected Surgical Modified DRGs, in 30 Maine Hospital Markets

Dealing with the Effectiveness Problem

The third part of my plan is to design and implement a program to deal with the unanswered questions concerning the outcomes of many common diagnostic and therapeutic interventions. The overriding question is whether a specific intervention undertaken to treat a condition with a known level of morbidity gets a better result than an alternative treatment. High levels of uncertainty cost billions of dollars nationwide and involve potentially thousands of lives. Reducing the level of uncertainty demands a concerted effort on the part of the private sector as well as government, and we have the means to achieve that objective.

The extent of the variation in use of most medical and surgical treatments, as well as a critical review of the literature supporting the assertion for efficacy of specific treatments, indicates that the number of outcome studies to be done is very large. Priorities will need to be set, new cost-effective health services research methodologies for evaluating outcomes must be invented and adopted, resources to conduct the studies must be made available, and the interest of practicing physicians in carrying out the studies and responding to the results must be cultivated.

I think we can count on physician participation in the design and implementation of such studies. By virtue of their inclination as well as their training, physicians want to practice scientifically sound medicine. That is what is expected of physicians and what physicians expect of themselves. When resources are available to support their participation, they respond in a very positive way. I submit as evidence the program of the Maine Medical Association to evaluate practice variations and cite in particular their program to investigate the outcome implications of prostatectomies undertaken for benign prostatic hypertrophy. After becoming aware of the extensive variation in prostatectomy rates among Maine communities, the urologists in Maine, under the leadership of Dr. Robert Timothy, undertook an extensive examination of the indications for the operation. As is typical for many common treatments, they could find no studies that provided a longer term, systematic follow-up of unselected patients. Because of this defect in the literature, the probabilities for specific kinds of outcomes—both the good and bad ones—could not be estimated in a meaningful way. To correct the situation, the physicians have undertaken a prospective evaluation of the response of patients to this treatment in order to document the changes in morbidity and functional status that relate to the operation. The study, which will provide information on events for up to a year after surgery, is making an important contribution to reduce uncertainty and ignorance concerning the expected outcomes following this operation.

What Can We Do To Make Such Efforts Routine?

Let me deal first with the medical schools. While the country has made a massive investment in basic biomedical science, both the Congress and the nation's medical schools have largely ignored the disciplines that deal directly with the problems of improving clinical decision making and evaluating health care outcomes—clinical epidemiology, biostatistics. and clinical decision analysis. Research to improve medical decision making is an important part of the agenda of schools of Public Health and has received scattered interest from enlightened physicians in many parts of the country. Yet, career opportunities are extremely limited in these disciplines and funding for specific outcome studies seems to be the last on everyone's agenda, except perhaps for randomized trials in selected fields such as cancer chemotherapy. The underdevelopment of these quantitative disciplines in the faculties of the medical schools not only affects the quality and volume of research in this area; it also means that the medical students are receiving little training in the very subjects that promise to make them better evaluators of evidence concerning alternative choices of treatment and more sophisticated participants in studies designed to improve the knowledge base of clinical medicine. If we wish to deal systematically with the clinical dilemmas evidenced by the practice variation phenomenon, we must adjust this imbalance.

How could the federal government help? In addition to the mobilization of the Medicare claims data base I mentioned before, the Department of Health and Human Services could help in a very direct way. Let me close this testimony by suggesting some specific objectives.

Foremost, the topic must be given visibility and priority. I suggest that HHS should make the goal of reducing uncertainty about the outcome implications of commonly used medical and surgical interventions a high departmental priority.

Second, a lead agency should be designated with responsibility for organizing a national strategy for implementing a program of outcome evaluation. The recent expansion of its mandate to include technology assessment suggests the National Center for Health Services Research for the role of lead agency, but, at the same time, Congress appropriated funds at a level below that available last year. Further, I want to underscore that the evaluative effort I am calling for applies to existing and commonly used medical practices. While assessment of new technology is obviously important, the lack of understanding of the value of existing practices needs special and ongoing attention.

Third, the national strategy should include the development in the medical schools of the quantitative disciplines essential to this task, including epidemiology, biostatistics, decision analysis, and computer sciences. This will provide medical students the analytic tools they need to practice informed, cost-effective medical care. The government could promote this needed instruction by directly supporting educational programs in these areas and by linking government awards to medical schools to the establishment of training programs in these vital areas.

Fourth, as part of this strategy, HHS should design and implement an intra- and extra-mural research program that seeks specifically to improve the knowledge base for services purchased under the Medicare program. My suggestion is that a fixed percentage of the Medicare and Medicaid patient care dollars be earmarked for this purpose. In 1984, expenditure from the Medicare Trust Fund totaled about $33 billion, nearly all spent on hospital care. Industries commonly invest directly in development of better products. If one-half of one percent of this amount were invested to find out what portion of this $33 billion is well spent and what represents unnecessary and even harmful uses of public resources, the long-term cost containment strategies of the federal government would not only be more successful, they would truly promote better health.

5. Continuous Improvement As an Ideal in Health Care

Donald M. Berwick

Imagine two assembly lines, monitored by two foremen.

Foreman 1 walks the line, watching carefully. "I can see you all," he warns. "I have the means to measure your work, and I will do so. I will find those among you who are unprepared or unwilling to do your jobs, and when I do there will be consequences. There are many workers available for these jobs, and you can be replaced."

Foreman 2 walks a different line, and he too watches. "I am here to help you if I can," he says. "We are in this together for the long haul. You and I have a common interest in a job well done. I know that most of you are trying very hard, but sometimes things can go wrong. My job is to notice opportunities for improvement—skills that could be shared, lessons from the past, or experiments to try together—and to give you the means to do your work even better than you do now. I want to help the average ones among you, not just the exceptional few at either end of the spectrum of competence."

Which line works better? Which is more likely to do the job well in the long run? Where would you rather work?

In modern American health care, there are two approaches to the problem of improving quality—two theories of quality that describe the climate in which care is delivered. One will serve us well; the other probably will not.

Source: Adapted from the *New England Journal of Medicine,* Vol. 320, No. 1, pp. 53–56, with permission of the Massachusetts Medical Society, © 1989.

THE THEORY OF BAD APPLES

The theory used by Foreman 1 relies on inspection to improve quality. We may call it the Theory of Bad Apples, because those who subscribe to it believe that quality is best achieved by discovering bad apples and removing them from the lot. The experts call this mode "quality by inspection," and in the thinking of activists for quality in health care it predominates under the guise of "buying right," "recertification," or "deterrence" through litigation. Such an outlook implies or establishes thresholds for acceptability, just as the inspector at the end of an assembly line decides whether to accept or reject finished goods.

Those in health care who espouse the Theory of Bad Apples are looking hard for better tools of inspection. Such tools must have excellent measuring ability—high sensitivity and specificity, simultaneously—lest the malefactors escape or the innocent be made victims. They search for outliers—statistics far enough from the average that chance alone is unlikely to provide a good excuse. Bad Apples theorists publish mortality data, invest heavily in systems of case-mix adjustment, and fund vigilant regulators. Some measure their success by counting heads on platters.

The Theory of Bad Apples gives rise readily to what can be called the my-apple-is-just-fine-thank-you response on the part of the workers supervised by Foreman 1. The foreman has defined the rules of a game called "Prove you are acceptable," and that is what the workers play. The game is not fun, of course; the workers are afraid, angry, and sullen, but they play nonetheless. When quality is pursued in the form of a search for deficient people, those being surveyed play defense. They commonly use three tactics: kill the messenger (the foreman is not their friend, and the inspector even less so); distort the data or change the measurements (whenever possible, take control of the mechanisms that may do you harm); and if all else fails, turn somebody else in (and divert the foreman's attention).

Any good foreman knows how clever a frightened work force can be. In fact, practically no system of measurement—at least none that measures people's performance—is robust enough to survive the fear of those who are measured. Most measurement tools eventually come under the control of those studied, and in their fear such people do not ask what measurement can tell them, but rather how they can make it safe. The inspector says, "I will find you out if you are deficient." The subject replies, "I will therefore prove I am not deficient"—and seeks not understanding, but escape.

The signs of this game are everywhere in health care. With determination and enormous technical resourcefulness, the Health Care Financing Administration has published voluminous data for two consecutive years about the mortality profiles of Medicare recipients in almost every hospital in the United States—profiles that are adjusted according to complex multivariate models to show many important characteristics of the patient populations.[1] Such information, though by no means flawless, could be helpful to hospitals seeking to improve their effectiveness. Yet the hundreds of pages of data are dwarfed by the thousands of pages of responses from hospitals, trying to prove whatever hospitals need to prove to build their defenses. What else should we expect?

The same game is being played between aggressive Boards of Registration in Medicine and other regulators that require hospitals and physicians to produce streams of reports on the contents of their closets. In Massachusetts, for example, merely talking with a physician about his or her involvement in a mishap may commit a hospital administrator by law to report that physician to the Board of Registration in Medicine.

The sad game played out in this theory and the predictable response to it imply a particular view of the nature of hazard and deficiency in health care, as it does in any industry playing such a game. The view is that problems of quality are caused by poor intentions. The Bad Apple is to blame. The cause of trouble is people—their venality, incompetence, or insufficient caution. According to this outlook, one can use deterrence to improve quality, because intentions need to be changed; one can use reward or punishment to control people who do not care enough to do what they can or what they know is right. The Theory of Bad Apples implies that people must be made to care; the inevitable response is the attempt to prove that one cares enough.

What a waste! The Theory of Bad Apples let American industry down for decades. It took some visionary theorists, many of them statisticians, in companies with great foresight to learn that relying on inspection to improve quality is at best inefficient, and at worst a formula for failure.[2-6] The Japanese learned first—from American theorists, ironically—that there were far better ways to improve quality, and the result is international economic history.[7] Today, no American companies make videocassette recorders or compact-disc players or single-lens-reflex cameras; we have simply given up. Xerox engineers visiting Japan in 1979 found copiers being produced at half the cost of those manufactured at Xerox's facilities, with only 1/30 the number of defects.[8]

THE THEORY OF CONTINUOUS IMPROVEMENT

What Japan had discovered was primarily a new, more cogent, and more valid way to focus on quality. Call it the Theory of Continuous Improvement. Its postulates are simple, but they are strangely alien to some basic assumptions of American industry—assumptions fully evident in health care today. These postulates have been codified most forcefully by two American theorists, W. Edwards Deming[9,10] and Joseph M. Juran[11,12]—heroes in Japan today, and among enlightened American companies. Juran and Deming, guided largely by a visionary group of mentors at Western Electric Laboratories (later AT&T Bell Laboratories) in the 1930s, drew on a deepened understanding of the general sources of problems in quality. They discovered that problems, and therefore opportunities to improve quality, had usually been built directly into the complex production processes they studied, and that defects in quality could only rarely be attributed to a lack of will, skill, or benign intention among the people involved with the processes. Even when people were at the root of defects, they learned, the problem was generally not one of motivation or effort, but rather of poor job design, failure of leadership, or unclear purpose. Quality can be improved much more when people are assumed to be trying hard already, and are not accused of sloth. Fear of the kind engendered by the disciplinary approach poisons improvement in quality, since it inevitably leads to disaffection, distortion of information, and the loss of the chance to learn.

Real improvement in quality depends, according to the Theory of Continuous Improvement, on understanding and revising the production processes on the basis of data about the processes themselves. "Every process produces information on the basis of which the process can be improved," say these theorists. The focus is on continuous improvement throughout the organization through constant effort to reduce waste, rework, and complexity. When one is clear and constant in one's purpose, when fear does not control the atmosphere (and thus the data), when learning is guided by accurate information and sound rules of inference, when suppliers of services remain in dialogue with those who depend on them, and when the hearts and talents of all workers are enlisted in the pursuit of better ways, the potential for improvement in quality is nearly boundless. Translated into cultural norms in production systems and made real through sound statistical techniques, these lessons are at the core of the Japanese industrial revolution.[13] They have proved their worth.

In retrospect, their success is not all that surprising. Modern theories of quality improvement in industry are persuasive largely because they focus on the average producer, not the outlier, and on learning, not defense. Like Foreman 2, the modern quality-improvement expert cares far more about learning and cooperating with the typical worker than about censoring the truly deficient. The Theory of Continuous Improvement works because of the immense, irresistible quantitative power derived from shifting the entire curve of production upward even slightly, as compared with a focus on trimming the tails. The Japanese call it *kaizen*—the continuous search for opportunities for all processes to get better.[14] An epigram captures this spirit: "Every defect is a treasure." In the discovery of imperfection lies the chance for processes to improve.

How far from *kaizen* has health care come! Not that the idea of continuous improvement is alien to medicine; self development, continuous learning, the pursuit of completeness are all familiar themes in medical instruction and history. Yet today we find ourselves almost devoid of such thinking when we enter the debate over quality. The disciplinarians seek out Bad Apples; the profession, and its institutions by and large, try to justify themselves as satisfactory. It is the rare "customer" and "supplier" of health care today who function as partners in continuous improvement; for the most part, they are playing a different game.

It would be naive to counsel the total abandonment of surveillance and discipline. Even in Japan, there are police. Politically, at least, it is absolutely necessary for regulators to continue to ferret out the truly avaricious and the dangerously incompetent. But what about the rest of us? How can we best be helped to try a little *kaizen* in our medical back yards? What follows are a few small steps.

First, leaders must take the lead in quality improvement. Those who speak for the profession, for health care institutions, and for large-scale purchasers must establish and hold to a shared vision of a health care system undergoing continuous improvement. The volleys of accusation and defense badly need to be replaced by efforts to clarify the goals that producers and payers share, beginning with this assumption: "Health care is very good today; together, we intend to make it even better."

Second, investments in quality improvement must be substantial. In other industries, quality improvement has yielded high dividends in cost reductions;[15] that may occur in health care as well. For the time being, however, improvement requires additional investments in managerial time, capital, and technical expertise. With the high discount rate in health care planning today, such investment calls for steadfast long-term vision. The most important investments of all are in education and study, to understand the complex production processes used in health care; we must understand them before we can improve them.

Third, respect for the health care worker must be reestablished. Physicians, hospital employees, and health care workers, like workers anywhere, must be assumed to be trying hard, acting in good faith, and not willfully failing to do what they know to be correct. When they are caught in complex systems and performing complex tasks, of course clinicians make mistakes; these are unintentional, and the people involved cannot be frightened into doing better. In fact, if they are afraid, they will probably do worse, since they will be wasting their time in self-defense instead of learning.

Fourth, dialogue between customers and suppliers of health care must be open and carefully maintained. As an incentive to improve quality, the threat of taking one's business elsewhere is pale compared with the reminder that one is committed to a long-term relationship. Quality improves as those served (the customers) and those serving (the suppliers) take the time to listen to each other and to work out their inevitable misunderstandings. Just as marriages do not improve under the threat of divorce, neither, in general, will health care.

Fifth, modern technical, theoretically grounded tools for improving processes must be put to use in health care settings. The pioneers of quality improvement—Shewhart,[16,17] Dodge, Juran,[18,19] Deming,[20,21] Taguchi,[22] and others[23]—have left a rich heritage of theory and technique by which to analyze and improve complex production processes, yet until recently these techniques have had little use in our health care systems. The barriers have been cultural in part; physicians, for example, seem to have difficulty seeing themselves as participants in processes, rather than as lone agents of success or failure. The techniques of process flow analysis, control charts, cause-and-effect diagrams, design experimentation, and quality-function deployment, to name a few, are neither arcane nor obvious,[24,25] they require study, but they can be learned. Many will be as useful in health care as they have been in other industries. Processes that can be improved by means of systematic techniques abound in medicine. Those within institutions are obvious, such as the ways in which hospitals dispense medications, transfer information, or equip and schedule operating rooms. But even individual doctors create and use "production processes." In this sense, the way a physician schedules patients constitutes a process, as does the way he or she prescribes medicines, gives a patient instructions, organizes office records, issues bills, or ensures that high-risk patients receive influenza vaccine.

Sixth, health care institutions must "organize for quality." When other types of companies have invested in quality improvement, they have discovered and refined managerial techniques requiring new structures, such as are not currently found in the American hospital or health maintenance organization. Quality engineers occupy a central place in such structures, as quality is brought to center stage in the managerial agenda, on a par with finance. Flexible project teams must be created, trained, and competently led to tackle complex processes that cross customary departmental boundaries. Throughout the organization, a renewed investment must be made in training, since all staff members must become partners in the central mission of quality improvement.

Furthermore, health care regulators must become more sensitive to the cost and ineffectiveness of relying on inspection to improve quality. In some regulatory functions, inspection and discipline must continue, but when such activities dominate, they have an unfavorable effect on the quality of care provided by the average worker. This is not to argue against measuring quality and developing tools to do so; without them, artisans could not improve their craft. The danger lies in a naive and a theoretical belief, rampant today in the orgy of measurement involved in health care regulation, that the assessment and publication of performance data will somehow induce otherwise indolent care givers to improve the level of their care and efficiency. In other industries, reliance on inspection as the agent of change has instead more commonly added cost and slowed progress toward improvement. So it will be in health care.

Without doubt, regulators who willingly learn and respect modern principles of quality improvement can have a helpful role. They can do so as the partners of care givers in developing sound measurement tools that represent common values and are for use primarily by the producers themselves; by aggregating data centrally to help care givers learn from each other; by providing technical support and training in methods of quality improvement; and by encouraging and funding studies of efficacy of technologies and procedures and thus expanding the scientific basis for specifying rational processes of care.

In addition, professionals must take part in specifying preferred methods of care, but must avoid minimalist "standards" of care. Linked closely to the reliance on inspection to improve quality is the search for standards of care, which usually implies minimal thresholds of structure, process, or outcome above which one is safe from being labeled a Bad Apple. Quality-control engineers know that such floors rapidly become ceilings, and that a company that seeks merely to meet standards cannot achieve excellence. Specifications of process (clear, scientifically grounded, continuously reviewed statements of how one intends to behave) are essential to quality improvement, on the other hand, and are widely lacking in medical care. Health care producers who commit themselves to improvement will invest energy in developing specific statements of purpose and algorithms for the clinical processes by which they intend to achieve those purposes. For example, they will specify rules both for routine procedures (e.g., "What is our system for dispensing medications correctly?") and for the content and evaluation of clinical practices (e.g., "What is our best current guess about the proper sequence of tests and therapies for back pain, and how well are they working?"). Ideally, such specifications are guidelines that are appropriate locally and are subject to ongoing assessment and revision.

Finally, individual physicians must join in the effort for continuous improvement. It may seem at first that the Theory of Continuous Improvement, coming as it does from experience in large manufacturing companies, has little relevance to individual physicians, at least those not involved in managed care organizations. But the opposite is true. At the very least, quality improvement has little chance of success in health care organizations without the understanding, the participation, and in many cases the leadership of individual doctors. In hospitals, physicians both rely on and help shape almost every process pertaining to patients' experience, from support services (such as dietary and housekeeping functions) to clinical care services (such as laboratories and nursing). Few can improve without the help of the medical staff.

Furthermore, the theory of quality improvement applies almost as well to small systems (such as a doctor's office) as it does to large ones. Individual physicians caring for individual patients know that defects in the care they provide do not usually stem from inattention or uninformed decisions. Yet hazards and defects do occur. Often they originate in the small but complex sequences on which every doctor depends, even sole practitioners. A test result lost, a specialist who cannot be reached, a missing requisition, a misinterpreted order, duplicate paperwork, a vanished record, a long wait for the CT scan, an unreliable on-call system—these are all-too-familiar examples of waste, rework, complexity, and error in the doctor's daily life. Flawless care requires not just sound decisions but also sound supports for those decisions. For the average doctor, quality fails when systems fail. Without the insights and techniques of quality improvement embedded in their medical practice, physicians are like anyone else who depends on others to get a complicated job done. They can remain trapped by defects they do not create but will nonetheless be held accountable for. The solo doctor who embodies every process needed to ensure highest-quality care is now nearly a myth. All physicians depend on systems, from the local ones in their private offices to the gargantuan ones of national health care.

Physicians who doubt that methods designed to improve quality can help them in daily practice may consider several questions. When quality fails in your own work, why does it fail? Do you ever waste time waiting, when you should not have to? Do you ever redo your work because something failed the first time? Do the procedures you use waste steps, duplicate efforts, or frustrate you through their unpredictability? Is information that you need ever lost? Does communication ever fail? If the answer to any of these is yes, then ask why. How can it be changed? What can be improved, and how? Must you be a mere observer of problems, or can you lead toward their solution? Physicians and health care managers who study and apply the principles of continuous improvement daily will probably come to know better efficiency, greater effectiveness, lower cost, and the gratitude and loyalty of more satisfied patients. They will be able to make better decisions and carry them out more faithfully.

CONCLUSION

We are wasting our time with the Theory of Bad Apples and our defensive response to it in health care today, and we can best begin by freeing ourselves from the fear, accusation, defensiveness, and naiveté of an empty search for improvement through inspection and discipline. The Theory of Continuous Improvement proved better in Japan; it is proving itself again in American industries willing to embrace it, and it holds some badly needed answers for American health care.

NOTES

1. Health Care Financing Administration, *Medicare Hospital Mortality Information.* (Washington, D.C.: Government Printing Office, 1988.) GPO Publication No. 1987 0-196860.

2. W.A. Shewhart, The Application of Statistics As an Aid in Maintaining Quality of a Manufactured Product, *J Am Stat Assoc* 20 (1925): 546–8.

3. W.A. Shewhart, *Economic Control of Quality of a Manufactured Product* (New York: D. Van Nostrand, 1931).

4. J.M. Juran, F.M. Gryna, Jr., and R.S. Bingham, Jr., eds. *Quality Control Handbook* (New York: McGraw-Hill, 1979).

5. W.E. Deming, *Quality, Productivity, and Competitive Position* (Cambridge, Mass.: Massachusetts Institute of Technology, Center for Advanced Engineering Study, 1982).

6. A.V. Feigenbaum, *Total Quality Control,* 3rd ed. (New York: McGraw-Hill, 1983).

7. D.A. Garvin, *Managing Quality: The Strategic and Competitive Edge* (New York: Free Press, 1988).

8. P.H. Abelson, Competitiveness: A Long-Enduring Problem, *Science* 240 (1988): 865.

9. Deming, *Quality, Productivity, and Competitive Position.*

10. W.E. Deming, *Out of the Crisis* (Cambridge, Mass.: Massachusetts Institute of Technology, Center for Advanced Engineering Study, 1986).

11. Juran, et al., *Quality Control Handbook.*

12. J.M. Juran, *Managerial Breakthrough* (New York: McGraw-Hill, 1964).

13. Garvin, *Managing Quality.*

14. M. Imai, *Kaizen—The Key to Japanese Competitive Success* (New York: Random House, 1986).

15. P.B. Crosby, *Quality is Free: The Art of Making Quality Certain* (New York: McGraw-Hill, 1979).

16. Shewhart, The Application of Statistics.

17. Shewhart, *Economic Control of Quality.*

18. Juran, et al., *Quality Control Handbook.*

19. Juran, *Managerial Breakthrough.*

20. Deming, *Quality, Productivity, and Competitive Position.*

21. Deming, *Out of the Crisis.*

22. R.N. Kackar, Off-Line Quality Control, Parameter Design, and the Taguchi Method, *J Qual Technol* 17 (1985): 176–88.

23. H.M. Wadsworth, K.S. Stephens, and A.B. Godfrey, *Modern Methods for Quality Control and Improvement* (New York: John Wiley, 1986).

24. Ibid.

25. K. Ishikawa, ed., *Guide to Quality Control* (White Plains, N.Y.: Kraus International Publications, 1986).

PART II.

TODAY

From "Yesterday" to "Today," we have moved rapidly on the continuum from Quality Assurance (QA) to Quality Improvement (QI); building on the strengths of QA. Quality Assurance refers to the internal and external methods of assessing the incidence and levels of quality problems and attempts to assure that quality is improved. The hospital conducts reviews based on definite criteria, as well as reviews based on specific incidents. The orientation is to look for the "bad apples."[1] This mode of inspection rarely motivates anyone to study systematically how to improve the quality of the entire group, rather it emphasizes the outliers. Most of QA staff time is spent on meeting minimum external requirements. Quality Assurance does not focus on common cause or system variation—how to improve the whole.[2] Instead, it focuses on the tail of the distribution, the people who do not meet minimum standards. On the surface, the difference between QA and QI may appear fuzzy but in implementation they are very different, as we will see in the discussion in Chapter 14. Quality Improvement involves a major cultural change in organization, plus senior management commitment and involvement, employee participation, and the use of scientific tools—Statistical Process Control (SPC).[3]

In Chapter 6 George Whetsell answers the question, "What is Total Quality Management (TQM)?" and provides a good overview of the process. In Chapter 7, Paul Plesk goes further in explaining the process of TQM. There are many quality improvement models and, while it may seem that they are quite different, they are all built on the same conceptual base. He examines the basic concepts and shows how to use them in a practical way. Quality Improvement holds promise for major changes in health care organizations and among practitioners. Few doubt that QI applies to services (turnaround time, patient flow, material flow). Less clear, however, is the evidence of its impact on standardizing clinical work and improving clinical quality.[4] In Chapter 8, Bolster, Falter, and Hooper, however, clearly demonstrate that QI is effective in the clinical area when treating stroke patients.

73

The Outcomes Management (OM) movement, clinical practice guidelines, and critical paths may point the way and speed up the process. They all attempt to identify, decrease variation, and thus improve quality. Critical paths are detailed day-by-day descriptions of the care plan. "They define the optimal sequencing and timing of intervention by physicians, nurses, and other staff for a particular diagnosis or practice. They are designed to minimize delays and resource utilization and to maximize care. Critical paths have been shown to reduce variation in care provided, facilitate expected outcomes, reduce delay, reduce length of stay, and improve cost-effectiveness. The approach and growth of critical paths are consistent with Total Quality Management."[5] This concept is discussed at length in Chapter 9 by Richard Coffey, et al. In Chapter 10, Dr. James discusses implementing practical guidelines through Clinical Quality Improvement (CQI). QI theory provides a set of tools to understand, measure, and manage the health care delivery process and their associated costs. As a methodology for process management QI theory merges case management, practice guidelines, and outcomes research into a single coordinated effort. He explains how practical guidelines can be used as a decision support and management tool. In Chapter 11, Dr. Epstein considers the forces that have brought about the outcomes movement and the direction it has taken so far. He then examines the goals of the movement and the likely impediments to its progress. The goal is to have a national program in which clinical guidelines are based systematically on patient outcome. In Chapter 12, Dr. Donabedian further elaborates on the role of outcomes in assessing and assuring quality. He stresses that there is no reason to debate the relative superiority of process over outcome or structure—we need information on all three.

Outcomes Management is deeply rooted in clinical issues that interrelate concerns about quality with cost effectiveness. OM is not simply the evolution of the end products of the health care system. It goes beyond Donabedian's tripod of structure, process, and outcome,[6] as shown here, and as reviewed in Chapter 12. Outcomes data are an important tool of outcomes management programs, but more is involved than simply collecting data on mortality, disability, and cost. Large data bases are needed to establish monitoring systems. Variations in outcomes in different areas and the interventions that are associated with these differences in outcome are identified. These data can then be used to inform practitioners about process components that are related to outcome. Clinical outcomes can be used to make more informed decisions. The use of severity measures to adjust for differences in case mix is one of the fundamental components of outcome research.[7] We have evolved from looking at the quality tripod from Donabedian's point of view, to the tripod as described by Nash. Both are shown as follows.

The emphasis in TQM is on "doing things right" the first time. Outcomes Management is equally concerned with "doing the right thing." Thus, TQM and

STRUCTURE PROCESS OUTCOME

Donabedian's Quality Tripod

OUTCOMES PRACTICE   CQI
RESEARCH PATTERN
         ANALYSIS

Nash's Quality Tripod

OM are integrally related components of a cohesive organization's wide focus on enhancing the health status of the population. Such a population-based view demands that individual institutions devise means of following patterns over time. Managing outcomes over time often requires modifying patient behavior (Chapter 17), as well as physician practice patterns (Chapter 18). The challenge for the organization's leadership is to support information networks and interactive clinical-management structures that will produce, monitor, and act systematically on outcomes information.

The method of evaluating quality has gone from the linear approach to the circular approach to the multidisciplinary approach, as shown in Figure II–1. The organization has the ability to link financial and clinical data to health outcomes.[8] There is a natural fit between the use of practice guidelines (from outcomes research) and the Total Quality (TQ) cycle of plan-do-check-act (P-D-C-A). In the P-D-C-A cycle, processes are studied to plan change, changes are tried, their effectiveness is checked, and if successful, they are enacted into regular operations. One can even think of practice guidelines, TQM, and outcomes as a kind of physiological feedback loop, each integrated with the other continuously cycling.[9] (See Figure II–2.)

The recognition, analysis, and reduction in variation—the intellectual core of TQM—allow health care organizations to make important advances by developing sound clinical guidelines based on rigorous analysis of variation in *outcome and processes.*[10]

Brook believes that three main forces are pushing toward the development of practice guidelines

1. increased financial pressure in the health care system
2. rapid introduction of new technology
3. new data showing high levels of inappropriate care and the resultant waste of billions of dollars worth of resources[11]

Benchmarking, as discussed in Chapter 13, is a process designed to assess the competition in comparison to an organization's own performance.[12] It is the search for the best practice that will lead to superior performance. It encourages

Since yesterday we have gone from the linear approach:

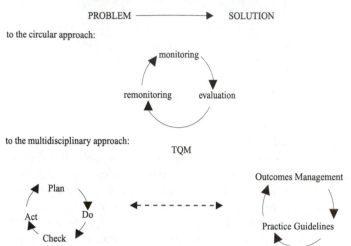

to the circular approach:

to the multidisciplinary approach:

TQM

Figure II–1 Quality Evaluation

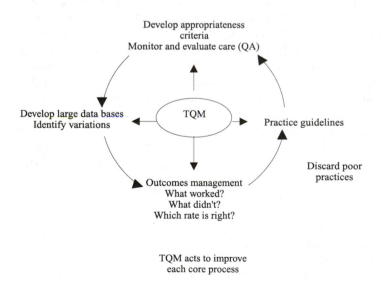

Figure II–2 Feedback Loop for Quality

the organization to learn from the best and to improve continuously. Chapter 14 provides insight on automated information systems and their potential to track usable information. Durbin, et al., in Chapter 15 discuss strategic planning and TQM in a multi-institutional system. The concepts of TQM are important for organizing quality in a complex system. In times of rapid change, the need to learn continually is certainly accelerated. Peter Senge in Chapter 16 discusses the need to build a learning organization. Much of what we need to learn about quality management in health care exists in the literature from other industries. The last chapter in this section (Chapter 19) discusses the barriers to implementation of TQM.

Some of the forces driving the change from QA to QI are double-digit inflation in the cost of health care, variations in practice, lack of access to health care, competition, and the demand for professional accountability. Methods of QA have evolved over the years from implicit peer review to medical audits, to monitoring and evaluation, to continuous quality improvement. The shift to continuous QI is the next logical step. Quality Assurance has been motivated by external requirements, focusing on the outlier or "bad apple" and fosters a department-oriented approach to quality. Quality Improvement focuses on finding the root cause, the importance of cross-functional and multidisciplinary approach to process improvement. TQM recognizes that the entire organization must be committed to improvement.[13] (See Exhibit II–1.)

QUESTIONS FOR THOUGHT, DISCUSSION, AND RESEARCH

1. What are the characteristics of the organization that has successfully implemented quality improvement?

Exhibit II–1 A Schematic of TQM/CQI

Attitude +	*Method* +	*Tools = TQM/CQI*
Prevention vs. detection	Process improvement	Flow chart
Customer centrality	Systems approach	Run chart
Do right things right the first time	Team and teamwork	Scatter diagram
Top commitment	Decrease variation	Cause and effect
Empowerment		Pareto
		Histogram
		Control chart

Attitude + Method + Tools = TQM/CQI

2. To what extent are guidelines based on real information instead of national myths?
3. How do you change practice behavior?
4. How does the implementation of clinical guidelines affect the quality of care?
5. What difference do guidelines make in terms of cost and patient outcome, including functional status?
6. Are certain organizational structures able to move more readily to adopt quality improvement methods?
7. How do you get the medical staff involved?
8. How do you solve the problem of affordable data?
9. How do you assure quality or improve the process when it crosses institutions?
10. What do you do if you find out that quality is poor and change is unlikely?
11. How can we more effectively teach scientific and statistical thinking to health care workers?
12. What are the effects of automated systems on quality improvement?

NOTES

1. D. Berwick, Continuous Improvement As an Ideal In Health Care, *NEJM* 320, no.1 (1989): 53–56.

2. V.K. Sahney and O.L. Warden, The Quest for Quality and Productivity in Health, *Frontiers of Health Services Management* 7, no.4 (1990): 2–40.

3. Sahney and Warden, The Quest for Quality.

4. R.H. Palmer, Quality Improvement/Quality Assurance Taxonomy: A Framework, in *Putting Research to Work in Quality Improvement and Quality Assurance* (Summary Report), eds. M. Grady, J. Bernstein, S. Robinson (Washington, D.C.: U.S. Department of Health and Human Services, Public Health Service, Agency for Health Care Policy and Research, 1993), 13–37.

5. R. Coffey, et al., An Introduction to Critical Paths, *Quality Management in Health Care* 1, no.1 (1992): 45–54.

6. A. Donabedian, The Epidemiology of Quality, *Inquiry* 22 (1994): 292.

7. D.D. Nash and L.E. Markson, Managing Outcomes: The Perspective of the Players, *Frontiers of Health Services Management*, 8 no.2 (1991): 3–51.

8. D.A. Conrad, Editorial, *Frontiers of Health Service Management* 8, no.2 (1991): 1–2.

9. D. Bohr and B. Bader, Medical Practice Guidelines: What They Are and How They Are Used, *The Quality Letter* 3 no.1 (February 1991).

10. G. Laffel and D. Blumenthal, The Case for Using Industrial Quality Management Science in Health Care Organizations, *JAMA* 262, no. 20 (1989): 2869–73.

11. R. Brook, Practice Guidelines and Practicing Medicine, *JAMA* 262 (1989): 3027–30.

12. Sahney and Warden, The Quest for Quality.

13. F. Appel, From Quality Assurance to Quality Improvement: The Joint Commission and the Quality Paradigms, *Journal of Quality Assurance* 13, no.5 (1991): 26–29.

6. Total Quality Management

George W. Whetsell

Producing higher-quality products and services has become a major competitive issue in America for two reasons:

1. Organizations that produce higher-quality products or services than their competitors can expect to capture a greater share of the market.
2. Organizations that produce higher-quality products and services have lower unit costs and, as a result, greater pricing flexibility. Some experts argue that lower unit costs result from capturing greater market share and producing greater volumes, while others contend that the result comes from improving the quality of the production process and eliminating delays, duplication, and errors.

The fact is, both of these factors, which can occur simultaneously, lead to lower unit costs. The idea that increasing quality results in competitive advantage is not new. Dr. W. Edwards Deming originally proposed this concept to American manufacturers in the late 1940s; however, at the close of World War II, competition was not a major concern of U.S. manufacturers. In 1950, Dr. Deming took his concepts to Japan where they were adopted with an almost religious commitment. The Japanese spent the next 40 years applying, refining, and expanding the quality-improvement principles of Dr. Deming, Dr. Joseph Juran, and other "quality gurus." As a consequence the term "made in Japan" was transformed from implying "cheap junk" to embodying the quality benchmark. Beginning in the 1970s and continuing through the 1980s, Japanese products (including automobiles, electronic appliances, and a host of other manufactured goods) emerged as global leaders in quality; by delivering the highest-quality

Source: Reprinted from *Topics in Healthcare Financing,* Vol. 18, No. 2, pp. 12–20, Aspen Publishers, Inc., © 1991.

products at a competitive price, the Japanese significantly increased their share of the worldwide market.

Quality as a competitive advantage is not new in the United States. One does not have to look back very far in history to find a period when "made in the U.S.A." was synonymous with "the highest quality"; however, beginning in the late 1970s and continuing throughout the 1980s, this perception was not always the case. U.S. manufacturers lost domestic and global market shares to Japanese and European competitors.

This situation did not occur because U.S. quality declined or U.S. prices were not competitive. Nor did it happen because global competitors developed more sophisticated technology; in fact, in many instances, U.S. manufacturing technology is identical. It happened because foreign competitors steadily increased the quality of their products until it surpassed this country's. The quality levels of Japanese products in particular, which are now beginning to be seen in U.S. products, are the result of implementing a management system called "Total Quality Management" (TQM).

TQM utilizes elements of human behavior theory, statistical-process control, and classical industrial engineering to create a process for improving the quality of products and services produced by an organization. Improving quality has become a major goal of U.S. organizations during the past few years. The Malcolm Baldrige Award for quality excellence is now a coveted prize for many companies. In fact, the quality improvement concepts embodied in TQM are gaining such acceptance that the Joint Commission on Accreditation of Healthcare Organizations announced recently that it will begin seeking evidence that TQM principles are being applied as part of its accreditation process.

WHAT IS TOTAL QUALITY MANAGEMENT?

TQM is a structured, systematic process for creating organizationwide participation in planning and implementing continuous improvements in quality. TQM is a means to an end, with the end being the long-term success of an organization. According to TQM, quality is defined as meeting or exceeding the customer's expectations at a price that is reasonable to the customer. The logic behind TQM is intuitively simple—if the entire organization is dedicated to meeting customer expectations, to continuously looking for new ways of exceeding customer expectations, and to delivering products and services at a competitive price, then success is virtually guaranteed.

TQM combines a set of management principles with a set of tools and techniques that enable employees to carry out these management principles in their daily work activities. Individually the TQM principles are not particularly complex. Implementing them (and they all have to be implemented for TQM to work), however, is a real challenge. The principles and tools that define TQM follow.

Customer Focus

Within TQM, satisfying the customer is the key to success. The TQM definition of quality implies that meeting internally imposed specifications or standards may not be sufficient to satisfy the customer. An organization must know who its customers are, what they expect, and how well their expectations are being met. Surveys, focus groups, and other market-research tools are often used to develop an understanding of external customers' expectations. However, in TQM meeting the quality expectations of internal customers is an equally important goal. In TQM, any department, function, or employee receiving and relying on input from another part of the organization is a customer; the entire organization must be committed to serving internal and external customers.

Organizations that have begun to compete on the basis of quality have discovered that customer expectations are not always easy to understand. One TQM theory separates quality into two dimensions: (1) "expected" and (2) "unexpected" quality. Expected quality includes quality characteristics that result in a decline in customer satisfaction if they are omitted or poorly performed but do not significantly increase customer satisfaction when they are present. Unexpected quality includes characteristics that the customer does not expect, but that result in a significant increase in customer satisfaction when they are delivered. Because these features are not expected, they are not missed when they are not delivered and have little impact on customer satisfaction. Of course, TQM recognizes that customer expectations change. What was unexpected becomes expected shortly after it becomes available, and the unexpected extras your competitors offer will quickly become expected by your customers.

Quality First and Quality in Everything

TQM places quality before costs, budgets, and schedules. Within TQM, there are no acceptable excuses for compromising quality. Although a customer-focused definition of quality is a key tenet of TQM, in TQM nothing is left to chance. TQM requires that quality be defined and measured for every characteristic of a product or service with which a customer might be concerned. Basic operating characteristics and performance measures, aesthetics (such as look, feel, taste, sound, smell), reliability, durability, and availability are all considered to be dimensions of quality. But, just as TQM recognizes external and internal customers, TQM expects quality to be defined and measured for both internal and external activities.

Process Management

TQM focuses on understanding and improving the process used to produce products and services. Every product or service is produced through a series of related work activities involving people, methods, materials, and equipment. A key TQM axiom is that the quality of the output is determined by the quality of the production process, and that improvements in quality result primarily (almost exclusively) from improvements in the process.

In TQM, quality is improved by systematically documenting a process, analyzing its operating characteristics, and identifying ways of improving it. The concept of focusing on the process is simple, but it is one of the most important principles of TQM. It implies that setting quotas, offering incentives, or trying to motivate employees through slogans will have little impact on quality, because it is the process that determines the quality of the outputs, *not* the workers.

Cross-Functional Management

Most businesses (including hospitals) use a hierarchical, bureaucratic organizational structure with several layers of management, formal policies and procedures that establish authority and responsibility, well-defined departmental boundaries, and clear supervisor and subordinate reporting relationships. Unfortunately, the process for producing products and services typically does not follow the organizational hierarchy but rather cuts across the organization.

The service delivery process creates a series of supplier-customer interfaces between functions or departments. TQM recognizes that often the most promising opportunities for improving a process are at these interface points. TQM addresses this issue by having cross-functional teams, comprised of representatives of all of the functions and departments that are involved in a process, work together to improve the process.

Employee Involvement and Teamwork

TQM recognizes that the employees directly involved in the current process are the "experts" in the process and the best source of information on weaknesses and areas for improvement. In TQM, employees actively participate in identifying and implementing improvements in the production process. In fact, TQM takes advantage of the fact that employees enjoy participation and are more receptive to change when they help identify the changes.

TQM also recognizes that the processes organizations use to produce products and services are complex and often cross-functional, and as a result, one person seldom has sufficient expertise to deal with all aspects of a process. For this reason, TQM emphasizes the use of teams commonly referred to as "Quality Improvement Teams" (QITs).

Because all of the key people involved in a process work together, the prospects for successfully identifying and implementing improvements are greatly enhanced. Employee involvement is one of the most important and challenging elements of TQM. It often requires managers to change their management style, as well as their relationship with workers. TQM expects managers to be leaders rather than administrators.

Employee involvement is also a challenge, because the employees must be given the means to be involved. QIT meetings take time, and training employees to be effective team members requires an investment of time and money.

Continuous Improvement

TQM requires continuous improvement and the means to this improvement is the plan, do, check, act (P-D-C-A) cycle depicted in Figure 6–1. In TQM, every process can be improved, and the goal is to have every employee continuously looking for process improvements. Traditionally, management has focused its attention on innovative breakthroughs—dramatic new inventions, technology, or automation. TQM focuses on finding small, incremental improvements (although innovative breakthroughs are welcome) by applying the P-D-C-A cycle to every process used to produce products and services. And TQM has demonstrated that the gains from continuous improvement will equal or exceed the gains from innovation.

Standardization

While the use of quotas or other numerical standards is not compatible with the TQM culture, TQM requires standardization. TQM focuses on standardizing the process. The standardization principle simply states that at any point in time, the best way for a process to work should be known, and everyone involved in the process should be using the best approach. Combining continuous improvement with standardization is one of the more difficult TQM concepts to understand and implement. Through continuous improvement, QITs look for better ways to carry out the process; through standardization, TQM expects that improvements will be immediately communicated to all employees and implemented.

- Define measures of quality
- Measure current performance
- Analyze process
- Identify improvement actions

Plan

Standardize
actions and   Act
repeat

Implement
Do improvement
actions

Check
Measure benefits of
improvement actions

Figure 6–1 P-D-C-A Cycle

Tools and the Use of Data

The P-D-C-A cycle provides the QITs with a mission—to continuously improve quality—but TQM does not leave carrying out the mission to chance. TQM includes a specific set of process-analysis tools that support the P-D-C-A cycle. TQM tools are based on the premise that "a picture is worth a thousand words" and, consequently, all of the tools provide visual outputs. While any analytical or problem-solving tools can be used in TQM, TQM "purists" have defined seven basic tools:

1. Flow charts (Figure 6–2)—Flow charts are used to document all of the activities involved in a process in the sequence they occur. Flow charts are powerful tools for defining the current process, facilitating group consensus on what the current process is, and identifying delays, redundancies, and bottlenecks inherent in the process.
2. Cause-and-effect diagram (Figure 6–3)—Also known as a "fishbone" diagram, this tool supports a brainstorming process for identifying the causes of problems. It is designed to facilitate a team process that starts with a problem and works backward to the cause(s) by repeatedly asking

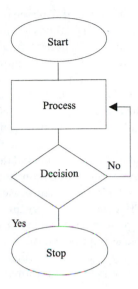

Figure 6–2 Flow Chart

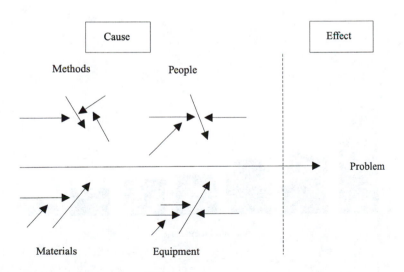

Figure 6–3 Cause-and-Effect Diagram

the question "why?" The standard fishbone initially classifies causes into four categories: (1) people, (2) methods, (3) materials, and (4) equipment. Each response to the "why?" question is written as a branch on the diagram. The cause-and-effect diagram is a very powerful tool that supports an important TQM concept—finding the "root" cause of a problem.

3. Pareto charts (Figure 6–4)—Pareto charts are bar graphs that display data on the frequency of the causes of problems. A QIT utilizing the cause-and-effect diagram typically identifies a wide range of causes of a problem. The Pareto principle states that approximately 20 percent of the causes account for 80 percent of the occurrences of the problem. The Pareto chart displays the frequency of causes of a problem in descending order using a bar chart, so that the most frequent causes clearly stand out. Pareto charts support another TQM concept—an organization should first focus its energies on eliminating the most frequent causes of a problem, because this will result in the greatest improvement.

4. Histograms (or frequency distributions) (Figure 6–5)—Histograms are bar charts that display quality and other performance measurements associated

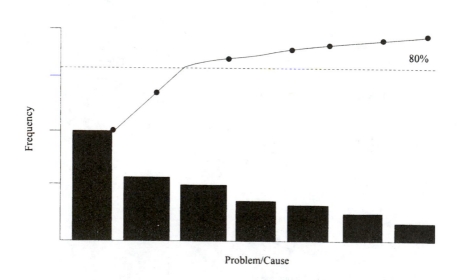

Figure 6–4 Pareto Chart

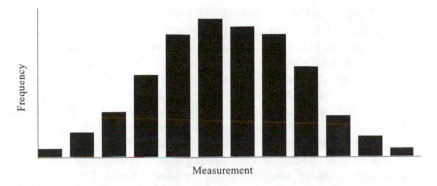

Figure 6–5 Histogram

with a process. They document the range of current performance levels and by segmenting the data (by person, machine, day-of-week, month, etc.), in many cases, help pinpoint problems. They are also used to assess the impact of process improvements.

5. Scatter diagrams (Figure 6–6)—Scatter diagrams assess and display relationships between two variables. Essentially a simple form of correlation analysis, scattergrams can be very useful in pinpointing the cause of problems as well as identifying the potential impact of improvement actions.

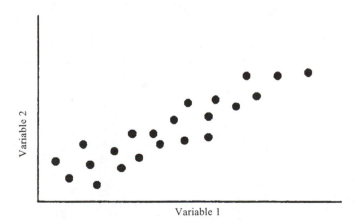

Figure 6–6 Scatter Diagram

6. Run charts (Figure 6–7)—Run charts display the results of a process in production order. In a run chart, measurements are plotted in sequence and then connected to form a line graph. The graph provides a visual tool for highlighting trends that suggest that the process has changed.

7. Control charts (Figure 6–8)—Run charts provide a simple way of monitoring the results of a process. The control chart adds statistical limits to a run chart to assess whether the observed variation is reasonable. The upper and lower control limits are calculated using actual measurements from the process (they are *not* specifications or standards). The process is considered to be under control and functioning as well as should be expected so long as the measurements fall inside the control limits.

The tools also support the data-driven philosophy of TQM. Carrying out the P-D-C-A cycle requires that data be collected and that the data be used to identify potential improvements. Under TQM, opinions, anecdotes, and personal preference are replaced with facts.

Training

Another key TQM philosophy is providing the means to achieve an objective. The objective is continuous improvement through application of the P-D-C-A

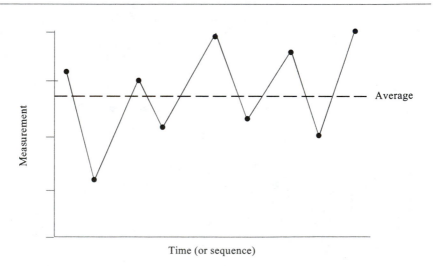

Figure 6–7 Run Chart

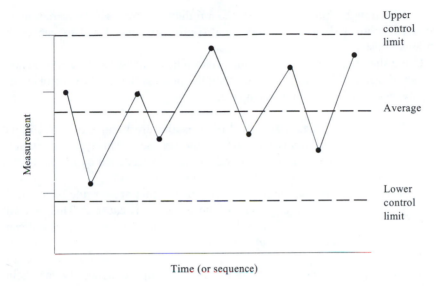

Figure 6–8 Control Chart

cycle. To meet this objective, TQM requires that all employees receive training on the TQM philosophy and the application of the process-improvement tools. While the tools are not particularly complicated, the need for training cannot be overestimated. Application of the tools in the context of the P-D-C-A cycle often requires a level of patience and discipline to which many managers and employees are unaccustomed. The training reinforces the importance of using data and getting to the "root" cause of a problem. In addition to training on the analytical tools, managers and employees require training on how to work in, and lead, teams.

Variation and the Use of Statistics

TQM recognizes that variation is an inherent characteristic of any process. The time required to perform an activity, even when performed exactly the same way, will vary each time it is performed. The quality of process outputs also varies, even when the process is performed in an identical or standardized manner every time.

But TQM also recognizes that there are statistical characteristics of the variation that can be measured. While variation cannot be eliminated, it can be reduced through improvements in the production process. As variation is reduced, delays and waste due to poor quality are also reduced, and this can result in lower costs.

Using statistical tools, the range of variation in a process can be analyzed and insight developed into ways of improving the process. Using the control chart, two types of variation can be identified:

1. Variation in the measurements of a process that are within the control limits is referred to as variation due to "common causes." This type of variation is caused by the process itself and can only be reduced by *changing the process.*
2. Variation in the measurements of a process that are outside the control limits is referred to as variation due to "special causes." This type of variation is caused by factors that are independent of the process and can only be reduced by *eliminating the cause.*

The concepts of special and common causes are important, because they help focus improvement efforts. In fact, most of the opportunities for improving quality require improvement in the process. Consequently, TQM focuses on reducing variation due to common causes and improving quality by improving the production process, while at the same time looking for ways to eliminate special causes of variation.

Prevention

Traditional approaches to quality management are designed to find and correct errors, defects, or other quality shortfalls. This detection approach requires inspecting some or all of the outputs of a process. Another TQM axiom is that quality cannot be inspected into a product or service. To improve quality, the process must be improved so that the number of errors, defects, and quality shortfalls is reduced. In this respect, TQM focuses on preventing quality shortfalls rather than fixing them after they occur.

It is through prevention that TQM delivers its tremendous economic advantage. TQM experts estimate that 15 to 40 percent of an organization's costs are incurred in finding and fixing quality problems. By improving the production process, TQM directly reduces the number of quality problems and their associated costs.

Measurement and Monitoring

The P-D-C-A cycle, the use of data, and a focus on understanding and improving the production process are all elements of TQM's scientific approach to managing quality. The TQM approach also requires measurement and monitoring. Current quality levels must be measured to provide a benchmark for gauging the effect of improvement actions, and quality must be monitored on an ongoing basis to ensure that processes are not changing unexpectedly.

CONCLUSION

This article provides a brief outline of some of the key concepts that define TQM. For the most part, these concepts are based on longstanding research findings that have often been ignored. When put to the test, these concepts work, as the Japanese have proved. Many American corporations, in fact many hospitals, are now implementing TQM, because the evidence is overwhelming that high quality is more marketable, costs less, and leads to long-term success.

SUGGESTED READINGS

Brassard, M. *The Memory Jogger*. Methuen, Mass.: GOAL/QPC, 1988.

Carnegie, D. *How To Win Friends and Influence People*. 3rd ed. New York, N.Y.: Simon & Schuster, 1981.

Crosby, P.B. *Quality is Free: The Art of Making Quality Certain*, New York, N.Y.: McGraw-Hill, 1979.

Deming, W.E. *Out of the Crisis*. 2nd ed. Cambridge, Mass.: Massachusetts Institute of Technology Center for Advanced Engineering Study, 1986.

Grazier, P. *Before It's Too Late: Employee Involvement an Idea Whose Time Has Come*. Chadds Ford, Penn.: Teambuilding, Inc., 1989.

GOAL/QPC. *The Memory Jogger*. Methuen, Mass.: GOAL/QPC, 1988.

Gordon, T. *Leader Effectiveness Training*. New York, N.Y.: Bantam Books, 1980.

Harrington, H.J. *Poor-Quality Cost*. New York, N.Y.: Marcel Dekker, 1987.

Harrington, H.J. *The Improvement Process: How America's Leading Companies Improve Quality*. New York, N.Y.: Marcel Dekker, 1987.

Imai, M. *Kaizen-The Key to Japan's Competitive Success*. New York, N.Y.: Random House, 1986.

Juran, J.M. *Juran on Planning for Quality*. New York, N.Y.: Free Press, 1988.

Peters, T. *Thriving on Chaos*. New York, N.Y.: Knopf, 1988.

Scherkenbach, W.W. *The Deming Route to Quality and Productivity: Road Maps and Roadblocks*. Rockville, Md.: Mercury Press, 1988.

Scholtes, P.R. *The Team Handbook*. Madison, Wis.: Joiner Associates, 1988.

Walton, M. *The Deming Management Method*. New York, N.Y.: Pedigree Books, 1986.

7. Tutorial: Quality Improvement Project Models

Paul E. Plsek

A quality improvement project is a structured team effort to either address a problem, respond to an opportunity, or design a new process. The project is typically conducted by a multidisciplinary team, using the concepts of modern quality management and employing a set of simple process- and data-analysis tools.[1,2] A quality improvement project also typically follows a well-defined "roadmap," called a "quality improvement project model," that everyone on the project team (and perhaps everyone in the organization) agrees to use as a unifying framework to guide the effort. Unfortunately, there are many, seemingly different, models to choose from in the quality management literature. So, while a quality improvement project model can provide a unifying improvement methodology and common language to build collective learning within a team, this learning might not be readily accessible to other teams or other organizations that have chosen to use a different model. In other words, a team studying how to reduce waiting time or unplanned returns to surgery has difficulty learning from the work of other teams who have already made improvements in these areas simply because their projects were conducted in a different "language."

In this tutorial, we will explore the basic concepts underlying all effective quality improvement project models. We will then use these concepts to analyze some common models, discussing their similarities and differences and exposing the strengths and weaknesses of each. The objective of this tutorial is to improve the potential for collective learning from case studies that appear in the quality management literature, and to help readers make informed decisions when choosing an existing model or developing a unique one for use in their organizations.

Source: Reprinted from *Quality Management in Health Care*, Vol. 1, No. 2, pp. 69–81, Aspen Publishers, Inc., © 1993.

BASIC CONCEPTS UNDERLYING QUALITY IMPROVEMENT PROJECT MODELS

Exhibits 7–2 through 7–5 present four of the many quality improvement project models that are available for use in health care organizations. (We will review each of these models in detail in a later section.) While they may seem dissimilar at first glance, these models are not fundamentally different. It turns out that all effective quality improvement project models share a common conceptual and theoretical basis, an understanding of which enables one to work with and learn from these different models. The elements of this common conceptual framework are listed in Exhibit 7–1. These concepts, and their role in shaping an effective quality improvement project model, are described below.

Principles of Quality Management

Effective quality improvement project models reflect the basic values and principles that underlie all of quality management science.[3-6] The summary below presents these principles in generic language and describes how each should be reflected in an effective quality improvement project model.

Exhibit 7–1 Key Concepts in Quality Improvement Project Models

Principles of quality management	Principles of projects
Processes	Universal sequence of breakthroughs
Customers	Four phases of improvement
Variation	
Continuous improvement	Pareto principle
Prevention	Convergent/divergent thinking cycle
Scientific method (PDCA cycle)	Creative/empirical thinking cycle
Positive view of people	
Leadership	

Processes

All work involves the execution of processes. A process is a sequence of steps in which something is passed along and modified, producing some eventual output. The "something passed along" might be a patient (the admissions process), information (the lab results reporting process), materials (the process for stocking exam rooms), or thought (the process for clinical or administrative decision making). An effective quality improvement project model guides the team to define explicitly the process under study and to identify and eliminate waste and unnecessary complexity in that process.

Customers

Processes exist to produce outputs and services that provide a benefit to, or meet the needs of, someone. In quality management theory, these beneficiaries are called "customers."[7,8] These customers can be external to the organization (for example, the patient is the customer of the medication delivery process, and the payor is the customer of the billing process) or internal (for example, the nurse who must administer the medication is also a customer of the medication delivery process, and the senior administrator who reviews accounts receivable reports is also a customer of the billing process). If a process does not produce a benefit or meet a need for someone, it is pointless and should not exist. It follows, therefore, that if an organization is going to carry out a process, then it should seek to provide the greatest benefit to the customers of that process. A good quality improvement project model encourages such "customer thinking" within the team.

Variation

The outcomes of processes are naturally variable. For example, patients will not have exactly the same response to a given therapy, the time required to process a purchase order will not be precisely the same for all orders, etc. This variation in outcome is due to both the intended and unintended variation in the people, machines, materials, methods, and measurements that make up the process.[9] An effective quality improvement project model guides the team to a deep and thorough understanding of this variation and all of its potential sources.

Continuous Improvement

Organizations that implement modern quality management are seeking to push the performance of their processes beyond existing standards and industry norms. The goal is to achieve and maintain a never-before-achieved level of performance. This is typically accomplished through a series of incremental improvements.[10] A good quality improvement project model should facilitate such continuous, iterative, incremental improvements by encouraging alternating cycles of change, followed by stability, followed by more change, and so on.

Prevention

We do not fundamentally improve a process when we simply add steps to check for and screen out errors and problems after they occur.[11] This only makes the process more complex, while leaving intact the underlying causes of inefficiency, waste, and dissatisfaction. An effective quality improvement project model will encourage a project team to find the root causes of problems and develop processes that prevent error, waste, and customer dissatisfaction from occurring again.

Scientific Method or the Plan-Do-Check-Act Cycle

Fundamental to quality management is the commitment to using data and a logical process to build knowledge and make decisions. But effective improvement models go well beyond the shallow interpretation of this concept. Good models encourage the deliberate building of knowledge through the structure of the scientific method, familiar to many health care professionals.[12–14] For example, Newton's work on gravity illustrates the scientific method for systematically building knowledge. Newton observed an apple fall (or so the story goes), formed the theory that were was an attraction between the mass of the earth and the mass of other objects, tested his theory by conducting various experiments, and captured his new knowledge in the form of mathematical formulas that allowed him to predict the behavior of the world around him. Shewhart[15] developed a version of the scientific method, which he called the plan-do-check-act (PDCA) cycle, for use in quality improvement. Shewhart suggests that we can systematically build knowledge by *planning* a change, *doing* it, *checking* to see its effect, and then *acting* on what we have learned by either rejecting the change or making it a standard part of the process. The phrases PDCA cycle, Shewhart cycle, and Deming cycle all appear in the quality management literature and are synonymous. Unfortunately, some industrial and health care organizations have also made further trivial, but confusing, modifications by using other words and letters in the cycle. For example, the so-called PDSA and PDCL cycles are trivial modifications of Shewhart's work, where the word "study" has been substituted for "check" in the first case and the word "learn" has been substituted for "act" in the second.

Semantics aside, the concept of systematically building knowledge through disciplined data collection and deliberate experimentation lies at the foundation of all effective quality improvement projects models. During the course of a project, a team typically conducts multiple iterations of Shewhart's PDCA cycle in building knowledge about the process and the actions necessary to improve it. The quality improvement project model should guide and remind the team about the importance of this disciplined and deliberate study.

Positive View of People

While some managers see people as the ultimate cause of all problems, inefficiencies, and missed opportunities, quality management theorists view the people who work in the process as the ultimate source of knowledge about how to improve it.[16] The quality improvement project model should remind the organization and the project team about the importance of constructively involving the people who actually do the work in activities designed to improve that work.

Leadership

The need for effective leadership is a central theme in quality management theory.[17,18] Without strong effective leadership and an infrastructure to support quality management, improvement efforts may not happen or, if they do happen, may quickly dissipate because of neglect and lack of integration with other activities in the organization. The mere presence of an agreed-upon model supports this leadership principle because it provides a predictable path for improvement efforts. This path gives leaders the opportunity to become involved through initiation, review, and coaching of improvement efforts. Beyond this, an effective quality improvement project model should at least offer no barriers to constructive and active leadership (for example, it should not suggest that the project team conduct its work in secrecy).

It is important to note that the principles described above apply to all quality management efforts, not just improvement projects. We would expect to see these same principles reflected in the way an organization does its strategic planning or the systems it sets up for routine measurement. The point here is that a good quality improvement project model should also explicitly reflect these principles, or at least not suggest actions that would be counter to them.

Principles of Projects

As noted earlier, a quality improvement project is a structured and team-oriented effort that can involve many diverse people and departments within an organization. Because of this, quality improvement project models must go beyond the general principles of quality management and incorporate other key concepts that address the different points of view and ways of thinking present in complex organizations. These additional principles are described below.

Universal Sequence of Breakthroughs

Underlying all effective quality improvement project models is Juran's "universal sequence of breakthroughs."[19,20] Juran asserts that breakthroughs in process performance in complex organizations require a universal sequence of subordinate breakthroughs. The quality improvement project model should guide the team through this complete sequence of breakthroughs. First, Juran suggests that there must be a *breakthrough in attitude*. Here, the team and the organization challenge the historical standard of performance and come to believe that there is both a need and a means to do better. Next, Juran suggests the need for a *breakthrough in organization*. Since most significant processes and problems involve multiple functions and departments within an institution, we must create a representative quality improvement team to provide a thorough understanding and analysis of the process. Achieving a new level of performance in a process also often requires a *breakthrough in knowledge*. Here, the team reaches new plateaus in its knowledge of how the process operates and what causes poor performance. Then, because the people who work in the process are accustomed to the historical level of performance and the traditional ways of doing things, Juran suggests the need for a *breakthrough in cultural patterns*. This involves such things as dealing with resistance to change and providing training in new methods. Finally, we need to implement the changes and verify a *breakthrough in results*. This includes setting up measurement systems to monitor and sustain the new level of performance. The key point here is that the quality improvement project model should remind the quality improvement team to address each of these breakthroughs during the improvement effort.

Four Phases of Improvement

The need for the breakthroughs noted above leads to four phases of activity that should be included in any effective quality improvement project model. Each phase is important; no phase can be excluded.

The first phase of an improvement effort involves *identification and selection of improvement opportunities*. Most organizations can come up with a long list of problems and improvement opportunities based on consideration of customer feedback, imperfect outcomes, high costs, poor utilization, or waste in processes. But, in order to make effective use of the organization's limited improvement resources, a leadership group should take initial steps to set priorities among these opportunities, gather and publish data to show proof of the need for improvement and to stimulate breakthroughs in attitude, and establish a project team to generate a breakthrough in organization. Quality improvement project models typically reflect this early phase of activity through the use of key words like focus, define, clarify, organize, charter, etc., in the initial steps of the model.

Following this is the second phase of the project effort: *determination of the causes of the problem or barriers to improvement*. In this phase, breakthroughs in knowledge lead to identification of the underlying causes of poor process performance, or the conceptual barriers that stand in the way of realizing an improvement opportunity. The analysis work is done by the improvement team and typically involves repeated cycles of the scientific method or PDCA cycle (described above). Quality improvement project models typically use key words like diagnose, analyze, understand, root cause, key factors, etc., to describe activities in this phase of the effort.

Having identified the underlying causes or barriers, the team can now enter the third phase of the effort: *development and implementation of improvements*. Here, the team works together with the responsible departments and individuals to develop appropriate process changes, implement those changes, and achieve breakthroughs in cultural patterns. Effective project models use key words and phrases like design, remedy, process change, countermeasure, etc., to describe this third phase of the effort.

In the final phase of a quality improvement project, *establishment of ongoing control*, the operating departments and the quality improvement team collect and analyze data on the performance of the new process and confirm a breakthrough in results. The operating departments then continue to monitor the new control system in order to maintain the breakthrough in performance. The quality improvement project model might use words and phrases like check, measure, monitor, stabilize, hold the gains, institutionalize, etc., to indicate what needs to be done in this final phase of the improvement effort.

Pareto Principle

The Pareto principle states that in any group of items that contribute to an effect, a relative few of the contributors will account for the majority of the effect.[21,22] For example, while patients might experience many different processes in their interaction with a health care organization, their experience in a few of these processes might correlate most strongly with their overall satisfaction. Or, while team members might have many theories about what causes delays in a process, data might show that a few of these potential causes account for the majority of the delays. The key point here is that by isolating and focusing on these so-called "vital few" factors, a team or organization can make maximal use of its limited improvement resources. An effective quality improvement project model should, therefore, guide the team and the organization to identify and focus on the vital few problems, opportunities, customers, processes, causes, barriers, changes, and control variables.

The Divergent/Convergent Thinking Cycle

Effective quality improvement project models guide the team in logical thinking. In addition to the discipline of the scientific method and the other concepts cited above, another important aspect of such logical thinking is the divergent/convergent thinking cycle.[23–26] This refers to the cycle of first expanding the team's thinking (divergent thinking) and then narrowing it to a focus (convergent thinking). For example, a leadership group might initiate projects by first formulating a long list of problems (divergent thinking) and then selecting a few for focused effort (convergent thinking). A quality improvement team might list various theories of cause in order to expand its knowledge and understanding of the problem. But following this, they need to converge and focus their efforts on the major root causes. Similarly, the team might consider a variety of solutions before converging on a single design; they should consider all the barriers to change before getting down to specific implementation tasks.

This cycle between divergent and convergent thinking is key to effective improvement. Quality improvement projects can get bogged down due to continual divergent thinking. Team meetings can be consumed with "yet another discussion" of various problems, the latest incident, or other theories of cause. The team will not progress unless these discussions converge to focus on a specific project or to the design of tests needed to confirm or disprove a theory. At the other extreme lies the danger of too much convergent thinking too early in the project. For example, the latest problem might not be the most important one to devote the organization's energies to, the one theory advanced by the senior person on the team might not be the best explanation of what is causing the problem, and the solution that leaps first to mind might not be the most effective or economical. Effective problem-solving teams are keenly aware of the need to balance between divergent and convergent thinking. They recognize the need to focus their attention and energies in order to move on after broad discussion of general facts and opinions. But they also recognize the need to spend time answering the "what else?" question before devoting their attention to a specific course of action. Therefore, an effective quality improvement project model should contain some steps that direct the team into divergent thinking and some steps that direct them into convergent thinking.

The Creative/Empirical Thinking Cycle

A second, related thought cycle is that between creative and empirical thinking. This too is foundational to an effective quality improvement project model.[27–29] There are points during problem solving when the team needs hunches, guesses, and opinions. Creative (or intuition-driven) thinking is needed when listing problems, theories of cause, possible solutions, and potential barriers to change. But there is an equally important need to rely solely on the facts at other points in the improvement effort. Such empirical (or data-driven) thinking is mandatory when prioritizing problems, analyzing symptoms, testing theories of cause, checking performance, and monitoring the control system. As with divergent/convergent thinking, effective project teams are also keenly aware of the need to balance between creative and empirical thinking. They create an environment on the team that makes it easy and acceptable for team members to express opinions or unique ideas. They are not so driven by scientific method that they refuse to think beyond the narrow confines of the available data. But they do not make key decisions based solely on intuitions, opinions, or hunches. Instead, they get the data and facts before making final conclusions or permanent changes. The quality improvement project model should reflect this balance between creative and empirical thinking.

It should be noted that while the divergent/convergent thinking, creative/empirical thinking, and PDCA cycles are related concepts, they are not the same. The divergent/convergent thinking cycle refers to the need to alternate and balance the *scope* of our thoughts: between broad ("long list") views and focused ("short list") views. The creative/empirical thinking cycle refers to the need to alternate and balance the *sources* of our thoughts: between intuition-driven ("hunches") and data-driven ("just the facts, ma'am") thinking. The PDCA cycle refers to the *technique* of our thoughts and knowledge building, but it does not explicitly call for any particular type of thinking. For example, our plan (the "P" in PDCA) might come from intuition or from analysis of data, and we might have converged to it quickly or arrived at it by combining many divergent ideas. Therefore, it is important that the project team implement all three of these concepts—an effective quality improvement project model will guide them or remind them to do so.

ANALYSIS OF SOME COMMON QUALITY IMPROVEMENT PROJECT MODELS

Having catalogued in the preceding section the basic concepts underlying all effective quality improvement project models (Exhibit 7–1), we can now use these concepts to examine some common models and identify their similarities, differences, strengths, and weaknesses. For example, Exhibit 7–2 presents a quality improvement project model that originated in instructional materials published by the Juran Institute.[30] This model is referenced in the book *Curing Health Care*[31] and is used in seminars sponsored by the Institute for Healthcare Improvement. [The Juran Institute (Wilton, Connecticut) recently updated this model. The update appears in Appendix 7-A.][32,33]

Exhibit 7–2 Juran Institute's Quality Improvement Project Model

Project Definition and Organization	List and prioritize problems Define project and team
Diagnostic Journey	Analyze symptoms Formulate theories of causes Test theories Identify root causes
Remedial Journey	Consider alternative solutions Design solutions and controls Address resistance to change Implement solutions and controls
Holding the Gains	Check performance Monitor control system

Source: Juran Institute, Inc., Wilton, Connecticut, 1989.

Examining the model relative to the foundational concepts described above, one is immediately struck with the prominence of the four phases of improvement. The model also encourages divergent/convergent and creative/empirical thinking cycles by showing separate steps for activities such as "formulate theories of cause" (divergent and creative), "test theories" (convergent and empirical), "consider alternative solutions" (divergent and creative), and "design solutions and controls" (convergent and creative). Words like "theories" and "tests" remind the team to use the scientific method and the PDCA cycle. The five breakthroughs occur when we do such things as "define a project and team" (breakthrough in organization) or "address resistance to change (breakthrough in cultural patterns). And phrases such as "prioritize problems" and "identify root causes" encourage the team to apply the Pareto principle throughout the improvement effort.

   While the model in Exhibit 7–2 has some obvious strengths, it also has some weaknesses. A subtle but potentially troublesome one is that the connotation of the word "problem" in the first step might limit the kinds of improvement efforts an organization undertakes. For example, an organization might not consider a few delays or some waste to be a "problem" if patients are not complaining and the organization is enjoying relative fiscal health. But such was the attitude of the American automobile industry when it began its decline in the 1970s. For an organization to use this model effectively, it must have already had a break-through in attitude about what constitutes a problem, and it must reflect this thinking in careful project selection. Another weakness of this model is that it assumes that the principles of quality management are well understood in the organization. Note, for example, that the concepts of customers, process, variation, and leadership are not explicitly addressed in the steps of the model. Of course, nothing in the model precludes the application of these principles; we can select projects based on their impact on our customers, we can proceed by analyzing the symptoms of failures in the process, we can address all of the potential sources of variation when we list our theories of cause, etc. So, this quality improvement project model can be effective in an organization where the principles of quality management are well understood, or where members of the improvement team are otherwise adequately reminded of these principles through training classes, posters in meeting rooms, or the presence of a trained facilitator or advisor to guide the team.

Exhibit 7–3 shows another quality improvement project model popular in health care, the FOCUS-PDCA® model developed by the Quality Resource Group at Hospital Corporation of America (HCA) in Nashville.[34] This model is widely used in health care both because there are a large number of HCA hospitals and because of the commendable practice of the HCA Quality Resources Group to be open and willing to share their training materials.

Exhibit 7–3 Hospital Corporation of America's FOCUS-PDCA® Strategy for Improvement

Find a process improvement opportunity

Organize a team who understands the process

Clarify the current knowledge of the process

Uncover the root cause of variation and poor quality

Start the "plan-do-check-act" cycle

Plan the process improvement

Do the improvement, data collection, and analysis

Check the results and lessons learned

Act by adopting, adjusting, or abandoning the change

Source: HCA Quality Resources Group, Nashville, Tennessee. © 1992, HCA. Used with permission.

In contrast to the Juran model, notice the prominence of quality management principles in the FOCUS-PDCA model. Words and phrases like "process," "variation," "data collection," and "organize a team" are clear reminders of these principles. The model emphasizes the Pareto principle and scientific method with phrases such as "clarify current knowledge," "uncover the root cause," and "start the PDCA cycle." It also guides the team through the sequence of breakthroughs (although, as noted below, there are no steps that explicitly address resistance to change and breakthroughs in cultural patterns). Finally, the phrase "process improvement opportunities" places no conceptual bounds on our thinking about potential topics for improvement projects.

While this model is strong in its emphasis on the principles and conceptually sound overall, it too has potential weaknesses that users should be aware of. Note that most of the steps are stated in convergent and empirical terms. The model assumes that team members will be adequately aware of the need for divergent and creative thinking as they work through the steps. The model does not discourage or preclude divergent or creative effort; it simply does not explicitly remind the team to do so. Also note that the model gives little guidance on implementing the eventual process change and securing a breakthrough in cultural patterns. The team and the organization would need to take additional steps to assure adequate involvement of impacted staff and appropriate attention to potential resistance to change. Again, these weaknesses can easily be overcome through training, good facilitation and coaching, or other reminder mechanisms.

Exhibit 7–4 lists the steps of the quality improvement project model used by Florida Power and Light (FP&L)[35] and its consulting subsidiary, Qualtec Quality Services, Inc. This model is also conceptually sound with only a few, easily addressable weaknesses. It encompasses the four phases of improvement, encourages scientific method, and emphasizes the Pareto principle. But, like the Juran model, it too assumes some prior knowledge of the principles of quality management and may restrict thinking through its repeated use of the word "problem." Furthermore, it is a bit vague about when, how, and by whom a team should be formed to achieve a breakthrough in organization. (Note: FP&L uses the model for both cross-functional and intrafunctional teams.[36] In the case of a cross-functional team, a leadership group might perform step 1 of the model and then form a team to address steps 2 through 7. In the case of intrafunctional improvement, a standing committee of department members might perform all seven steps.) It should also be noted that most of the steps are stated in convergent terms; the team would need to recall the need to diverge and be creative. Again, these issues are minor, provided the organization using the model is aware of them and takes steps to address them.

There are also a few unique and interesting features of this model that I would like to point out before moving on. Note that the opportunity identification phase

Exhibit 7-4 Florida Power and Light's Quality Improvement Project Model

1. Reasons for improvement
   To identify a theme (problem area) and the reasons for working on it

2. Current situation
   To select a problem and a target for improvement

3. Analysis
   To identify and verify the root causes of the problem

4. Countermeasures
   To select countermeasures (proposed solutions) that will correct the identified root causes of the problem

5. Results
   To confirm that the problem and its root causes have been decreased and the target for improvement has been met

6. Standardization
   To prevent the problem and its root causes from recurring

7. Future plans
   To plan what is to be done about any remaining problems and to evaluate the team's effectiveness

Source: Qualtec Quality Services, Inc., Miami, Florida. *Team Leader Participant Manual,* © 1992.

has two distinct elements: a broad "theme" and a specific "problem and target for improvement" under that theme. This concept of first selecting a broad area for improvement (for example, patient information flow in a clinic) and then identifying a smaller, more focused target within that area (for example, availability of the medical record for patients seen by a referring physician on the previous day) might be useful in organizations that historically feel frustrated by improvement efforts that fail because they attempt to address too broad an issue. Also note the last step of the FP&L model—"Future Plans." This commitment to thoughtful reflection at the end of the project is entirely consistent with efforts underway in many health care organizations that are striving to become "learning organizations."[37]

The next model I wish to examine here is a bit different from the others. While you may not have been aware of it, the models presented thus far have implicitly assumed that a work process already exists, and that the improvement project involves eliminating some chronic cause of waste or taking advantage of some opportunity for enhancement. This assumption of an existing process is reflected in phrases such as "analyze the symptoms" (Exhibit 7–2) and "clarify the current knowledge of the process" (Exhibit 7–3). The model in Exhibit 7–5, however, makes no such assumption and, therefore, represents a special case among quality improvement project models—the steps of a process design project. This happens to be a model that I developed and teach in courses sponsored by the Institute for Healthcare Improvement.[38] Juran[39] presents a conceptually similar model; I have chosen my model here simply because it is easy to compare to the earlier figures. A team might use this model to either design a new process (for example, design the work flows in a new satellite pharmacy) or completely redesign an existing one (for example, design a standardized process to replace the current *ad hoc* procedures for transporting oncology patients or redesign a manual paperwork process to take advantage of available automation).

Note that this design model is built on the same concepts as the other improvement models. The principles of quality management are prominent, especially the principles associated with customers, process, and prevention.

Exhibit 7–5 Process Design Project Model

Project Definition and Organization	List and prioritize problems Define project and team
Conceptual Design	Clarify customers and purpose Develop process flows Perform customer needs analysis
Problem Prevention	Consider potential problems Consider potential causes Develop prevention Design control system Implement new process
Holding the Gains	Check performance Monitor control system

Source: Reprinted with permission from Paul E. Plsek & Associates © 1989 Paul E. Plsek & Associates, Atlanta, Georgia.

The team must also remember to work through the universal sequence of breakthroughs; for example, they must seek a breakthrough in knowledge as they design the new process rather than simply replicating a process used elsewhere (more about this below). And the team must balance divergent/convergent thinking and use the Pareto principle by, for example, thinking first of many potential problems and then focusing on those that would be the most detrimental and most likely to occur.

While the design model in Exhibit 7–5 is similar to the other improvement models, there is one key conceptual difference. Notice that the design model transposes the second and third phase of improvement. For example, in the models in Exhibits 7–2, 7–3, and 7–4, detailed analysis of the current process precedes the design of the changes to that process. But, in the model in Exhibit 7–5, the process design (or redesign) is done first, and then it is subjected to systematic analysis. This subtle difference becomes a pitfall that teams must be aware of before using any design model. Design models seem to offer the team a way to make quick improvements by completely redesigning an existing process, rather than taking the time to collect the data needed to isolate the causes of the deficiencies in the current process. But, if the team does not really know what causes the flaw in the current process (that is, they have no breakthrough in knowledge), they may simply carry the sources of flaw over into the new process. This pitfall can be avoided by conducting some analysis of the existing process, even if it seems to be completely *ad hoc*, before deciding to embark on any redesign project. This suggestion applies to the design of new processes as well; the team would be well advised to study similar processes in their own or others' organizations before beginning the design of a new process. (Studying others' processes and applying that knowledge to one's own process is referred to in the quality management literature as "benchmarking."[40])

As a final example, Ishikawa notes the steps commonly undertaken by quality control circles in some Japanese companies in his book *What Is Total Quality Control?*[41] According to Ishikawa, the "quality control circle process" requires that a team:

- Determine the problem
- Select the subject for discussion
- Fix a time limit
- Study the current situation
- Analyze the factors
- Work out a policy
- Implement the policy
- Confirm the results

Analysis of the model is left to the reader; it is reasonable and effective. I include it here to illustrate how a thoughtfully constructed model can be used to avoid expected pitfalls that a team might encounter. The developers of this model were clearly concerned about the efficiency and time-effectiveness of the quality circle process. While nothing in the previously described models precludes a team from setting a time limit on its efforts, this model does not leave that matter to the discretion of the team.

THE NEED FOR AND VALUE OF QUALITY IMPROVEMENT PROJECT MODELS

The preceding discussion makes it clear that the various available quality improvement project models are more similar that they are different. The same basic concepts—the principles of quality management and the principles of projects—form the theoretical basis for all such effective quality improvement project models. So, what is the point of such models? Do we really need them? Why are there so many of them? What value do they add? Indeed, if everyone in an organization thoroughly understood and practiced the fundamental concepts, there would be no need for quality improvement project models! Effective, quality-oriented improvement would occur naturally in such an organization. Common understanding and logic would guide the team members forward as one. In such an organization, the "roadmap" provided by the quality improvement project model would be as unnecessary as a roadmap directing you to your favorite restaurant in the town where you live.

Unfortunately, while the basic foundational concepts are simple and logical, they are not thoroughly understood nor routinely practiced in most organizations. This is true for both general industry and health care. So, the quality improvement project model is needed as a unifying guide or a reminder of these important ideas so that they will not be overlooked during the intensity of effort that often characterizes improvement projects.

This is an important point, with subtle implications, so I want to pause here and restate it to assure that it is understood. The specific words or format of a quality improvement project model are not so important, but the concepts that lie behind the model are critical. So, no matter what the model says, if the concepts are not understood, accepted, or practiced by the team and the organization at large, the team's improvement efforts will fall short. Having the "right" quality improvement project model is not a guarantee of success, any more than having an up-to-date driving map is a guarantee that you will arrive at your destination. While driving, you may get lost, you may choose to ignore the map and go in the direction that seems right to you at the moment, or your inability to cope with unanticipated circumstances may prematurely end your journey. Similarly, no matter which quality improvement project model you choose, the team may not be able to follow it, they may revert to their instincts, or circumstances may arise that make improvements difficult to achieve. Blaming the roadmap—the model—for the failure of an improvement effort is as illogical as blaming the driving map for an ill-fated journey. (Although, I must admit, I have resorted to this tactic once or twice to salve my bruised ego.)

Quality improvement project models are not "magical," and, we must admit, neither are they new or profound. But this does not mean that they should be rejected, as some have scornfully suggested, as "merely common sense." The models are certainly sensible, because the concepts that lie behind them are sensible. But, these concepts are often not at all common in their application within organizations. Pointing out that a quality improvement project model is a list of obvious steps for good problem solving does not negate the value of such a list if good problem solving is not routinely practiced within the organization.

So, why bother with quality improvement project models? First, the quality improvement project model provides a common framework for improvement that allows otherwise disparate functional groups like physicians, nurses, administrators, and housekeepers to speak the same language and work together for the improvement of the processes in which they each play a part. Second, the quality improvement project model serves as a reminder of those quality management concepts that people have learned but might tend to forget when under pressure to perform in solving a longstanding problem, achieving a goal, or designing a new process. Third, the quality improvement project model can be used to preempt logistical or organizational pitfalls that the developer believes are likely to occur. (The explicit requirement to "set a time limit" in the quality control circle model described previously is an example of this.)

The quality improvement project model is, then, an important tool in the implementation of quality management in an organization. Since it functions primarily as a reminder of things that people should know anyway, the need for such models should, theoretically, go away over time. But, after a decade or more of improvement work, leading companies like IBM, AT&T, Hewlett-Packard, and FP&L still use quality improvement project models to guide and report their team efforts.

ON BECOMING MULTILINGUAL IN UNDERSTANDING QUALITY IMPROVEMENT PROJECTS

Understanding the fundamental concepts behind the various quality improvement project models helps quality management practitioners to cut through the jargon and learn from the improvement projects of others, regardless of the model used. So, when reading a case study, hearing a conference presentation, or discussing efforts with colleagues in other organizations, concentrate on learning the answers to questions such as those listed below.

- How were customers and their needs identified and addressed?
- What did the team learn about the process?
- What key sources of variation did they identify?
- What incremental improvements were made?
- What future improvement efforts are planned?
- What data did the team use in its decision making?
- How were both staff and leadership involved?
- How did the team use the scientific method to build knowledge?
- How did they stay focused on the "vital few"?
- How were breakthroughs accomplished?
- Who was on the team?
- How did they break through the prevailing attitude and cultural patterns?
- What results did they achieve?
- What steps did they undertake in analyzing the process?
- How did the team go about generating creative, effective, and acceptable recommendations?
- How did they implement their recommendations?
- What ongoing monitors and controls did they put in place?
- How did the team demonstrate and balance divergent, convergent, creative, and empirical thinking?

Looking beyond the specific quality improvement project model that a team used and understanding the concepts of effective improvement are the keys to being able to learn from others' projects, regardless of the "language" they speak.

SELECTING A QUALITY IMPROVEMENT PROJECT MODEL

Understanding the concepts behind effective quality improvement project models and realizing that the model is primarily a reminder of things that might otherwise be overlooked by teams in an organization, enables one to make informed choices in selecting among existing models or developing one's own model. In selecting or designing a quality improvement project model, organizational decision makers should:

- Examine the organization's overall quality management training curriculum to assure that all of the fundamental concepts described earlier are covered.
- Reflect on their organization's past experience at improvement to identify concepts that are typically inadequately addressed and pitfalls that are frequently encountered.
- Review existing models relative to their potential value in helping teams remember key concepts and avoid past difficulties.
- Select an existing quality improvement project model, or develop a new one, to match the specific needs and past experience of the organization.
- Critically analyze the model chosen to identify its weaknesses. (Note: Every model has its imperfections—even the ones I have developed! I believe that it is impossible to capture concisely in a model everything there is to know about effective improvement efforts. If you think that the model you have chosen has no weaknesses, perhaps you have not really thought about it deeply enough.)
- Develop a plan to address the weaknesses in the selected model (through, for example, supplemental training, project advisors, reminders in meeting rooms, etc.).
- Develop a plan to publicize the quality improvement project model and teach members of the organization how to use it as a shared framework and language for improvement.
- Continually stress the importance of understanding the underlying principles of quality management, rather than simply memorizing the steps of the model.

While choosing a quality improvement project model for use in one's organization is an important decision in the implementation of quality management, don't agonize unnecessarily over it. Realize that there is no perfect model. Also realize that the model itself does not bring about improvement; hard, diligent, and sincere effort will be required from leaders, trainers, and organizational members, regardless of the model chosen. Simply choose a model that seems to fit your organization (using the process described above) and get on with the never-ending task of explaining what it means and how it is to be used.

New quality improvement project models are sure to appear in the years to come as more and more organizations and consultants become involved in quality management in health care. However, the fundamental concepts of quality management are less likely to change. Organizations and individuals who make the effort to understand these basic concepts will more quickly develop and internalize the habit of continuous improvement than those who rely solely on their chosen quality improvement project model as their only guide.

Interested readers can learn more about the concepts behind quality improvement project models by reading the books listed in Suggested Readings.

NOTES

1. J.M. Juran, *Managerial Breakthrough* (New York, N.Y.: McGraw-Hill, 1964).

2. P.E. Plsek, A. Onnias, and J.F. Early, *Quality Improvement Tools* (Wilton, Conn.: Juran Institute, Inc., 1989).

3. V.K. Sahney and G.L. Warden, "The Quest for Quality and Productivity in Health Services," *Frontiers of Health Services Management* 7, no. 4 (1991): 2–38.

4. G. Laffel and D. Blumenthal, "The Case for Using Industrial Quality Management Science in Health Care Organizations," *Journal of the American Medical Association* 262, no. 20 (1989): 2869–2873.

5. P.R. Scholtes, *The Team Handbook* (Madison, Wis.: Joiner Associates, 1988).

6. D.M. Berwick, A.B. Godfrey, and J. Roessner, *Curing Health Care* (San Francisco, Calif.: Jossey-Bass, 1990).

7. K. Ishikawa, *What Is Total Quality Control: The Japanese Way*. Translated by David J. Lu (Englewood Cliffs, N.J.: Prentice-Hall, 1985).

8. J.M. Juran, *Juran on Planning for Quality* (New York, N.Y.: The Free Press, 1988).

9. K. Ishikawa, *Guide to Quality Control* (New York, N.Y.: UNIPUB, 1985).

10. Juran, *Managerial Breakthrough*.

11. D.M. Berwick, "Continuous Improvement As an Ideal in Health Care," *New England Journal of Medicine* 320 (1989): 53–56.

12. C.I. Lewis, *Mind and the World Order* (New York, N.Y.: Scribner's, 1929).

13. T.S. Kuhn, *The Structure of Scientific Revolution* (Chicago, Ill.: University of Chicago Press, 1962).

14. H.R. Neave, *The Deming Dimension* (Knoxville, Tenn.: SPC Press, 1990).

15. W.A. Shewhart, *Economic Control of Quality of Manufactured Product* (New York, N.Y.: Van Nostrand, 1931).

16. W.E. Deming, *Out of the Crisis* (Cambridge, Mass.: Center for Advanced Engineering Study, 1986).

17. Deming, *Out of the Crisis*.

18. D. Bush and K. Dooley, "The Deming Prize and Baldrige Award: How They Compare," *Quality Progress* 22, no. 1 (1989): 28–30.

19. Juran, *Managerial Breakthrough*.

20. Plsek, et al., *Quality Improvement Tools*.

21. Juran, *Managerial Breakthrough*.

22. J.M. Juran, "The Non-Pareto Principle, Mea Culpa," *Quality Progress* 8, no. 5 (1975): 8–9.

23. Plsek, et al., *Quality Improvement Tools*.

24. C. Kepner and B.S. Tregoe, *The Rational Manager* (New York, N.Y.: McGraw-Hill, 1963).

25. H.D. Shuster, *Teaming for Quality Improvement: A Process for Innovation and Improvement* (Englewood Cliffs, N.J.: Prentice-Hall, 1990).

26. H.J. Brightman, *Group Problem Solving: An Improved Managerial Approach* (Atlanta, Ga.: Business Publishing Division, Georgia State University, 1988).

27. Plsek, et al., *Quality Improvement Tools.*

28. Kepner and Tregoe, *The Rational Manager.*

29. E. de Bono, *Serious Creativity* (Toronto: HarperCollins Publishers, 1992).

30. Juran, *Managerial Breakthrough.*

31. Berwick, et al., *Curing Health Care.*

32. *Improving Health Care Quality* (Boston, Mass.: The Institute for Healthcare Improvement, 1989).

33. *Methods and Tools for Quality Improvement* (Boston, Mass.: The Institute for Healthcare Improvement, 1990).

34. J.E. McEachern and D. Neuhauser, "The Continuous Improvement of Quality at the Hospital Corporation of America," *Health Matrix* 7, no. 3 (1989): 5–11.

35. *Managing Quality Improvement* (Miami, Fla.: Qualtec Quality Services, Inc., 1991).

36. *Managing Quality Improvement.*

37. P.M. Senge, *The Fifth Discipline: The Art and Practice of the Learning Organization* (New York, N.Y.: Doubleday, 1990).

38. *Methods and Tools for Quality Improvement.*

39. J.M. Juran, *Juran on Quality Design* (New York, N.Y.: The Free Press, 1992).

40. R.C. Camp, *Benchmarking: The Search for Industry Best Practices That Lead to Superior Performance* (Milwaukee, Wis.: Quality Press, 1989).

41. Ishikawa, *What Is Total Quality Control.*

SUGGESTED READINGS

Berwick, D.M., Godfrey, A.B., and Roessner, J. *Curing Health Care.* San Francisco, Calif.: Jossey-Bass, 1990.

Juran, J.M. *Managerial Breakthrough.* New York, N.Y.: McGraw-Hill, 1964.

Appendix 7-A. The Quality Improvement Process

1. Identify a Project

- Nominate projects
- Evaluate projects
- Select a project
- Ask: Is it quality improvement?

2. Establish the Project

- Prepare a mission statement
- Select a team
- Verify the mission

3. Diagnose the Cause

- Analyze symptoms
- Confirm or modify the mission
- Formulate theories
- Test theories
- Identify root cause(s)

4. Remedy the Cause

- Evaluate alternatives
- Design remedy
- Design controls
- Design for culture
- Prove effectiveness
- Implement

5. Hold the Gains

- Design effective quality controls
- Foolproof the remedy
- Audit the controls

6. Replicate Results and Nominate New Projects

- Replicate the project results
- Nominate new projects

Source: Quality Improvement in Health Care, Juran Institute, Inc., Wilton, Connecticut, 1993.

8. Bringing Theory into Practice— Applying Improvement Thinking

C.J. Bolster, Elizabeth Falter, and Laura Hooper

Part I

INTRODUCTION

Organizational interest in quality improvement explodes as results from clinical improvement teams achieve demonstrable improvements in patient outcomes. Is this your organization's headline on quality improvement? Or has your organization invested heavily in quality improvement only to experience limited results due to a focus on small, less than critical process improvements? Juran teaches a key lesson in quality improvement: focus on the vital few.[1] He describes the vital few as those processes or customers that account for most of the impact on an organization or product. In the interest of safe start-ups, many in health care have misapplied Juran's advice and focused improvement efforts on less than vital processes. Nothing is more vital to health care organizations than the delivery of patient care—this is especially true for high-volume diagnoses. Continuous efforts to improve these high-impact care delivery processes will yield significant benefits to patients as well as leverage the benefits of improvement throughout the organization.

Stroke is one of the leading diagnoses treated in health care organizations across the United States. For most tertiary and community health care facilities, undertaking an improvement project focused on the care of stroke patients could potentially produce significant results. For these same organizations, undertak-

Source: Part I reprinted from *Clinical Performance and Quality Health Care*, Vol. 1, No. 2, pp. 97–100, with permission of Slack, Inc., © 1993. Part II reprinted from *Clinical Performance and Quality Health Care*, Vol. 1, No. 3, pp. 163–171, with permission of Slack, Inc., © 1993.

ing an improvement effort in stroke care also presents a formidable challenge; improvement efforts must seek to balance the impact of a disease that has highly variable underlying etiologies and clinical outcomes with the interests and practices of multiple physician groups and a multidisciplinary health care team.

The purpose of this two-part report is to demonstrate that focusing improvement efforts on patient care processes—the vital few—will leverage results into improved organizational performance, offer a specific approach to improving patient care processes while reducing the risk of focusing on key diagnoses, and apply the improvement process to the care of stroke patients.

OVERALL APPROACH

The overall approach to applying quality improvement principles to enhance the care and outcomes of stroke patients results from a simple hypothesis: The outcomes from an episode of care are the result of a complex and highly integrated series of processes performed by the medical staff and the health care organization. To improve stroke patient outcomes fundamentally (e.g., reduce mortality and complication rates, enhance patient satisfaction, return the patient to an optimal lifestyle, reduce resource consumption), one must identify and improve those processes that directly impact the outcomes of stroke patients.[2] Adapted from quality improvement theory, this hypothesis guides the improvement effort.

Recognizing the need to achieve sustainable results from improvement efforts, the overall approach must be expanded to include key principles of organizational change. Combining an understanding of the behavioral and cultural aspects of change with the principles of quality improvement yields a powerful combination of ideals. When such an approach is used to drive change, there is an increased likelihood that recommended changes will be implemented and benefits realized. Adapted from Weisbord's work on productive workplaces[3] and the authors' experience with organizational change projects, the key principles that must be integrated into the overall improvement approach include the determination of economic need, a focus on whole systems, and the involvement of stakeholders.

Economic Need

Building the necessary commitment and performing actual work to improve patient care consumes significant resources. Because resources are scarce in all health care organizations, improvement efforts must be focused on those systems or processes vital to each facility's economic interests. The opportunity for clear returns to all stakeholders must be easily demonstrated. Because the care of stroke patients typically falls across several formal and informal department/ discipline lines (e.g., neurology, internal medicine, family practice, numerous nursing units, other ancillary services, and allied caregivers), there are inherent opportunities to achieve new levels of efficiency and effectiveness in the care process. As a high-volume diagnosis demanding complex cross-functional, multidisciplinary involvement, the stroke patient care process easily meets the test of economic need.

Focus on Whole Systems

Systems thinking[4] suggests that improvement efforts focus on the whole system. In hierarchical and functional organizations, improvement traditionally has been focused on individual cells of responsibility. Often, these traditional improvement efforts yield changes that were in conflict with the larger system, especially relative to cost-reduction efforts.

The process of caring for stroke patients presents a unique opportunity to pursue improvement of a whole system. Initially, the process may be defined as beginning from the time a stroke patient enters the health system until the time the patient is discharged from the acute-care setting. However, this system paradigm may be expanded to include preventive care and postacute, rehabilitative, or maintenance care. Viewing the care of stroke patients from a more comprehensive perspective promotes a higher degree of collaboration between multiple stakeholders. Using the whole system paradigm, process stakeholders more accurately can see the continuum of care from the patient's perspective.

Involve Process Stakeholders

Both quality improvement and organizational change principles underscore the necessity of creating improvement teams consisting of process stakeholders, because their knowledge and emotional dedication to the existing process are critical to ultimate improvement. "Externally" imposed improvement initiatives by management, outside consultants, or other caregivers will, in all likelihood, not produce the desired benefits.

DETAILED APPROACH—THE KEY ELEMENTS

Incorporating organizational change and quality improvement principles into successful efforts to improve patient outcomes requires a systematic and disciplined approach. The remainder of this report seeks to describe the key elements of this approach and apply them to improving the care of stroke patients.

Adapting the PDCA Cycle to Foster Clinical Improvement

As mentioned in the first of a series of articles,[5] key quality improvement principles will be applied to the improvement of vital, clinical processes. As you will see, we have adapted Deming's plan-do-check-act (PDCA)[6] cycle to guide clinical improvement efforts. (See Figure 8–1.)

The PDCA cycle has its foundation in the Deming wheel. Deming saw the need to have constant interaction among research, design, production, and sales in conducting company business. He recommended that these four processes be rotated constantly, with quality as the top criterion. "Turning the wheel" for constant improvement became the basis for Japanese management and subsequently the PDCA cycle in all improvement efforts.

The plan stage is when an improvement team applies its process analysis and problem-solving skills. The team members really need to become "system" thinkers and may use the seven statistical tools (Pareto charts, cause-and-effect diagrams, histograms, control charts, scatter diagrams, graphs, checksheets) to help explain processes and system activity. The team may use flow-charting either in a detailed form or in a top-down approach.

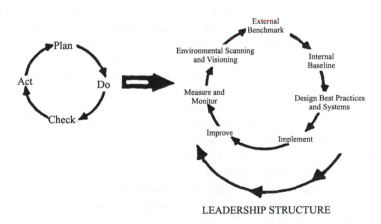

Figure 8–1 Applying PDCA to Clinical Improvement

Whatever tools are used, it is most critical that the team define the current process and its customers, document the process, measure it, understand it, and identify improvement opportunities. The team may in fact find the current process to be so bad, it literally dumps it and designs a new one. The team may experience the "aha" response in this stage as the process it is analyzing is usually so wrought with problems and inefficiencies that the team can no longer in good conscience blame anyone for bad results. The team discovers here that in fact the 85/15 rule is true; 85% of an organization's problems are due to faults in the system. Workers can control less than 15% of the problems.[7]

Before engaging in the do step, the team needs to identify process improvement opportunities by challenging the way things are done. The team will study the process and ask what can be changed, where the bottlenecks are, who is aware, trained, responsible for doing, what (or who) can be resequenced, repackaged, reassigned, taken on, automated, substituted, eliminated, standardized, crosstrained, combined, shared, used as an outside supplier, unbundled, bundled, reused, changed (hours), reinventoried, or renegotiated, and why, why, why, why, why?

Once improvements are identified, the team moves into the do step. Ironically, the do step has as much planning as the plan step. In fact, teams need to plan before piloting an improvement. If it has not already done some measurement in the plan stage, the team clearly needs to do some at this point, or defining measurable improvement will be difficult. After measuring, the team will control implementation by doing the right things right the first time on a unit or division that is most apt to succeed. Implementation involves decisions about what, when, where, how, and who will make improvements.

Prior to implementation, the team should define each step of the new process to avoid "fix and repair" work as much as possible—mounting rework is often what triggers the need for improvement. The team then needs to communicate the results of the pilot to the organization at large, but most importantly train those involved in the new process. Careful monitoring of initial implementation is essential. Because change is painful, visible evidence of support must be apparent to the doers. Simply put, improvement may be reducing length of stay from 7 to 6 days, reducing missing medications by 30%, or starting surgery on time 95% of the time versus 80%. Improvements is improving outcomes—for the patient and the organization.

The check stage requires the team to identify results, analyze them, and verify outcomes. Critical indicators reflecting the key process outcomes must be carefully chosen and measured to determine improvement effectiveness. Because change requires resources, it is important to know the impact of any improvement interventions.

Finally, if a quality outcome is proven or the team's efforts have moved it closer to the desired outcome, the team moves into the act stage, where the new process is standardized and the cycle is repeated for further improvement. A cautionary word here—improvement is not always transferable; for example, before implementing an improvement found for orthopedics in oncology, reapply the PDCA cycle. The environment, population, and illness have changed requiring a customized process for that area.

TEAM BUILDING—AN ESSENTIAL INGREDIENT

While part of the improvement process is data driven, the importance of establishing group cohesion, respect, and trust among members cannot be underestimated. Intellectualizing change will help align rational issues with rational solutions, but only healthy group dynamics will allow a team to cut through the inevitably emotionally charged, many times irrational responses that accompany the politics of change. Perhaps the most important differentiation between process improvement and conventional scientific methodology is the paramount role of the team. Therefore, great importance is placed on group dynamics and achieving levels of group consensus and productivity otherwise not experienced in conventional bureaucracies. Many opportunities for improvement have been squelched by dysfunctional group dynamics. Improvement means moving forward with consensus and support and cannot be sustained by a lone champion. Adversarial behavior and hidden agendas must be openly identified and recognized as resistance to change.

Upon the team's inception, the members must find their common ground. In clinical improvement teams, this common ground is improving the health status of populations and assuring the viability of the organization. Group member resistance or the formation of factions or coalitions can be metered and assessed relative to the fundamental charge of the team. It is helpful for the team to establish ground rules for behavior that provide for defusing or reconciliation of dysfunctional trends. While many consensus building techniques are named in direct association with continuous improvement, nothing works better than to deal with resistance as it arises. The team process should not provide for harboring of ill will or persistent divisive behaviors. Teams should agree, up front, that they will be open to confrontation and honesty as the team moves forward. Managing the complexity of human behavior will prove many times to be just as challenging as the operational details of the most troublesome process.

The PDCA cycle has been used to guide the improvement activities across a variety of industries, including health care. There are, however, special considerations when teams endeavor to improve clinical processes. These considerations require modifications to the PDCA cycle that expand the plan stage to include environmental mapping, the collection and analysis of external and internal data, and designing the best practices. The remaining stages in the PDCA cycle are essentially unchanged: do includes implementation, check is referred to as measure and monitor, and act is improvement in response to new findings. Figure 8–1 illustrates how the PDCA cycle has been modified to drive clinical improvement.

Part II

INTRODUCTION

Part I of this report described an adaptation of the traditional plan-do-check-act (PDCA) cycle to include steps that enhance the success of clinical improvement efforts. Each of these steps have assisted clinically based groups in analyzing performance and identifying improvements in the care processes that have yielded long-term improvements in patient outcomes. After establishing a leadership structure, the clinical improvement process begins with environmental mapping and visioning as team members assess the environmental forces affecting the care of stroke patients. This effort promotes the evolution of an answer to why the process must change and where change may take the organization. Establishing an external benchmark builds a quantitative outcome-based comparison with other health care providers. Recognizing an internal baseline focuses the group efforts on the current system of caring for stroke patients and on the degree of variability among interdependent processes and caregivers. Designing best practices focuses the group on defining how patients with stroke will be treated in their health systems. Implementation is the next step. The measure-and-monitor step determines how process changes and expected improvements in patient outcomes will be measured and monitored. The improvement step closes the circle and suggests that improvements in the care processes for stroke patients must continuously evolve and efforts must be focused on the process and how it relates to the outcomes of this patient population. Each of these elements of the clinical improvement process will be discussed in the following sections.

LEADERSHIP STRUCTURE

Achieving real improvement in the patient care process begins with a leadership structure that establishes a legitimate climate for initiating a patient care (diagnosis-based) improvement effort. Recognizing that improvement in patient outcomes must result from an integrative, multidisciplined assessment of clinical and operational processes, the leadership structure must include representatives of the key stakeholders in the process. Given the uniqueness of this approach, typically the initial leadership structure includes representatives from the board of directors, senior hospital management, and senior leaders of the medical staff. While these individuals will not actually improve the process, they will empower a process design team, define the boundaries and scope of improvement efforts, identify and reduce barriers to implementation, and communicate, organization-wide, the importance of developing improvement ideas. Perhaps the most important role of leadership is to reinforce the importance of implementation and the realization of benefits.

The suggested leadership structure may seem extensive, but the inclusion of board members offers several important advantages. They will be able to encourage and reinforce the need for broad-based improvement efforts. This commitment often reduces the level of resistance from individual members of the medical staff. In their role as stewards of community health resources, they will be able to better communicate improvement efforts and results to a community desperate for reduced health care costs and improved health care value. Finally, involvement in improvement efforts like these will yield an understanding of the difficulty of trying to change an organization and key operating processes.

Regarding the stroke improvement process, the leadership group empowers a design team to begin focused improvement. Members appointed to the design team should have ownership in the process. In other words, team members should have intimate knowledge of the disease process and the current process of caring for a stroke patient. The 10 to 12 members typically include physicians from neurology, internal medicine, and rehabilitation medicine departments; nursing staff from units that treat stroke patients; allied health professionals from rehabilitation services, respiratory care, and pharmacy; and support personnel from quality assurance (QA) and finance.

Environmental Mapping and Vision

The leadership structure creates and empowers a team to study the stroke process and develop a series of recommendations designed to improve the process and the outcomes of stroke patients. Within these broad guidelines, over a series of eight to 10 meetings, the team studies the current process and outcomes and develops suggestions for improvement. A key first step in initiating this process is to assess quickly the environmental forces affecting stroke patient outcomes. These forces could include an aging population, the lack of neurologists, reduced state funding for Medicaid patients, increased managed care activity with a focus on patient outcomes, or a local business alliance looking into outcomes and resource use. Developing a group consensus on these issues lays the foundation for future improvements in the process. More importantly, this exercise begins to build a group understanding as to why improving stroke care is important at all. Having the "why change?" question answered early in the process focuses the team's attention and develops the justification for change that becomes vital during implementation.

Incorporating the Affinity Diagram in Environmental Mapping Efforts

The affinity diagram and group process is a tool particularly suited to an environmental mapping exercise. The affinity diagram allows a team to gather large amounts of language-based data (ideas, opinions, issues, etc.) and then organize the data into groupings based on the natural relationship between each item. While the affinity diagram is considered one of the seven management and planning tools, it is largely a creative rather than a logical process. For this clinical improvement team, the affinity exercise is used to support a structured brainstorming session. Essentially, the team is asked to identify the environmental forces that affect the care and outcomes of patients receiving treatment for strokes. A description of the affinity exercise follows.

Each team member is supplied with small pads of note paper and a thick black pen (a black pen is used for legibility). The team member is instructed to write a response to the question using a noun and verb. There is one response allowed per sheet of paper, and as the ideas are generated they are placed on a flip chart, posterboard, or the wall. The idea-generating portion is done in silence to stimulate and encourage free thinking. The team members can generate as many ideas as they want until, as with popcorn, the "kernels" are done popping. It is important to note that the noun and verb are used so that the readers of the ideas understand what the writer means. Too often we write something like "time" but never explain that what we actually mean is "the healing process takes time." In team brainstorming it is imperative that no one owns ideas but that everyone works to create an atmosphere that fosters better ideas.

After the team has generated as many ideas as possible, the members gather around the flip chart, posterboard, or wall and quietly arrange the sheets in relationship rows. All ideas having to do with *time-related* are put in one column while all ideas having to do with *physician-related* or *nurse-related* or *patient-related* go in another column. Members may move the sheets back and forth and may, in fact, have to create more ideas. Once all the columns are in place, the team openly identifies headers for each of the columns. The affinity has its most powerful effect in cross-functional teams where members really hear thoughts from others for the first time. At first there is an "aha!" and then a realization that team members agree much more than they disagree. The affinity is then entered into the minutes and quality journal and can be referred to any time it is needed in the improvement process.

EXTERNAL BENCHMARK

Heightened public awareness of health care issues and an economic-driven focus on prevention and control of chronic illness have far-reaching epidemiologic implications. Television documentaries, public service announcements, politicians, and malpractice attorneys are but a few sources of testimony of how modern health care interventions impact disease distribution and frequency in the United States. Hospitals and other health care providers face mounting pressures to improve their performance as it increasingly impacts the financial and health status of the population.

As this report proposes, viewed from an improvement mindset, the outcomes of episodes of health care can be linked causally to clinical and organizational/operational processes. Because some organizations are improving at faster rates than others, there is an experience base reflected in patient-level comparative outcome data that can be used to benchmark or meter organizational performance. In the growing study and management of outcomes, data compared across national and local health care facilities have been used effectively to compare performance across institutions, initiate improvement efforts with facts (adjusted outcome comparisons), and identify specific opportunities for improvement (areas of focus). While many methods of risk-adjusting outcome data are available, each organization must decide on its level of comfort and available resources to commit to risk adjustment. For our purposes, risk-adjusted outcome data, whether operational (costs, charges, length of stay) or medical (complication/infection rates, morbidity, mortality), were compiled into homogeneous clinical categories and Diagnosis-Related Groups (DRGs) for comparative analysis. These clinically adjusted groups were developed by expert panels and applied to publicly available data sets (primarily Medicare billing files). For example, patients with a principle diagnosis of stroke were subdivided into patients with stroke secondary to cerebral thrombosis, intracerebral/intracranial hemorrhage, subarachnoid hemorrhage, or subdural hemorrhage. Patients with stroke were further modified by the following severity modifiers: cardiovascular/pulmonary disease, diabetes, and age.[8]

We used a method in which the ratio of observed (unadjusted) hospital data to the risk-adjusted expected values was used to provide a statistically adjusted index. In this method, any variance from 1.00 indicates outcome or resource use different from the risk-adjusted average to provide relative comparisons between health care facilities. Graphic displays of such data among peer organizations often convince team members that opportunities for improvement exist.

Figure 8–2 and 8–3 illustrate an actual comparison of outcomes between peer hospitals for DRG 14 (cerebrovascular disorders except transient ischemic attacks). Higher-than-average mortality rates, average lengths of stay, and total costs were evident for this patient population at the medical center (MC). The leadership structure identified this DRG as an area of opportunity for focused clinical process improvement. The external data comparison communicated the opportunity and specific areas of stroke care on which to focus.

INTERNAL BASELINE

With the improvement target broadly established, the next step includes identifying, understanding, and measuring the critical subprocesses that interrelate to produce outcomes of the health care system. Performing an analysis of internal data serves to establish the organization's baseline performance. This baseline reveals valuable information regarding the source and degree of opportunities for improvement and provides a reference point for measuring the direction and magnitude of change. Often, the internal baseline indicates a high degree of variability among all caregivers and significant opportunities to learn.

For clinical processes, a randomly selected sample of recent medical records is perhaps the richest source of process information. Other supporting data sources may include QA/quality assessment and utilization review reports, risk management statistics, case management variance reports, and the hospital

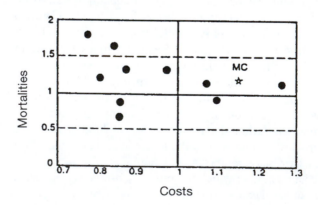

Figure 8–2 Statistically Adjusted Comparisons between Hospital Mortality Rates and Total Costs Associated with the Care of Stroke Patients

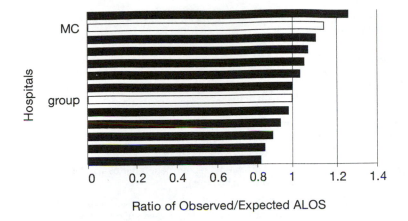

Figure 8–3 Statistically Adjusted Hospital Average Length of Stay Comparisons for Stroke Patients

---

information system. Coupled with the personal knowledge and expertise of a multidisciplinary team whose members are involved in the process, the intricacies of a complex care network can be closely and effectively examined. Using a scientific, data-driven approach is "really just a systematic way for individuals and teams to learn about processes. It means agreeing to make decisions based on data rather than hunches, to look for root causes of problems rather than react to superficial symptoms."[9]

Referring again to process improvement theory, understanding the variability in a process is the first step in reducing it. Outcomes cannot be improved unless the processes that produce it are consistently performed. The treatment of stroke at the MC provides a good example of how sources of variability were identified and specifically targeted for change. A selected group of professionals comprised of a neurologist; radiologist; dietitian; social worker; two internists; two respiratory, physical, and speech therapists; and staff and quality review nurses met for two hours every two weeks to collaboratively improve stroke patient outcomes. After reviewing the external comparative data, the multidisciplinary stroke process improvement group agreed on the key internal sources of process variability in the care and treatment of acute strokes. A preliminary issues list was compiled and used to develop a medical chart review form to measure baseline performance and process variability. This issues list is displayed as Table 8–1. The key findings and process variability of the baseline stroke medical record review are presented in Table 8–2.

Table 8–1   Medical Center Stroke Process Improvement Work Group
Preliminary Issues List

Source of Variability	Description
Patient admission status	Source of admission Duration of deficit Age Patient psychosocial assessment Family psychosocial assessment Existing patient comorbidities
Discharge planning	Date of discharge assessment (after evaluation of stroke; after diagnostic tests)
Physicians	Variability exists in many physician practices—some conventional methods still being used with variable effectiveness
Nursing	The unit where the patient receives care Early intervention strategies with dysphagic patients (nursing does swallowing assessment) Timing of speech therapy referral for swallowing assessment Timing and quality of nutritional intake Complications (pneumonia, urinary tract infections, decubitus ulcers, contractures)
Diagnostic tests	The tests deemed necessary The tests that are done (emergency computerized tomography [CT] scans, cerebral arteriograms, and magnetic resonance imaging are common first-line tests) Timing of diagnostic tests (initial diagnostic and follow-up) Routine lab tests ordered Cerebral arteriograms (estimated 60% use rate) should not be done in cases of a completed stroke Echocardiograms not needed on all stroke patients New technology to be explored ("spiral" CTs)
Anticoagulation therapy	Heparin use: timing, dose, duration, route Other anticoagulant use
Respiratory care	Oxygen use Treatment of pulmonary complications (eg, pneumonia) Tracheostomy patients
Patient/family teaching	Degree of family involvement post-stroke How patient/family teaching is organized Appropriateness of teaching material
Physical rehabilitation	When rehabilitation can start (physical, speech, and occupational therapies) When rehabilitation does start

Table 8–1 continued

Source of Variability	Description
Rehabilitation medicine (physiatry)	Timing of consults Goal-setting for each stroke patient
Long-term rehabilitation placement	Medicare/Medicaid/no-pay patients experiencing problems with long-term placement Swing bed availability for interim placement Transfer back to local hospital for post-acute stroke care
Communication	Documentation practices by person Documentation practices by unit Referral protocol Interdepartmental communication Interdisciplinary communication Family/patient involvement in the care process Generally seeking a comprehensive understanding of how to care for the stroke patient

Table 8–2 depicts process variability that is likely the result of common-cause variation, typically due to a large number of small sources of variation. For example, relating the preliminary issues list (Table 8–1) to the data collected (Table 8–2), group members inherently knew that variations in nursing practices on different units contributed to variable lengths of stay, and no doubt, variable outcomes. Indeed, some of that variability involves caregiver proficiency and expertise and some can be attributed to other sources like interdepartmental and interdisciplinary communication mechanisms, patient/family teaching patterns, ancillary service productivity, nurses' personal comfort level with various physicians, and physician practice variability. Experience indicates that one can learn by comparing performance and processes across physicians, nurses, and other caregivers. Insights into designing the best practices can usually be found embedded in process variability. Figure 8–4 illustrates variability in length of stay by MC physicians for stroke patients.

DESIGN BEST PRACTICES

The complexity of health care processes combined with high levels of human involvement make understanding variability much more difficult than simply identifying it. Due to the nature of the services provided and a history of inefficient systems, health care processes tend to have layers, or "band-aids"

Table 8–2 Stroke Medical Record Review Baseline Findings and Process Variability

Patient Admission Status

Demographics	
Average age (years)	71.7
Male (%)	61
Female (%)	39
Average length of stay (days)	8.9
Documented comorbidities (%)	
Hypertension	61
Atherosclerotic coronary vascular disease, myocardial infarction, coronary bypass surgery	30
Previous stroke	30
Degenerative joint disease	22
Atrial fibrillation	22
Congestive heart failure/cardiomyopathy	17
Diabetes	17
Chronic obstructive pulmonary disease	13
Acuity assessed on admission (%)	
Definite functional limitations, high probability of complications	76
High risk for increased morbidity/mortality during hospitalization	14
Moribund patient—unlikely to survive hospitalization	10

Discharge Planning	*(%)*
Timing of social service referrals	
Total patients referred	74
Referral on day of admission	12
Referral on day 1-2 of stay	24
Referral on day 3-5 of stay	29
Referral on day 6-7 of stay	18
Referral after day 7	18
Discharge disposition	
Home	39
Rehabilitation facility	26
Died	17
Home health referral	13
Nursing home	4

Table 8–2 continued

Diagnostic Tests	Patients (%)	Positive (%)	Negative (%)
Computed tomography (CT) scan of brain with contrast medium	57	67	33
Patients with > 1 CT scan	8		
CT scan of brain without contrast medium	83	48	52
Patients with > 1 CT scan	26		
Magnetic resonance imaging (MRI) of brain	30	86	14
MRI and CT scan	30		
CT first result negative	86		
Carotid angiography	13	100	
Carotid ultrasound	65	69	31
Angiography and ultrasound	4		
Echocardiogram	87	37	63

Admitting Unit	Patients (%)	Average Length of Stay (Days)†
Neurology	50	8.1
Medical/surgery I	14	9.3
Medical/surgery II	14	9
Intensive care unit	9	8
Surgical	5	15
Medical/surgery III	5	11
Medical/surgery IV	5	6

Complications Documented	(%)
Urinary tract infection	9
Pneumonia	4
Decubitus ulcer	4
Sepsis	4
Other (single cases)	
falls, seizures, pulmonary embolus, syncope, obstructive apnea	20

Patient/Family Teaching	(%)
Patients with any teaching documented	50
Type of teaching documented	
Dietary instructions	40
Medication instructions	20
Rehabilitation teaching	40
Other (various topics)	70

continues

Table 8–2 continued

Anticoagulation Therapy	(%)
Heparin	61
Coumadin	43
Aspirin	35

Therapeutic Interventions	(%)
Oxygen therapy	39
Urinary catheter	22
Respiratory therapy	17
Tube feedings	4

		Day Ordered (%)		
Consultation	Ordered (%)	Admission Date	Day 1-2	Day 3-5	On or After Day 6
---	---	---	---	---	---
Neurology	87	91	10		
Neurosurgery	4	100			
Social services	74	12	24	29	36
Physical therapy	78	28	44	22	6
Speech therapy	43	30	50	20	

Acute Phase Nursing Documentation (%)	Day 1	Day 2	Day 3
Mental status, level of consciousness	100	91	86
Affect/personality	86	55	45
Speech/language	95	82	73
Sensation/perception	50	45	45
Motor control	95	91	68
Bladder function	82	68	59
Nutritional intake	55	64	55
Skin integrity	59	59	55
Breath/lung sounds	73	50	45
Bowel sounds	41	18	23
Level of the head of the bed	23	41	41

14% of annual Medical Center volume for DRG 14, June 1, 1991 to May 31, 1992.
†Excludes deaths.

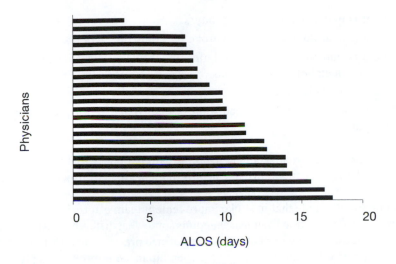

Figure 8–4 Average Length of Stay by MC Physicians for Stroke Patients

which, once established, are difficult to change. An important part of moving toward the best practices is identifying existing system band-aids. Some of these include the following:

- organizational policies that serve to support a bad system design,
- non-value-added activities,
- work and data redundancy,
- buffers and intermediaries that fill communication or other gaps,
- chronic inefficiency.

Continuing with the example for the improvement of the care of stroke patients, once external benchmarking and internal baselining have been performed, the next challenge is designing a system to realize improvement. New system design focuses on the essence of caring for typical stroke patients, including clinical practices and support systems. Again, a major component of success is designing the variability out. In clinical improvement efforts, this can be accomplished effectively by getting the team to begin with the end in mind. In other words, the team first identifies those endpoints in the stroke care process that reflect the patient's readiness for discharge from the hospital. Then, the best way to achieve those endpoints is mapped out for each discipline involved.

In the case reported here, the stroke team agreed on the following medical endpoints, or discharge criteria, for their stroke patients.

- Patient is medically stable for 48 hours.
- Patient is neurologically stable (stroke is "complete") for 48 hours.
- Patient is nutritionally stable and nutritional intake is sufficient to meet individual metabolic requirements.
- Someone is ready to receive the patient.
- Bowel/bladder control has been addressed sufficiently for postdischarge management.

These criteria were broad enough to allow for patient variability yet focused enough to direct attention to the details of managing key aspects of stroke care.

It is important to note that in stroke improvement team efforts in a variety of facilities, each team defined medical endpoints somewhat differently. Anecdotal evidence suggests that by respecting locally defined practices within an acceptable care framework, team cohesion and ownership in the improvement process is enhanced. Physician leaders are increasingly responsive to change when the practice dynamics of their community, rather than broad national guidelines, are considered.

In the case reported here, developing the interventional path required participants to rethink the care delivery process. Driven by the improvement opportunities revealed from the internal baselining process, the stroke team agreed that, for this patient population, the best practices would provide for early mobilization of resources and tightly interfaced, collaborative care. Although studies conducted on the effects of a coordinated program of stroke care suggest mixed results,[10] our physicians felt the best practices for stroke care should be provided using a programmatic approach driven by a unit-based, multidisciplinary stroke team. By building a broad-based consensus on the endpoints of care and the process for consistently achieving those endpoints, decisions to centralize or decentralize specific processes can be made. For example, centralizing stroke patients on one unit has made significant improvements in patient outcomes (ie, reducing complication rates and length of stay). Decentralizing radiology or laboratory services for this group of patients, however, has not yielded substantive improvements in outcomes.

A framework for treating stroke patients was defined to represent distinct phases of care, and the basic treatment goals of each phase were identified. The framework and basic treatment goals for stroke care are outlined in Table 8–3.

Identification of the medical endpoints and the overall framework for caring for stroke patients led to a number of additional considerations. Obtaining agreement on the point at which a patient is medically ready for discharge allowed the group to rapidly move toward answering the question of what in our process could be changed to move the patient and family or caretakers to the

Table 8–3 Framework and Basic Treatment Goals for Stroke Care

Acute Phase	Intermediate Phase	Rehabilitation Phase
Achieve medical stability (completed stroke)	Achieve neurological stability	Complete evaluations
Initial diagnostic testing (noncontrast computed tomography scan)	Complete diagnosis	Mobilize resources for aftercare
Ongoing neurological assessment	Stabilize comorbid states	Secure optimal long-term intervention (rehabilitation, home health, etc)
Initiate major, critical evaluations	Begin physical rehabilitation	
Assess patient/family psychosocial needs	Intensive discharge planning	

endpoints in less time with increased effectiveness. In answering this question, each discipline developed detailed plans addressing the arrangement of key interventions designed to achieve the respective treatment goals for each phase of care. Key interventions often consist of nursing interventions (physical, neurological, and psychosocial assessments, head and body positioning), medical interventions (timing and use of ancillary services, timing and use of diagnostic testing), allied health care interventions (speech, occupational, and physical therapy assessments and intervention), and health system interventions (bed assignments, turnaround times on lab/diagnostic testing, link with rehabilitation facilities, and the use of home care). Considering key interventions, what resulted were the implementable details of stroke protocol. The following guidelines were applied in developing the level of detail necessary to achieve a truly multidisciplinary stroke team and a program of care to produce the desired outcomes. These guidelines reflect both conventional and more recent principles of continuous improvement and process redesign.[11]

GUIDELINES FOR STROKE PROTOCOL DEVELOPMENT

The following points are guidelines to keep in mind when designing key interventions for stroke protocol.

- Focus on actually designing the work group's vision of the future. Remember the following: "seamless" care delivery; collaboration; consistent, early, multidisciplinary intervention; prevention of complications; reliable, accurate communication; more patient-focused interventions; and more patient/family involvement.

- When planning the structure and interventions for the stroke protocol, keep focused on the desired overall outcomes: increased patient satisfaction, improved health outcomes, and optimized/reduced resource use (wasted time, materials, costs).

- Organize the care process around endpoints, not tasks. Focus on the endpoints, then create the best way to achieve them. Try to eliminate turf considerations if possible. Think about the patient.

- Understand the current problems so that they are not repeated. Be honest with each other.

- Understand the existing rules, formal and informal. Determine which should be bypassed, broken, or replaced. Keep thinking about ways to achieve improvement.

- Keep it simple. Eliminate non-value-added activities.

- Link activities. Seek to integrate cross-discipline boundaries.

- Minimize the dependence on buffers and intermediaries. Identify and define roles of individuals needed to satisfy the coordination/teaching needs that cannot be done efficiently by day-to-day caregivers. Otherwise, try not to build systems on top of faulty systems. Design a protocol under the assumption that you are all competent people who, in a good system, can work toward getting it right the first time.

- Whenever possible, put the decision point where the work is performed and build control into the process. Try to increase the decision-making autonomy of the caregiver. Define interventions and contingencies (under what conditions physicians are notified, etc.). Focus on allowing caregivers to assume responsibility for routine patient care issues. Team care means maximizing efficiency by giving primary caregivers well-defined, yet broadened parameters within which to work. Build these ideas into the protocol by clearly defining the collaboration between disciplines to make informed decisions. For example, after a patient has entered the intermediate phase, their activity orders may be "advance as tolerated." This means that nursing and rehabilitation medicine communicate with each other to provide continuity of care, that the patient is involved, and that the physician is comfortable with the patient's progress. The same may apply to diet, bladder/bowel training, for example. Ideally, once the stroke protocol has been initiated, the physician knows what to expect, the right services are provided at the right time, and the patients receive levels of high-quality, efficient care from admission to aftercare.

- Clearly define the roles and responsibilities of each discipline during each phase of care.
- Whenever applicable, capture information once and at the source. Reduce redundancy of information and effort. Evaluate documentation practices. Seek a system where clarity of information is assured.
- Provide for the development of skills needed to match the demands of improvement. Integrated care means training and education. While these details need not be included directly in the stroke protocol, staff education needs must be addressed as an implementation issue to assure sustainable continuity of care.
- Finally, when you have great ideas, write them down, even if they do not relate directly to the protocol or if they seem impossible.

Following reorientation of key interventions, teams often have built a series of reminders for the medical staff and caregivers to more effectively coordinate the activities of multiple disciplines. Supporting stroke protocol were mechanisms designed to assure the necessary attention to the details of the care process. These key reminders often have taken the form of standing physician's orders for patients admitted with stroke. While not intended to be prescriptive, the orders are designed to remind physicians and caregivers of key steps in the care process while providing ample opportunity for modifications to meet particular patient needs. Other reminders include the development of multidisciplinary documentation tools designed to coordinate specific process details. Key intervention checksheets, patient and family teaching logs, care maps for variance analyses, and specific QA indicators can be used to shape the care process as well as provide a source of process feedback. Such instruments can serve as reminder systems if used concurrently and communication links are well established.

The structure of reminder systems will vary depending on organizational beliefs about health care delivery. For example, care maps, critical pathways, practice guidelines, or similar methods have been developed differently to present the expected course of treatment for the typical patient with the respective diagnosis. The major differences in approach will hinge on whether the health care facility focuses more on length of stay or optimizing incremental care interventions. Adopting a days focus, the timing of key interventions will be presented and executed following a day-1, day-2 format. Using an optimal care focus, the timings of key interventions are executed in a relational perspective to an individual patient's responses. While delays in the care process may signal a negative variance in the days approach, optimal care will assure that appropriate interventions are performed as efficiently as possible to achieve the desired endpoints. On the other hand, patients who are ahead of the days schedule may not progress as rapidly as their individual pace allows whereas optimal care will move continuously that patient through the care process more efficiently with the same or improved outcomes. The opportunities for optimizing the care process should not be measured relative to length of stay but, more importantly, by appropriateness of interventions. As technology changes, biomedical research discoveries are made and health care delivery continues to shift to alternative systems, expected lengths of stay will change. Health care facilities designing care using a days approach are facing a moving target.

After several meetings, the stroke team will have completed the design of how a patient with stroke will be treated in its organization. Given the highly participative nature of the analysis and design process, a significant amount of learning already has occurred in the group. Often, for the first time, the entire improvement team has a broadened understanding of the endpoints and the system for achieving superior patient outcomes. This team-based knowledge must now be expanded to include the extended caregiving team.

IMPLEMENT

Realizing change requires attention to implementation details. The cumulative effect of the previous steps in the clinical improvement process will provide the analytical details for actually improving the status quo. Planing the remaining details is perhaps the single most important part of implementation. All steps in the stroke care process require in-depth planning of what will be done, who will do it, how it will be done, how much it will cost, and over what time frame completion is expected. Staff development and training are essential to successfully operationalizing implementation plans. This includes education of physicians, multidisciplinary caregivers, ancillary services, and support departments.

In planning implementation, special consideration must be given to effective communication of anticipated change. The goal of communication strategies should be to gain widespread acceptance of required changes in behavior as a result of improvement activities. Managing change effectively requires anticipating, recognizing, and responding to resistance. While the leadership structure provides the support and guidance for organizationwide communication of improvement initiatives, stroke improvement team participants reinforce this communication by building support at their respective organizational levels. Their combined display of commitment facilitates a positive initial transition from current to improved practices.

In general, the scope of improvement efforts will determine whether pilot testing in a limited, controlled environment is necessary. For diagnosis-driven clinical improvement efforts such as stroke care, the scope for implementation should be self-limiting. However, planning should consider the magnitude of change and assure its manageability. Because process improvement inevitably will provide some ideas that are transferable on a broad scale, full organizational implementation of such improvements is possible after proven results are in. For example, in developing protocols for magnetic resonance imaging testing, the stroke improvement team saw an opportunity for hospital-wide application. Though initial use of the protocol would be implemented to screen stroke patients, plans were made to expand the protocol to the entire organization through the hospital information system.

Depending on improvement objectives, results of clinical improvement efforts applied in unique situations manifest in a variety of ways. For stroke care, implementation of improvement ideas had decreased hospital length of stay, decreased clinical practice variability; increased patient satisfaction, reduced ancillary resource use (especially laboratory and radiology costs), and provided transferable benefits to other departments. Most importantly, teams develop, many for the first time, a broad understanding of the stroke care process. This learning has translated into more satisfying job environments.

MEASURE AND MONITOR

Two questions are central to the clinical improvement process. First, have changes in the care process improved the outcomes of the intended patient group, in this case, stroke patients? Are there demonstrable changes in mortality and complication rates, length of stay, use of resources, pace of return to optimal lifestyle, and patient satisfaction? Second, are the key process changes occurring uniformly throughout the care process? Has process variability been reduced?

Depending on the nature of the organization, responsibility for measuring and monitoring could be assigned to one of several groups. In a traditional environment, responsibility could be assigned to QA or utilization review. In a more team-oriented environment, measurement and monitoring could be assigned to the work team accountable for delivering the care, in essence, unit-based monitoring. In these transitional times, overall outcomes monitoring could be assigned to a centralized group whereas responsibility for process monitoring could be assumed by the care team. Whatever the method chosen, both outcomes and key process monitoring should occur. One caveat exists, however. Design teams should avoid overmonitoring. It will not be efficient or productive for organizational learning to involve measuring and monitoring every single process change and outcome. The work groups should focus measurement efforts on those key process indicators that will assure implementation is occurring and outcomes are improving.

IMPROVE

After significant effort and success with redesigning stroke care processes, the tendency often would be to move toward other diagnoses and improvement efforts. It is not likely, however, on the first pass of the improvement effort, that the stroke team will design the perfect process and achieve perfect outcomes. If the care of patients with stroke is indeed one of the vital few where continued improvement will improve significantly the performance of the organization, then after initial implementation, the improvement process should be repeated.

CONCLUSION

This article discusses how focusing on improving high-volume patient care processes would result in improvement opportunities that would leverage overall organizational performance, describe a specific process for improving clinical performance, and apply that process to the care of stroke patients. Applying this process across several organizations, we remain convinced that improvement efforts must focus on the vital few and that the care of patients with specific diagnoses meets the test of those vital few. Patients with stroke illustrate this idea especially well. They account for a high volume of cases and revenue, involve a broad spectrum of medical staff and allied caregivers, and represent, especially for community-based caregivers, a highly visible care process.

Designing an improvement process that encompasses quality improvement, organizational development, and change principles has led to the successful design of new methods of care delivery and also to the successful implementation of these ideas. The combination of these principles yields a powerful approach for achieving the types of breakthroughs necessary to flourish in the future health care system.

NOTES

1. J.M. Juran, *Juran's Quality Control Handbook* (New York, NY: McGraw Hill: 1974).

2. C.J. Bolster and J. Dawson, Clinical Engineering: Integrating All Caregivers in the Design of High Quality Patient Care Delivery Systems, *Aspen's Advisor for Nurse Executives* 7, no. 8 (1992): 1–6.

3. M.R. Weisbord, *Productive Workplaces* (San Francisco, Calif: Josey-Bass; 1991).

4. P.M. Senge, *The Fifth Discipline* (New York, NY: Doubleday/Currency, 1990).

5. C.J. Bolster and E. Falter, Quality: An Improvement Tool for the 21st Century, *Clinical Performance and Quality Health Care* 1 (1993): 55–57.

6. P.R. Scholtes, *The Team Handbook: How to Use Teams to Improve Quality* (Madison, Wisc: Joiner Associates, 1990).

7. Scholtes, *The Team Handbook*.

8. *Quality-Based Performance Analysis Software* (Atlanta, GA: Hay Group).

9. Scholtes, *The Team Handbook*.

10. M. Pasquarello, Measuring the Impact of an Acute Stroke Program on Patient Outcome, *Journal of Neuroscience Nursing*, 22 no. 2 (1990): 76–82.

11. S.L. Huff, Reengineering the Business, *Business Quarterly* (Winter 1992): 38–42.

9. An Introduction to Critical Paths

Richard J. Coffey, Janet S. Richards, Carl S. Remmert,
Sarah S. LeRoy, Rhonda R. Schoville, and Phyllis J. Baldwin

A critical path is an optimal sequencing and timing of interventions by physicians, nurses, and other staff for a particular diagnosis or procedure, designed to minimize delays and resource utilization and to maximize the quality of care. Critical path methodologies originated in the construction and engineering fields, and they have been in use in these fields for many years. For those applications, several excellent methodologies and computer programs are available that compute beginning and ending times, critical path(s), slack times, and other useful data. Most programs allow either tabular or graphic formats of outputs. Some programs add in optimistic, expected, and pessimistic time estimates for each activity to address the variability in times. Critical path methods have proven to be a very valuable approach to manage large, complex projects.

In health care, concepts related to critical paths were discussed and researched in the early 1970s, but the environment for implementation was not receptive. In 1974, for example, Shoemaker stated that "Routines or patient protocols are useful means to standardize care, to facilitate completeness of services, and to evaluate both the patient's progress and the therapeutic efficacy of the program. They are also an educational tool. In essence, the development of protocols is the first step leading from anecdotal to scientific medicine." He further stated that, "Protocols, routines and other standards do not insure excellence, but sometimes they prevent disasters."[1] Although some of the research showed promise, the environment was not supportive of full implementation and expansion. At that time, hospitals were reimbursed on a dollar-for-dollar basis for their full costs by most payors. Hence, there was no financial incentive to optimize resource

Source: Reprinted from *Quality Management in Health Care*, Vol. 1, No. 1, pp. 45–54, Aspen Publishers, Inc., © 1992.

utilization. In addition, many physicians resisted formal efforts to restrict their freedom to practice as they wished.

Beginning in the early 1980s, however, hospital reimbursement systems began to feature prospective payment and competitive bidding. These changes stimulated renewed interest in critical paths and related subjects such as clinical guidelines and algorithms. Other factors that stimulated renewed interest were the increasing evidence of unacceptable variation in clinical care and outcomes,[2,3] a trend toward increasing input from multiple professions in the decision-making process for patient care, and increasing malpractice costs.

The University of Michigan Medical Center (UMMC) began researching critical paths in the late 1980s. Separate development efforts were initiated within University Hospital, the adult medical-surgical hospital, and the C.S. Mott Children's Hospital. At University Hospital, critical paths were implemented on the thoracic surgery, neurosurgery, and neurology inpatient units in January 1991. One key motivation to develop critical paths was to reduce length of stay and costs associated with specific diagnoses and procedures. From the beginning, the critical path effort has included physicians, nurses, and other health care providers.

At the C.S. Mott Children's Hospital, the initial pilot began in May 1991. Nineteen critical paths pertinent to cardiology and thoracic surgery were developed. Five of the pathways were developed for new procedures in which no prior experience was available. Currently there are 36 critical paths being used at UMMC, and many others are being developed.

CONCEPTS, DEFINITIONS, AND ROLES

There are a number of different terms associated with the general concepts of critical paths. The following paragraphs define the terms critical paths, variances, case coordinator or case manager, and physician and clarify the differences and similarities between related terms.

Critical Paths

A critical path defines an optimal sequencing and timing of interventions by physicians, nurses, and other staff for a particular diagnosis or procedure, designed to better utilize resources, maximize quality of care, and minimize delays. It can be thought of as a visualization of the patient care process. Typically, critical paths are developed for high-volume, high-risk, and high-cost diagnoses and procedures. The following aspects of the care process are typically tracked: consults and assessments, tests, treatments, nutrition, medications (both intravenous and other), activity or safety, teaching (patient, significant other), discharge planning and coordination, and other additional categories based on the specific diagnosis or procedure.[4] The analysis begins with a study of the complete process; TQM also begins in this fashion.

Several different terms are used to describe methods to achieve better coordinated care similar to critical paths. These terms include critical pathways, critical paths of care, and care maps. It is more important to look at the characteristics of the process in which critical paths are used than the specific terminology. These characteristics distinguish them from algorithms and practice parameters. Unlike these applications, critical paths feature:

- *Comprehensiveness*. Critical paths deal not just with physician decision making, but with the decision making, services, and interactions among all providers of services for the patients covered by the critical paths.
- *Timelines*. Critical paths contain specific timelines for interventions to occur.
- *Collaboration*. Critical paths are jointly developed by multiple health care professionals.
- *Manager*. Patients on critical paths have a case manager or case coordinator, usually a nurse.

Although a critical path represents the typical or expected progression of interventions, it can and must be adjusted to meet the patient's individual needs. Algorithms and practice guidelines are also adjusted to accommodate the needs of the patient.

A useful extension of the carefully orchestrated multidisciplinary interventions and actions in the critical path is to include an analysis of patient and family actions in terms of responses to the staff's interventions.[5] These problems or responses or outcomes are shown on the same form as the critical path itself. The combination of the actions and responses produces essentially "cause and effect grids, i.e., staff actions should result in patient/family reactions or responses, which over time are 'transformed' into desired outcomes. Staff actions are equivalent to standards of practice; patient reactions are equivalent to standards of care."[6]

Currently, most critical paths are developed by health care professionals, with little direct input from patients. The increasing focus on patients and other customers as part of a continuous quality improvement or total quality management process may result in a movement toward patient input in developing critical paths, particularly for long-term conditions.

Variances

Variances are deviations or "detours" from the critical path. They may be positive or negative, avoidable or unavoidable. Variances may be caused by:

- *Patient or family:* Patient refuses test, patient develops fever or pain, patient advances quicker than expected, or family unable to come to hospital to learn how to do wound care at home.
- *Clinician:* Physician decides patient does not need a magnetic resonance imaging (MRI) scan, or parent teaching of nasal gastric feeds for a pediatric patient is not indicated early in the hospital stay.
- *System:* Computed tomography (CT) scanner breaks down, patient consult is lost, no general care bed available to transfer patient from intensive care unit, or test results are received earlier than expected.
- *Community:* Ambulance delayed or skilled nursing facility (SNF) bed unavailable.

When variances are noted in a timely fashion, investigations or corrective actions can be initiated sooner. In the case of variances resulting from the patient's condition, analyses can contribute to more timely interventions, which may decrease complications or resource utilization. Analysis of variance data may also lead to changes in the critical path—a form of continual process improvement. Predictable variances in a patient population leads to earlier intervention or prevention, or a change in the critical path.

Case Coordinator or Case Manager

The case coordinator or case manager is usually a registered nurse who is responsible for the ongoing coordination, monitoring, and evaluation of the patient's progress on the critical path. The case coordinator typically serves in this role for the duration of inpatient stay or the episode of illness. Variations in the scope of responsibility and case load vary with individual institutional models. As an example, for children's heart disease in the C.S. Mott Children's Hospital, the case managers are clinical nurse specialists and are involved in the direct patient care. Thus, the case manager not only monitors patient progress, but can intervene as needed to ensure timely interventions. These case managers also have both outpatient and inpatient responsibilities, which facilitates continuity of care. The case coordinator may also be responsible for the aggregation and analysis of variance data for his or her patient population.

Physicians

Physicians directly participate in, and may initiate, development of critical paths. Although the critical paths are collaboratively developed, at UMMC physicians continue to direct the overall care. They make the ultimate decisions concerning the medical interventions included in the critical path. The activities that currently require a physician's order continue to do so.

DIMENSIONS OF CRITICAL PATHS

A large number of health care organizations are actively developing critical paths. The development process and outputs may vary along several important dimensions.

Scope

Scope refers to the range of application, or period of care, for which the critical path is developed. Applications of the general principles of critical paths may cover one or more of the following scopes:

- *Inpatient care.* These critical paths are initiated either at the time of admission or at the time of a surgical procedure; they end at the time of discharge. This scope is the most common one. Critical paths for inpatient care are currently being used by the Alliant Health System, Louisville, Kentucky; Lee Memorial Hospital, Fort Myers, Florida; New England Medical Center, Boston, Massachusetts; Robert Wood Johnson University Hospital, New Brunswick, New Jersey; Sinai Hospital, Detroit, Michigan; the Toronto Hospital, Toronto, Ontario, Canada; the UMMC, Ann Arbor, Michigan; Vanderbilt University Hospital and Clinic, Nashville, Tennessee; and many others.
- *Complete episode of care.* These critical paths begin at the time the patient presents at the physician's office and end at the termination of posthospitalization follow-up.
- *Specialized applications.* These include critical paths such as those for ambulatory surgery patients or renal dialysis patients. An example currently being developed at UMMC is a coordinated care model for managing the care of outpatients in a new cough and dyspnea clinic.
- *Life and health management.* These are critical paths for the management of chronic conditions. Consider a person with chronic hypertension. A

critical path could be developed by a team including the patient, physician, nurse, dietitian, and possibly a recreational therapist. The person may then serve as the case manager, assisted by a nurse or other health care professional. New York University Medical Center, New York, New York; and Vanderbilt University Hospital and Clinic, Nashville, Tennessee, are developing critical paths of this type.

Conditions Addressed by Critical Paths

Critical paths are developed for patients with common or specialized procedures or diagnoses. Separate paths are developed for sets of patients that are expected to have distinctly different treatment protocols or outcomes based on the patient's condition or clinical practices. Some hospitals have developed separate critical paths for different physicians treating similar diagnoses or procedures, although the goal is usually consensus on a common critical path. Critical paths can be used for any practice that is replicated for patients with similar, identifiable conditions. For example, a critical path could be developed for diagnostic workups for heart transplant patients.

Categories of Staff Actions

For ease of use, staff actions and interventions included in critical paths are typically organized into categories. Zander[7,8] defined one commonly used set of categories including consults and assessments, treatments, nutrition, medications, activity and safety, teaching, discharge planning, and others. The same categories are usually used for different critical paths within the same organization.

Problem and Outcome

In addition to the types of interventions, another characteristic included in an expanded version of critical paths is the expected problems, responses, and outcomes, as described above. The advantage to this approach is that the practitioners, patient, and family know the typical progress of a patient, along with the care provided. One of the types of critical paths includes the following categories of problems, responses, and outcomes: pain, activity intolerance, knowledge deficit, anxiety, potential for injury, and potential for change.[9,10] The categories of problems, responses, and outcomes may be tailored to each critical path.

Format

The format of a critical path is another characteristic that distinguishes different applications. The format for most clinical applications is a matrix of activities by day or hour. A sample is displayed in Exhibit 9–1. This format allows the critical path to be placed at the bedside or in the patient's medical record.

Documentation

The approach to documentation is another characteristic distinguishing different applications of critical paths. The critical paths may or may not be used as part of the permanent medical record. Many agree that including the paths in patients' medical records would reduce the time required for charting, especially for nurses. So far, however, critical paths have rarely replaced other parts of the medical record. Therefore, documentation related to the critical paths is redundant with other charting activities. Some hospitals that have implemented the critical paths discard them after the patient has left the hospital. Others keep the critical paths as quality assurance documents to document quality and variances.

USES OF CRITICAL PATHS

Critical paths are being used more frequently and by more institutions because they are perceived to be useful. The following paragraphs are some of the most important potential uses of critical paths.

Clarify the "Big Picture." Traditionally, physicians write orders each day, but few members of the health care team are aware of the overall care plan. Each day nurses, pharmacists, therapists, ancillary departments, and others carry out that day's orders. Collaboration across disciplines is uncommon and inconsistent. When something is not ordered, a delay may occur because other members of the care team cannot proceed. One common exception in medical centers involves patients on research care critical paths. Critical paths extend the benefits of daily orders by providing an integrated overall plan for everyone to use.

Provide Planning and Coordination of Care. During development of each critical path, physicians, nurses, and others plan and coordinate all aspects of care based on data, expert opinion, and consensus. Development of the critical path creates common expectations among physicians, nurses, and other care

Exhibit 9–1 Sample Critical Path for Cervical Spinal Cord Injury

CRITICAL PATHWAY: Cervical spinal cord injury with neurological deficit without respiratory complications

UNIVERSITY OF MICHIGAN NEUROSURGERY

ADMIT DIAGNOSIS: Cervical Spinal Cord Injury
DRG: 9
PROCEDURE: Spinal fusion
EXPECTED LOS: 4.5 days

PHYSICIAN:
DATE INITIATED
PATHWAY CODE: 9.1.1 MCLA 333.21515.20175
August 8, 1991

	DAY 1 (Admission)	DAY 2/3 (Surgery)	DAY 4/5 (Transfer)	DAY 6/7 (Discharge)
Date				
Consults	PMR, SCI social worker, SCI nurse, Orthotics, Rehabilitation engineering	Physical, occupational therapy	Dietitian	Transfer to PMR/ SCI service
Tests	Lateral C-spine, CXR, MRI ABG, Admission Profile.	PARU: CBC, CHEM A & B, ABG, CXR, Lateral C-spine	CBC, CHEM A & B, ABG CXR, Lateral C-spine with position change.	
Activity	Bedrest (if Stryker do not turn until lateral C-spines and residents orders) Turn q2h. ROM q4h. Consider roto test for pulmonary management.	Hospital bed turn q2h (logroll). HOB no greater than 30 degrees. ROM q4h. Splints per OT.	ROM q4h with progression to sitting. Splints per OT.	

Exhibit 9–1 continued

	DAY 1 (Admission)	DAY 2/3 (Surgery)	DAY 4/5 (Transfer)	DAY 6/7 (Discharge)
Treatments	Vitals, spinal motor scale checks q1h. Pin level checks q1h Temperature q2-4h Respiratory assessment q2-4h with Respiratory parameters q2-4h Quad cough technique q3-4h Foley to DD	Vitals, spinal motor scale checks to q1-3 h Pin level checks q1-3h Discontinue Foley ISC q3-4h to Maintain <300cc of urine volume.	Vitals, spinal motor scale checks q4h. Pin level checks q4h	
	Assess need for P & PD Bowel program begun: LOC/SUPP O_2 per NC Antiembolitic socks with SCD IS q1h C & DB Nurse Call Device (rehab engineering) Prism Glasses (OT)	Discontinue O_2 if O_2 sat >96%.,	Continue bowel program	
	Maintain traction as ordered (check topknot q2h) Pin care q day.	Maintain Halo Vest. Pin care q day. Neck Dressing checked q1-3h.	Assess for Hyperreflexia (BP, Sweats, HA)	

continues

Exhibit 9–1 continued

	DAY 1 (Admission)	DAY 2/3 (Surgery)	DAY 4/5 (Transfer)	DAY 6/7 (Discharge)
Medications	Consider Heparin SQ IVF as ordered Antibiotics ×24h Histamine antagonists IV/NG Narcotic analgesics IV/IM/NG Benadryl PRN Consider Steroid	Discontinue Antibiotics → → → Discontinue steroid drip	Consider Heparin lock Histamine antagonist PO Analgesics PO ↑	
Diet	NPO × ice chips NG to LCS if nauseated - NPO	Advanced to clear liquids if Bowel sounds present.	Diet as tolerated (at preadmission level)	
Patient and family education	Teach anxiety relief measures (i.e. guided imagery, relaxation techniques) Preop education per unit policy. Orient patient and family to NICU policy, procedures and family support group. Assess discharge needs.	Assess family/patient knowledge of injury and consequences. Assess psychological stage of injury. Assess questions/concerns of sexuality.	Prepare for transfer to acute care unit. Reassess discharge needs. Consider rehabilitation tour. Patient and family. Prepare for transfer to rehabilitation unit.	

providers. Use of the critical path also ensures regular communication among caregivers and promotes early problem detection and intervention.

Reduce Variation in the Processes and Outcomes of Care. Work at Intermountain Health Care, Salt Lake City, Utah, and other hospitals has demonstrated that teams of physicians, nurses, and other staff have little knowledge of the clinical practices of others.[11,12] When presented with the different processes or practices and different outcomes for similar patient populations, health care professionals usually reach consensus on a standard critical path that reduces variation in care and substantially improves outcomes.

Education and Orientation. Critical paths provide an excellent tool to educate staff, students, and others regarding treatment plans and expected outcomes. Educational efforts should focus on house officers or residents, medical students, nurses, patients and their families, pharmacists, therapists, and other caregivers and disciplines involved in the care of the patient. New clinicians can learn to identify key interventions and attend to variances. In addition, clinicians can use critical paths to orient and educate the patient and family members. Patients and their families know at the onset of their admission how treatment is expected to progress.

Improved Working Environment. Development and use of critical paths encourage cooperation and mutual understanding of everyone's role in providing quality, cost-effective patient care. The critical path allows everyone to provide better answers to questions from patients and families about the care and planned outcomes. This ability improves communication and fosters mutual respect, which improves the working environment for everyone.

Recruitment and Retention. Recruitment and retention can be improved when staff have a more direct involvement in the overall care of patients, which also serves to improve the working environment. Etheredge states that "in interviews, nurses note the case management role as one indicator of a progressive and innovative environment in which to practice."[13] Nurses and other health care professionals seek out and remain in institutions that provide them with the opportunity to make a difference in the care and outcomes of their patients.

Benchmarking. Critical paths provide an excellent mechanism to study care plans and their relation to patient outcomes. Critical paths from other hospitals that have achieved "world class" results can theoretically be studied and emulated as a form of benchmarking. Of course, critical paths from other institutions will require thoughtful modification to reflect professional practices and local needs.

Communication with Payors. A critical path is an excellent tool to communicate the plan of care to third-party payors and can be used to gain approval for hospitalization and care. Critical paths also allow the hospital to anticipate the costs for a particular diagnosis or procedure. This information can be used to provide group rates to health maintenance organizations and other payors.

ESTABLISHING AND USING CRITICAL PATHS

The process for development and use of critical paths will vary among organizations. Nevertheless, the following actions (see Figure 9–1) are commonly involved.[14]

Select Diagnoses and Procedures for Critical Paths. Diagnoses or procedures can be selected based on case volume, financial impact, profitability, quality assurance issues, and physician or payor interests. Selection criteria should be developed by hospital and clinical leadership. Not all diagnoses and procedures are suited to critical paths.

Appoint a Team to Develop Critical Path. As is the case in classic quality improvement projects, the team should include all key caregivers and affected personnel. Although any member may lead the team, most hospitals appoint nurses as the team leaders.

Select Characteristics for Critical Path. The team defines the scope and format of the critical path and selects other characteristics. Categories of staff actions, for example, must be specified.

Document Current Process. Most critical path efforts begin by documenting current practices and outcomes through chart review. This approach helps team members understand the complexities and dependent relations in the process before instituting change. It also demonstrates differences between perceived and actual practices. Current practices are usually documented in substantial detail, including the sequence of timing of specific procedures, treatments, consults and assessment, medications, diet, teaching, and other aspects of care. Flow charts and time estimates may be used to clarify understanding.

Study Internal and External Practices. Research at this stage helps the team to clarify their understanding of practice variations and to visualize what an "ideal" path would encompass. Critical paths from other organizations are helpful during this phase. Key questions include: What is done? Why? Does it contribute value? Why? Could it be done in an easier or faster way? Why? What are the barriers to changing practices?

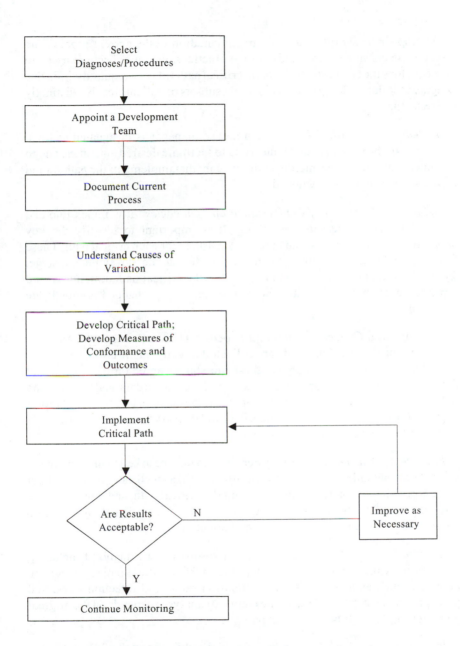

Figure 9–1 Developing and Implementing Critical Paths: Key Steps

Develop Critical Path. Based on documentation of the current process and research concerning internal and external practices, the multidisciplinary team then develops the critical path. Separate critical paths may be required within one Diagnosis-Related Group (DRG) if distinct subsets of patients receive distinctly different care.

Implement the Critical Path. Often a case manager is designated to track adherence to the critical path, to intervene to facilitate desired outcomes, and to document variances. The interdisciplinary team that implements the path should be the same group that developed it.

Define Key Measures of Conformance and Outcomes. It is impossible and wasteful to try to measure everything. It is important to identify the key processes, decision criteria, and outcome measures for each critical path. These factors should be determined by the team during the development stage. Typically, measures include compliance with the critical path, timeliness, and types of variances from the path. These measures may be changed as knowledge is gained.

Develop Data Collection Tools and Process. Data collection is often over-looked, unfortunately. Some data are collected directly on the critical path. For the other measures defined above, the team should agree on the operational definitions, how data will be collected, who will collect the data, and how the data will be used. There is no point collecting data if they cannot be used. One helpful approach is to create some hypothetical data and then ask the team how these data will help them improve the critical path.

Educate All Affected Staff. Every person who may be asked to implement the critical path should be oriented to the critical path, as well as to how to collect data, how to handle patients who vary from the critical path, and how to use the critical path (if at all) for documentation purposes. This orientation should be completed before the critical path is implemented.

Analyze Results. A number of different results can be analyzed including changes in utilization of resources; variations from critical paths; changes in outcomes such as length of stay, readmission rates, and infection rates; and perceptions of patients and staff. The choice of analyses depends on the original goals for implementing the critical path.

Improve Critical Path As Required. Critical paths can and should be modified based on the above analyses or on the availability of new knowledge and technologies. Key reasons for variations from the critical path provide useful information to improve the critical path continually.

RESULTS

Investigators have documented some of the benefits detailed above. These benefits include reduced length of stay, reduced costs and charges, and improved communication.

Reduced Length of Stay

Reductions in length of stay have been documented by several authors.[15,16] As a result of their critical path efforts, New England Medical Center has reduced its average length of stay for myocardial infarction from nine to seven days. For cardiac catheterization, length of stay has been reduced from five to two days.[17] For ischemic stroke patients there was a 29 percent drop in average length of stay and a 47 percent drop in the average number of intensive care unit (ICU) days.[18]

In another study, Cohen reported on the use of critical paths for caesarean section patients in a large, acute institution. Cohen found that "a significant reduction in patient length of stay was achieved (p <.0001) on the experimental unit, which reported a mean length of stay of 4.86 days. The control group reported a mean length of stay of 6.02 days. Length of stay declined by 1.16 days (19 percent) between the experimental and control groups.[19] This study provides better proof of efficacy, because it compared sample and control groups over the same time period.

At Carondelet St. Mary's Hospital and Health Center, investigators documented reductions in length of stay, and financial benefits from their critical path program. "Since 1986, the year in which nurse case management was initiated, length of stay for individuals with DRG #88 has decreased 8.1 days resulting in a savings of $1,552 per case."[20] This DRG occurred frequently at the hospital.

Reduced Costs and Charges

Alliant Health System in Louisville, Kentucky, has implemented over 200 critical paths to date. Investigators there have reported "the estimated financial impact was primarily due to anticipated LOS [length of stay] reduction."[21]

Cohen stated that, "Data analysis indicated a decrease in inpatient resources, changes, and expenditures related to their use on the experimental unit. The experimental group charged an average $5,147.05 per case, whereas the control group charged $6,198.90 per case."[22] Furthermore, "Data analysis indicated that the total aggregate direct nursing care hours (including all professional skill mix) were significantly higher (p<.0001) with the nursing case management model (mean of 16.84 hours) compared with the conventional mode of patient care delivery (mean of 12.28 hours).[23] Thus, nurses are spending a larger proportion of their time in direct patient care.

Improved Communications

Virtually all authors commented that there appear to be improvements in communications among the physicians, nurses, and other staff. The impact has not been measured, however. Unanticipated benefits were improved communications with patients and families and acceptance of the critical paths. Mosher, et al., stated, "One patient told us, 'The pathway helped relieve some of my anxiety because I knew what to expect each day. It also helped motivate me to get where I needed to be by the time I was discharged. My husband enjoyed reading the pathway too. It made him feel involved.'"[24] At UMMC, most critical paths are posted where they can be seen by patients and families; patients and families have made positive comments about this information.

Results from the critical path efforts at UMMC are similar to those reported above. Length of stay data for seven types of cases are summarized in Table 9–1, before and after implementation of critical paths. This table includes only cases from University Hospital with significant sample sizes in both the pre- and post-critical path periods. In all of these cases, the average length of stay decreased; in some cases it decreased dramatically.

Table 9–1 Comparison of Average Length of Stay (LOS) Before and After Critical Paths

Type of case	Pre-critical Path Period 18 Jan 1990– 19 Jan 1991		Post-critical Path Period 20 Jan 1991– 19 Jan 1992		Decrease in Average LOS	
	Sample Size	Average LOS	Sample Size	Average LOS	Days	%
Coronary artery bypass graft	435	13.07	467	10.92	2.15	16.5
Esophagectomy	62	16.31	52	13.83	2.48	15.2
Hernia repair	39	8.05	34	7.94	0.11	1.4
Heart transplants	31	26.74	21	26.29	0.46	1.7
Lobectomy	72	9.60	55	8.09	1.51	15.7
Mechanical valve replacement	57	15.68	51	11.73	3.96	25.2
Tissue valve replacement	27	16.26	50	14.90	1.36	8.4

The charge data are more difficult to interpret because the data crossed three fiscal years and prices increased; no adjustments were made for severity. Nevertheless, average daily services charges decreased 13.8 percent and the ancillary service charges decreased 2.6 percent. Analysis of the length of stay, charge, and other results from these and other critical paths is continuing.

Qualitatively, development and use of critical paths have improved communication and the working relationships among the care providers and others related to the care of patients, as indicated by many positive comments. The perceptions of physicians, nurses, and others are very important to the long-term success of the critical paths.

CONCLUSION

Critical paths establish optimal resource utilization and improve communication among physicians, nurses, and other staff. They reduce unnecessary variation in the delivery of and outputs from care. They have been shown to reduce length of stay, improve teaching, reduce costs, and improve the working environment of physicians, nurses, and others.

Reducing unnecessary variation, improving the quality of care, and improving collaboration among physicians, nurses, and other staff are all highly consistent with TQM. It would appear, therefore, that critical paths can be folded into, or even serve to stimulate, TQM efforts.

NOTES

1. W.C. Shoemaker, Critical Path Medicine, *Critical Care Medicine* 2, no. 5 (September–October 1974): 279.

2. J.E. Wennberg, et al., Changes in Tonsillectomy Rates Associated with Feedback and Review, *Pediatrics* 59, no. 6 (June 1977): 821–26.

3. J.M. Eisenberg, *Doctors' Decisions and the Cost of Medical Care* (Ann Arbor, Mich.: Health Administration Press Perspectives, 1986).

4. K. Zander, Care Maps: The Core of Cost/Quality Care, *The New Definition* 6, no. 3 (Fall 1991): 1–3.

5. Zander, Care Maps, 1–3.

6. Zander, Care Maps, 1.

7. Zander, Care Maps.

8. K. Zander, Nursing Case Management: Strategic Management of Cost and Quality Outcomes, *Journal of Nursing Administration* 18, no. 5 (May 1988): 23–30.

9. Zander, Care Maps.

10. C. Stetler and A. DeZell, *Case Management Plans: Designs for Transformation* (Boston, Mass.: New England Medical Center Hospitals, 1987).

11. B.C. James, *Quality Management for Health Care Delivery* (Chicago, Ill.: Hospital Research and Educational Trust, 1989).

12. D.C. Classen, et al., The Timing of Prophylactic Administration of Antibiotics and the Risk of Surgical-Wound Infection, *New England Journal of Medicine* 326, no. 5 (30 January, 1992): 281–86.

13. M.L.S. Etheredge, ed. *Collaborative Care: Nursing Case Management* (Chicago, Ill.: American Hospital Publishing, 1989).

14. E. Gaucher and R.J. Coffey, *Total Quality Management in Health Care: From Theory to Practice* (San Francisco, Calif.: Jossey-Bass, 1993).

15. Zander, Nursing Case Management.

16. Etheredge, *Collaborative Care.*

17. Ibid.

18. Zander, Nursing Case Management.

19. E.L. Cohen, Nursing Case Management: Does It Pay? *Journal of Nursing Administration* 21, no. 4 (April 1991): 20–25.

20. P. Ethridge and G.S. Lamb, Professional Nursing Case Management Improves Quality, Access and Costs, *Nursing Management* 20, no. 3 (March 1989): 30–35.

21. K. Zander, Estimating and Tracking the Financial Impact of Critical Paths, *Definition* 5, no. 4 (Fall 1990): 1–3.

22. Cohen, Nursing Case Management, 22.

23. Ibid, 22–23.

24. C. Mosher, et al., Upgrading Practice with Critical Pathways, *American Journal of Nursing* (January 1992): 41–44.

10. Implementing Practice Guidelines through Clinical Quality Improvement

Brent C. James

American health care is changing. Ten years ago most American hospitals worked under a cost-plus system. Long-term financial survival required that a hospital's leaders manage *revenues*: They had to be certain that patients came to their facility to receive care (they tried to increase utilization) and they had to ensure that they added the right amount of financial margin to each service they provided. The natural unit of analysis in such an environment was a department. Many hospitals built sophisticated computer systems to track financial data at a departmental level, and used those systems as their primary source of management information and decisions. The medical staff bore responsibility for clinical quality, largely independent of administrators. Physicians also controlled the flow of patients into most hospitals. Therefore, hospital administrators often treated their medical staffs as their primary customers.

Then came 1983. That's the year the federal government first began to implement the Diagnosis Related Group (DRG) Prospective Payment System (PPS). Suddenly, for about 30 percent of a typical hospital's case load, the size of the cost-plus margin no longer mattered. The government paid a flat rate per case regardless of the hospital's charges or costs. Hospitals initially shifted revenue shortfalls from government programs to other health care payer segments (a major factor in apparent hospital price inflation.[1] In response, many large private purchasers began to develop their own "provider-at-risk" strategies (i.e., managed care—per capita or per case payment) to limit health care expenses. Under those new structures, health care purchasers and third-party payers began to supplant physicians' control of patient flow. Payers and patients became the hospitals' primary customers.

Source: Used with permission from *Frontiers of Health Services Management*, Vol. 10, No. 1, pp. 3–32, Health Administration Press, Ann Arbor, MI, © 1993, Foundation of the American College of Healthcare Executives.

As the decade progressed hospitals saw larger and larger proportions of their patient volume shift to the provider-at-risk column. The phenomenon is most prominent on the West Coast, where some community hospitals currently report that more than 90 percent of their inpatient volume comes through managed care contracts. It is gradually sweeping toward the East Coast, engulfing localized pockets of heavy activity (such as the Minneapolis/St. Paul area) as it goes. And the trend is accelerating. For example, strategic planners at Intermountain Health Care (IHC—a 24-hospital system in Utah, Idaho, and Wyoming) initially estimated that provider-at-risk contracts would increase from their current 60 percent penetration to about 85 percent of the system's total inpatient volume by the turn of the century. But vigorous political efforts to control health care costs, at both a national and local level, may reduce the time required to reach that level of managed care penetration to just three or four years.

As the provider-at-risk environment grows, hospitals are trying to use accounting adjustments to adapt their old revenue-based financial systems to the new reality. "Contractual allowance" or "deductions from revenue" measures what hospitals are *not* paid, relative to their charges. If managed care contracts account for most of a hospital's business, administrators can easily set their contractual allowance to any desired level by adjusting the hospital's charges, without affecting their net (real) revenues. In a provider-at-risk environment hospitals can no longer guarantee their long-term financial survival by managing revenues. Revenues are a fixed value, established through highly competitive, price-sensitive contract negotiations. Survival lies on the other side of the financial equation: Hospitals must begin to manage *costs*.

PROCESS MANAGEMENT

In a provider-at-risk, cost-based environment the natural unit of analysis and management is a *process*, not a department. A process is a series of linked steps, often (but not necessarily) sequential, designed to *cause* some set of outcomes to occur. The idea of a process not only aptly describes health care delivery but any repetitive human activity designed to add value, transform inputs into outputs, or cause some set of specified outcomes to occur. Processes usually span departments and facilities. Failures, which damage quality and increase costs, usually cluster around the interfaces, where one department or group hands off to another in the course of a single process.

Start with the idea of a process. Add to it fundamental knowledge of systems (processes interacting together), basic human psychology in a work setting, variation (statistics), and a theory for systematically acquiring and applying new knowledge.[2,3] Build a method to efficiently, effectively manage processes over time. The end result is the *methodology* (as opposed to the complementary philosophy) of quality improvement theory. In fact, implementing a total quality management strategy can be viewed as systematically redesigning a health system's infrastructure—its clinical data systems, financial data systems, human resources (policies and training), and culture—so that it is possible to manage and improve health care processes within a provider-at-risk environment.

Process management is also a common thread that brings together a number of current national health care initiatives: When focused on clinical processes of care, process management *is* case management. It blurs the line between operations and research, and provides a direct link between health care delivery systems and outcomes research.[4] Finally, practice guidelines are explicit descriptions of preferred clinical processes. From that viewpoint practice guidelines are just a form of process management. Clinical quality improvement methods supply a set of tools to iteratively implement and modify such practice guidelines.

In 1989, the Congress of the United States formed the Agency for Health Care Policy and Research (AHCPR). Within its enabling legislation AHCPR has two specific missions: It must initiate studies to measure the outcomes of common health care interventions, and it must generate practice guidelines that codify research and consensus findings regarding best health care practices. These activities were mandated in the (untested) belief that they could eliminate inappropriate medical interventions and reduce health care costs.[5] In addition to AHCPR, many professional groups, health care purchasers, and commercial enterprises are working to generate practice guidelines—often, though, with different objectives, different definitions, different levels of sophistication, and unequal quality in their final products.

It is hard to generate good guidelines. Special literature review methods, formal consensus techniques, sophisticated meta-analyses, and a very significant amount of effort are usually required. But many hospitals have the same hopes that prompted the U.S. Congress to launch AHCPR: They believe that, if they are to survive in the growing provider-at-risk environment, they must manage costs. They believe that practice guidelines may help them to document better patient care while controlling costs. Under many different names, hospitals therefore are trying to implement practice guidelines to manage health care delivery, whether they generate the guidelines themselves or obtain them from a third party.

The purpose of this article is to explore practical issues surrounding the physicians' role in the *implementation* of practice guidelines in American hospitals. It leaves the *generation* of practice guidelines to other sources.[6,7] It also largely ignores the practical aspects of information systems and organizational structures to handle the data associated with guideline implementation. With regard to physicians and guideline implementation, this article makes three key arguments to two crucial groups:

- **Physicians:** It is more important that you do it the same than that you do it "right."
- **Administrators:** It is more important how you implement than what you implement. The aim is to manage clinical processes, not to manage physicians.

To that end, this article first reviews several important quality improvement concepts central to any discussion that touches on cost, quality, and practice management. It then defines practice guidelines and introduces tools to document and manage them in a practical setting. It next presents a real-world case study in which a practice guideline was used to successfully manage a care process, simultaneously reducing costs and improving patient outcomes. Finally, it draws from the case study to discuss practical issues related to generating and implementing practice guidelines.

This article does not distinguish between *protocols* and *guidelines*—it uses the terms interchangeably. Many presently available guidelines (e.g., those published by AHCPR) lack sufficient detail to allow direct implementation. A potential user must first add a level of detail and definition that allows specific practice recommendations and measurement: With that level of detail a guideline becomes a protocol. But in terms of the physician relationships discussed here, the distinction is not critical.

Because of the physician focus of this article, all of the discussions and examples it uses center on clinical care delivery. But exactly the same techniques apply to nonclinical (administrative) support processes. Very often key clinical processes succeed or fail depending on the quality of the support processes upon which they rest. Further, it is not uncommon to find cost savings within administrative support processes that match or exceed those found in clinical processes. As a methodology, quality improvement and practice guidelines apply just as well to a hospital's administrators as to its clinicians.

IMPLEMENTING PRACTICE GUIDELINES: BACKGROUND PRINCIPLES

This article assumes that the reader is familiar with, and understands the implications of, several central principles of quality improvement theory. Those background principles are briefly outlined here, with references that provide detailed discussions of their rationale and characteristics.

- *Quality controls costs.* Stated more accurately, quality and cost are two sides of the same coin. They are so tightly intertwined that it is impossible to act on one without acting upon the other.[8] Quality interacts with cost through three explicit mechanisms: Quality waste (costs fall as quality improves), productivity/efficiency (costs fall as quality holds stable), and cost-effectiveness (quality improves but at a higher cost). Quality also affects costs through secondary mechanisms such as the costs of attracting new customers, warranty (malpractice) costs, employee replacement costs, the costs of low employee morale, and long-term effects of low quality on an organization's standing within a community (the "ripple effect").

Quality waste alone accounts for 25 to 40 percent of all hospital operating costs.[9] It is a particularly useful concept: As quality improves, it *causes* costs to fall—a very favorable combination for attracting new patients. The idea of quality waste also provides a means (by seeking waste and rework) to identify areas for improvement.

- People show a consistent, predictable response when confronted with data that purport to document substandard performance. Scherkenbach[10] called that reaction *The Cycle of Fear*[11] The first phase of the Cycle is *denial* ("kill the messenger" or shift the blame)—"my patients are sicker." During the second phase, those individuals being measured begin to *filter the data* ("game the system")—as they generate the data that others will later use to evaluate them, they change how they assess and record that information so as to cast themselves in a more favorable light. The final phase is *micromanagement*—they know that they are outliers, but have no idea how they came to such a position. They therefore try anything they can imagine that might improve their apparent performance. Even though the vast majority of such efforts are ineffectual, and though some may do active harm, at least they are showing a good effort.

  Many quality assurance programs bog down in the Cycle of Fear, devolving into meaningless measurement and reporting. In such situations the aim is to meet regulatory requirements—a subtly different goal than patient care improvement. Those being measured soon become cynical. They lose all faith that the process can ever produce better patient care. More importantly, most of the energy expended on quality goes to arguments about methodology, rather than improvement.

- Traditional quality assurance uses thresholds (standards) to define acceptable and unacceptable performance. Providers who do not fall below the standard are judged "good enough"—their quality is acceptable. Most providers approach quality from that viewpoint, in order to pass regulatory review. But often it is possible to perform at levels far better than a standard that defines lowest acceptable performance. Every time a provider fails to be the best they can be, they harm their patients and they waste money (through quality's relationship to cost). Within health care *"good enough" is never good enough*—the only acceptable goal is to find, implement, and consistently perform the best possible care processes.[12]

- Finally, *"find and implement the best"* is a more effective strategy than *"find and eliminate the worst"* to improve patient outcomes and reduce costs.[13] It's not that traditional quality assurance doesn't work; it just doesn't work very well when compared to quality improvement. Two principles are involved in quality improvement: Process operators use measurement tools to: (1) eliminate *inappropriate* variation (usually in care process steps) then (2) *document* continuous improvement (usually in outcomes). "Find and implement the best" redirects energy from finding fault (and the natural defensive response that it provokes) to finding solutions. It creates a much more positive atmosphere within which to measure, criticize, and improve health care processes.

IMPLEMENTING PRACTICE GUIDELINES: DEFINITIONS

In 1989, AHCPR commissioned the Institute of Medicine (IOM) to assess practice guideline development and evaluation. The IOM's 1990 report defined practice guidelines as "systematically developed statements to assist practitioner and patient decisions about appropriate health care for specific clinical circumstances." The report catalogs many of the conflicting definitions of practice guidelines found in the medical literature and in practice, and attempts to distinguish among them. Eddy[14] adds an important distinction to the IOM's definition of practice guidelines. He defines *practice policies* as "preferred recommendations issued for the purpose of influencing decisions about health interventions." In contrast, *performance policies* (or clinical algorithms) "guide or review the performance of interventions, without concern for whether the intervention should have been performed in the first place." Practice policies describe "doing the right thing"—clinical indications that lead to a decision to apply a particular medical test or treatment. Performance policies define "doing it the right way." They describe the manner in which the test or treatment should be executed. Eddy further distinguishes three levels of practice policies, depending upon the degree of professional certainty about the outcomes of a particular practice and patients' preferences for the practice's predictable results: *Standards* describe practices with well-documented outcomes and virtual unanimity among patients about their desirability. A standard is a relatively strict rule that embodies a "best" clinical decision in essentially all circumstances. On that basis, deviations from standards should be rare. *Guidelines* apply to clinical interventions that have well-documented outcomes, but whose outcomes are not clearly desirable to all patients. They therefore should be followed in most cases, but must be modified for individual patients. Deviations from guidelines may be relatively common, as dictated by differences in individual patient circumstances. *Options* describe medical interventions for which outcomes are not known, patient preferences are not known, or about which patients are indifferent. Options are neutral with respect to recommending a particular medical intervention—they simply provide a list of credible choices.

Practice policies and performance policies are obviously tightly interlinked. Eddy notes that correct performance of an intervention is immaterial if that intervention is not appropriate.[15] But patients and clinicians choose a particular practice based on its documented outcomes. Those outcomes cannot be accurately established if the practice is not performed correctly. Seen another way, the "decision to intervene" and the "performance of the intervention" are sequential steps within a single process, with patient outcomes completing a feedback loop to inform the initial decision. Guideline implementation centers on performance policies, but draws from practice policies for source material.

Flow charts are a generic tool to document processes (several medical publications have recommended flow charts as a professional standard for recording, comparing, discussing, and systematically improving practice guidelines.[16–18] When a guideline is laid out as a flow chart, an important feature found in all processes becomes evident: Processes are inherently hierarchical. In other words, every box in a flow chart hides another, more detailed, sub-flow chart.

To illustrate, Figure 10–1 shows the process used at IHC's LDS Hospital (in Salt Lake City, Utah) to manage deep post-operative wound infections. Each step in the highest level process (Prevention → Detection → Treatment) is the outcome of a subprocess, with its own series of steps. Similarly, each step in every subprocess is the outcome of an even more detailed sub-subprocess, and so on down to an arbitrary level of detail. That means that every box in a flow chart is both a process step (of its superior process) and an outcome (of its subprocess). The terms "outcome" and "process step" are interchangeable, depending on the level of abstraction employed to manage a particular subprocess at a particular point in time. Hierarchical flow charts are useful tools to focus attention and manage complexity. Starting with a high-level flow chart, detail is added within a focused area by expanding appropriate subprocess flow charts. When detail is no longer needed, the subprocess flow charts are collapsed back into their superior process steps. Flow charts play another essential role: They are the foundation for effective communications and systematic improvement within a clinical team. Without a written paradigm, differences in mental models, perceptions, and terminology make it extremely difficult to even discuss a complicated care process. With a written model guideline team members can identify differences in practice style, criticize specific steps in the model, and recommend improvements. Finally, when monitoring a clinical process, a flow chart identifies measurement points. It shows the data that are needed to track both performance and outcomes within a particular process.

Decisions (practice policies) and execution (performance policies) are embedded throughout a clinical flow chart. For example, the use of Antibiotic Prophy-

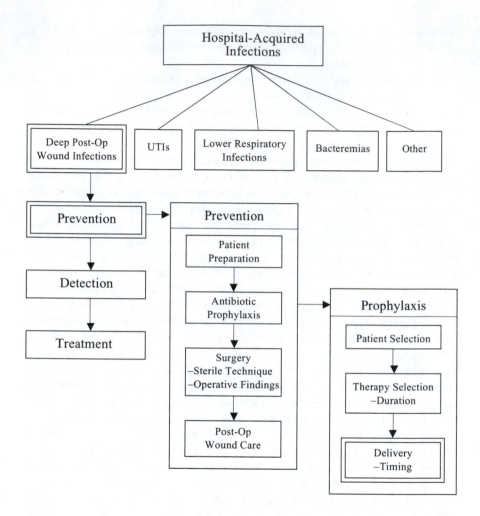

Figure 10–1 Hierarchical Process of Care. A flow chart describing a hierarchical process of care used to manage deep post-operative wound infections. Such flow charts can be used both to control complexity when describing a clinical process, and to identify appropriate measurement points to monitor critical care processes. In some instances the simple act of documenting a process flow will improve coordination and reduce variation among care providers.

laxis is the second performance step in the Prevention subprocess for deep post-operative wound infections. But the first step in the Prophylaxis subprocess is Patient Selection. That step requires a decision. Clinical indications (a practice policy) identifies patients who should receive prophylaxis. Collecting and evaluating the information necessary to decide whether to use prophylaxis for a particular patient is a process in itself, with its own decision and performance steps. Nearly every performance step depends on underlying decisions, while nearly every decision step depends on underlying performance.

Eddy[19,20] has championed the use of meta-analytic methods to extract and synthesize important scientific information to guide clinical decisions. His work provides a critical service in those instances when scientific data are available. Leape, Kosecoff, Chassin, Brook and other researchers at RAND have developed formal consensus techniques for use when scientific data are not available.[21] But given a practice guideline that describes a performance policy, based on appropriate practice policies, how can a hospital work with a clinical team to manage the process and document (for patients, purchasers, and regulators) that effective, efficient care results?

IMPLEMENTING PRACTICE GUIDELINES: A CASE STUDY

Adult Respiratory Distress Syndrome (ARDS) is a disease of the lungs. It often appears as a complication of an underlying pneumonia or shock and multiorgan failure. For example, one common precipitating cause is a simple viral pneumonia—a chest cold, of the sort that many individuals experience during the winter. For reasons that are not clearly understood, some patients' lungs react to the pneumonia by secreting fluid into their air spaces. As the lung's air spaces fill with fluid the lungs are not able to move oxygen into the blood (hypoxemia). The fluid also makes the lungs stiff (noncompliant), difficult to inflate and deflate as the patient breathes. Traditional treatment depends on mechanical respiration (ventilator support), with high oxygen concentrations and constant high air pressure to force oxygen into the blood despite the fluid. If the patient remains alive until the underlying pneumonia or shock resolves then their ARDS will often clear. Those who live usually achieve a complete recovery and regain normal health.

While ARDS affects both genders and all ages, it concentrates mainly within young men, in their twenties and thirties. Each year it accounts for about 15,000 cases in the United States. Historically, among all patients who developed ARDS only about one third survived.

During the mid-1970s pulmonary researchers developed an alternative therapy to use in place of stand-alone ventilator support. Called extra-corporeal membrane oxygenation (ECMO), it used a heart-lung machine, connected through the patient's femoral artery and vein, to oxygenate the patient's blood outside their body. In theory, that would keep the patient alive until their underlying pneumonia or shock resolved and their ARDS cleared. The researchers also established metrics (the ECMO criteria) that identified a subgroup of ARDS patients who were at a particularly high risk for death. Historically, about 10 percent of patients who met the ECMO criteria survived. Clinical trials conducted on patients who met the ECMO criteria eventually demonstrated that ECMO was no better in preventing ARDS deaths than standard ventilator therapy. The ECMO therapy was therefore abandoned. But pulmonary researchers have continued to identify and track ARDS patients who meet ECMO criteria. Recent estimates of survival among ARDS patients who meet ECMO criteria reach as high as 15 percent.

In the 1980s an Italian pulmonary research group reported a variant of ECMO that they claimed significantly improved survival in ARDS patients. In addition to oxygenating a patient's blood outside the body, they added equipment to simultaneously remove CO_2 and other waste products (extra-corporeal CO_2 removal, or $ECCO_2R$). A pulmonary research team at LDS Hospital received a grant from the National Heart, Lung, and Blood Institute to test the new therapy in the United States. They planned a randomized clinical trial to compare $ECCO_2R$ (the treatment arm of the trial) to standard mechanical ventilation (the control arm) for ARDS patients who met ECMO criteria.

A key factor in clinical trial design centers around the idea of consistency. If a clinical trial is to accurately compare two competing treatments, then each of the treatments must be applied in a consistent fashion. Otherwise it is impossible to judge whether differences in patient outcomes are due to the treatments or to variations in their application. Trials therefore usually use protocols to describe, in detail, the manner in which each treatment will be delivered. As the LDS Hospital research team began to construct the $ECCO_2R$ clinical trial they had an important insight: They recognized that, despite the fact that they had practiced together for many years, cross-covering each other on the same patients, they didn't manage ventilators in a consistent fashion. Those differences went beyond variation among the physicians, nurses, and therapists in the group. Individual clinicians showed differences in practice patterns from patient to patient. In fact, it appeared that a single clinician sometimes was inconsistent when treating the same patient from day to day, or even from morning to evening rounds.

The team therefore decided to generate a detailed protocol—a practice guideline—to oversee ventilator management on the control arm of their clinical trial. They first performed a careful literature review to identify important research findings that should guide their decisions and care practices. They then used formal consensus techniques to fill in those parts of the guideline not covered by the scientific literature, and represented their new guideline as a flow chart. It described ventilator management for ARDS in detail, being more than 35 pages long with an average of more than 20 major decision nodes per page.

But when they had completed the guideline they had a second important insight: Much of their new ventilator management guideline was based upon consensus— "expert" opinion, generated as a theoretical exercise far from the treatment of real patients. They had no *data* to demonstrate that the consensus portions of their guideline were correct. Because of the consensus process, they had no scientific basis to argue that the guideline represented best care for real patients.

The ECCO$_2$R team therefore chose to use their new ventilator guideline in a very innovative way. They reviewed the guideline with all involved clinicians (nurses, physicians, and other allied health professionals) so that everyone understood its content. They built a measurement system to track whether the clinicians followed the guideline's recommendations, at the level of each detailed decision covered in the document. Finally, they placed a copy of the guideline at the bedside of every ARDS patient being treated with a mechanical ventilator, and asked that the clinicians follow it. But if a clinician disagreed with a guideline recommendation, the team instructed the clinicians to follow their own judgement, not the guideline. In such circumstances they assumed that the guideline was probably wrong, not the clinician. After all, they knew and trusted the clinicians on the team. It was the guideline that had yet to prove itself with demonstrated results.

The research team then carried their reasoning to the next logical step: If a clinician failed to follow the guideline, leading to the assumption that the guideline was probably wrong for that particular decision, then they had an opportunity to correct the guideline. They therefore automatically added that clinical case and the associated guideline-based decision to the agenda for their next weekly staff meeting. That meant that they were able to discuss each questionable guideline recommendation as a group, in the context of a real case. In those meetings they stripped identifying information from the cases in order to avoid the Cycle of Fear. Their aim was to fix the system, not fix blame. They wanted to agree upon "best" treatment processes as a group, not single individual team members out for criticism.

Three possible courses of action are possible in such a setting:

1. As the team examined a guideline recommendation, they could conclude that the guideline was wrong and change it.
2. The team could agree that the guideline was right. That sends a message not only to the clinician who had made the original decision, but to all members of the team, concerning their group consensus about best patient care, as codified in the guideline.
3. They could decide that the case was an outlier for that particular decision. No guideline can reasonably cover all patient variants.

Figure 10–2 shows guideline compliance rates as the team used their iterative review process.[22] Over a period of about four months, guideline compliance increased from under 40 percent to more than 90 percent.[23–25] In the early stages changes to the guideline were common. Note that the team never achieved perfect guideline compliance. No guideline will ever perfectly match every patient, or supplant clinical judgement.[26] Statistical process control (SPC) provides an ideal tool to track noncompliances in a process, separating treatment deviations arising from differences in patient presentation (appropriate, common, or random vari-

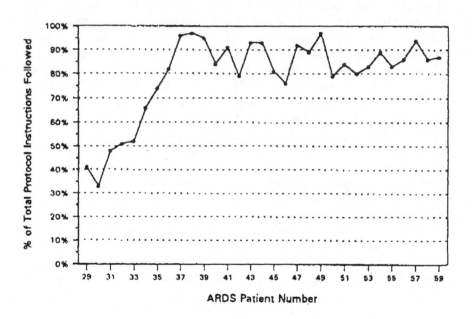

Figure 10–2 Ventilator Protocol Compliance (9/14/88–1/20/90). Percentage of protocol-based recommendations followed for Adult Respiratory Distress Syndrome (ARDS) patients, starting with the first patient (Patient Number 29, admitted to LDS Hospital's Pulmonary ICU on August 14, 1988) for whom the protocol was used through 30 consecutive patients (Patient Number 59, admitted on January 1, 1990). A typical treatment episode involved more than 200 protocol-based treatment recommendations. Roughly four months elapsed between Patient Number 29 and Patient Number 37. From Patient Number 37 on, most protocol noncompliances occurred either (1) when a patient was removed from the ICU (usually for either surgery or imaging), (2) as further improvements to the protocol were tested, or (3) as a consequence of the fact that few protocols are perfect (nearly all guidelines show some level of random noncompliance as clinicians address patient factors not anticipated by the protocol or factors that are so rare as to not justify inclusion in the protocol).

ation) from those arising from external practice patterns that intrude into the treatment process (inappropriate, special, or assignable variation).[27]

Upon completion of the randomized clinical trial, $ECCO_2R$ achieved 38 percent survival for patients who met ECMO criteria. Stabilized ventilator management (as produced by the ventilator protocol) achieved 44 percent survival for the same patient group, better than the $ECCO_2R$ treatment arm and much better than the 9 to 15 percent survival expected for ventilator management from historical experience.[28,29] Figure 10–3 compares ARDS survival experience from several pulmonary research groups, covering cases beyond the LDS Hospital $ECCO_2R$ clinical trial.[30,31]

The team's experience with a practice guideline produced other interesting results:

- Physician time to manage these complex cases fell. That was because common, day-to-day decisions were pushed down into the system, where physicians did not have to consider them one case at a time. It wasn't that the physicians didn't think about the patient care issues involved, but that they addressed them for groups of patients, instead of case by case. That freed physicians to deal with the patients' interesting problems, that required a physician's oversight, or allowed the physician to see other patients. It also made the members of the team (physicians, nurses, and technicians) more predictable to one another, which may reduce friction and improve efficiency.
- If a patient lived, they may have left the intensive care unit (ICU) faster than similar patients had before the introduction of the ventilator protocol. That is probably because the patients could advance on the protocol 24 hours per day, rather than waiting for a physician to come on rounds and change orders.
- Stabilized ventilator management cost about $120,000 per patient who lived. $ECCO_2R$ (the next best therapy) cost more than $160,000 per patient who lived, not counting physician fees.

The LDS Hospital pulmonary research team is now supervising a follow-up randomized clinical trial that compares traditional ventilator management for ARDS patients to stabilized ventilator management as produced by their ventilator protocol.

IMPLEMENTING PRACTICE GUIDELINES: LESSONS LEARNED

Lesson 1: The Core Problem Is Variation in Clinical Practice

When members of the LDS Hospital ARDS research team recognized the variability of their own ventilator management practices, they built upon a long

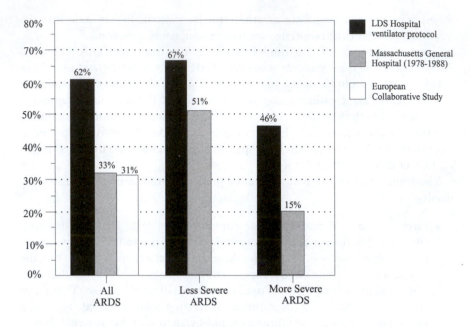

Figure 10–3 Percent Survival for ARDS Patients. Survival among Adult Respiratory Distress Syndrome patients by risk class, comparing LDS Hospital's experience with stabilized ventilator management (a detailed practice protocol) with that of other major pulmonary research groups who did not use the ventilator protocol.

line of studies that demonstrate variation in medical practices. Glover first measured differences in the rates of tonsillectomy among various regions of England, beyond what could be explained by population differences, in 1938.[32] Lewis provided additional evidence of the phenomenon in the United States in the late 1960s.[33] During the 1970s and 1980s, Wennberg formalized and extended analytic techniques for examining differences in surgical procedure use rates or hospitalization rates among communities. He called those methods small area variation analysis (SAVA). His studies again demonstrated that hospital admissions for some surgical procedures and medical diagnoses occurred at a much higher rate in some communities than other, similar communities, even after controlling for underlying population factors.[34–36] Wennberg also showed that the range of inter-community variation was related to specific surgical procedures and medical diagnoses. When examining the rates of use for the same procedures and diagnoses in other countries, he found that some showed consistently low ranges of variation within all countries examined, while others showed consistently high ranges of variation within all countries examined. This was true even though the average use rates for each procedure or diagnosis varied significantly between the countries included in the study.[37]

The RAND team[38] hypothesized that SAVA differences among communities could be explained by higher rates of inappropriate treatment in communities with high use rates. The RAND team developed formal methods to generate measurable indications for several surgical procedures and medical hospitalizations. For each condition they examined, they first performed a structured review of the medical literature. They then presented the resulting scientific information to a panel of expert physicians, drawn from the appropriate specialty area. Within each expert panel they used formal consensus techniques to derive extensive lists of appropriate, equivocal, or inappropriate indications for the treatment under study. Finally, they used their indications to measure the rates of appropriate versus inappropriate use of the targeted conditions in communities that showed high rates of utilization and communities that showed low rates of utilization for the procedure or hospitalization in question. They discovered that high use rates were not consistently associated with high rates of inappropriate indications.[39] That is, geographic areas that showed low utilization rates for a particular surgical procedure or medical hospitalization often had as high a rate of inappropriate indications as other geographic areas that showed high utilization rates for the same medical decision. They also demonstrated that inappropriate surgical procedure use and inappropriate hospitalization for medical conditions are surprisingly common, and that some procedures or hospitalizations show consistently high rates of inappropriate application, while others show consistently lower rates of inappropriate use.[40,41]

Wennberg's small area variation analysis and the RAND team's measures of appropriateness addressed a single class of issues: Both examined the decision to treat a patient, at the level of Eddy's practice policies (indications for treatment). A further set of studies investigated variations in what happens to patients after they enter a hospital (at the level of Eddy's performance policies).[42,43] Their Quality, Utilization, and Efficiency (QUE) studies tracked patients with comparable presenting disease, comorbidities, and outcomes hospitalized for transurethral prostatectomy (TURP), cholecystectomy, total hip arthroplasty, and permanent pacemaker implantation.[44,45] Those studies showed that physicians used widely different amounts of specific care factors to treat similar patients, with differences among physicians ranging from 60 to 460 percent. Figure 10–4 illustrates two important process of care factors for TURP—true surgical procedure time and grams of prostatic tissue removed—among 16 urologic surgeons, across a group of comparable patients at four hospitals. Each factor varies by more than 200 percent across the physician group.

While well-designed studies document wide variations among physicians with regard to their decisions to apply treatment to patients and the manner in which those treatments are applied, anecdotal information suggests that practice variation may extend even further. Individual physicians appear to vary in how they

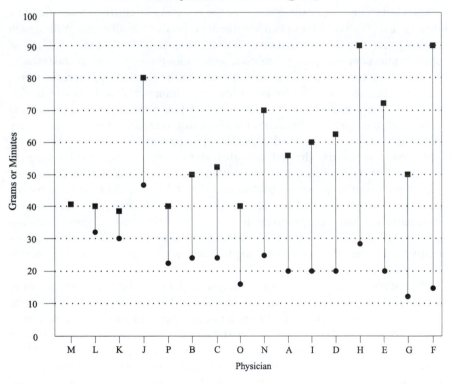

Figure 10–4 Variation in Transurethral Resection of the Prostate (TURP) Practice Patterns among 16 Urologists. Variation among urologic surgeons for two important process of care factors when performing a transurethral prostatectomy (TURP): true surgical procedure time and grams of prostatic tissue excised. The cases in the study were similar in terms of the presence and severity of comorbidities on admission to the hospital and in terms of medical outcomes (complications and therapeutic goals). The surgeons are shown in order of grams removed per minute of surgery. Both factors (surgery time and grams of tissue) showed more than two-fold variation across the physician group. The length of surgery had a strong statistical association with grams of tissue removed: The longer a surgeon's procedure time, the smaller amount of tissue removed.

diagnose and treat similar, sequential patients, beyond what would be expected from patient factors. Observation of very complicated patients (for example, ARDS patients on ventilators as described in the case study) suggests that physicians may vary from contact to contact, morning to night, in how they treat individual patients.

Eddy, Wennberg, and others have summarized possible causes of practice variation.[46–49] The combined list is extensive, running to more than 60 different items. Interestingly, many of the most prominent causes are not under physicians' control. They arise from professional uncertainty:

- *80 to 90 percent of common medical practices have no basis in published scientific research.* In 1979, Williamson tracked common medical practices for three subspecialties of internal medicine back to the medical literature. He estimated that fewer than 10 percent of the medical practices examined had any foundation in published research.[50,51] Follow-up studies by the federal Office of Technology Assessment in 1985[52,53] and the Office of Medical Applications of Research in 1990,[54,55] generated estimates of 10 to 20 percent and less than 20 percent, respectively.

  That does not mean that 80 to 90 percent of medical practices are wrong. They are based on a long history of medical tradition and experience, and probably help most patients. But it does mean that for most medical practice we do not know what is best. Practitioners can hold legitimate differences of opinion about best practices.

- *Much of the scientific research that does exist is not available to medical practitioners.* Williamson, et al., also documented that even when scientific research regarding best medical practices does exist, its diffusion into actual medical practice is slow and uneven.[56,57] Given the size, complexity, and lack of methodologic consistency of the medical literature, that finding is not unexpected. An effort to find, evaluate, and synthesize appropriate scientific articles for a particular medical topic requires special expertise. Most practitioners lack the tools, resources, and time for such an undertaking. Williamson, Lincoln, and Turner[58] recommended a set of formal methods (called information synthesis) for that purpose.[59] Eddy has published meta-analytic techniques, and produced and distributed computer software, to address the same issue.[60,61]

- *Even such limited scientific information as is available may overwhelm the capacity of the unaided human mind.* The human mind is limited in its capacity to synthesize complex information to optimize outcomes. When working with the ventilator guideline presented in the case study, Morris[62] found that experienced physicians were not able to manage more than four concurrent variables to maximize patient outcomes. Unfortunately, a typical

ARDS case presented more than 200 active variables. A physician's patient care decisions depended on which small subset of variables the physician chose to analyze. As different variables thrust themselves into the physician's attention at different points in time, the physician's practices changed. Thus, a physician could vary from morning to evening in managing the same patient. While ventilator management for ARDS patients in an ICU is admittedly complex, most patient care decisions involve far more than four variables.

American medical practice is based on the notion of a physician-patient relationship. That ideal asserts that best patient care occurs when an individual physician advises a patient on factors affecting their physical and mental well-being, available health care responses, and likely outcomes, so that the patient can make informed decisions about their own health. A major corollary is the assumption that an individual physician can *subjectively* integrate hundreds of disparate factors to accurately advise patient decisions. At a minimum, a physician must correctly synthesize the patient's underlying disease processes, their individual physiologic response to each of those diseases, various treatment options, likely outcomes for each possible treatment, and the patient's personal values and preferences, in order to provide an accurate list of options from which the patient can chose. But that model is incompatible with knowledge of the limited capabilities of the unaided human mind.

Perhaps Eddy said it best: "It is simply unrealistic to think that individuals can synthesize in their head scores of pieces of evidence, accurately estimate the outcomes of different options, and accurately judge the desirability of those outcomes for patients. . . . All confirm what would be expected from common sense: The complexity of modern medicine exceeds the inherent limitations of the unaided human mind."[63]

- *Humans are inherently fallible information processors.* McDonald demonstrated that, regardless of training or intent, humans make errors when handling data.[64] Some types of errors, such as digit transpositions when writing numbers or misplacement of decimal points, occur more frequently. An individual's error rate is affected by stress levels (e.g., lack of sleep), complexity, and whether that individual is operating within their domain of specific knowledge. Simple errors can introduce variation into patient care. Carefully designed, robust processes can catch and correct or reduce the effect of human errors when they do occur.

- *Differences in observation—measurement error—can lead to differences in assessment and differences in treatment among physicians.* Koran documented frequent differences among physicians in physical examination findings, interpretation of diagnostic procedures, diagnosis, recommended treatments, and evaluations of the quality of care. He notes, "The physicians studied almost always disagreed at least once in 10 cases, and often disagreed more than once in five cases, whether they were eliciting physical signs, interpreting roentgenograms, electrocardiograms or electroencephalograms, making a diagnosis (from incomplete information), recommending a treatment or evaluating the quality of care. Disagreements of this magnitude, if characteristic of clinical practice in general, cannot safely be regarded as inconsequential."[65]

Beyond differences in patient care that arise from professional uncertainty, human limitations, unequal allocation of health care resources, and variation in measurement, patients differ from one another and individually differ over time. Among other inconsistencies, they have different values, different preferences, different symptoms, different physiologic response to disease, and different ways of interacting with health care providers. All of these factors cause appropriate differences in practice patterns. Any clinical process management system must group patients together in a way that takes those differences into account.

Lesson 2: Real Benefits Accrue to Patients, Payers, and Providers When *Inappropriate* Practice Variations Decline

Quality improvement uses statistical process control to separate *assignable* from *random* variation. Random variation arises from differences in a process's inputs (i.e., differences in patient presentation) or the sum of many small variations in process steps that cannot be tracked to specific, preventable causes. It is a physical, measurable attribute, representing the random noise in any real process. Assignable variation arises from identifiable causes that can be tracked and eliminated. Statistical process control graphs the probability that variation in a specific process measurement arises from assignable, rather than random, causes. In quality improvement jargon, assignable variation represents *inappropriate* variation. Random variation is not only appropriate, but expected. When it does not appear something is probably wrong.

It is important to distinguish between the two types of variation because each requires a different management approach. With assignable variation, the aim is to track the outlier points to their root causes then eliminate them, so they never intrude in the process again. On the other hand, random variation is a physical attribute of the process and its inputs. To reduce random variation, a provider must design a new process (usually a variant of the old process, generated by changing specific process steps), then scientifically compare its performance against the old approach. Quality improvement theory calls such a test the Shewhart Cycle, and summarizes its steps as "PDCA": Plan a change, Do it in a small subgroup, Check its performance against prior outputs, then Act (discard the change or fully implement it). Traditional medicine calls the same approach a clinical trial.

Quality improvement theory defines a *stable process* as a process that shows only random variation over time, with no assignable variation. *Process capability* is the ability of a process to achieve its stated goals. For example, a process designed to prevent infections has an absolute goal of no infections. If only two percent of cases develop infections, then the process is 98 percent capable—it achieves its goal 98 percent of the time.

Quality improvement theory notes that it is impossible to measure a process's true capability unless that process is stable. Otherwise, variation in performance can alter (for the worse) the apparent efficacy of the process (the actual outcomes of an uncontrolled process in a community setting is called effectiveness). That is exactly the same idea embodied in the treatment protocols that define each arm in a controlled clinical trial. Such protocols guarantee that the trial's treatments are consistent from case to case. Otherwise, it is impossible to tell whether differences in patient outcomes arise from true differences in the capabilities of the treatments, or just variation in how they were applied.

In other words, if a clinical process shows inappropriate variation, it is impossible to even measure its true outcomes, let alone apply the scientific method (clinical trials) to systematically improve. But American medicine is rife with assignable variation. Much of it arises from practice differences among physicians. But for 80 to 90 percent of common medical practices, physicians' assertions of what is "right" for their patients is just a matter of opinion.

Hence the statement to physicians regarding their patient treatment practices: It is more important that you do it the same than that you do it "right." For when, as a group, physicians develop consistent practices based on the best scientific information and peer consensus, they can accurately measure patient outcomes and apply the scientific method to systematically improve. No matter where a group starts, iterative application of the scientific method, informed by comparisons with other professional groups, will eventually lead to documented best patient care. But without consistent care delivery practices it is not even possible to accurately measure outcomes, let alone systematically improve.

The costs associated with a health care process are just one more outcome of the process. As such, process management techniques apply to them just as well as to medical outcomes. This is the basis for the widely held but unproven view that efforts to eliminate variation will produce less costly as well as better care.

In an increasingly competitive medical marketplace, it is critically important to physicians and hospitals that they are able to *document* effective, efficient patient care, improve both quality and cost over time, and share the results with patients, purchasers, and regulators. In a very real sense, within a provider-at-risk environment a provider's financial success is tied directly to the provider's professional success. Both depend upon the provider's ability to measure and manage variation.

Lesson 3: For Most Physicians, Financial Rewards Are Secondary to Good Patient Care. For That Reason Practice Management Efforts That Emphasize Patient Care Quality Are Much More Successful, Even for Managing Costs, Than Those That Focus on Costs Alone

The foregoing list of major sources of physician practice variation overlooks one oft-cited factor: Financial incentives clearly affect medical decision making.[66–71] But financial incentives exist within the broader context of professional uncertainty. When forced to choose between good patient outcomes (as supported by credible clinical data) and their own financial gain, most physicians consistently elect to maximize patient outcomes (consider, for example, Maine's experience with falling surgical rates following publication of outcomes data.[72]) More than that, physicians almost exclusively use the language of quality when they argue practice issues among themselves. Even financial arguments are usually couched in quality terms.[73] By concentrating on quality of care (at the level of professional uncertainty) process management can align the moral weight of the entire medical profession with its goals, and control the context within which financial decisions take place.

Physicians' response to financial incentives may arise partly from nonphysicians' fixation on costs: Many practicing physicians perceive that health care administrators, regulators, and payers care *only* about reducing costs. If an administrator's ill-considered cost control efforts damage patient care, the patient and the physician are left to face the ethical and legal consequences alone. But as quality improvement theory (and related experience) clearly demonstrates, quality controls costs. One of the best ways to control costs is to manage quality. One of the biggest hurdles IHC faced in implementing clinical process management (in order to improve both quality and costs) was overcoming the distrust that years of monomaniacal cost control efforts had built among physicians. As IHC's administration has shifted its emphasis to best patient outcomes (with secondary cost control in a quality improvement setting) physicians' willingness to collaborate on clinical process management has steadily increased.

Lesson 4: Guidelines Are Nothing New to American Medicine

When the LDS Hospital research team began to develop a protocol to control ventilator management for ARDS patients, they followed models that have seen continuous use in American medicine since the early 1900s. Physicians routinely use guidelines in daily practice (even though they often apply them subjectively) because it helps them deal with complex decisions and makes them more efficient (guidelines save time, as the LDS Hospital ARDS team so clearly demonstrated). As an extreme example, residents and interns routinely purchase, carry, and rely on books of medical guidelines specifically designed to quickly summarize the diagnosis and treatment of common conditions.

Lesson 5: "Control" Is a Central Issue

Why, then, would physicians resist the implementation of practice guidelines at a hospital level? One major reason is that they fear a loss of control. They see hospital-level practice guidelines as straitjackets that mandate decisions, fail to recognize the full complexity of real patient care, and eliminate clinical judgement. More than that, they perceive that control is wrested from them only so that administrators can control costs. The responsibility for bad patient outcomes still rests with the physicians, even after their control over patient care (and, hence, patient outcomes) is gone.

In contrast, medicine's traditional guidelines are decision support tools that recognize the need for clinical judgement. The LDS Hospital ARDS team addressed this issue by giving the clinical team control over the guideline. The use of statistical process control to measure guideline compliance, which inherently recognizes a range of appropriate (random) variation while still preventing inappropriate (assignable) variation, reinforces the critical role of clinical judgment.

Lesson 6: Implementing Process Management Requires a Partnership Between Physicians and Administrators

The idea of continuous improvement/process management is a central tenet of the medical profession. Every physician, upon entering the practice of medicine, ethically commits to examine the treatments they give to patients and the outcomes they achieve, with an aim to improve their treatments for future patients. In medical school and residency training every physician also forcefully learns that they cannot trust subjective data—objective information and evaluation are essential to good treatment decisions. But for some reason, when physicians leave training and enter the practice of medicine, they begin to evaluate their treatments and outcomes subjectively, in their heads. Because of that subjectivity their practices often resemble a series of small, unplanned, uncontrolled human experiments, based on the last journal article the physician had time to scan or the last drug representative who visited the clinic. Obviously, that kind of medical practice—the kind practiced by almost all American physicians—has no chance of generating viable information about best patient care.

The central question, then, is "Why?" If physicians know that objective information is critical to the practice of medicine, why do they base their practice of medicine on subjective evaluations? As we implemented clinical process management within IHC, we had the opportunity to ask that question of many community-based and academic physicians, as well as examine its meaning in our own medical practices. We concluded that practicing physicians do not have the resources, the time, or the training to deal with the masses of data required for objective practice management. But data management is a well-established ability within health care organizations.

Effective guideline implementation requires a partnership. Physicians, working as a peer group, supply clinical leadership. They have the clinical understanding necessary to oversee the content and direction of clinical guidelines. They can meet (as a group) to discuss best patient care and to review guideline compliance. The hospital supplies staff support. Hospital staff collect, collate, and analyze the clinical data, and support the generation and maintenance of other guideline-related documents (such as flow charts).

Lesson 7: Local Consensus Is Essential for Implementing Guidelines

Because most clinical practices have no firm basis in published scientific research, those who generate practice guidelines are often forced to rely on expert consensus to complete their work. But even when generated through formal methods, expert consensus is an inexact tool. Different consensus groups have different goals and use different techniques. They often generate different, even conflicting, guidelines on the same topic.[74–76] Within a single consensus panel the experts often disagree, and their assessments change when they apply guidelines generated in a theoretical setting to real patients.[77] Perhaps most troubling, physician experts show wide disagreements when asked to assess underlying probabilities that are essential to consensus judgments.[78,79] For example, Eddy asked thoracic surgeons, sponsored by a professional society, to assess the chance of a particular outcome for a well-defined group of patients within a specific time period after surgery.[80] The outcome was an essential element to determine when the procedure was appropriate. The surgeons' assessments ranged from zero to 100 percent. In light of many similar examples, there is real doubt that such a thing as a "medical expert" truly exists.

As the LDS Hospital ARDS team recognized, expert consensus suffers from the same deficiency that produces practice variation in the first place: There are no data to show that consensus guidelines are correct. In such a setting, if the aim is to stabilize a care process then systematically improve, local consensus among the complete care delivery group is far more important than the consensus of an expert panel. An expert consensus panel can provide a jumping off point, to get a practice guideline started. But that expert consensus must translate into local consensus if the guideline is to modify physician practices.

Lesson 8: Effective Guidelines Require Feedback on Compliance and Outcomes, Using Credible Clinical Data

In 1989, Lomas, et al., tracked the implementation of a practice guideline covering repeat caesarean sections in Canada.[81] The guideline was developed and widely distributed by the major professional society that represented obstetricians in the country. In a survey, 87 to 94 percent of obstetricians told Lomas that they "agreed with the content" of the guideline; 33 percent said that, as a result of the guideline, they had changed their practice of medicine. But in a follow-up test only 67 percent of the obstetricians in the survey understood the guideline's contents. The actual repeat C-section rate was 15 to 49 percent above the rate reported by the obstetricians. Lomas concluded that the guideline had produced only "slight change in actual practice." Other investigators, upon evaluating the impact of dissemination for other guidelines, have found similar results.[82-84]

The LDS Hospital ARDS team generated data through which members of the team could objectively evaluate their performance against the guideline. In the face of credible clinical data, in a supportive environment, guideline compliance changed. Several other projects within IHC have shown the same effect, and other investigators have reported similar results.[85]

Subjective data works no better for guideline implementation than for care delivery. Successful guideline implementation appears to rest upon the availability of an adequate data system. But such a data system serves many other concurrent purposes in addition to helping establish guideline compliance. It provides information to assess outcomes and systematically improve, and generates reports for use with regulators and health care purchasers.

Lesson 9: Physicians Will Lead Guideline Implementation If the Subject Is Approached through Existing Professional Values, Structures, and Realities.

The values and standards of the American medical profession are a ready foundation upon which a successful guideline implementation program can securely rest. But to take advantage of that foundation, administrators must approach guideline implementation from the medical perspective, using structures and language that physicians understand. For example, physicians already have a structure to implement clinical management. It's called the medical staff. Therefore, as the LDS pulmonary research team began to implement their ventilator guideline, they did not add another layer of meetings. Instead, they used their existing clinical staff meetings. Similarly, time is a limited commodity for most practicing physicians. Asking community physicians to attend team meetings, outside of their existing quality structure, is tantamount to asking hospital employees to attend quality team meetings without compensation outside of regular work hours. At IHC, we therefore involve physicians in a supervisory role. Hospital employees invest the hours of staff work necessary to implement a guideline, regularly contacting physician leaders for oversight, direction, and approval. We call meetings of the entire subspecialty medical staff only after the staff work for a guideline or practice analysis is well advanced, and after physician leadership has already had a chance to review and criticize it.

CONCLUSION

In 1989 Linder[86] interviewed 104 clinical and administrative leaders at 31 hospitals in the United States. All 31 hospitals used a large commercial severity-of-illness measurement system to compare the health outcomes achieved by individual physicians. All claimed to use the system as part of a quality improvement effort. But Linder concluded that 45 percent of the hospitals in the study used these tools primarily to avoid meaningful change. Their outcomes measurement and quality improvement programs were a facade, a barrier to deflect outside criticism while they practiced "business as usual" behind their shield. For an additional 35 percent, the hospital administration used outcomes measurement and quality improvement to exert control over physicians. Only 20 percent of the hospitals surveyed used their systems to manage care processes—to build a partnership with physicians, and manage quality and cost through an informed and open discussion of difficult medical issues.

Linder's findings underscore a central issue in guideline development and implementation. Because most medical decisions have no basis in published scientific research, consensus techniques are essential to build practice guidelines. But for a significant subgroup of health care leaders, some opinions are more valuable than others. On one side is a group of "experts" (members of the guideline development team) who can think, while on the other side (practicing clinicians) are those who can only do what they are told.

A group of "experts" can generate a practice guideline. A hospital administration can mandate that practicing physicians follow its rules. But given the realities surrounding the science of medicine, consensus methods, and the practice of medicine, effective implementation will occur only when clinicians and administrators team together to find the best patient care. That union is the sole safe haven in an increasingly competitive provider-at-risk environment. It not only creates the means to manage costs and improve patient outcomes; it generates the information necessary to market effective, efficient care to purchasers.

For the next generation of American health care systems, success will depend on the ability of health care leaders to create a culture of cooperation among all members of the health care team. Those leaders will not manage physicians. Instead, they will organize clinicians then supply them with the necessary tools, so that physicians can manage themselves and the health care processes they oversee. In creating that collaborative culture, it is obviously far more important how health care leaders implement practice guidelines, than the particular set of guidelines that they use to initiate implementation.

NOTES

1. D. Dranove, M. Shanley, and W.D. White, How Fast Are Hospital Prices Really Rising?, *Medical Care* 29, no. 8 (August 1991): 690–96.

2. W.E. Deming, Personal communication, June 1990.

3. D.M. Berwick, TQM: Refining Doctoring, *The Internist* 34 (March 1993): 8–10.

4. B.C. James, S.D. Horn, and R.A. Stephenson, *Management by Fact: The Relationship of Quality Improvement to Outcomes Management, Practice Guidelines, and Randomized Clinical Trials* (Unpublished manuscript, 1992).

5. Institute of Medicine, *Clinical Practice Guidelines: Directions for a New Program* (Washington, DC: National Academy Press, 1990).

6. Institute of Medicine, *Clinical Practice Guidelines*.

7. D.M. Eddy, *A Manual for Assessing Health Practices & Designing Practice Policies* (Philadelphia, PA: The American College of Physicians, 1992).

8. B.C. James, *Quality Management for Health Care Delivery* (Chicago, IL: Hospital Research and Educational Trust [American Hospital Association], 1989).

9. C.A. Anderson and R.D. Daigh, Quality Mind-Set Overcomes Barriers to Success, *Healthcare Financial Management* 45 (February 1991): 21–32.

10. W.W. Scherkenbach, *The Deming Route to Quality and Productivity: Road Maps and Roadblocks* (Washington, DC: CEEPress Books, 1991).

11. B.C. James, Good Enough? Standards and Measurements in Continuous Quality Improvement, in *Bridging the Gap Between Theory and Practice* (Chicago, IL: Hospital Research and Education Trust [American Hospital Association], 1992).

12. James, Good Enough?

13. Ibid.

14. Eddy, *A Manual For Assessing Health Practices*.

15. Ibid.

16. Society for Medical Decision Making Committee on Standardization of Clinical Algorithms, Proposal for Clinical Algorithm Standards, *Medical Decision Making* 12 (April–June 1992): 149–54.

17. S.D. Pearson, et al., The Clinical Algorithm Nosology: A Method for Comparing Algorithmic Guidelines, *Medical Decision Making* 12 (April–June 1992): 123–31.

18. D.C. Hadorn, K. McCormick, and A. Diokno, An Annotated Algorithm Approach to Clinical Guideline Development, *Journal of the American Medical Association* 267 (24 June 1992): 3311–14.

19. Eddy, *A Manual for Assessing Health Practices*.

20. D.M. Eddy, The "Clinical Decision Making: From Theory to Practice" series in the *Journal of the American Medical Association:* Volumes 263–268 (1990–1992).

    1. The Challenge, *Journal of the American Medical Association* 263, no. 2 (12 Jan. 1990): 287–90.

    2. Anatomy of a Decision, *Journal of the American Medical Association* 263, no. 3 (19 Jan. 1990): 441–43.

    3. Practice Policies—What Are They?, *Journal of the American Medical Association* 263, no. 6 (9 Feb. 1990): 877–78, 880.

    4. Practice Policies: Where Do They Come From?, *Journal of the American Medical Association* 263, no. 9 (2 March 1990): 1265, 1269, 1272.

    5. Practice Policies—Guidelines for Methods, *Journal of the American Medical Association* 263, no. 13 (4 April 1990): 1839–41.

    6. Guidelines for Policy Statements: The Explicit Approach, *Journal of the American Medical Association* 263, no. 16 (25 April 1990): 2239–40.

    7. Comparing Benefits and Harms: The Balance Sheet, *Journal of the American Medical Association* 263, no. 18 (9 May 1990): 2393, 2498, 2501.

    8. Designing a Practice Policy: Standards, Guidelines, and Options, *Journal of the American Medical Association* 263, no. 22 (13 June 1990): 3077, 3081, 3084.

    9. Resolving Conflicts in Practice Policies, *Journal of the American Medical Association* 264, no. 3 (18 July 1990): 389–91.

    10. What Do We Do about Costs?, *Journal of the American Medical Association* 264, no. 9 (5 Sept. 1990): 1161, 1165, 1169–70.

    11. Connecting Value and Costs: Whom Do We Ask, and What Do We Ask Them?, *Journal of the American Medical Association* 264, no. 13 (3 Oct. 1990): 1737–39.

    12. Rationing by Patient Choice, *Journal of the American Medical Association* 265, no. 1 (2 Jan. 1991): 105–8.

    13. What Care Is "Essential"? What Services Are "Basic", *Journal of the American Medical Association* 265, no. 6 (13 Feb. 1991): 782, 786–88.

    14. The Individual vs. Society: Is There a Conflict?, *Journal of the American Medical Association* 265, no. 11 (20 March 1991): 1446, 1449–50.

    15. The Individual vs. Society: Resolving the Conflict, *Journal of the American Medical Association* 265, no. 18 (8 May 1991): 2399–2401.

    16. What's Going on in Oregon?, *Journal of the American Medical Association* 266, no. 3 (17 July 1991): 417–20.

    17. Oregon's Methods: Did Cost-Effectiveness Analysis Fail?, *Journal of the American Medical Association* 266, no. 15 (16 Oct. 1991): 2135–41.

    18. Oregon's Plan: Should It Be Approved?, *Journal of the American Medical Association* 266, no. 17 (17 Nov. 1991): 2439–45.

    19. Cost-Effectiveness Analysis: A Conversation with my Father, *Journal of the American Medical Association* 267, no. 12 (25 March 1992): 1669–75.

    20. Cost-Effectiveness Analysis: Is It Up to the Task?, *Journal of the American Medical Association* 267, no. 24 (24 June 1992): 3342–48.

    21. Cost-Effectiveness Analysis: Will It Be Accepted?, *Journal of the American Medical Association* 268, no. 1 (1 July 1992): 132–36.

    22. Applying Cost-Effectiveness Analysis: The Inside Story, *Journal of the American Medical Association* 268, no. 18 (11 Nov. 1992): 2575–82.

21. R.E. Park, et al., *Physician Ratings of Appropriate Indications for Six Medical and Surgical Procedures*, R-3280-CWF/HF/PMT/RW (Santa Monica, CA: RAND Corporation, 1986).

22. S.E. Henderson, et al., Computerized Clinical Protocols in an Intensive Care Unit: How Well Are They Followed?, *Proceedings of the Fourteenth Annual Symposium on Computer Applications in Medical Care (SCAMC)* (Los Alamitos, CA: IEEE Computer Society Press, 1990).

23. S.E. Henderson, et al., Performance of Computerized Protocols for the Management of Arterial Oxygenation in an Intensive Care Unit, *International Journal of Clinical Monitoring and Computing* 8, no. 4 (1992): 271–80.

24. Henderson, et al., Computerized Clinical Protocols.

25. T.D. East, et al., A Strategy for Development of Computerized Critical Care Decision Support Systems, *International Journal of Clinical Monitoring and Computing* 8, no. 4 (1992): 263–69.

26. T.D. East, et al., A Successful Computerized Protocol for Clinical Management of Pressure Control Inverse Ratio Ventilation in ARDS Patients, *Chest* 101 (March 1992): 697–710.

27. T.P. Ryan, *Statistical Methods for Quality Improvement* (New York, NY: John Wiley and Sons, 1989).

28. A.H. Morris, et al., Final Report: Computerized Protocol Controlled Clinical Trial of New Therapy Which Includes $ECCO_2R$ for ARDS, *American Review Respiratory Disease* 145, no. 4 (1992): AJ84.

29. A.H. Morris, Protocols, $ECCO_2R$, and the Evaluations of New ARDS Therapy, *Japanese Journal of Intensive Care Medicine* 16 (1992): 61–63.

30. W.M. Zapol, et al., The Adult Respiratory Distress Syndrome at Massachusetts General Hospital: Etiology Progression and Survival Rates, 1978–1988, in *Adult Respiratory Distress Syndrome*, ed. F. Walz (New York: Marcel Dekker, Inc., 1991).

31. A. Artigas, et al., Clinical Presentation, Prognostic Factors, and Outcomes of ARDS in the European Collaborative Study (1985–1987), in *Adult Respiratory Distress Syndrome*, eds. W. Zapol and F. Lemaire (New York: Marcel Dekker, Inc., 1991).

32. J.A. Glover, The Incidence of Tonsillectomy in School Children, *Proceedings of the Royal Society of Medicine* 31 (1938): 1219–36.

33. C.E. Lewis, Variations in the Incidence of Surgery, *New England Journal of Medicine* 281, no. 16 (1969): 880–84.

34. J.E. Wennberg and A. Gittelsohn, Small Area Variations in Health Care Delivery, *Science* 182 (14 December 1973): 1102–8.

35. J.E. Wennberg, Variations in Medical Practice and Hospital Costs, *Connecticut Medicine* 49, no. 7 (1985): 444–53.

36. J.E. Wennberg, B.A. Barnes, and M. Zubkoff, Professional Uncertainty and the Problem of Supplier-Induced Demand, *Social Science and Medicine* 16, no. 7 (1982): 811–24.

37. K. McPherson, et al., Small-Area Variations in the Use of Common Surgical Procedures: An International Comparison of New England, England, and Norway, *New England Journal of Medicine* 307 (18 November 1982): 1310–14.

38. Park, et al., *Physician Ratings*.

39. L.J. Leape, et al., Does Inappropriate Use Explain Small-Area Variation in the Use of Health Care Services?, *Journal of the American Medical Association* 263 (2 February 1990): 669–72.

40. R.H. Brook, et al., Predicting the Appropriate Use of Carotid Endarterectomy, Upper Gastrointestinal Endoscopy, and Coronary Angiography, *New England Journal of Medicine* 323 (25 October 1990): 1173–77.

41. C.M. Winslow, et al., The Appropriateness of Performing Coronary Artery Bypass Surgery, *Journal of the American Medical Association* 260 (22 July 1988): 505–9.

42. B.C. James, et al., *Final Analysis of the IHC "Transurethral Prostatectomy" Utilization Study: Intermountain Health Care Department of Medical Affairs Technical Report* No. 1 (Salt Lake City, UT: Intermountain Health Care, Inc., 1987).

43. B.C. James, et al., *Final Analysis of the IHC "Uncomplicated Cholecystectomy" Quality, Utilization, and Efficiency (QUE) Study: Intermountain Health Care Department of Medical Affairs Technical Report* No. 2 (Salt Lake City, UT: Intermountain Health Care, Inc., 1988).

44. M.L. Baird, et al., *Final Analysis of the IHC "Uncomplicated Total Hip Arthroplasty" Quality, Utilization, and Efficiency (QUE) Study,* (Salt Lake City, UT: Intermountain Health Care Inc., 1988).

45. M.L. Baird, et al., *Final Analysis of the IHC 1987 "Permanent Pacemaker Implant" Quality, Utilization, and Efficiency (QUE) Study* (Salt Lake City, UT: Intermountain Health Care, Inc., 1989).

46. D.M. Eddy, Variations in Physician Practice: The Role of Uncertainty, *Health Affairs* 3 (Summer 1984): 74–89.

47. D.M. Eddy and J. Billings, The Quality of Medical Evidence: Implications for Quality of Care, *Health Affairs* 7 (Spring 1988): 19–32.

48. Wennberg, Barnes, and Zubkoff, Professional Uncertainty.

49. James, Horn, and Stephenson, *Management By Fact.*

50. J.W. Williamson, M. Alexander, and G.E. Miller, Priorities in Patient Care Research and Continuing Medical Education, *Journal of the American Medical Association* 204 (22 April 1968): 303–8.

51. J.W. Williamson, P.G. Goldschmidt, and J.A. Jillson, *Medical Practice Information Demonstration Project: Final Report*, Office of the Asst. Secretary of Health, DHEW, Contract #282-77-0068GS (Baltimore, MD: Policy Research Inc., 1979).

52. J.P. Bunker, Is Efficacy the Gold Standard for Quality Assessment?, *Inquiry* 25 (Spring 1988): 51–58.

53. Institute of Medicine, *Assessing Medical Technologies* (Washington, DC: National Academy Press, 1985).

54. J.H. Ferguson, Research on the Delivery of Medical Care Using Hospital Firms, *Medical Care* 29, no. 7 (Supplement 1991): JS1–2.

55. M. Dubinsky and J.H. Ferguson, Analysis of the National Institutes of Health Medicare Coverage Assessment, *International Journal of Technology Assessment in Health Care* 6, no. 3 (1990): 480–88.

56. Williamson, et al., Priorities in Patient Care Research.

57. Williamson, et al., *Medical Practice Information.*

58. J.W. Williamson, M. Lincoln, and C.W. Turner, Personal communication, May 1991.

59. P.G. Goldschmidt, Information Synthesis: A Practical Guide, *Health Services Research* 21 (June, Part 1 1986): 215–37.

60. Eddy, *A Manual for Assessing Health Practices.*

61. D.M. Eddy, V. Hasselblad, and R. Shachter, *Meta-Analysis by the Confidence Profile Method: The Statistical Synthesis of Evidence* (San Diego, CA: The Academic Press, 1992).

62. A.H. Morris, Computer Applications, in *Principles of Critical Care*, eds. J.B. Hall, G.A. Schmidt, and L.D.H. Wood (New York: McGraw–Hill, Inc., Health Professions Division, 1992).

63. Eddy, Clinical Decision Making: From Theory to Practice, Series in *JAMA*, 263, no. 9 (2 March 1990):1265, 1269, 1272.

64. C.J. McDonald, Protocol-Based Computer Reminders, the Quality of Care and the Non-Perfectibility of Man, *New England Journal of Medicine* 295 (9 December 1976):1352–55.

65. L.M. Koran, The Reliability of Clinical Methods, Data and Judgments, *New England Journal of Medicine* 293 (25 September 1975 [Part 1], 2 October 1975 [Part 2]):642–46; 695–701.

66. Wennberg, Barnes, and Zubkoff, Professional Uncertainty.

67. Eddy, Variations in Physician Practice.

68. B.J. Hillman, Physicians' Utilization and Charges for Outpatient Diagnostic Imaging in a Medicare Population, *Journal of the American Medical Association* 268 (21 October 1992): 2050–54.

69. J.M. Mitchell and E. Scott, Physician Ownership of Physical Therapy Services: Effects on Charges, Utilization, Profits, and Service Characteristics, *Journal of the American Medical Association* 268 (21 October 1992): 2055–59.

70. J.M. Mitchell and J.H. Sunshine, Consequences of Physicians' Ownership of Health Care Facilities—Joint Ventures in Radiation Therapy, *New England Journal of Medicine* 327 (19 November 1992): 1497–1501.

71. A. Swedlow, et al., Increased Costs and Rates of Use in the California Workers' Compensation System as a Result of Self-Referral by Physicians, *New England Journal of Medicine* 327 (19 November 1992): 1502–6.

72. P. Caper, Population-Based Measures of the Quality of Medical Care, in *Health Care Quality Management for the 21st Century*, ed. J. Conch (Tampa, FL: American College of Physician Executives, 1991).

73. J.E. Wennberg, et al., Changes in Tonsillectomy Rates Associated with Feedback and Review, *Pediatrics* 59 (June 1977): 821–86.

74. S.E. Kellie and J.T. Kelly, Medicare Peer Review Organization Preprocedure Review Criteria, *Journal of the American Medical Association* 265 (13 March 1991): 1265–70.

75. A.M. Audet, S. Greenfield, and M. Field, Medical Practice Guidelines: Current Activities and Future Directions, *Annals of Internal Medicine* 113 (1 November 1990): 709–14.

76. L.L. Leape, et al., Group Judgments of Appropriateness: The Effect of Panel Composition, *Quality Assurance in Health Care* 4, no. 2 (1992): 151–59.

77. R.E. Park, Physician Ratings of Appropriate Indications for Three Procedures: Theoretical Indications vs. Indications Used in Practice, *American Journal of Public Health* 79 (April 1989): 445–47.

78. Eddy, Variations in Physician Practice.

79. G.T. O'Connor, et al., What Are My Chances? It Depends on Whom You Ask. The Choice of a Prosthetic Heart Value, *Medical Decision Making* 18 (October–December 1988): 341.

80. Eddy, *A Manual for Assessing Health Practices*.

81. J. Lomas, et al., Do Practice Guidelines Guide Practice?: The Effect of a Consensus Statement on the Practice of Physicians, *New England Journal of Medicine* 321 (9 November 1989): 1306–11.

82. J. Kosecoff, et al., Effects of the National Institutes of Health Consensus Development Program on Clinical Practice, *Journal of the American Medical Association* 258 (20 November 1987): 2708–13.

83. B. Merz, High Consensus, Low Compliance on Cancer Screening Guidelines, *American Medical News* September 23/30 (1991).

84. M.M. Cohen, et al., Assessing Physicians' Compliance with Guidelines for Papanicolaou Testing, *Medical Care* 30 (June 1992): 514–28.

85. Caper, Population-Based Measures.

86. J.C. Linder, Outcomes Measurement: Compliance Tool or Strategic Initiative?, *Health Care Management Review* 16 (Fall 1991): 21–33.

SUGGESTED READING

Flanagin A., and Lundberg, G.D. "Clinical Decision-Making: Promoting the Jump From Theory to Practice." (Editorial laying out the start of the Eddy series), *Journal of the American Medical Association* 263, no. 2 (12 Jan 1990): 279–80.

11. The Outcomes Movement: Will It Get Us Where We Want To Go?

Arnold A. Epstein

Arnold Relman, editor-in-chief of the *Journal*, has dubbed it "the third revolution in medical care."[1] That description of what I call the outcomes movement may be hyperbole, but clearly we have entered an era of unprecedented growth in activity directed at the assessment of outcomes, the analysis of effectiveness, and quality assurance.

There are many conspicuous manifestations of this type of activity. For example, the Joint Commission on Accreditation of Hospitals, moving away from its traditional reliance on structural measures, has formally embraced quality assessment based on severity-adjusted outcomes as the cornerstone of its future strategy for monitoring hospitals.[2,3] Paul Ellwood, who popularized the concept of health maintenance organizations, has now called for a major initiative in what he terms "outcomes management"[4]—a national program in which clinical standards and guidelines are based systematically on patient outcomes.

In line with this vision, the federal government, through the Health Care Financing Administration[5] and the newly established Agency for Health Care Policy and Research,[6] has launched a program directed at gauging the effectiveness of medical interventions and developing guidelines for medical practice through the assessment of patient outcomes. These activities will be pursued with the help of substantial increases in research funding. Two years ago federal funding devoted to this kind of activity, through the National Center for Health Services Research, was limited to $1.9 million; last year it rose to $5.5 million. More than $30 million is allotted for such research in this year's budget.

Proponents of the new emphasis on measuring the outcomes of medical practice[7,8,9] predict myriad social benefits, including better information for both

Source: Reprinted from the *New England Journal of Medicine*, Vol. 323, No. 4, pp. 266–269, with permission of the Massachusetts Medical Society, © 1990.

physicians and patients, improved guidelines for medical practice, and wiser decisions by purchasers of health care. But will these efforts really pay off? Will the era of outcomes assessment and accountability actually provide what Ellwood says we need—"a central nervous system that can help us cope with the complexities of modern medicine"?[10]

I believe that research on outcomes can tell us more about the effectiveness of different interventions and may help increase the efficiency of existing systems for monitoring the quality of care. At the same time, I question whether this information is all we need to formulate guidelines that will serve as a rational basis for decision making and make medical care for a broad range of conditions more efficient. In this article I shall first consider the forces that have brought about the outcomes movement and the directions it has taken thus far. I shall then examine the goals of the movement and the likely impediments to its progress. I hope that the recognition of these impediments will lead us to modify our expectations appropriately and will help us funnel our efforts into the activities that will be most productive.

THE ORIGINS OF THE OUTCOMES MOVEMENT

At least three important factors have led to the current emphasis on the assessment of effectiveness and outcomes. The first is the need for cost containment. Growth of managed care and the initiation of state and federal prospective-payment systems have engendered substantial fear that administrative and payment policies designed to control the increase in medical services will have deleterious effects on the quality of care. In the context of cost containment, the emphasis on outcomes is seen in two ways: as an index of the relative effectiveness of different interventions that allows the elimination of unnecessary expenditure and as part of a vital monitoring system directed not so much to improving the quality of care as to detecting its deterioration.[11]

The second factor is a renewed sense of competition. Since 1970, the number of health maintenance organizations has grown nearly 20-fold.[12,13] Using a variety of structures, these insurers now compete vigorously for the industrial buyer's dollar. Without question this competition has taken place on the battlefield of price, but there is concern that price alone is an inadequate basis for competition. Buyers need, in Walter McClure's words, to "buy right," to compare outcomes and quality, and to incorporate their findings into their ultimate buying decisions.[14]

The third, and perhaps the most important, factor leading to the outcomes movement has been the work of researchers such as John Wennberg, who have documented substantial geographic differences in the use of various medical procedures.[15–17] These differences, which appear to persist even after control for the severity of illness, raise questions about whether they reflect unnecessary costs in high-use areas or less-than-optimal care in low-use areas; the focus on outcomes is the obvious first step in answering these questions.

NEW DIRECTIONS IN ASSESSING OUTCOMES

The surge of interest in outcomes has not meant simply an increase in the amount of attention paid to outcomes. Rather, the movement has taken some very specific directions that affect the types of data that are collected and used, the types of studies that are performed, and the types of outcomes that are assessed.

First, there has been a much greater emphasis on the use of large computerized data bases—for several reasons. One is the continuing accumulation of data by state rate-setting commissions and third-party payers, including the Health Care Financing Administration, that use computerized clinical and billing data in determining reimbursement. At the same time, the availability of portable computers and workstations now facilitates the analysis of these data. There are currently 40-pound computers that can easily be used to analyze treatment patterns for literally hundreds of thousands of patients. Finally, vested interests have become involved. Government research initiatives have clearly been directed toward making use of the Health Care Financing Administration's files on Medicare beneficiaries, among other data.[18]

The existence of large computerized data bases also offers the potential for natural experiments of tremendous size. We have seen the resurgence of the quasi-experimental design or the nonrandomized study over the randomized, controlled trial. The latter is excellent for assessing efficacy—that is, for determining whether an intervention will reliably produce the desired effect under well-controlled, essentially ideal circumstances. On the other hand, randomized, controlled trials may not tell us much about how effective treatments are when they are used in everyday practice by ordinary clinicians and patients. The Lipid Research Clinics Coronary Primary Prevention Trial, for example, showed that cholestyramine is extremely efficacious in lowering cholesterol levels and diminishing the risk of coronary heart disease under controlled circumstances.[19,20] Yet many clinicians have questioned whether its adverse side effects will limit its effectiveness in everyday practice.

There are, of course, obvious trade-offs when one uses a nonrandomized design. Randomization allows one to compare different interventions while controlling for both known and unknown confounders. In nonrandomized trials, we can use statistical techniques such as matching, stratification, and structural modeling for this purpose. However, these techniques are most effective when the data available include detailed measures of the severity of illness. Thus, there has been a growing interest in expanding the data on coexisting diseases and severity that are routinely incorporated into large data bases.

Perhaps the most important effect of the outcomes movement has been a broadening of our focus to include a wider range of outcomes. For many years we have studied differences in the use of medical services; it was only a short step to the consideration of differences in the rates of mortality, readmission, and complications and in other traditional measures of clinical outcome. During the past few years, however, we have seen a dramatic expansion in the range of outcomes that physicians and policy makers are willing to consider valid indicators of health. These go far beyond traditional clinical indexes and include a series of variables assessed through interviews: functional status, emotional health, social interaction, cognitive function, degree of disability, and so forth. There is growing appreciation in the medical community that, although they are still imperfect, instruments based on subjective data from patients can provide important information that may not be evident from physiologic measurements and may be as reliable as—or more reliable than—many of the clinical, biochemical, or physiologic indexes on which doctors have traditionally relied.[21]

THE GOALS AND LIMITATIONS OF THE OUTCOMES MOVEMENT

Proponents of the increased emphasis on outcomes believe this approach may help us achieve several related goals. These include increased understanding of the effectiveness of different interventions, the use of this information to make possible better decision making by physicians and patients, and the development of standards to guide physicians and aid third-party payers in optimizing the use of resources.

The effort to determine the outcomes and effectiveness of different medical interventions and to use that information as an aid to clinical decision making is, I believe, a useful extension of basic clinical research. We are seeing efforts not only to expand our medical knowledge but also to develop more effective ways to communicate new findings to physicians and make them accessible to patients. In recent years, for example, we have learned a substantial amount about the efficacy of prostatectomy to relieve the symptoms of benign prostatic hypertrophy, in terms of both the probability of success and the risk of mortality and adverse consequences such as impotence. A group of researchers, including Michael Barry, Floyd Fowler, Al Mulley, John Wennberg, and colleagues, have recently developed innovative videotapes to convey more accurately to patients who are considering prostatectomy the broad range of possible outcomes and the impact they may expect on their quality of life if they undergo the procedure (personal communication). Efforts to educate patients are, of course, not new. Yet the emphasis on outcomes that may be more meaningful to patients (i.e., the presence or absence of dribbling rather than urine-flow measurements) and the use of sophisticated audio-visual aids appear to be improvements on previous efforts. Additional work is now under way to refine this approach and apply it in other clinical situations—for example, for patients with breast cancer who are considering mastectomy and for patients with chronic low back pain who are considering orthopedic surgery.

A much more controversial aspect of the outcomes movement is the effort to develop guidelines that can be used by physicians in providing care and by third-party payers attempting to ensure the appropriate use of services.[22-25] In a review of more than 4,500 hospital records of Medicare patients, Chassin, et al., found that one sixth of those undergoing coronary angiography and upper-gastrointestinal endoscopy and one third of those undergoing carotid endarterectomy had procedures that a consensus panel considered inappropriate.[26] Because this study, carried out at the Rand Corporation, was based on a retrospective review of charts, some proportion of the identified instances probably represented inadequate documentation of appropriate care rather than truly inappropriate care. Nevertheless, the reported results suggest the potential magnitude of the problem.

Conceptually, the steps in the process of moving from outcomes to guidelines are straightforward.[27] We first use large data bases to establish monitoring systems; we identify variations in outcome in different areas and differences in procedures or interventions that are associated with the differences in outcome; we use nonrandomized trials or, if necessary, meta-analyses, decision analyses, or randomized, controlled trials to assess the results of the different interventions; we incorporate the results of data analysis into appropriate guidelines; and we use education and feedback to modify the behavior of physicians in the appropriate direction. Throughout the process we continue to monitor care, with the goal of modifying the initial guidelines over time as practice changes and as new technologies are developed.

Although the path to progress appears clear, numerous difficulties are likely to limit our ability to apply this approach to a broad range of conditions. The production of guidelines will be expensive and time-consuming and therefore will be justifiable only for common procedures or those that have a substantial impact on cost or outcome. It will also be most appropriate to develop guidelines for interventions in cases in which therapeutic options are stable.

The development of guidelines may be especially difficult when patients' preferences are an important factor in clinical decision making. In the case of prostatectomy, a 70-year-old man may have nocturia and urinary hesitancy and dribbling because of benign prostatic hypertrophy. Data show that prostatectomy is likely to relieve his symptoms but that the procedure entails a low risk of surgery-related death and a 5 to 25 percent risk of impotence.[28] Patients clearly differ in how they evaluate these potential benefits and risks. Better information on effectiveness may help determine the best decision for individual patients, but formal guidelines will be difficult to establish when appropriate care for persons with identical clinical characteristics differs because of their different priorities.

Progress in assessing the relative effectiveness of interventions may also be slow. Variations often arise in situations in which different groups of physicians believe different approaches are preferable. This is not a random occurrence. Controversies in medicine occur when, for one reason or another, effectiveness is difficult to gauge and the available data conflict. Should one perform a transurethral prostatectomy or an open prostatectomy for patients who need prostate surgery? Several studies have shown that the transurethral approach (used in approximately 95 percent of prostatectomies[29]) can be effective.[30–32] Other studies show, however, that open prostatectomy is more effective.[33] Will additional studies give a definitive answer?

Moreover, generally accepted standards for an appropriate level of cost effectiveness are still lacking. Today the results of hundreds of studies tell us that the cost effectiveness of various interventions ranges from a few thousand dollars to many hundreds of thousands of dollars per year of life saved. At the extremes, the decision is relatively simple. What do we do, however, for most interventions, which fall in the middle? We know, for example, that the use of cholestyramine to lower the serum cholesterol level of a 35- to 64-year-old male smoker with a serum total cholesterol level of 7.50 mmol per liter (290 mg per deciliter) and a low-density lipoprotein cholesterol level of 4.65 mmol per liter (180 mg per deciliter) will cost somewhere between $65,000 and $200,000 per year of life saved, depending on the patient's exact age.[34] Consensus guidelines developed by the National Cholesterol Educational Program tell us to treat that patient with cholestyramine,[35] but other consensus guidelines disagree.[36] Which set of guidelines is correct? Unfortunately, at present we have no universally accepted standards to help us develop appropriate clinical guidelines.

The consensus process will certainly be a focal point in the development of standards. To the extent that consensus merely provides an algorithm for clinical behavior that is supported by strong and consistent evidence, the task will be straightforward and worthwhile. When the data conflict or when cost effectiveness is not extreme, however, the process will be more problematic. In these situations, a panel of experts may be able to reach consensus on a guideline, but this agreement will not necessarily define the most appropriate course of care. Clearly, different panels of experts often disagree. We still have a surprisingly limited understanding of important aspects of the consensus process, including the impact of specialty training and geographic region in the composition of panels and the effects of structuring existing data in different ways.

Finally, there are potential difficulties with implementation and monitoring. Ideally, the promulgation and enforcement of guidelines should be designed strictly to make the use of health care services more appropriate. But virtually all studies on appropriateness so far and much of the attendant dialogue have focused on patients who undergo unnecessary procedures rather than on patients who do not receive appropriate care. I suspect that a reduction in the cost of care is high on the silent agenda of many who promote the use of guidelines. As a result, administrative efforts are more likely to be focused on decreasing inappropriate care than on increasing access to beneficial procedures.

Even if efforts at implementation are balanced, physicians are likely to resist unless the guidelines can be made sufficiently comprehensive to incorporate all the data that bear on the clinical decision. The establishment of such all-encompassing guidelines will, in some instances, be difficult. Previous study has shown that even when physicians view particular guidelines favorably, they are slow to change their patterns of practice.[37] This reluctance will be especially evident in controversial areas, in which guidelines may be arbitrary and open to challenge on the basis of contradictory data. In addition, our understanding of how to induce physicians to change their patterns of practice is incomplete.[38] Education, monitoring, and feedback may be helpful strategies but are costly in terms of administrative effort and expense.

Although none of these problems are insurmountable, collectively they represent a substantial impediment. Numerous studies have documented the prevalence of inappropriate use.[39,40] Although I am sympathetic to those who would move now to curtail practice patterns that fall outside the usual range,[41] I worry that extending this approach to a broad range of conditions will be difficult.

IMPLICATIONS FOR THE FUTURE

The outcomes movement is well underway. The increased allotment of funds for research is real. Already greater attention is being devoted to determining the outcomes of different interventions, and this research is likely to yield insights into efficacy and rational behavior. I believe that expanding our research focus to a broader set of outcomes will reap rewards, since traditional physiologic and clinical indexes have important limitations. Understanding how different inter-ventions affect such factors as physical and emotional function, social activity, and return to work will provide a more sensitive gauge. Developing new and more effective methods to convey such information to doctors and patients can only lead to wiser decisions. At the same time, however, we must realize that clinical research is not a new endeavor. Will the expansion of our research effort and the development and increased accessibility of larger computerized data bases lead to a revolutionary increase in our understanding? Will these changes truly be instrumental in creating a "central nervous system" for health care? Certainly they will help, but I believe our expectations should be modest.

What about guidelines? The political tide here is strong. Images of the "rogue surgeon" practicing beyond the acceptable bounds argue strongly for an aggressive approach. The proponents of guidelines would have us develop, implement, and enforce standards for a broad set of therapies now. Is that feasible? Clearly, the consensus process can provide an answer, and when the education of physicians is ineffective in changing practice, stronger administrative and financial levers can be used. But will such efforts make the provision of care more rational and lead to a more efficient system?

I believe the call for increased assessment and accountability is healthy, but in many instances guidelines are not likely to produce more rational or more efficient care. Our efforts should continue, but our energy should be focused and metered; progress will be made, but slowly. Our expectations must be moderate if we are to avoid disappointment. The danger we face is that we will undermine a healthy evolution and allow revolutionary zeal to lead us to carry a good thing too fast and too far.

NOTES

1. A.S. Relman, Assessment and Accountability: The Third Revolution in Medical Care, *N Engl J Med.* 319 (1988): 1220–2.

2. D.S. O'Leary, The Joint Commission Looks to the Future, *JAMA* 258 (1987): 951–2.

3. J.S. Roberts, J.G. Coale, and R.R. Redman, A History of the Joint Commission on Accreditation of Hospitals, *JAMA* 258 (1987): 936–40.

4. P.M. Ellwood, Outcomes Management: A Technology of Patient Experience, *N Engl J Med* 318 (1988): 1549–56.

5. W.L. Roper, et al., Effectiveness in Health Care: An Initiative to Evaluate and Improve Medical Practice, *N Engl J Med* 319 (1988): 1197–1202.

6. Public Law 101–239. The Omnibus Budget Reconciliation Act of 1989.

7. Relman, Assessment and Accountability.

8. Ellwood, Outcomes Management.

9. Roper, et al., Effectiveness in Health Care.

10. Ellwood, Outcomes Management.

11. L. Wyszewianski, Quality of Care: Past Achievements and Future Challenges, *Inquiry* 25 (1988): 13–22.

12. T.R. Mayer and G.G. Mayer, HMOs: Origins and Development, *N Engl J Med* 312 (1985): 590–4.

13. *HMO Industry Profile. Vol. 1. Benefits, Premiums and Market Structure in 1988* (Washington, D.C.: Research and Analysis Department, Group Health Association of America, 1989).

14. J.K. Iglehart, Competition and the Pursuit of Quality: A Conversation With Walter McClure, *Health Aff* (Milwood) 7, no. 1 (1988): 79–90.

15. J. Wennberg and A. Gittelsohn, Small Area Variations in Health Care Delivery, *Science* 182 (1973): 1102–8.

16. J.E. Wennberg, et al., Hospital Use and Mortality Among Medicare Beneficiaries in Boston and New Haven, *N Engl J Med* 321 (1989): 1168–73.

17. J.E. Wennberg, J.L. Freeman, and W.J. Culp, Are Hospital Services Rationed in New Haven or Over-Utilised in Boston? *Lancet* 1 (1987): 1185–9.

18. Ellwood, Outcomes Management.

19. Lipid Research Clinics Program. The Lipid Research Clinics Coronary Primary Prevention Trial Results. I. Reduction in Incidence of Coronary Heart Disease, *JAMA* 251 (1984): 351–64.

20. Lipid Research Clinics Program. The Lipid Research Clinics Coronary Primary Prevention Trial Results. II. The Relationship of Reduction in Incidence of Coronary Heart Disease to Cholesterol Lowering, *JAMA* 251 (1984): 365–74.

21. K.N. Lohr, Advances in Health Status Assessment: Overview of the Conference, *Med Care* 27, Suppl. 3 (1989): S1–S11.

22. Relman, Assessment and Accountability.

23. Ellwood, Outcomes Management.

24. Roper, Effectiveness in Health Care.

25. P.R. Lee, et al., The Physician Payment Review Commission Report to Congress, *JAMA* 261 (1989): 2382–5.

26. M.R. Chassin, et al., *The Appropriateness of Use of Selected Medical and Surgical Procedures and Its Relationship to Geographic Variations in Their Use* (Ann Arbor, Mich.: Health Administration Press, 1989).

27. Ellwood, Outcomes Management.

28. F.J. Fowler Jr, et al., Symptom Status and Quality of Life Following Prostatectomy, *JAMA* 259 (1988): 3018–22.

29. N.P. Roos, et al., Mortality and Reoperation After Open and Transurethral Resection of the Prostate for Benign Prostatic Hyperplasia, *N Engl J Med* 320 (1989): 1120–4.

30. T. Kolmert and H. Norlen, Transurethral Resection of the Prostate: A Review of 1111 Cases, *Int Urol Nephrol* 21 (1989): 47–55.

31. W.K. Mebust, Surgical Management of Benign Prostatic Obstruction, *Urology* 32 Suppl. 6 (1988): 12–15.

32. M. Abddalla, et al., Complications de la résection Transurétrale Dans la Cure de l'Hypertrophie Prostatique Bénigne: A Propos d'Une Serie de 1 180 Adénomes—1976–1986, *J Urol (Paris)* 95 (1989): 15–21.

33. Roos, Mortality and Reoperation.

34. G. Oster and A.M. Epstein, Cost-Effectiveness of Antihyperlipemic Therapy in the Prevention of Coronary Heart Disease: The Case of Cholestyramine, *JAMA* 258 (1987): 2381–7.

35. The Expert Panel, Report of the National Cholesterol Education Program Expert Panel on Detection, Evaluation, and Treatment of High Blood Cholesterol in Adults, *Arch Intern Med* 148 (1988): 36–69.

36. Task Force on the Use and Provision of Medical Services, Report on the Detection and Management of Asymptomatic Hypercholesterolemia. Ontario Ministry of Health and the Ontario Medical Association, 1989.

37. J. Lomas, et al., Do Practice Guidelines Guide Practice? The Effect of a Consensus Statement on the Practice of Physicians, *N Engl J Med* 321 (1989): 1306–11.

38. J.M. Eisenberg and S.V. Williams, Cost Containment and Changing Physicians' Practice Behavior: Can the Fox Learn to Guard the Chicken Coop?, *JAMA* 246 (1981): 2195–201.

39. M.R. Chassin, et al., Does Inappropriate Use Explain Geographic Variations in the Use of Health Care Services? A Study of Three Procedures, *JAMA* 258 (1987): 2533–7.

40. L.L. Leape, et al., Does Inappropriate Use Explain Small-Area Variations in the Use of Health Care Services?, *JAMA* 263 (1990): 669–72.

41. R.H. Brook, Practice Guidelines and Practicing Medicine: Are They Compatible?, *JAMA* 262 (1989): 3027–30.

12. The Role of Outcomes in Quality Assessment and Assurance

Avedis Donabedian

The purpose of this article is to explain the role of outcomes in assessing and assuring quality in health care. In order to do so, a few fundamental preliminaries must be agreed on.

First, the definitions of *assessment* and *assurance* must be clarified. In spite of the confusion caused by partisans of one term or another in an ever-changing terminology, this need not be a difficult matter. I shall take *assessment* to mean determining the degree of quality in health care, whereas I take *assurance* to comprise all the measures used to protect, maintain, and improve the quality of care.

Assessment and assurance are separable activities; however, most of the time they are combined. Usually we assess quality in order to see if something needs to be done about it, and once we have done that something, we assess quality to see if we have succeeded. This being the case, I shall from now on speak of assessment only, while implying assurance as well.

The second preliminary task, one that is both more fundamental and more difficult, is to agree on what *quality* means. What are the properties, characteristics, and attributes of care that lead us to a judgment that care is of good or poor quality? Exhibit 12–1 presents a list of what some of the more important properties might be. With regard to assessment and assurance, I would like to make the following observations:

- Quality has many aspects;
- In any given situation, attention usually will focus on some of these aspects in preference to others; and

---

Source: Reprinted from *Quality Review Bulletin*, Vol. 18, No. 11, pp. 356–360, with permission of Mosby-Year Book, © 1992.

Exhibit 12–1 Some Attributes of Quality in Health Care

1. **Effectiveness**
   The ability to attain the greatest improvements in health now achievable by the best care

2. **Efficiency**
   The ability to lower the cost of care without diminishing attainable improvements in health

3. **Optimality**
   The balancing of costs against the effects of care on health (or on the benefits of health care, meaning the monetary value of improvements in health) so as to attain the most advantageous balance

4. **Acceptability**
   Conformity to the wishes, desires, and expectations of patients and responsible members of their families

5. **Legitimacy**
   Conformity to social preferences as expressed in ethical principles, values, norms, laws, and regulations

6. **Equity**
   Conformity to a principle that determines what is just or fair in the distribution of health care and of its benefits among the members of a population

- The specific outcomes chosen as indicators of quality will vary to some degree depending on the aspect of quality being assessed, but the role of outcomes in assessment will be fundamentally the same in all cases.

The third preliminary task is to agree on what we mean by *outcome*. Here we are on rather slippery ground. In one sense, any consequence of health care is an outcome. But perhaps it is more useful to take a more limited view; for purposes of this article, we will define outcomes as states or conditions of individuals and populations attributed or attributable to antecedent health care. They include changes in health states, changes in knowledge or behavior pertinent to future health states, and satisfaction with health care (expressed as opinion or inferred from behavior).

Exhibit 12–2 presents a list of the more usual outcomes pertinent to quality assessment. Needless to say, this list is open to expansion and modification as each situation requires. In any given situation perhaps the best way to identify the relevant outcome is to ask, "If we are successful in what we are doing, what change in patients or populations can we expect to achieve and detect? In what ways will they be different, as compared to before?"

Exhibit 12–2 A Classification and Listing of Some Outcomes of Health Care

A. **Clinical**
  1. Reported symptoms that have clinical significance
  2. Diagnostic categorization as an indication of morbidity
  3. Disease staging relevant to functional encroachment and prognosis
  4. Diagnostic performance—the frequency of false positives and false negatives as indicators of diagnostic or case-finding performance
B. **Physiologic-biochemical**
  1. Abnormalities
  2. Functions
      a. Loss of function
      b. Functional reserve—includes performance in test situations under various degrees of stress
C. **Physical**
  1. Loss or impairment of structural form or integrity—includes abnormalities, defects, and disfigurement
  2. Functional performance of physical activities and tasks
      a. Under the circumstances of daily living
      b. Under test conditions that involve various degrees of stress
D. **Psychologic, mental**
  1. Feelings—includes discomfort, pain, fear, anxiety (or their opposites, including satisfaction)
  2. Beliefs that are relevant to health and health care
  3. Knowledge that is relevant to healthful living, health care, and coping with illness
  4. Impairments of discrete psychologic or mental functions
      a. Under the circumstances of daily living
      b. Under test conditions that involve various degrees of stress
E. **Social and psychosocial**
  1. Behaviors relevant to coping with current illness or affecting future health, including adherence to health care regimens and changes in health-related habits
  2. Role performance
      a. Marital
      b. Familial
      c. Occupational
      d. Other interpersonal
  3. Performance under test conditions involving varying degrees of stress
F. **Integrative outcomes**
  1. Mortality
  2. Longevity
  3. Longevity, with adjustments made to take account of impairments of physical, psychologic, or psychosocial function: "full-function equivalents"
  4. Monetary value of the above
G. **Evaluative outcomes**
  1. Client opinions about, and satisfaction with, various aspects of care, including accessibility, continuity, thoroughness, humaneness, informativeness, effectiveness, cost

Reprinted with permission from Donabedian, A: *Explorations in Quality Assessment and Monitoring, Volume 2, The Criteria and Standards of Quality*. Ann Arbor, MI: Health Administration Press, 1982, pp 367–368.

The final preliminary task is to differentiate between two closely related activities that could be termed quality assessment: *technology assessment*, or activities meant to determine the right things to do (or the right ways to behave); and *quality* or *performance assessment*, or activities meant to determine if the things known (or presumed) to be the right things to do (or the right ways to behave) have in fact occurred.

Sometimes the term *quality assessment* is used to mean the first of these activities, sometimes the second, and sometimes both, simultaneously or alternately. Most of the confusion in our thinking about the role of outcomes in quality assessment arises from confusing these two kinds of evaluational activities.

When our purpose is to find out what the right thing to do is, we are engaged in technology assessment. Often technology is defined narrowly—for example, when we ask what surgical procedure to perform, what diagnostic tasks to carry out, or what drugs to prescribe. But technology can also be defined broadly—for example, how to organize an emergency service, what educational methods to use, what kind of appointment system to set up, or what style of interaction with patients to adopt. There is only one way to take on such problems: to measure the outcomes relevant to each proposed intervention and to compare these outcomes. Outcomes are the paramount criterion of good quality either by themselves or as related to costs if efficiency and optimality are to be determined. There are no other criteria except, of course, those of ethical or moral valuation.

But most of us are not involved in technology assessment. We are not responsible for advancing the science and art of health care; we do not set out to invent new ways of caring for patients. Rather we are interested in finding out whether what is already known or accepted to be the best care is being implemented. This is the more usual meaning of quality or performance assessment. And when *this* is the objective of our evaluational activity, the role of outcomes changes markedly.

THE STRUCTURE-PROCESS-OUTCOME PARADIGM

When we evaluate the quality of performance (as contrasted to the quality of the underlying science or technology) we are looking for evidence, direct or indirect, that the best strategy of care was selected and that it was implemented in the most skillful way. There are three kinds of evidence of information available to us—these can be called structure, process, and outcome.[1,2] These are not attributes of quality; rather they are only kinds of information from which inferences can be made about the quality of care. *Structure* is defined as physical and organizational properties of the settings in which care is provided, *process* is what is done for patients, and *outcome* is what is accomplished for patients.

In Figure 12–1, the progression shown first embodies the essential, fundamental characteristic of the structure-process-outcome paradigm. These three kinds of information can be used to assess quality only when and to the extent that they are causally related: structure leads to process, and process leads to outcome.

The lower part of the diagram shows that the structure-process-outcome paradigm presented first is highly simplified. In fact, there is a chain of events and even interrelated chains in which A leads to B, B to C, and so on. It is to some degree arbitrary where we stop and say, "This is an outcome"; and sometimes it is not easy to say, "Here structure ends and process begins or process ends and outcome begins." This difficulty of clearly distinguishing the three categories in our paradigm occurs more frequently when we separate it from the clinical setting for which the paradigm was designed and try to use it for other kinds of evaluation. This ambiguity will be much reduced if we ask the key question, "In what way have individuals or groups become different?" And if we are still not sure how to classify any given manifestation, we should not worry unduly as long as we understand how A leads to B, B to C, and so on. What is essential is that this chain of events be clearly modeled and understood before quality assessment begins. Figure 12–2 offers an illustration of how the structure-process-outcome paradigm might be applied in identifying the phenomena that may be subject to assessment. Some attributes of the structure-process-outcome paradigm that govern its evaluative use are as follows:

• The paradigm is a simplified version of a more complex reality;
• There must be a causal relationship between adjacent pairs;

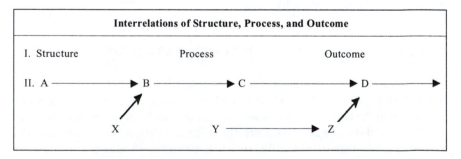

Figure 12–1 The Progression Shown First is the Essential Characteristic of the Structure-Process-Outcome Paradigm. The lower diagram demonstrates that the paradigm is a highly simplified presentation of a complex reality. (The concept of means-ends chains typified by item II derives from H.A. Simon, *Administrative Behavior*, New York: Macmillan Co, 1961, pp. 62–66.)

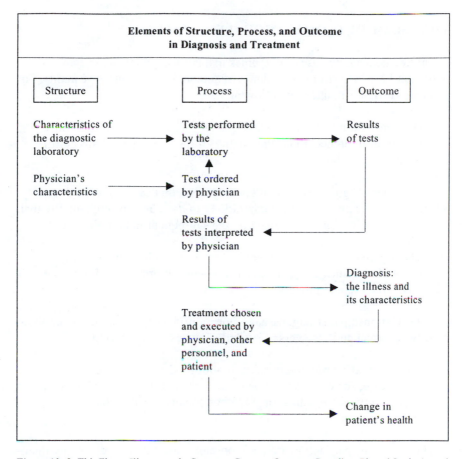

Figure 12–2 This Figure Illustrates the Structure-Process-Outcome Paradigm Played Out in Actual Practice

---

- The existence of and degree of causal relationship is established or pre-sumed *before* quality assessment can begin;
- The causal relationships are probabilities, not certainties;
- The probabilities can vary widely in magnitude (they are particularly low for structural characteristics); and
- The presence and strength of causal probabilities determine the validity and usefulness of any piece of information as an indicator of quality.

THE USE OF OUTCOMES IN QUALITY ASSESSMENT

The key issues in the use of outcomes in quality assessment are summarized in Exhibit 12–3 in the form of attributes of outcomes as indicators of quality. For example, attribute 1 states the following:

> Outcomes do not directly assess quality of performance. They only permit an inference about the quality of the process (and structure) of care.

If outcomes are good, we cannot say for certain that care was of high quality. All we can say is that the care is more likely to have been of high quality than not. The reason for this is explained by the subsequent item in the list:

> The degree of confidence in that inference depends on the strength of the predetermined causal relationship between process and outcome (and structure and process).

If the relationship is strong, we have more confidence that our inference about quality is correct and vice versa. Attribute 3 states the following:

> Because that causal relationship is modified by factors other than health care, corrections must be made for the effects of these factors, by case-mix standardization or other means, so that like can be compared with like.

These intercurrent factors are an important reason that outcomes by themselves can be very misleading as indicators of quality. To the extent that we make corrections for these factors, our confidence in inferences from outcomes improves. But we do not as yet have sufficiently complete methods of case-mix standardization to allow us to make conclusions about quality simply on the basis of outcomes. Confirmation by process analysis is needed. Still, prior standardization will reduce the number of cases in which costly, time-consuming process verification will be required. Attribute 4 states the following:

> Because the relationship between process and outcome is a probability, it is necessary to collect an appropriately large number of cases before one can infer if care is better or worse or meets specified standards.

The standards of outcomes are only expectations of achievement. We cannot use the outcome in an individual case as proof of quality. Care could be excellent

Exhibit 12–3 Some Attributes of Outcomes as Indicators of Quality

1. Outcomes do not directly assess quality of performance. They only permit an inference about the quality of the process (and structure) of care.

2. The degree of confidence in that inference depends on the strength of the predetermined causal relationship between process and outcome (and structure and process).

3. Because the causal relationship is modified by factors other than health care, corrections must be made for the effects of these factors, by case-mix standardization or other means, so that like can be compared with like.

4. Because the relationship between process and outcome is a probability, it is necessary to collect an appropriately large number of cases before one can infer if care is better or worse or meets specified standards.

5. But poor outcomes can identify a set of cases that merit analysis of the process (and structure) of care in search of possible causes for the poor outcomes.

6. Outcomes have the important advantage of being "integrative." They reflect the contributions of all those who provide care, including the contributions of patients to their own care. Outcomes also reflect skill in execution as well as appropriateness of choice of a strategy of care.

7. The integrative property of outcomes is necessarily accompanied by an inability to isolate with certainty the specific errors or virtues that have contributed to bad or good outcomes. First process analysis and then structure analysis are needed for that.

8. Outcome measurement requires specification of the appropriate "time window," which is the time when outcome differences caused by degrees of quality in health care are most manifest.[3]

9. The varying time windows of specific outcomes determine the manner and degree of their usefulness in assessments. Immediate outcomes can be used for concurrent monitoring of care so that modifications in care can be made accordingly. Delayed outcomes are useful for retrospective monitoring, leading to improvements in future care.

10. Outcomes, if poor, indicate damage already done.

11. Outcomes as indicators of quality are more comprehensible to patients and the public at large than are indicators of the process of technical (but not interpersonal) care. But outcomes are also open to misrepresentation and misunderstanding by the public if the problem of multiple causation is not understood.

12. As in all evaluational activities, the availability of information, its completeness, its accuracy, its susceptibility to manipulation, and the cost of its acquisition are important considerations. Information about delayed outcomes (after the patient is discharged) is often difficult to get; but some outcomes are susceptible to direct verification by an outside observer, in addition to being experienced and reported by patients.

13. Health care professionals are less willing or able to establish valid normative standards for outcomes as compared to process.

even if the patient dies. It is excellent because in that kind of patient the care given is most likely to do the most good.

Still, outcomes can contribute to case-by-case quality assessment, as stated in the fifth item in the list:

> But poor outcomes can identify a set of cases that merit analysis of the process (and structure) of care in search of possible causes for the poor outcomes.

This is, in fact, one of the most important uses of outcomes in quality assessment. Poor outcomes ring a warning bell, alerting us to the need for further investigation. They make it easier to identify substandard care and especially so if prior case-mix standardization has been performed. The more complete the standardization, the more precise and accurate the warning.

> Outcomes have the important advantage of being "integrative." They reflect the contributions of all those who provide care, including the contributions of patients to their own care. Outcomes also reflect skill in execution as well as appropriateness of choice of a strategy of care.

Attribute 6 highlights perhaps the most distinctive property of outcomes as indicators of quality. Outcomes reflect the effects of all the inputs into care, adjusting for the relative importance of each of several inputs as a contributor to health and welfare. In particular, outcomes reflect skill in execution of health care interventions, an aspect difficult (but not impossible) to incorporate into criteria of process.

We often wonder if we will ever have a single overall measure of the quality of care: a single number that stands for quality. Of course we do not have such a number now; but we do have a model that *could* lead to such a number. If we could say how many years of life, adjusted for differences in the quality of life, our health care intervention has produced, that number could be a measure of the effectiveness of care, though not necessarily of other attributes of quality. We have made considerable progress in developing such a number ("quality-adjusted year of life"), but there are still many problems to solve, some of which may prove insuperable.

Attribute 7 shows the other side of the coin:

> The integrative property of outcomes is necessarily accompanied by an inability to isolate with certainty the specific errors or virtues that have contributed to bad or good outcomes. First process analysis and then structure analysis are needed for that.

It looks as if for every advantage there is a corresponding disadvantage. Because outcomes are integrative, they conceal the detail needed to find out precisely what went wrong, where, and why. For that, we need further analysis of process and structure. But outcomes are useful, as mentioned earlier, in prompting such analysis.

Attributes 8 and 9 demonstrate the importance of time as an attribute of outcome indicators:

> Outcome measurement requires specification of the appropriate "time window," which is the time when outcome differences caused by degrees of quality in health care are most manifest.[3]

> The varying time windows of specific outcomes determine the manner and degree of their usefulness in assessments. Immediate outcomes can be used for concurrent monitoring of care so that modifications in care can be made accordingly. Delayed outcomes are useful for retrospective monitoring, leading to improvements in future care.

The more an outcome is delayed in its appearance, the more difficult it is to obtain information about it and the more opportunity there has been for factors other than quality to have influenced the outcome. Also, poor outcomes indicate that the damage we would have wished to prevent has already occurred, as shown in attribute 10:

> Outcomes, if poor, indicate damage already done.

Attribute 11 shows a property of outcomes very important to patient management and to public policy:

> Outcomes as indicators of quality are more comprehensible to patients and the public at large than are indicators of the process of technical (but not interpersonal) care. But outcomes are also open to misrepresentation and misunderstanding by the public if the problem of multiple causation is not understood.

Government agencies have believed that by publishing poor and good outcomes of care for individual hospitals, they can bring about public pressure to improve care. I have doubts about the efficacy of this approach. I do believe, however, that the information is essential if hospitals are to review and correct their own practices. I also believe that the public should know about hospitals that, after process analysis, have been shown to have deficiencies that they are unable to correct.

The remaining two items in the list, attributes 12 and 13, deal with more specific, technical issues of measurement:

> As in all evaluational activities, the availability of information, its completeness, its accuracy, its susceptibility to manipulation, and the cost of its acquisition are important considerations. Information about delayed outcomes (after the patient is discharged) is often difficult to get; but some outcomes are susceptible to direct verification by an outside observer, in addition to being experienced and reported by patients.

> Health care professionals are less willing or able to establish valid normative standards for outcomes as compared to process.

Issues of accuracy in measurement are often more important than whether an indicator is an item of outcome or process. In selecting any item as an indicator of quality the two key questions are (1) Does this indicator tell me what I want to know about this aspect of quality? and (2) Can I easily get complete, accurate information about the indicator?

Whether the indicator belongs to structure, process, or outcome is secondary in importance. The ability to formulate credible standards is, of course, important.[4] At present, health care professionals find it easier to offer standards of good

---

Exhibit 12–4 Why Combine Structure, Process, and Outcome Data in Quality Assessment and Assurance?

1. Helps conduct a multidimensional assessment of quality, since certain categories of information may be more indicative of certain aspects of the quality of care.
2. Helps identify sites and causes of failures in quality and suggests appropriate action (modifications in structure and process).
3. Agreement in the inferences drawn from several types of indicators increases confidence in the validity of the inferences about quality.
4. Disagreement in the inferences drawn from several types of indicators suggests presence of problems that include the following:
   a. Data are incomplete, inaccurately measured, or deliberately falsified.
   b. Outcomes have been measured at the inappropriate time window, or in an insufficient number of cases, or without adequate case-mix standardization.
   c. The model of the relationships among structure, process, and outcome used to guide the assessment is faulty because
      (1) existing knowledge has been misapplied,
      (2) existing knowledge is properly used, but that knowledge is itself faulty. (This means new research is needed.)

care. But, as our understanding of outcomes improves, our ability to specify standards will also improve. Until then, we can always make comparisons in outcome attainment among different sources of care.

One can easily infer from the attributes enumerated in Exhibit 12–3 that outcomes offer a mix of strengths and weaknesses as indicators of the quality of care. Process measures offer their own corresponding mix of strengths and weaknesses, as do measures of structure.[5] Consequently, the best strategy in quality assessment is to select a mix of indicators drawn from each of these approaches. Some of the reasons for this conclusion are offered in Exhibit 12–4.

The single most important conclusion to draw from all of this is one of reconciliation and harmony. There is no reason whatever to engage in a divisive debate on the relative superiority of process over outcome or of outcome over process in measurements of quality. We need information about both and about structure as well. The secret of success in quality assessment is the proper choice of the relevant indicators and not in unthinking partisanship for one kind of indicator over another.

NOTES

1. A. Donabedian, Evaluating the Quality of Care, *Milbank Mem Fund Q* 44, Pt 2 (Jul 1966): 166–203.

2. A. Donabedian, *Explorations in Quality Assessment and Monitoring: The Definition of Quality and Approaches to Its Assessment*, Vol. 1 (Ann Arbor, MI: Health Administration Press, 1980).

3. R.H. Brook, et al., Assuring the Quality of Medical Care Using Outcome Measures: An Overview of the Method, *Med Care* 165, Suppl. (Sept 1977): S1–165.

4. A. Donabedian, *Explorations in Quality Assessment and Monitoring: The Criteria and Standards of Quality*, Vol. 2 (Ann Arbor, MI: Health Administration Press, 1982).

5. Donabedian, *Explorations in Quality Assessment*, Vol. 1.

13. Benchmarking

Craig Anderson and Peggy A. Rivenburgh

Benchmarking: Who? What? When? Where? Why? How? Those are the questions being asked today by leading health care organizations. Benchmarking is undoubtedly one of the most significant and important topics in the quality arena, as well as a key activity in the many fundamental steps of total quality management. World-class organizations that have received coveted quality awards have all excelled at benchmarking.

In its simplest form, *benchmarking is merely comparing oneself against others*. However, benchmarking may be defined in a number of ways. David T. Kearns, chief executive officer (CEO) of Xerox Corporation, the recipient of the 1989 Malcolm Baldrige National Quality Award, defines benchmarking as "the continuous process of measuring products, service, and practices against the toughest competition or those companies recognized as industrial leaders."[1] A more strategic definition of benchmarking is "measuring an organization's performance against that of best-in-class companies, determining how the best in class achieve those performance levels and using the information as the basis for one's own company's targets, strategies, and implementation."[2] Regardless of how the definition is worded, the underlying principles are the same: (1) gain insight into the "best of the best" operations and (2) use this knowledge to gain a competitive advantage through identifying, understanding, measuring, and implementing improvements in all areas of the organization.

TYPES OF BENCHMARKING

The benchmarking process is not a new concept. The IBM Corporation, recipient of the 1990 Malcolm Baldrige National Quality Award, began identi-

Source: Reprinted from *Total Quality Management: The Health Care Pioneers* by M.M. Melum and M.K. Sinioris, pp. 325–334, published by American Hospital Publishing, Inc., © 1992. All rights reserved.

fying its best management processes during the 1960s by comparing *internal* practices worldwide. Xerox performed a similar comparison in the late 1970s. Both of these organizations initiated internal benchmarking and utilized it as a management tool for determining the best practices within their organizations. Internal benchmarking is common in most health care organizations and involves comparing the organization's functions and processes over time to track improvements. Internal benchmarking does not, however, challenge the potential maximum effectiveness of an organization's processes. Accordingly, the concept of external benchmarking was conceived.

After mastering internal benchmarking, Xerox began *external* benchmarking against competitors. The term *competitor* is used in the broadest sense. External benchmarking can be performed against any organization, from one's own industry or other industries, that has achieved excellent standards for a particular function.

In general there are two types of external benchmarking:

- *Competitive benchmarking* involves comparing an organization to competitors marketing the same direct product or service. Competitive benchmarking could be as simple as comparing a hospital's length of stay by service to that of competing institutions in the same service area. More advanced competitive benchmarking might include identifying the best patient outcomes for each service, measured by such factors as mortality rates, nosocomial infections, patient mobility, and so on. Comparison of practice patterns and resource consumption profiles against those of competitors will begin the process of planning for improvement.

- *World-class benchmarking* involves benchmarking against organizations outside of one's specific industry. This type of external benchmarking can be applied to a particular process (such as patient discharge) or to an individual activity (such as order fulfillment and supplier relations). A prime example of world-class benchmarking that is immediately apparent in health care is the billing and collection function, which is similar across numerous industries.

The objective of world-class benchmarking is to identify similar processes between one organization and other organizations that excel at those processes. The best service-oriented billing and collection function may well exist in a non-health care environment; however, these "best" functions will help a health care organization identify its "benchmarking gaps."

A benchmarking gap is the difference between an organization and the industry averages compared to world-class functions. Consider again, for example, the billing and collection function. One could compare the number of bills processed and collected per full-time equivalent (FTE) position. Initially this may seem like a rudimentary comparison. However, recognizing the "gap" between one organization and other organizations may initiate creative concepts of process improvement. An illustration of a benchmarking gap is shown in Figure 13–1.

Limiting the comparison to industry averages limits its potential effectiveness. Comparing an organization's process to that of other industries begins to identify improvement techniques such as:

- improved information collection techniques
- automated process capabilities
- patient (customer) collection approaches
- other unanticipated techniques

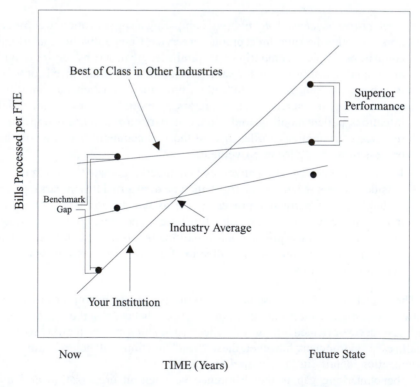

Figure 13–1 Benchmarking Gap. *Source:* Reproduced, with permission, from R.C. Camp, *Benchmarking: The Search for Industry Best Practices That Lead to Superior Performance,* Milwaukee, WI: ASQC Quality Press, 1989.

These studies also lead to the integration of other TQM principles, such as empowerment of employees and error-free attitudes, which are more common in the management of world-class processes.

External benchmarking is foreign to most health care organizations but is a common practice of other world-class organizations. Well-documented examples of external benchmarking used by Xerox Corporation include using the American Hospital Supply system to benchmark automated inventory control, the L.L. Bean system to benchmark warehousing and distribution, and the American Express system to benchmark billing and collection processes and procedures. Each of these other businesses has excelled in the identified areas. Xerox was prudent in turning to the best of the best to evaluate and benchmark its processes.

The health care industry has a number of processes that warrant benchmarking, in addition to the billing and collection function. Some of the processes are:

- reward and recognition programs
- recruiting programs and costs
- inventory turns
- medication costs
- case-mix index
- new service introduction process
  - orientation program
  - benefits
- training
- suggestion program
- building and equipment maintenance

THE BENCHMARKING PROCESS

The benchmarking process is a systematic approach to gaining superior information and is not simply comparing oneself to a set of standardized procedures. World-class leaders in benchmarking have identified three generic benchmarking phases:

1. planning
2. data collection and analysis
3. process improvement

The three phases can be applied to both the internal and external benchmarking processes. Following is a summary of the steps to be performed in each phase.[3] (The phases and steps of benchmarking are outlined in Exhibit 13–1.)

Exhibit 13–1 Phases and Steps in the Benchmarking Process

Phase	Internal	External
I. Planning	• Identify what to benchmark	• Identify what to benchmark
	• Determine benchmark measurements	• Determine benchmark measurements
	• Develop a data collection plan	• Develop a data collection plan
	• Select internal locations/departments	• Identify best external organizations
II. Data Collection and Analysis	• Collect data	• Research data elements
	—————	• Interview/surveys
	• Form a corporate benchmarking committee	—————
	• Location visits	• Location visits
	—————	• Select and collect data
	• Data analysis	• Data analysis
III. Process Improvement	• Process change plan	• Process change plan
	• Implement and measure changes	• Implement and measure changes
	• Updating the data base	• Updating the data base
	• Ongoing reporting	• Ongoing reporting

Phase 1: Planning

The planning phase is the backbone of the entire benchmarking process. Benchmarking plans that are organized and properly designed provide a much better set of results. The steps in the planning phase are very similar for both internal and external benchmarking. During this phase the services, processes, and/or activities to be benchmarked are identified, as are the internal-external benchmarking partners. In addition, the methods of data collection are determined at this time. Some examples of data collection methods include telephone or personal interviews, surveys, research, and focus groups.

Phase 2: Data Collection and Analysis

At this stage, implementation begins for the steps developed in the planning phase. The final selection of the external benchmarking partners is based on research. Once the data have been collected, the data analysis process begins.

The process of translating collected data into usable information is a critical component. It is important to utilize qualitative data as well as quantitative data in performing the analysis. The "best" processes may not come solely from one organization. It may be necessary to combine the activities of several organizations in order to determine a new best practice.

Phase 3: Process Improvement

In this phase, the organization determines the changes, if any, needed to achieve improvement. If changes are implemented, they should be done one at a time in order to evaluate the impact of each change independently. An internal report should be developed and issued periodically that compares performance by location or department. Also, a system should be established to periodically update the data base.

APPLICATION OF THE BENCHMARKING PROCESS

When an organization adopts benchmarking, it usually begins with an internal process and then expands to external organizations. World-class organizations perform external benchmarking on a cross-industry basis. The benchmarking process can require a significant commitment for an organization. For that reason, it is imperative to obtain management approval and commitment to change before beginning the process. In general, the benchmarking process will help an organization achieve its quality vision and objectives through observing what the competition is currently doing and then projecting that performance for the future.

Obviously, the planning phase is essential to an effective benchmarking effort. It is during this phase that the majority of common problems arise. Typically, it is conceptually difficult to identify benchmarking organizations outside of one's industry. If they are identified, comparable data are often unavailable and must be constructed. The analysis and process improvement phases often require visiting other organizations to study their activities. These organizations are often unwilling to spend the time to assist another organization in its study. If they are diligently pursued, however, the end result can be significant.

THE MALCOLM BALDRIGE NATIONAL QUALITY AWARD

The importance of benchmarking has been amplified with its identification as one of the major elements successful TQM organizations must demonstrate in applying for the Malcolm Baldrige National Quality Award (MBNQA). The benchmarking category of the Baldrige Award asks an organization to describe its approach to selecting quality-related competitive comparisons and benchmarks. Specifically, the areas to address include the rationale and criteria the organization used in making choices; the current scope of its data; and the organization's evaluation and improvement process of the scope, sources, and uses of the data. On the basis of the Baldrige Award examination criteria, the benchmarking process demands a great deal of time and planning. However, if the process is implemented in the proper way, the payback to an organization can be immeasurable.

THE STATUS OF BENCHMARKING IN HEALTH CARE

Benchmarking is not a new business strategy concept, but it has been refined significantly over the years. Although health care organizations have been comparing themselves with other health care providers for many years, classical benchmarking is relatively new to the health care industry. Numerous health care data bases are available in the public domain that show comparisons of various hospital components. But is this really benchmarking? Some of the most common types of data bases available are based on total costs, salaries and wages, case-mix index, and materials management. Although all of these appear to be adequate bases for rudimentary comparisons, there are limitations associated with each of them. For example, the majority of the data bases consist of only statewide data, thereby limiting the richness of the potential comparative information. To gain a better understanding of what is currently being done in the health care industry, it is necessary to look at a few types of data bases in detail. Three data bases—statewide, department-specific, and financial—are discussed briefly in the following text.

- *Statewide Data Base.* One well-known and frequently used statewide data base is the *Maryland Database*. It consists of total and component costs for each Maryland hospital and is maintained by the rate-setting commission. The Maryland rate-setting commission has built this data base by mapping the chart of accounts to relative value units. These units are based on procedure levels by department. The data base uses four categories for comparisons:
  - salaries and wages
  - productivity
  - nonlabor costs
  - other

One benchmarking limitation of this data base is that it utilizes only statewide data and contains averages of hospital statistics instead of determining the best of each category.

- *Department-Specific Data Base*. Another type of health care data base, developed for a specific function, is department-specific. A good example of this type is based on the survey conducted by Ohio Hospital Management Services (OHMS). Ohio Hospital Management Services distributes an annual survey to all Ohio hospitals requesting information on their materials management system (such as purchasing, receiving, central sterile supply, and so forth). These data are summarized by question, and the results are reproduced as a comparative data base.
- *Financial Data Base*. The American Hospital Association (AHA) has developed a financial data base that captures utilization statistics, revenue statistics, labor utilization, labor cost, capital, total expense, and operating margin. These data can be manipulated so that they are comparative by year, bed size, and region to determine how hospitals of a defined bed size compare operationally with other hospitals. This information, however, does not identify the processes associated with the best outcomes; it only provides comparisons.

These and other similar data bases are what the health care industry has been using for its comparisons. Raw comparisons within an industry are a first step for advancing understanding, but true benchmarking requires an organization to go one step further. The question to ask is: What is the organization comparing its practices with—best, good, adequate, or poor practices? These "benchmarking" questions may not be answered with simple comparative information that is readily available to the public. The health care industry needs to consider a formal benchmarking process in order to answer classic quality questions. What is the difference between what the health care industry is doing—called competitive analysis—and benchmarking? It goes back to this chapter's opening comments about who, what, when, where, why, and how, which are the questions answered by classic benchmarking, whereas competitive analysis answers only the questions who and what. The chart depicted in Exhibit 13–2 begins to demonstrate the differences between simplified competitive analysis and comparison benchmarking.

The most significant benchmarking issue hospitals face is the identification of world-class data sets to benchmark against. One needs to look outside as well as inside the health care industry to identify these data sets. Two of the fundamental principles of total quality management are "management by fact" and "continuous improvement." Benchmarking is essential to successful performance in each of these criteria. Management by fact requires organizations to collect meaningful data to use as a basis for cutting-edge decision making.

Exhibit 13–2 Summary Differences among Approaches for Competitive Analysis and Benchmarking

Item	Competitive Analysis	Benchmarking
Generic Purpose	Analyze competitive strategies	Analyze what, why, and how well competition or leading companies are doing
Usual Focus	Competitive strategies	Business practices that satisfy customer needs
Application	Marketplace and products	Business practices as well as products
Usually Limited To	Marketplace activities	Not limited, competitive, functional, and internal benchmarking are used
Information Sources	Industry analysts, etc.	Industry leaders as well as competitors

Source: Reprinted, with permission, from R. C. Camp, *Benchmarking: The Search for Industry Best Practices That Lead to Superior Performance*. Milwaukee, WI: ASQC Quality Press, 1989.

Continuous improvement requires a belief that, no matter how well something is done, it can always be done better. Benchmarking is a key to the successful application of these TQM principles.

BENCHMARKING IN THE FUTURE

To advance the potential of benchmarking for the field of health care in relation to determining best management practices, the American Quality Foundation is conducting the International Quality Study (IQS). The American Quality Foundation, an independent, nonprofit entity formed under the auspices of the American Society for Quality Control, examines the cross-cultural implications of quality improvement efforts. The International Quality Study will seek to understand the best management practices across four industries—health care, banking, automotive, and computer—and four countries—Canada, Germany, Japan, and the United States. More than 250 hospitals have completed surveys and are included in this data base.

This is the first such study ever conducted of this magnitude, complexity, and international significance. The results produced will serve as a benchmark for quality progress. One of the most interesting features of this study is that it demonstrates that service sectors (health care and banking) and manufacturing sectors have many common practices contributing to world-class quality production and service delivery. The study also demonstrates that it is possible to learn a superior approach to performing specific processes from unrelated industries. This is particularly important to the health care industry in that it has always used data bases that were exclusively health care based.

The International Quality Study consists of more than 125 questions in five basic categories:

- business organization
- service development
- delivery process and customer satisfaction
- quality and strategic positioning
- culture

Each question has been answered by each industry participant in each country. The resulting data base will be subjected to "causal" modeling to determine the relationships among various factors that result in "world-class" performance.

The International Quality Study is both an assessment tool and an external benchmarking tool to identify benchmark gaps between a hospital's existing processes and the best performance processes. Completing the IQS has provided hospitals with a starting point to build a quality improvement plan to achieve world-class performance in all of their processes. This benchmarking function is yet another valuable and essential step toward improvement.

Initial analysis has been performed on the data base. The initial findings have been organized into four areas:

- *Business Performance.* In the area of business performance, the data show that hospitals expect to increase their emphasis on using quality as an assessment criterion for management performance. For example, 51 percent of U.S. hospitals and 48 percent of Canadian hospitals believe that within the next three years the quality performance of the organization will be a primary criterion in assessing the performance and compensation for senior management. If this statement is to become a reality, hospitals must begin defining and measuring quality. In other words, quality defined in measurable terms must become an integral part of the management process. The current mind-set of management is to review only financial data. In addition to well-established financial indicators, management must develop measurement systems that also link quality to performance. In Germany and Japan, the anticipated percentage of hospitals indicating quality performance as being of primary importance as an assessment criterion for senior management is much less: 7 and 27 percent, respectively. This raises more questions, which will require additional analysis.

- *Customer Focus*. The second area probed in the International Quality Study is customer focus. In today's competitive environment, strategic planning is a critical element in the management process. Although the voice of the customer is proclaimed to be heard and embedded into organizations' strategic planning, the IQS results show that only 31 percent of U.S. hospitals place primary importance on this element. United States hospitals predict that in the future more than 70 percent of the hospitals will view customer satisfaction as a primary criterion in the strategic planning process. In Canada, hospitals currently view customer satisfaction as a primary criterion 25 percent of the time but predict that in the future 50 percent of Canadian hospitals will focus on customer service as a primary indicator in building strategic plans. The plan to increase customer involvement demonstrates the need to have an advanced understanding of customer expectations in order to be competitive.

  In support of this finding is a related question on the importance of the use of technology in meeting customer expectations. When trends for countries over time are examined, Japanese hospitals not only currently lead other nations at 43 percent in the use of new technologies to meet patient expectations, but also are planning to increase the use of this approach to 58 percent to continue their leadership position in this area. Canadian hospitals placing primary emphasis on technology are projecting greater than a threefold increase, from 11 to 36 percent, over the next three years. German hospitals are also planning an increase, from 19 to 36 percent. United States hospitals are intending an increase of 165 percent (from 17 to 45 percent) in the use of technology to meet customer expectations.

- *Process Improvement*. Process improvement, as defined in this study, applies not only to service development but also to all business functions within an organization. Canadian and U.S. hospitals have only minimally embraced the practices of process improvement, including cycle time reduction and process simplification. Only 4 percent of Canadian hospitals and 5 percent of U.S. hospitals currently use process simplification on a routine basis to improve business processes. Further, Canadian and U.S. hospitals report that 50 and 48 percent of the hospitals, respectively, seldom or never use cycle time analysis (a tool to compress time in business processes). There is a need for North American hospitals to recognize the value of these practices as the competitive pressures continue from declining reimbursements, alternative health care sources, and shortages of skilled medical professionals.

- *Employee Involvement*. One of the basic principles of total quality management is employee involvement. Traditional management styles emphasize the use of departmental teams. However, many organizations are beginning to see the value of cross-functional teams as a method of solving business problems and plan to use them in the future. Sixty percent of Canadian hospitals and 84 percent of U.S. hospitals report that 25 percent or less of their employees are currently involved in quality-related programs. Interesting to note, Canada and the United States anticipate that three years from now the percentage of hospitals with employees in this category will decrease to 29 and 41 percent, respectively. Another aspect of employee involvement is participation in regular meetings about quality. Only 14 percent of North American hospitals indicate that 75 percent or more of their employees participate in quality meetings. These statements show that,

Exhibit 13–3 Key Objectives and Expected Results from Benchmarking

Without Benchmarking	With Benchmarking
Defining customer requirements	
Based on history or gut feel	Market reality
Perception	Objective evaluation
Low fit	High conformance
Establishing effective goals and objectives	
Lacking external focus	Credible, unarguable
Reactive	Proactive
Lagging industry	Industry leading
Developing true measures of productivity	
Pursuing pet projects	Solving real problems
Strengths and weaknesses not understood	Understanding outputs
Route of least resistance	Based on best industry practices
Becoming competitive	
Internally focused	Concrete understanding of competition
Evolutionary change	New ideas of proven practices and technology
Low commitment	High commitment
Industry best practices	
Not invented here	Proactive search for change
Few solutions	Many options
Average of industry progress	Business practice breakthrough
Frantic catchup activity	Superior performance

Source: Reproduced, with permission, from R. C. Camp, *Benchmarking: The Search for Industry Best Practices That Lead to Superior Performance*. Milwaukee, WI: ASQC Quality Press, 1989.

although health care organizations are talking about changing their management style, it has not yet become a reality.

These initial findings touch on only a small portion of the total potential information, insight, and data that have been developed—and are still in process—as part of this landmark study. The American Quality Foundation believes that, when the rich data base becomes available, it will be able to determine the management practices that constitute the best practices within each industry group, as well as the world-class practices that transcend industries. This study should encourage the health care industry to take a look at current practices and begin to think about where it is heading in the future relative to world-class performance.

Once the benchmarking process is complete, an organization will have a data base that contains information that will enable it to evaluate its practices and processes against existing world-class organizations. In turn, the organization will be able to develop goals and objectives for the future based on projections of today's world-class organizations. By accomplishing this task, the organization will be on its way to becoming one of the very best—and only the very best organizations will survive the 1990s.

Key objectives and expected results from benchmarking are identified in Exhibit 13–3.

NOTES

1. H.J. Harrington, *Business Process Improvement: The Breakthough Strategy for Total Quality, Productivity, and Competitiveness* (New York City: McGraw–Hill, 1991), 218.

2. K. Bemowski, Benchmarking Bandwagon, *Quality Progress* 24, no. 1 (Jan 1991): 19.

3. Harrington, *Business Process Improvement,* 233.

14. Quality Assurance and Quality Improvement in the Information Age

Kathryn L. Coltin and David B. Aronow

INTRODUCTION

The increase in "value-driven" competition among health care providers and insurers, coupled with renewed pressure on third-party payers to ensure that cost-containment initiatives do not compromise quality of care, has increased the demand for information on the quality and efficiency of care delivered in all settings. The demand for usable information is likely to escalate with the continued diffusion of quality management techniques in the health care industry. The operative term is "usable information." Most health care managers and clinicians are drowning in data, but data are not necessarily information and not all information is usable.

Usable information, in the context of both quality assurance (QA) and quality improvement (QI) activities, is timely, reliable, and actionable. It empowers managers and clinicians to: fix what goes wrong; learn from what goes right; reach increasingly higher levels of service, efficiency, and technical quality; achieve better outcomes for their "customers"; and know when they have done so.

Automated information systems and technologies can be powerful tools for producing usable information, but are we using these systems to their full potential? This paper addresses the following questions:

- How do QA and QI differ with respect to their information needs?
- To what extent can currently available information systems provide potentially usable information for QA and QI? What types of information are

Source: Excerpted with permission of the Harvard Community Health Plan, Brookline, Massachusetts, 1993.

being used now, and how are automated information systems being used to provide that information?

- What additional types of data are needed through automated information systems if QA/QI needs for usable information are to be met in a low-cost, timely, and reliable manner?
- To what extent are information technologies being used to access, analyze, and disseminate information from single or multiple linked information systems? What industry practices facilitate or impede such efforts?
- How can emerging information technologies be used to increase the range and quality of data available through automated information systems and the options available for data linkage, processing, analysis, display, and transmission? What new technologies are needed?
- What are the pragmatic and policy issues that must be addressed to realize the potential of current and emerging information technologies to improve health care quality and efficiency?

AUTOMATED INFORMATION SYSTEMS AND QUALITY ASSURANCE/QUALITY IMPROVEMENT

QA has been described by Steinwachs as involving the measurement of quality as one step in a process that "monitors quality of care indicators; conducts quality assessments where indicators suggest potential problems may exist; makes recommendations for improving care based on the assessment; and continues to monitor the problems into the future."[1]

QI may be described as the application of scientific methods to understand and continuously improve the ability of all processes to meet the needs of customers. The principal steps in the QI process include:

- Identifying an opportunity for improvement, typically resulting from the measurement of defects in the output of a process or inefficiencies in the process itself (for example, cost, cycle time).
- Diagnosing the root causes of defects in products or services (outputs) or inefficiencies in processes and differentiating systemic from extra-systemic causes.[2]
- Exploring alternative interventions to achieve improvements.
- Implementing solutions.
- Monitoring performance to hold the gains.

On the surface, the QA and QI process descriptions appear very similar, but in implementation, they generally have been quite different. This is particularly true in hospitals, where the majority of QA activities have been mandated and where QA has typically been translated into "peer review." Several authors have described the differences between QA and QI[3-6] which are summarized in Table 14–1. These differences in customers, goals, focus, objectives, measures, actions, and other features all contribute to differing information needs.

INFORMATION NEEDS FOR QI/QA: SIMILARITIES AND DIFFERENCES

In health care, QI encompasses both clinical and operational processes and includes as customers all of the following: the "users" (patients and their

Table 14–1 Quality Assurance vs. Quality Improvement in Health Care Institutions

Characteristic	Quality Assurance	Quality Improvement
Customers	Regulators	External: patients, enrollees, families, payers, etc. Internal: caregivers, managers, technicians, support staff, etc.
Goal	Regulatory compliance	Meet customer needs
Direction	Central coordinator or committee	Decentralized through the management line
Focus	Physician	Processes
Performance measure	External standards	Capability/need
Objective	Control	Breakthrough
Defects studied	Outliers/special causes ("extra-systemic")	Common ("systemic") and special causes
Viewpoint	Reactive	Proactive
Participants	Peers	All
Functions involved	Few—mainly physician	Many—clinician and support system
Tampering	Common	Rare
Review method	Summary	Analysis
Action taken	Recommend improvements	Implement improvements
Measurement and reporting	Ad hoc, sporadic	Routine, periodic

Source: Adapted from Berwick (1990) and Fainter (1991).

families), "nonusers" (the population for whom an insurer or a health care delivery organization assumes responsibility), public and private payers of services or insurance benefits, and all of the clinical and nonclinical staff involved in direct care or operational support processes.

While QA programs have relied on data to identify problems in the quality of care provided by health care services, historically they have ignored the issue of underutilization in their service area, enrolled population, or patient base. Often this has resulted from a lack of data on the nonutilizing population. This is particularly true among fee-for-service providers who have difficulty updating and maintaining patient files, given the migration of patients among providers and geographic regions. For products or services that are population based, such as screening or immunization rates, effective QI efforts will require information on both users and nonusers of a provider's services.

Although QA activities generally have been undertaken primarily to comply with regulatory requirements, the goal of QI is to meet customer needs more effectively. Data on the needs of both external customers (enrollees and patients) and internal customers (staff working within the care process who must depend on other staff to carry out their part of the process) are crucial to QI analyses. QA departments, especially in hospitals, have tended to see the collection and use of patient preference or satisfaction data as more in the domain of planners or market researchers than QA staff and the use of staff satisfaction survey data as principally a human resource department function. QI teams, however, recognize these data as important sources of information on unmet needs and/or deficiencies in care processes.

QA activities traditionally have focused on physician decisions and actions and ultimately on identifying the poor performers and improving or removing them. QI philosophy recognizes that people work within processes and that their ability to work up to their capabilities can be limited by the constraints of those processes.[7] Thus, data on process capability and performance are a requirement for QI analyses.

While QI does identify individual outliers in performance, that is not its principal focus. The improvement or removal of statistical outliers yields lesser gains than does improving the process capability for all performers. Thus, the central focus of QI is on achieving breakthroughs in process performance, rather than identifying "bad apples." To improve a process, QI efforts depend not only on the outcome (or proximate outcome) measures typical of QA indicators, but also on the availability of detailed data about the inputs to the process and the steps, characteristics, and temporal relationships of the process itself.

QA activities tend to be centralized and removed from the day-to-day activities of health care organizations, while QI activities engage the efforts of all members of the organization to improve their products and services by improving the processes in which they work. The QI process includes the implementation of solutions to process problems by those who work in and manage the process. QA managers, on the other hand, may recommend solutions only, and many such recommendations are never implemented. Data on the chronology of QI process initiatives must be documented to ensure consistent data on process performance measures (such as defect rates in products or services, cycle time, and cost per cycle) that will be used to assess their effectiveness over time—a quality control function.

In summary, QA programs generally have focused on what went wrong and who was responsible, not on why things went wrong. Nor have they used benchmarking techniques to examine why those same things go right in another population, delivery setting, or care context. Providing those responsible for the quality of care with information only on what went wrong often leaves them without a clue as to how care might be improved. It is the answers to the "why" questions that can provide managers and clinicians with the information they need to improve services and care outcomes.

QI focuses on the why questions by systematically analyzing characteristics of the processes that resulted in the observed defects in care. By understanding why, how, and when these processes fail, managers can act to redesign the processes and thereby improve care for all affected patients.

Recent changes in the focus of some of the regulatory agencies, such as the Joint Commission on Accreditation of Healthcare Organization's Agenda for Change, may bring the QA and QI processes closer together. In any event, many of the defects identified through QA monitoring can provide grist for the QI process, and many of the quality measurement techniques developed for QA can be used in a QI model. The data required to support the QI process, however, are both broader in scope and deeper in detail than those used for QA.

USEFULNESS OF AUTOMATED INFORMATION SYSTEMS

To answer questions about the quality and efficiency of health care delivery, accurate, reliable data are needed. Changes in technology and medical practices require that the data be relatively current (in some cases, concurrent) with care. In addition, the range of data collected must be expanded to determine whether differences in quality are due to differences in the population or the care process and to understand the causes of known quality problems.

A basic tool of quality management is "benchmarking." Benchmarking involves seeking out successful innovations in other settings and implementing them in one's own setting when appropriate, as well as identifying the top performers in each process area and striving to exceed their performance levels.

There is increasing interest in benchmarking among institutions, health care plans, and delivery settings.[8,9] For benchmarking to be effective, however, greater uniformity of coding practices, improved consistency in data definitions, and greater comparability in performance measures are necessary.

These factors, plus the escalating demand for data both from within and outside health care delivery settings, add urgency to calls for further development and implementation of accurate, efficient, and low-cost automated data collection, processing, and analysis techniques.

While automated information systems have been used extensively in health care to support QA monitoring and—in some settings—interventions, only recently have they been used to support formal QI initiatives.

PRAGMATIC AND POLICY ISSUES

The most difficult issue facing the field of information science is that of protecting the privacy and confidentiality of data. Issues related to the development and adoption of uniform standards for information exchange have technologic solutions near at hand, and leadership in adopting a specific set of standards for [medical information] MI systems at the federal, state, and professional society levels can greatly accelerate the widespread implementation of uniform standards. The adoption of a common patient identifier is methodologically and technically quite simple but legally and ethically complex. Such an action will make the linkage of multiple data bases at the patient level a straightforward technologic procedure that can be executed at any site having access to the necessary data bases. Likewise, emerging information technologies offer new capabilities to access and manipulate that data. Our current inability to safeguard the security, privacy, and confidentiality of such patient data stands out as a formidable barrier to widespread adoption of technologic advances in information processing to support QA and QI.

Concern over widespread computer access to private information is growing among the general public and among professionals in the information technology field.[10,11] The development of technologic solutions for ensuring data security and confidentiality is becoming a high priority, not only in health care, but in many other industries that collect and process sensitive information.[12] Recent advances in information technology offer some promising improvements in data and systems security, such as call-back modems for remote dial-up access and relational DBMSs [data base management systems] that allow controlled access at the row, column, or cell level, depending on the user ID and device. However, additional work in this area is needed if the widespread use of shared data bases for QA and QI is to become a reality.[13-18]

Another issue is related to the data itself. Two sets of activities are needed; first, we must accelerate the definition of uniform minimum data sets, and their development and reporting by institutions must be mandated by policy, as with UHDDS [Uniform Hospital Discharge Data Set], or the data bases necessary to support QA/QI efforts will not be available for linkage. Second, we must improve data quality through the widespread adoption of uniform coding practice standards and the auditing of compliance with these standards. Roper and Hackbarth[19] stated that one of HCFA's most important goals should be to increase the volume and quality of information available to the public. However, many authors have cited data quality problems in currently available administrative data bases and have called for improvements in both the kinds of data available[20–22] and the accuracy and consistency of coding practices.[23,24] Data quality is a fundamental concern. It will be a hollow victory if we succeed in addressing the legal, ethical, and technologic barriers to data base linkage and access only to find that the resulting diamond is really coal.

NOTES

1. D.M. Steinwachs, J.P. Weiner, and S. Shapiro, Management Information Systems and Quality, in *Providing Quality Care: The Challenge to Clinicians*, eds. N. Goldfield and D.B. Nash (Philadelphia: American College of Physicians, 1989), 160–182.

2. S.B. Kritchevesky and B.P. Simmons, Continuous Quality Improvement: Concepts and Applications for Physician Care, *Journal of the American Medical Association* 266 (1991): 1817–1823.

3. S.L. Andrews, QA vs. QI: The Changing Role of Quality in Health Care, *Journal of Quality Assurance* (Jan–Feb 1991): 14, 15, 38.

4. D.M. Berwick, Peer Review and Quality Management: Are They Compatible?, *Quality Review Bulletin* 16 (1990): 246–251.

5. J. Fainter, Quality Assurance Not Quality Improvement, *Journal of Quality Assurance* (Jan–Feb 1991): 8, 9, 36.

6. G. Laffel and D. Blumenthal, The Case for Using Industrial Quality Management Science in Health Care Organizations, *Journal of the American Medical Association* 262 (1989): 2869–2873.

7. D.M. Berwick, Continuous Improvement As an Ideal in Health Care, *New England Journal of Medicine* 320 (1989): 53–56.

8. M.R. Chassin, Quality of Care: Time to Act, *Journal of the American Medical Association* 266 (1991): 3472–3473.

9. A.L. Siu, E.A. McGlynn, H. Morgenstern, and others, A Fair Approach to Comparing Quality of Care, *Health Affairs*, (Spring 1991): 62–75.

10. V. Brannigan and B. Beier, Standards for Privacy in Medical Information Systems: A Technico-legal Revolution, in *Proceedings of the Fourteenth Annual Symposium on Computer Applications in Medical Care*, ed. R.A. Miller (Los Alamitos, CA: IEEE Computer Society Press, 1990), 266–270.

11. J. Weingarten, Can Confidential Patient Information Be Kept Private in High-Tech Medicine?, *MD Computing* 9 (1992): 79–82.

12. N. Cobb, The End of Privacy, *The Boston Globe Magazine*, 26 April 1992, 16, 17, 20.

13. Agency for Health Care Policy and Research, *The Feasibility of Linking Research-Related Data Bases to Federal and Non-Federal Medical Administrative Data Bases.* Rockville, MD: Author, 1991).

14. R.S. Dick and E.B. Steen, eds., *The Computer-Based Patient Record: An Essential Technology for Health Care* (Washington: National Academy Press, 1991).

15. General Accounting Office, *Medical ADP Systems: Automated Medical Records Hold Promise to Improve Patient Care* (Washington, D.C.: Author, 1991).

16. K.N. Lohr, S.D. Yordy, and S.O. Thier, Current Issues in Quality of Care, *Health Affairs* 7 (1988): 5–18.

17. B.G. Regan, Computerized Information Exchange in Health Care, *Medical Journal of Australia* 154 (1991): 140–144.

18. M. Walsh and F. Cortez, QA Systems Must Balance Functionality With Data Security, *Computers in Healthcare* 12 (1991): 35–36.

19. W.L. Roper and G.M. Hackbarth, HCFA's Agenda for Promoting High-Quality Care, *Health Affairs* 7 (1988): 91–98.

20. M.S. Blumberg, Comments on HCFA Hospital Death Rate Statistical Outliers, *Health Services Research* 21 (1987): 715–739.

21. M.R. Chassin, R.E. Park, K.N. Lohr, and others, Differences Among Hospitals in Medicare Patient Mortality, *Health Services Research* 24 (1989): 1–31.

22. K.L. Kahn, R.H. Brook, D. Draper, and others, Interpreting Hospital Mortality Data. How Can We Proceed?, *Journal of the American Medical Association* 260 (1988): 3625–3628.

23. M.S. Blumberg, Measuring Surgical Quality in Maryland: A Model, *Health Affairs* 7 (1988): 62–78.

24. Lohr, et al., Current Issues in Quality of Care.

15. Integrating Strategic Planning and Quality Management in a Multi-Institutional System

Steve Durbin, Claudia Haglund, and William Dowling

Integrating the concept of Total Quality Management (TQM) into the strategic planning process of a multi-institutional system presents an exciting opportunity to explore long-range quality goals across a continuum of facilities and services. In 1992, the Sisters of Providence Health System updated its system strategic plan with the specific intent of achieving a fuller integration of TQM into the life of the organization. This article describes the strategic planning process that was used, unique features and challenges of quality planning in a multi-institutional system, the system's philosophy regarding quality management, the quality strategies adopted, and planned implementation activities.

The Sisters of Providence Health System is a Catholic-sponsored, nonprofit system that has provided health and social services since 1856. Today, the system is one of the largest health care organizations in the western United States, with facilities in Alaska, Washington, Oregon, and California. At present, it operates 15 acute-care hospitals with a total of 3,637 beds, and 6 free-standing long-term care facilities and 5 hospital-based skilled nursing units with a total of 1,006 beds. The system's institutions range in size from 34 to 509 beds and are located in rural, suburban, and urban settings. In 1991, the system had a total of 135,282 admissions, over 2 million outpatient visits, 392,709 emergency room visits, and 233,541 home health and hospice visits. In addition, the system sponsors four managed care plans that serve over 400,000 individuals and manages several housing units for low-income elderly and disabled residents. Gross revenue for the system in 1991 was $1.3 billion. In that year, the system provided nearly $62 million in unsponsored community benefits to the poor, including $26.5 million in direct charity care.

Source: Reprinted from *Quality Management in Health Care*, Vol. 1, No. 4, pp. 24–34, Aspen Publishers, Inc., © 1993.

Quality management at the system level is broad in scope and designed to meet the oversight needs of the board of directors and support the quality improvement efforts of diverse institutions. Planning for system-level quality entails the articulation of a comprehensive philosophy regarding quality, development of policies to guide system activities, formulation of educational programs and training, establishment of mechanisms to exchange quality "intelligence," monitoring of selected quality measures, and creation of data bases to track information over time. At the system level, the main responsibility of the leadership is to encourage and support a culture and specific strategies that result in all aspects of organizational life being driven by the pursuit of quality.

Historically, the quality management efforts of our hospitals and nursing homes have been driven by accreditation and regulatory requirements. Since the late 1980s, we have taken steps to improve the effectiveness of the institution quality management programs, providing a strong base for the introduction of TQM. Each institution is responsible for carrying out an effective quality management initiative. Expectations for continuous quality improvement are reshaping how quality management is carried out and broadening the scope of those activities throughout the organization.

THE SISTERS OF PROVIDENCE PHILOSOPHY REGARDING QUALITY

The writings of Deming, Juran, and other quality leaders stress the importance of clear policies, in the form of vision, strategy, and plan statements, in leading an organization through the quality transformation. The first of Deming's 14 points is to create constancy of purpose for the improvement of products and services.[1] By stressing the need for constancy, Deming links quality improvement with planning for the future. The Sisters of Providence Health System Board of Directors adopted a quality philosophy and quality management guidelines in January 1990. The relevant documents make it very clear that our commitment to quality is rooted in our mission and values. Development of the philosophy and guidelines was led by the Quality of Care Committee of the board, which oversees the system's quality management reporting system. In drafting the philosophy statement, the committee deliberately integrated TQM principles with mission elements that address quality. At the time the statements were adopted, people within the system and institutions were actively learning and beginning to use TQM concepts. TQM concepts are reflected in the quality philosophy statement—in its call for continuous improvement and for the involvement of the medical staff and all employees across departmental lines in quality initiatives, and in its assertion that improving quality and lowering cost go hand in hand.

The philosophy statement was also accompanied by a definition of quality and a set of guidelines for quality management. The guidelines call for leadership involvement in improving quality, direct input from customer groups, use of teams, and attention to outcomes and effectiveness of care. During the development of the quality philosophy and guidelines, it was felt that these concepts were consistent with our core values. The Quality of Care Committee felt TQM principles and methods represented a positive, far-reaching alternative to the quality systems currently being used. Still, it was important to take the system's position on quality further. These quality statements were well crafted and we felt good about them, but without further work they were unlikely to have much impact on actual management behavior, care processes, and patient outcomes.

At the time these quality statements were developed, the system had not established an approach to TQM implementation, nor allocated the resources to support TQM methods. It began to do these things in late 1990. It is fair to say that the philosophy and guidelines did not create much change on their own, but their development and distribution contributed to a growing awareness of the principles and concepts of TQM throughout the Sisters of Providence Health System.

Some of the individuals who participated in the development of the quality philosophy were also pursuing the application of TQM within our own facilities. These individuals formed an informal network for sharing ideas and successes. The quality philosophy, networking across facilities, evidence from demonstration projects, and growing central support all contributed to increased interest in, learning about, and eventual adoption of TQM in many components of the system.

Like the health care industry in general, the Sisters of Providence Health System is aware of the forces for change in health care delivery. The external forces, discussed below, have led us to search continually for avenues of change and growth. The literature on TQM, its success in other industries, and its early applications in health care were effective in presenting TQM as a worthy alternative. Internally, leaders felt that TQM principles, because of their focus on individual needs and on participation, are very closely aligned with the system's core values. The alignment of values, the external pressures, and the successful internal demonstrations were strong contributing factors in the acceptance of TQM.

SITUATIONAL ASSESSMENT OF TQM IMPLEMENTATION

At the start of the system strategic planning cycle in 1992, awareness and application of TQM was growing rapidly. In 1991, system leadership had adopted a position on TQM designed to provide central support for our institutions to learn about, adopt, and apply its principles and methods. A planning task force recommended an approach to TQM implementation based on teaching, not mandating, TQM across the system's institutions and the system office. Such an approach was felt to be appropriate because of the system's culture, governance, and management systems. An extended study of the system characterized it as mostly analytic in its approach to the future, with a very strongly developed sense of culture and values. This characterization suggested that analysis and understanding of TQM would have to precede any significant move toward adoption and application of its principles and methods. The system's startup and adoption cycle is shown in Figure 15–1.

A study of TQM implementation conducted by system staff in fall 1992 concluded that a rapidly growing number of facilities are adopting TQM. They are implementing TQM at varying speeds based on a variety of factors. At present, central support through the system office includes training materials and

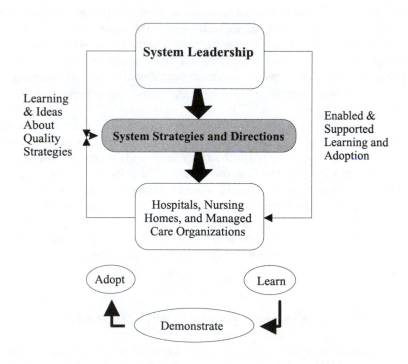

Figure 15–1 Total Quality Adoption and the Strategic Planning Process

support, links to consulting sources, networking among organizations inside and outside the system, consulting on startup and implementation, and participation in evaluative studies of TQM implementation.

While our supportive but decentralized approach to TQM adoption has created some variation in implementation at the institutional level, it is felt to engender increased institutional ownership of quality-driven strategies. One distinct disadvantage is that this approach is slower in creating a unified systemwide quality culture and may result in TQM implementation problems as individual institutions "re-learn" the common pitfalls of TQM implementation. The provision of central services is intended to minimize the disadvantages.

THE ROLE OF QUALITY IN THE STRATEGIC PLANNING PROCESS

Overview of the Strategic Planning Process

The components of the strategic planning process followed in the 1992 system plan are outlined in Figure 15–2.

The mission of the system has always emphasized respect for individual dignity and a commitment to provide compassionate, quality care that heals the total person. As expressed in the mission statement, "We continually seek to improve the quality of care we give and to maintain prudent stewardship of the human, physical, and financial resources that have been entrusted to us."

The strategic planning process for the system was carried out under the leadership of the Planning Committee of the board of directors. This group includes five members of the board, including the chairperson, the president, and a physician; representatives from a community and foundation board at the institutional level; a regional vice president for operations; the vice president for long-term care services and housing; the vice president for system finance; three institutional administrators; an assistant administrator for patient care services; a director of institutional planning; and three members of the Sisters of Providence religious community. The planning process was staffed by members of the system planning department. By contrast, the Quality Strategy Planning Committee included several institutional administrators and senior assistant administrators; the vice president for planning; two physicians; a medical director; and representatives from quality management, outcomes measurement, long-term care, and human resources.

One of the first steps in the strategic planning process was to assess trends in external, market, and internal performance (see Figure 15–3). The assessments involved the collection and analysis of demographic data, trending of utilization and financial information, and surveys of system leaders to identify key issues

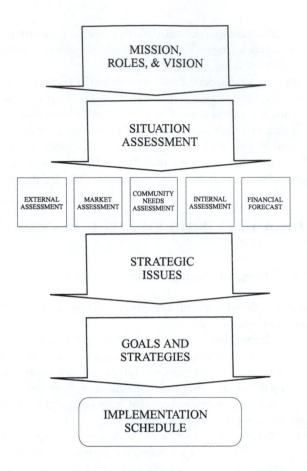

Figure 15–2 Components of the System Strategic Plan

and beliefs about the future of health care delivery. Key strengths of the system and areas requiring further attention and development are presented in the box entitled "Perceived System Strengths and Areas Requiring Attention." (Exhibit 15–1.) As shown, the leadership rated the system's mission of service, facilities, and financial systems very highly. However, the leadership was also very cognizant of the fact that health care delivery is on the brink of dramatic changes and challenges that will require organizations to develop closer relation-

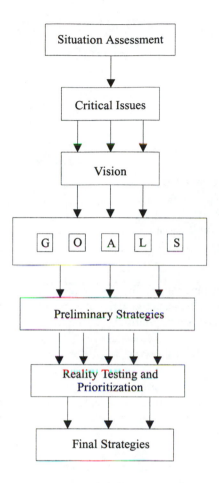

Figure 15–3 Process for Formulating Strategies

ships with physicians; more efficient delivery of care; greater coordination and integration of inpatient, outpatient, and long-term care services; and improved information systems to provide required information in a timely manner.

The Planning Committee next engaged in a visioning process to help clarify the preferred model for health care delivery and to pinpoint changes that would be required, both internally and externally, to realize the vision. The analysis of the strengths and limitations of the nation's health system and the internal capabilities and competencies of the Sisters of Providence Health System served

Exhibit 15–1 Perceived System Strengths and Areas Requiring Attention

Strengths
- Fulfillment of mission
- Quality facilities
- Financial systems and policies

Areas Requiring Attention
- Physician relations
- Development of regional delivery systems
- Delivery of cost-effective care
- Shift to outpatient services
- Information system development

to crystallize a vision for change. The resulting vision statement expresses the system's commitment to be an active participant in efforts to improve access to care, community health status, delivery cost-effectiveness, and outcomes of care.

In the strategic plan, the following definitions were used:

Vision: A short, inspiring statement of an organization's hopes, dreams, and beliefs about the future. It should communicate a picture of what the organization will look like in the years ahead and should guide the development of goals and strategies.

Goals: An expression of the fundamental commitments, directions, desired qualities, or market positions an organization seeks to achieve.

Strategies: Strategies indicate how goals will be achieved. Strategies are coherent, unifying, and integrating statements that reveal the organization's purpose in terms of priority actions and resource allocation decisions. Strategies position an organization in terms of values, quality, service or product lines, financial position, human resource requirements, and functional needs.

Many aspects of the system's vision touch upon quality as a comprehensive goal that unites the patient and provider in the search for improved processes and outcomes of care. Key aspects of the system's vision of the future that relate to quality include the following:

- guaranteed access by all individuals to quality health and social services that meet basic needs;

- healthier communities where care is organized around a coordinated continuum of services and providers;
- development of models of care that maximize health status and patient involvement;
- a rational and equitable system for managing health care costs;
- collaborative actions by physicians and other providers to maximize patient dignity, patient independence, and outcomes of care;
- significant progress in health education and disease prevention to improve the health status of the population;
- elimination of social causes of poor health status, such as poverty and discrimination;
- provision of work environments where employees are empowered to exercise their knowledge and skills; and
- involvement of the community in health planning.

The goals and strategies in the system's strategic plan were grouped into six key themes derived from the vision:

1. leading in changing times
2. improving community health
3. building comprehensive care systems
4. excelling in quality
5. commitment to people
6. managing for effective stewardship

Strategic needs and directions in the area of "excelling in quality" were the responsibility of a special task force described in the next section.

The Quality Subcommittee and the Quality Section of the Plan

Under the strategic planning model, the Quality of Care Committee of the board of directors was given the formal responsibility for developing strategies related to quality of care. The Quality of Care Committee in turn appointed a multidisciplinary subcommittee to draft concepts and recommended strategies. The subcommittee was purposely selected to bring together senior management with other experts in finance, information systems, and quality management as well as physician leaders and nurse executives experienced with TQM concepts and their application. Once formed, it was directed to develop strategies for improving clinical care and applying quality improvement methods to the broader strategic issues facing the system.

The subcommittee was presented with information on a variety of factors pertinent to its charge. These included descriptive inputs on quality issues from the situation assessment, an overview of present efforts toward implementing TQM; and information on future developments and ideas for TQM applications in health care settings, such as information on patient-focused delivery systems, case management, applications of systems thinking in modifying complex systems, principles and implications of integrated and managed care delivery systems, and developments in outcome and quality performance measurement. The subcommittee also was given the vision statement for the system and the quality philosophy statement described above.

In this planning cycle, we did not have any substantial data on system quality performance in the area of patient care quality. Nor did we have customer feedback at a system level. The situation assessment had information on market positioning and other volume and financial performance data. Essentially the subcommittee's work was based on descriptive information, not statistical data. As with many multihospital systems, data from quality indicators such as inpatient mortality, complications, and infections have been collected and trended for years. These data were not felt to be instructive regarding strategic aspects of quality performance.

Over several meetings, the subcommittee used techniques such as brainstorming, grouping by affinity diagrams, and multivoting to identify and consolidate issues into seven categories, which were divided into two groups: primary strategic issues and enabling and other issues. The three primary issues were assigned the highest priority by the subcommittee.

- Primary strategic issues:
    1. improving quality in organized, managed delivery systems
    2. providing person-centered, compassionate care
    3. improving appropriateness of, cost of, and access to care
- Enabling and other issues:
    4. improving the use of the quality data and best practices
    5. empowering caregivers
    6. addressing ethical issues
    7. providing education on total quality management

Using these issue groupings, the subcommittee next brainstormed strategic options to address the issues. This generated a long list of items, some with major long-range implications and others with an actionable, narrow focus. These were then synthesized and grouped down to a shorter, prioritized list.

DEVELOPMENT OF QUALITY GOALS AND STRATEGIES

After agreeing upon the major issues the system faced in the area of quality, the subcommittee proceeded with the development of goals and strategies to address these issues. To begin, the group agreed on a set of assumptions concerning the system's quality philosophy. These are summarized in the box entitled "Assumptions Guiding the Development of Quality Strategies." (Exhibit 15–2.)

The assumptions serve the purpose of communicating the system's beliefs about quality in a succinct manner within the strategic plan document. The assumptions also provided a framework for the development of goals and strategies and a means of testing whether the strategies were leading the system in the desired direction. The approved plan contains these assumptions, which is very helpful in communicating the central tenets of our approach to TQM and quality. Communicating the system strategic plan throughout the system and

---

Exhibit 15–2 Assumptions Guiding the Development of Quality Strategies

1. Total quality management is a means of furthering our mission and organizational culture. This means that:
   - Patients and others we serve are our highest priority and should have a strong voice in the design and delivery of care.
   - Quality results from continuously improving care and work processes.
   - Processes are improved by teamwork and involvement.
   - Decisions should be based on facts, but reflect compassion and caring.
   - Quality must flow from leadership and permeate all levels of the organization.
2. Total quality management is a unifying leadership philosophy that encompasses all that we do, not just the quality assurance function and clinical care.
3. Measurement of quality care must include:
   - Patient feedback and involvement
   - Determination of patient outcomes
   - Review of key internal processes
   - Assurance of appropriateness of care
   - Proper coordination of care across a continuum of services and providers
   - Cost effectiveness
4. Quality improvement requires timely access to accurate clinical data and the ability to analyze and interpret clinical pathways.
5. Our system will increasingly be responsible for the delivery of quality care to enrolled populations on a regional basis.

ensuring it has a meaningful effect on activities within the institutions is always challenging. The plan is communicated through distribution to senior institutional managers and institutional board members and also through special presentations and summary documents.

After lengthy discussion, the subcommittee agreed on four central quality goals and a number of strategies for each of the goals. These are described below.

Goal: Provide Person-Centered Compassionate Care That Respects Individual Dignity and Is Responsive to the Needs of Patients, Residents, Families, and Others Served

Strategies

- Maximize the involvement of patients and families in the care experience by improving patient involvement in care choices and by the use of shared decision making.
- Ensure the assessment of patient, medical staff, and employee satisfaction on a regular basis, incorporating survey standards and benchmarking.
- Implement recommendations concerning compassionate care of the dying.
- Address the spiritual needs of patients and families through pastoral care.

Goal: Engage Board Members, Employees, and Physicians in System Efforts to Implement TQM

Strategies

- Develop educational programs on TQM for board members, employees, and physicians.
- Involve physicians in the development of treatment protocols and the improvement of care systems.
- Develop and apply management models that engender effective teamwork and participatory decision making.

Goal: Develop a System Perspective on Analyzing and Communicating Information and Data on the Appropriateness, Quality, Outcomes, and Cost of Care

Strategies

- Document and share key quality performance and outcome studies throughout the system.

- Develop a system plan to address information needs associated with quality management, including common definitions, a core clinical data set, and enhanced analysis of available information.
- Further develop the skills and competencies of system personnel involved in quality management through users conferences and other means.
- Assess and evaluate the implications of new developments in the evolution of electronic medical records.

Goal: Support a Quality Management Approach That Furthers Coordination of Care Across the Continuum of Providers and Services

Strategies

- Further develop and apply case management models, especially across the continuum of services.
- Stimulate development of treatment protocols through collaborative efforts by our managed care plans and physicians.
- Determine how the development of integrated delivery systems can promote access and quality of care.

The quality section clearly included ideas based on TQM principles and concepts. Other subcommittees, including those looking at finance, operations, and human resources, also developed strategies that were based on TQM thinking. This resulted in broad incorporation of quality concepts throughout the plan. For example, the leadership section of the plan contains strategies related to transformational leadership, innovation, and systems thinking. The Subcommittee on Operations and Human Resources spent considerable time discussing the concepts of empowerment, learning, teamwork, and participation. This resulted in specific strategies to obtain employee input and involvement on a regular, systematic basis through quality of worklife surveys and representation on multidisciplinary teams. The Finance Committee focused on the value of clinical pathways, resource use analysis, and outcomes research in achieving more efficient and effective use of people and resources. The Finance Committee also identified the importance of greater interaction and teamwork among physicians, nurses, management, and other ancillary professionals for examining, critiquing, and improving the processes for delivering care.

IMPLEMENTATION OF QUALITY STRATEGIES

Implementation of the quality section of the plan is complicated by dilemmas facing our system over issues such as integration and centralization of directions and systems. Our historical tendency has been to give greater authority to the local CEOs, and our system is diverse in terms of types of organizations (hospitals, nursing homes, home health, and managed care organizations) and sizes (34 beds to over 400 beds). Many of the strategies outlined above require careful planning and integration with the operational systems of the facilities. One way to improve the link of system strategies to the individual organizations is through regional management structures. Regional forums to plan and implement strategies related to patient-focused care, patient satisfaction, pastoral care, use of clinical guidelines, and quality performance data can strengthen the link to the individual organizations.

Specific implementation tasks flowing from the quality strategies in the system plan include the following:

- providing more formalized direction, support, and modeling of TQM principles by the system's board of directors;
- developing an intensive TQM education program for top leadership within the system;
- providing greater standardization of the types of quality information gathered at the system level, including clinical data and patient or resident satisfaction surveys;
- strengthening existing mechanisms for collecting and disseminating quality studies and findings;
- providing support materials and resources for the care of dying patients;
- developing a framework for a system-level clinical database; and
- initiating research and further developing case management models.

MEASUREMENT OF QUALITY PERFORMANCE

Lack of sufficient, readily usable quality performance data was noted above as one of the concerns in this strategic planning cycle. This lack also affects the ability of the Quality of Care Committee and the board of directors to oversee the performance of the system. Present system-level quality measures are limited in scope but provide a sound base upon which to build. Further development of concepts and systems for measuring quality performance has implications for assessing plan implementation, governance, and future strategic planning cycles. The box entitled "Selected Quality Measures" lists measures called for in the plan to be used for evaluating the implementation of some of the strategies (Exhibit 15–3).

Exhibit 15–3 Selected Quality Measures

- Patient satisfaction
- Pain management as a major component of compassionate caring
- Spiritual needs assessment
- Measures of TQM implementation
- Quality of care outcomes and care process measures
- Clinical resource use improvement
- Appropriateness of care assessment
- Benchmarking to determine best practices
- Quality performance under capitated care systems

Work has started on two quality performance measurement models to help us frame and coordinate collection and analysis of data. The first model is based on three general categories of performance: effectiveness, efficiency, and economy. Establishment of a cross section of measures can provide a basis for broadly assessing quality performance. Under these three categories, critical success factors such as customer feedback, impact on health status, effectiveness of the care process, efficiency, and economic performance can be specified and measured for a given process. A number of present measures of quality can be incorporated into this framework and, where appropriate, aggregated into system-level measures. For example, a standardized patient satisfaction measure could be aggregated for a facility and then across facilities for the purpose of identifying trends and significant areas of variation.

These families of measures can also be used to assess the quality performance of key services or program groupings. The conceptualization of clinical program measures is moving forward in many health organizations across the country, as indicated in Figure 15–4, and the same general framework can be applied to defined care processes (e.g., total hip replacement) as well as clinical support and administrative processes. The family of measures framework has been demonstrated in the Admitting Benchmarking Study conducted by the Healthcare Forum and the American Quality and Productivity Association.

The family of measures framework is specifically suited to development of critical success factors and measures for processes that are common among organizations. As seen in the use of the framework for the Admitting Benchmarking Study, these measures can be defined and used for comparative performance evaluation across organizations. This makes the framework suitable for use at a system level in assessing quality performance. Where key processes and programs can be defined across organizations, a fair and rational basis for assessment and use of comparative information can be developed.

A Family of Measures
General Measurement Structure

Process Description

A Care Process–Patient Group

Measurement Group

| Effectiveness | | | | | Efficiency | | | | | Economy | | |

Critical Success Factors

Appropriate-ness of care	Patient Satisfaction	Long Term Health Status	Care Results	Readmissions, Complications, Errors	Effective Treatment	Care Process Variations	Errors & Rework	Length of Stay	Resource Use	Charges and Costs	Revenue and Net Revenue	Unit of Service Costs

Measurement Options

| Cases Meet Indications for Care | Survey Scores; Complaints | Health Perception-SF-36; Post-Care Functional Health | Discharge Health Status | Readmissions; Complications-Infections, Comorbidities; Physician Office Treatment of Complications | Time from Admit to Effective Care; Variations from Care Guidelines; Treatment Complications | Variations from Critical Path; Variations Due to Patient; Variations Due to Care Providers; Variations Due to Care System | Treatment Errors and Repeats | Time from Admit to Effective Care; Time Between Care Stages | Units of Service Used | Charges per Case; Cost per Case | Average Discount per Case; Capitation per Case; Contribution to Margin | |

Figure 15–4 Care Process Measurement Model. (Adapted from APQC and Healthcare Forum Admitting Benchmark Study.)

The initial work in this area uses an analysis of available data to look at significant program-specific care processes suitable for establishing measures as defined above. In the six Sisters of Providence hospitals in Washington, 12 inpatient program groups (cardiology, obstetrics, orthopedics, etc.) represent 80 percent of a combined index of case volume and total charges. Across these 12 program groups, 21 specific DRGs or combinations of clinically similar patients can be targeted based on their strategic significance to a program group. This analysis narrows the care processes down to a set that has a common definition across hospitals and that has like critical success factors. The model in Figure 15–4 can now be tailored for each of these processes, and measures can then be developed.

In a specific example using Pareto analysis, the orthopedics service line is third in ranking for volume and total charges among the Sisters of Providence hospitals in Washington. Orthopedics consists of 32 DRGs, of which DRG 209 (major joint procedure) accounts for 21 percent of cases and 43 percent of charges. Within DRG 209, hip and knee procedures account for most of the case volume and charges and are sufficiently homogeneous to allow the family of measures format to be applied. Improving performance of these care processes can have a strategic impact because of their significance within the orthopedics service line. This logic, applied across the 12 major service lines, allows greater strategic focus for quality improvement and measurement efforts. The selection of strategic "marker" conditions such as total hip replacement can also be tailored based on facility-specific data.

This measurement framework fosters the integration of measurement with the key TQM principles stated in the strategic plan (see the box entitled "Assumptions Guiding the Development of Quality Strategies," Exhibit 15–2). It brings together measurement methods and indicators such as outcome measures, patient satisfaction, current QA indicators (e.g., readmissions and complications), and other resource and economic measures. It also provides managers and care providers with a balanced approach for evaluating the performance of important care processes.

A second measurement approach is being used for evaluating managed care delivery systems. Development efforts are focused in two areas. One effort involves gathering useful, practical sets of health status data on enrollees in the Oregon managed care plan. A portion of this work is based on the SF-36 Health Perceptions Scale. Another measurement development effort involves tracking selected diseases and conditions across multiple care sites. For example, the health status of patients with chronic conditions such as hypertension can be tracked across different care sites and stages.

*   *   *

This article has described the approach used by a multi-institutional health system to create a unifying quality management system that bridges the gap between strategic direction setting and specific applications. The concepts inherent in TQM are valuable tools for organizing quality initiatives in a complex health system. Quality must be forcefully championed by the leadership, but it also must permeate all levels of the organization. Now that the Sisters of Providence Health System has established a framework for quality management through its strategic planning efforts, it must continue to pursue implementation and evaluate performance over time.

NOTE

1. M. Walton, *The Deming Management Method* (New York, N.Y.: The Putnam Publishing Group, 1986), 55.

16. Building Learning Organizations

Peter Senge

Without a unifying conceptual framework, the quality movement in the US risks being fragmented into isolated initiatives and slogans. *"The voice of the customer, fix the process not the people, competitive benchmarking, continuous improvement, policy deployment, leadership"*—the more we hear, the less we understand.

"Trying to put together the alphabet soup coming out of Japan of SPC, JIT, QIP, QFD, and so on can be hopelessly confusing without a unifying theme," says Analog Devices CEO Ray Stata. It is not surprising that, for many, it doesn't add up to much more than management's latest *flavor of the month* that must be endured until the next fad comes along.

Even those firms where there has been significant commitment to quality management for several years are encountering slowing rates of improvement. "We've picked all the low hanging fruit," as one Detroit executive put it recently. "Now, the difficult changes are what's left." The "difficult changes" are unlikely without a coherent picture of where we are trying to take our organizations through the quality management process.

Our Global Competitors. Equally troubling, the best of our international competitors are not fragmenting, they are building—steadily advancing an approach to improving quality, productivity, and profitability that differs fundamentally from the traditional authoritarian, mechanical management model.

Source: Reprinted from *Journal of Quality and Participation*, March 1992, pp. 30–38, with permission of the Association for Quality and Participation, Cincinnati, Ohio, © 1992.

"Total quality [TQ] is not a closed-ended methodology; its an open-ended methodology," says Shoji Shiba, of Japan's Tsukuba University. "TQ continues to develop according to the needs of society."

The tools American corporations are racing to master today, the frontier of the quality movement in Japan in the 1960s, are no longer the frontier. The "thought revolution in management," as quality pioneer Ishikawa called it, is still evolving.

Learning Organizations. I believe that the quality movement as we have known it up to now in the US is in fact the first wave in building *learning organizations*—organizations that continually expand their ability to shape their future.

The roots of the quality movement lie in assumptions about people, organizations, and management that have one unifying theme: to make continual learning a way of organizational life, especially improving the performance of the organization as a total system. This can only be achieved by breaking with the traditional authoritarian, command and control hierarchy where the top thinks and the local acts, to merge thinking and acting at all levels.

This represents a profound reorientation in the concerns of management—a shift from a predominant concern with controlling to a predominant concern with learning. Failure to come to grips with this shift plagues the efforts of many US firms eager to jump on the quality bandwagon.

Learning Organizations in Japan. Our Japanese competitors have no trouble with this shift. "Japan's greatest long-term comparative advantage is not its management system, Japan Inc., or quality," says C. Jackson Grayson Jr., of the American Productivity and Quality Center in Houston. "It's the Japanese commitment to learning." More specifically, as management practices in Japan have evolved over the past 40 years, there has been a steady spread of the commitment to learning—starting with statistical process control (SPC) for small groups of quality experts, to teaching quality improvement tools to frontline workers throughout the organization, to developing and disseminating tools for managerial learning.

Learning Waves. The evolution of learning organizations can be best understood as a series of waves. What most managers think of as quality management focuses on improving tangible work processes. This is the first wave.

The First Wave of Quality. In the first wave, the primary focus of change was frontline workers. Management's job was to:

- Champion continual improvement
- Remove impediments (like quality control experts and unnecessary bureaucracy) that disempowered local personnel
- Support new practices like quality training and competitive benchmarking that drive process improvement

The Second Wave of Quality. In the second wave, the focus shifts from improving work processes to improving how we work—fostering ways of thinking and interacting conducive to continual learning about the dynamic, complex, conflictual issues that determine system-wide performance. In the second wave, the primary focus of change is the managers themselves.

The Third Wave of Quality. These two ways will, I believe, gradually merge into a third, in which learning becomes *institutionalized* as an inescapable way of life for managers and workers alike (if we even bother maintaining that distinction).

We Are Still in the First Wave. American industry is, with a few exceptions, primarily operating in the first wave. "Despite all our improvements, the basic behavior of our managers, especially our senior managers, hasn't really changed much," laments the head of a major corporation's quality office.

Japan and the Second Wave. By contrast, the second wave is well underway in Japan, driven by their *seven new tools* for management, as distinct from their traditional *seven quality tools* that drove the first wave.

America's Challenge. The challenge today, as American companies endeavor to master the basic tools and philosophy of quality management, is not to be caught shortsighted with mechanical "quality programs." If we fail to grasp the deeper messages of the quality movement, we will one day awaken to discover ourselves chasing a receding target.

THE ROOTS OF THE QUALITY MOVEMENT

A close look at the roots of the quality movement shows that it has always been about learning.

"The prevailing system of management has destroyed our people," says Dr. [W. Edwards] Deming. "People are born with intrinsic motivation, self-esteem, dignity, curiosity to learn, joy in learning."

Intrinsic versus Extrinsic Motivation. Intrinsic motivation lies at the heart of Deming's management philosophy. By contrast, extrinsic motivation is the bread and butter of Western management.

The holiest of holy for the American manager, "People do what they are rewarded for," is actually antithetical to the spirit of quality management. This doesn't imply that rewards are irrelevant. Rather, it implies that no set of rewards, neither carrots nor sticks, can ever substitute for intrinsic motivation to learn. A corporate commitment to quality that is not based on intrinsic motivation is a house built on sand.

Motivate Them or Loose Their Own Motivation?

Consider, for example the goal of continuous improvement, which remains an elusive target for most American corporations.

Motivate Them. From an extrinsic perspective, the only way to get continuous improvement is to find ways to continually motivate people to improve, because people only modify their behavior when there is some external motivation to do so. Otherwise, they will just sit there—or worse, slide backwards. This leads to what workers perceive as management continually raising the bar to manipulate more effort from them.

Loose Their Motivation with Information and Appropriate Tools. However, from an intrinsic perspective, there is nothing mysterious at all about continuous improvement. If left to their own devices, people will naturally look for ways to do things better. What they need is adequate information and appropriate tools.

From the intrinsic perspective people's innate curiosity and desire to experiment, if unleashed, creates an engine for improvement that can never be matched by external rewards.

Learning and Intrinsic Motivation To Learn Have Always Been the Roots of Quality

A management system based on intrinsic motivation to learn is as befuddling to Western economists as it is to Western managers. Princeton economist Alan Blinder recently cited an impressive list of Japanese "violations" of economic orthodoxy—tolerated monopolies and cartels, single suppliers, salary scales that do not differentiate adequately between ranks, keeping promising young managers waiting too long for promotion, and "almost nothing gets you fired."

"We did the opposite of what American economists said," Blinder quotes a top Ministry of International Trade & Industry (MITI) official. "We violated all the normal rules." But the puzzle of how a nation that does so many things wrong can get so many things right dissolves when we realize that Western economic theories, from Adam Smith on, are based solely on extrinsic motivation.

The Way We Thought It Was. Adam Smith's *homo economicus* is presumed to maximize his income, not his learning. The following are some maxims of *US homo economicus:*

- If there is no opportunity for significant salary increase by climbing the corporate ladder, he will have little motivation to do his best or to improve.
- If there is no fear of dismissal, there will be nothing to drive him to be productive.
- If his company, made up of lots of greedy little buggers just like him, does not have to compete against other companies, they will have no motivation to continually lower costs of production, nor to improve their products.

In short, no competition, no innovation. But, if the drive to innovate comes from within, all this changes—especially if a management system can nurture and harness this drive.

Shewhart's and Dewey's Roots to Quality

But we don't have to look just to subtleties like intrinsic motivation to see that the quality movement has always been about learning.

PDCA. The famous PDCA cycle is evidence enough. No one ever gets far into any introduction to total quality management without learning about Plan-Do-Check-Act, the neverending cycle of experimentation that structures all quality improvement efforts.

Deming called it the *Shewhart cycle* when he introduced it to the Japanese in 1950, in honor of his mentor Walter Shewhart of Bell Labs. Eventually the Japanese called it the *Deming cycle.*

Of John Dewey, Learning and Quality. But the roots of the PDCA cycle go back further than Deming or Shewhart, at least as far as the educator, John Dewey. Dewey posited that all learning involves a cycle between four basic stages:

- Discover: the discovery of new insights.
- Invent: creating new options for action.
- Produce: producing new actions.

- Observe: seeing the consequences of those actions, which leads to new discoveries, continuing the cycle.

This is how we learned to walk, to talk, to ride a bicycle, to act skillfully wherever we have achieved some proficiency. The young child first must discover that they want to walk, invent ways of getting started, act, and observe the consequences of her or his action. Interrupting the cycle interrupts the learning. If the toddler is supported so they do not fall, they also do not learn.

Learning is Moving from Thought to Action. In effect, Dewey canonized the simple fact that all real learning occurs over time, as we move between the world of thought and the world of action. Learning is never simply an intellectual exercise. Nor is it a matter of changing behavior. It is an interactive process linking the two, in a spirit of continually expanding our capabilities.

It is not altogether irrelevant to note that this is a far cry from the common image of *learning* inculcated in the schoolroom, where most of us conclude that learning is synonymous with taking in information and being able to produce the right answer on cue—little wonder that for most adults, the word *learning* does not quicken the pulse.

The PDCA cycle takes Dewey's theory of learning one step further, saying, in effect, that in an organization it is often wise to distinguish small actions from widespread adoption of new practices.

The *do* stage then becomes pilot tests from which new data can be collected and analyzed (*checked*). Gradually, a series of such pilots results in more general learnings and the *act* stage moves to broader and broader application of new practices.

PDCA American Style. While simple in concept, the PDCA cycle is often practiced quite differently in the US and in Japan. Impatient for quick results, American managers often jump from plan to act.

The Rush To Act Undermines Efforts. We conceive new programs and then begin rolling them out throughout the organization. In fact, that's exactly what many US firms are doing with their total quality programs. While rolling out new programs makes us feel good about doing something (acting) to improve things in our business, in fact we are actually undermining possibilities for learning. Who can learn from an experiment involving thousands of people that is only run one time?

PDCA Japanese Style. By contrast the Japanese are masters of organizational experimentation. They meticulously design and study pilot tests, often with many corporations participating cooperatively.

Through repeated cycles, new knowledge gradually accumulates. By the time for organizationwide changes, people adopt new practices more rapidly because so many more have been involved in the learning.

For Americans, this whole process often seems unnecessarily time consuming and costly. As one manager pointed out to me recently, the statement "I'm running an experiment" in most American companies is a code word for "Don't hold me accountable for the results." Consequently, while we may go through the motions of quality improvement, we often get the facade without the substance. At best, we get limited bursts of learning.

IMPROVING HOW WE WORK

The First Wave

Improving tangible work processes (from the production line, to order entry, to responding to customer inquiries or coordinating the typing queue) was the predominant theme of the first wave in building learning organizations. The initial tools were derived primarily from statistics, including SPC, and related methods for diagraming, analyzing, and redesigning work processes to reduce variability and enable systematic improvement. As the first wave has unfolded, the focus has broadened to include more complex processes like product development. By and large, the customer was outside the system of production and the system was designed to meet customer needs.

First Wave Strength. The strength of the first wave lay in achieving measurable improvements in cost, quality, and customer satisfaction through rigorous and reproducible processes of improvement.

First Wave Limitation. The limitation lay in the relatively passive role of management and the limited impact on the larger systems whereby processes interact—for example, how sales, order entry, manufacturing, and customer satisfaction interact.

The Second Wave Unfolds

The initial profile of the second wave could be seen in Japan as early as the 1960s when leading firms began to undertake mass deployment of quality tools. Previously, only small groups of quality control experts learned how to analyze work processes, reduce variation, and improve quality and cost.

Japanese Quality Circles and Learning. "Beginning with quality circles," says Massachusetts Institute of Technology's Alan Graham, "that changed.

Everyone began to participate in quality improvement." This was the time when *kaizan* (organizationwide commitment to continuous improvement) was born. This also was the time when Japanese organizations began extensive training in team learning skills, to develop the norms and capabilities needed if quality circles were to be effective.

US Quality Circles and a Lack of Emphasis on Learning. Interestingly, when US firms began to organize production workers in quality circles, 10 to 15 years later, the emphasis was on forming teams, not on developing team learning skills. Consequently, "The skills and practices, both among workers and managers, necessary for QC circles to be effective," according to Graham, "were not present in the introduction of QC circles in the US. This has been typical of the general underemphasis here on skills and practices, as opposed to official programs and management goals."

The result was that many initial efforts at quality control circles in the US failed to generate lasting commitment or significant improvement. "Mid-level managers," says USC's Ed Lawler, "saw QC circles as a threat to their authority, and workers saw them as a gimmick to elicit increased effort and undermine union influence."

The Second Wave Arrives

In Japan, the second wave arrived in full force with the introduction of the seven new tools for management in 1979.

The Seven New Tools. These tools, the work of a committee of the Society for QC Technique Development that operated from 1972 to 1979, focus specifically on how managers think and interact. They particularly emphasize developing better communication and common understandings of complex issues, and relating that understanding to operational planning.

"There are a lot of methodologies for measuring, analyzing, and testing quantitative data," says the leader of the group that developed the new tools, Professor Shiba, "but the area of qualitative methodologies, how to create hypotheses, is very weak. Professor Jiro Kawakita, a Japanese anthropologist, developed methods for analyzing nonnumerical data and making sense of that data."

For example, the KJ method or affinity diagram, as taught by professor Shiba and other experts on the seven management tools, help teams gather large amounts of nonquantitative data and organize them into groupings based on natural relationships or affinities. Other tools help to clarify interrelationships, establish priorities, and think through and plan the complex tasks required for accomplishing an agreed upon goal.

A New Perspective of the Customer. Along with these new tools for thinking and interacting, a new orientation toward the customer has gradually emerged. The new perspective moved from satisfying the customer's expressed requirements to meeting the latent needs of the customer.

The Miata as a Second Wave Example. As one Detroit executive put it, "You could never produce the Mazda Miata from market research. You have to understand what the customer would value if he experienced it." In the second wave, the customer becomes part of the system. There is an interplay between what the firm seeks to produce and what the customer desires.

The Second Wave in America. Today, a small number of American companies are starting to experiment with the seven new management tools.

They are discovering a whole new territory for increasing organizational capabilities—how we think and interact around complex, potentially conflictual issues. This is the real message of the second wave—leverage ultimately lies in improving us, not just improving our work processes.

Engelbart's A, B, and C Work

"There are three levels of work in organizations," says computer pioneer and inventor of the *mouse* Douglas Engelbart, who has spent the better part of 20 years studying the nature of collaborative work.

"The most obvious level, *A work*, involves the development, production, and sale of a firm's products and services. Most of a company's people and resources are focused at this level. Effective A work would be impossible, however, without the next level, *B work*, which involves designing the systems and processes that enable a company to develop, produce, and sell its products and services. But, the subtlest and potentially most influential level is *C work*, improving how we think and interact. Ultimately, the quality of C work determines the quality of systems and processes we design and the products and services we provide."

The First Wave and B Work. The major contribution of quality management in the first wave was to focus time and energy systematically on Engelbart's B work, especially on improving processes, and to provide tools for the task.

The Second Wave and C Work. The major contribution of the second wave will be to systematically focus on Engelbart's C work. This, too, will require appropriate tools. But, before such tools can be developed, we must first understand the core competencies of learning organizations, those distinctive capabilities in thinking and interacting which will enable us to "continually improve the total behavior of organizations."

Core Competencies for Learning Organizations

The seven new tools point in the right direction. But, our work suggests that they are only a start to developing an organization's capabilities in:

- *Building shared vision.* There is no substitute for organizational resolve, conviction, commitment, and clarity of intent. They create the need for learning and the collective will to learn. Without shared visions, significant learning occurs only when there are crises, and the learning ends when the crises end.
- *Personal mastery.* Shared vision comes from personal visions. Collective commitment to learning comes from individual commitment to learning. An organization that is continually learning how to create its future must be made up of individuals who are continually learning how to create more of what truly matters to them in their own lives.
- *Working with mental models.* Organizations become frozen in inaccurate and disempowering views of reality because we lack the capability to see our assumptions, and to continually challenge and improve those assumptions. This requires fostering managerial skills in balancing *inquiry and advocacy* in organizations that have been traditionally dominated by advocacy.
- *Team learning.* Ultimately, the learning that matters is the learning of *groups of people who need one another to act* (the real meaning of team). The only problem is that we've lost the ability to talk with one another. Most of the time we are limited to discussion, which comes from the same roots as percussion and concussion and literally means to heave one's views at the other. What is needed also is dialogue, which comes from the Greek *dia logos* and literally means when a group of people talk with one another such that the meaning (logos) moves through (dia) them.
- *Systems thinking.* It's not just how we learn, but what we learn. The most important learning in contemporary organizations concerns gaining shared insight into complexity and how we can shape change. But, since early in life, we've been taught to break apart problems.

The resulting fragmentation has left us unable to see the consequences of our own actions, creating an illusion that we are victims of forces outside our control and that the only type of learning that is possible is learning to react more quickly.

Systems thinking is about understanding wholes, not parts, and learning how our actions shape our reality.

Creating an Organizational Symphony

The intrinsic limitations to each of these capabilities is only overcome if they are developed in concert:

- Empowering people (an organizationwide commitment to personal mastery) empowers the organization, but only if individuals are deeply aligned around a common sense of purpose and shared vision.
- Shared vision will energize and sustain an organization through thick and thin, but only if people think systemically: Once people are able to see how their actions shape their reality, they begin to understand how alternative actions could create a different reality.
- Individual skills in reflection and inquiry mean little if they cannot be practiced when groups of people confront controversial issues.
- Systems thinking will become the province of a small set of systems experts unless it is tied to an organizationwide commitment to improving mental models, and even then nothing much will change without shared visions.
- A commitment to seeing the larger system only matters when there is a commitment to the long term. In the short run, everyone can just fix their piece. Only with a long-term view can an organization see that optimizing the parts, one at a time, can lead to suboptimizing the whole.

A SHORT STUDY ON LEARNING AS A WAY OF ORGANIZATIONAL LIFE

In 1970, Royal/Dutch Shell was arguably the weakest of the big seven oil companies. Today, it is one of the strongest. A key to Shell's ascent has been reconceiving planning as learning, a conscious process of bringing operating managers' mental models to the surface and challenging those models.

Shell's Scenario Planning

This conceptual shift has been operationalized by tools like scenario planning. Through its use of scenarios, Shell's planners help managers continually think through how they would manage under multiple possible futures. Today, it is hard for a Shell manager to do business planning without engaging in a conscious learning process. Shell has become perhaps the first global corporation to realize the leverage of institutionalizing learning as the most effective approach to strategy in a turbulent world. "The corporate one-track mind," says former planning chief Arie de Geus, "is the single primary reason why so many once successful corporations fail to survive beyond their infancy."

From a Foreboding View to a New Form of Planning. Shell's innovations in institutional learning were driven by necessity. As early as 1971, Shell's planners became convinced that major shocks in supply and price were becoming a possibility in world oil markets. But, they were unable to convince managers conditioned by the stability of world markets in the 50s and 60s. This led the planners to develop scenario planning exercises, wherein managers thought through how they would manage if there were a shift from a buyer's market to a seller's market, where sudden changes in price would be a part of life, regardless of whether or not they expected such a change.

Prepared for Change in the 70s. When OPEC did become a reality and the first oil shocks hit in the winter of 1973 and 1974, Shell responded differently than any other big oil company. It increased local operating company control rather than increasing corporate control. It accelerated development of reserves, especially in its North Sea fields. While the other major oil companies saw a sudden, unexpected crisis and acted accordingly, Shell's managers perceived a sea change in the basic nature of the business, and acted differently.

Shell's Scenario Planning and the 80s. The discipline of thinking in terms of alternative futures served Shell equally well in the 80s. Shell planners created a $15 a barrel oil scenario in 1983, at a time when prices averaged around $30. They considered two alternative futures:

- *Alternative future one:* As managers considered how they would manage in a depressed price world, they quickly concluded that many of their present production processes would have to be shut down because they were too costly.
- *Alternative future two:* A few engineers suggested that radical redesign of their oil platforms using new miniaturization technologies could make them operable at prices as low as $11 per barrel.

As they considered the plan, it soon became obvious that such a redesign was in fact more desirable under any possible scenario! Their production people went ahead with the new design concepts. And when prices did fall, hitting an unbelievable $8 per barrel in 1984, Shell was, once again, one step ahead of its competitors.

Organizational Learning Alternatives

Institutionalizing learning as part of the planning process is one of many possible approaches. It's clear that many Japanese companies have institutionalized learning around quality improvement teams and related innovations. There is no shortage of ways by which learning may become a inescapable aspect of organizational life, once the nature of the commitment to learning is understood, and once appropriate tools are available.

Institutionalized Experimentation. "Institutionalizing experimentation can make an enormous difference," says Harvard's Dave Garvin. "For example, Allegheny Ludlum, one of the most profitable American steel companies, treats its entire production process as a laboratory for experimenting with new processes and technologies. Production managers can designate experiments they want to conduct and an entirely different set of measures and standards are used to evaluate their efforts."

Managerial Microworlds. Another means to institutionalizing learning, the focus of our research at MIT, involves developing *managerial microworlds*, practice fields for management teams.
   —*A financial services microworld:* For example, in a microworld designed for a leading property and liability insurance company, managers discover how many of their most-trusted practices, when they interact in the larger systems of which they are a part, actually contribute to runaway settlement and litigation costs. Using a computerized *management flight simulator*, they are then able to freely experiment in ways that would be difficult in real insurance offices, with a wide range of alternative personnel, workflow, and quality management practices to find where there may be leverage in reversing the growing insurance crisis.

Eventually, we envision such microworlds being as common place in organizations as meeting rooms. There will be places where we gather to think through complex issues and learn through experimentation when trial and error learning is impossible in the real system.

Activity-Based Cost Accounting. Another potential breakthrough lies in changing managerial accounting practices to reinforce learning rather than controlling. "Managers and manufacturing engineers," says Harvard's Robert Kaplan, "frequently comment that considerable operating improvements they achieve go unrecognized in their financial results."
   If the emphasis is on continuous, system-wide improvement, how can we have accounting practices based on historically determined standards? "Traditional cost accounting measures fail when they focus on small, local (but not system-wide) measures of efficiency and productivity."

WHY BECOMING A LEARNING ORGANIZATION MATTERS

Seeing quality management as part of a deeper and even more far-reaching shift leads to several realizations into why the unfolding changes in American management practices may not produce an enduring transformation.

First Wave Quality Is Still Not Well Understood in the US

Despite enormous attention, public commitment by prominent corporations, and even a national award, there is a distinct possibility that American management still does not understand what the quality movement is really all about. Specifically, we lack understanding of what is required for even first wave quality management practices to take root, and why they often fail to take root in American firms.

Confusion over the Connections between Learning, Teams, Standards, Motivations, and Innovation. The total quality management task force at one of America's most successful high-tech manufacturing firms recently came unglued around a question of standards. The external consultant brought in to help develop and implement the TQM strategy argued that standards and standardization were vital to gain better control of the organization's production processes, so that they could be improved. But, to some of the firm's managers, standardization meant rigidity, and a loss of freedom and respect for workers' creativity and individuality.

"Everything becomes vanilla," argued one manager. "We will kill the spark of individual creativity that has made this company what it is."

"If you're not operating in a learning orientation," observed MIT's Dan Kim, "you hear *standardization* differently than if you are. People internalize the need to improve as, *I must be deficient*. Naturally, they then resist what they perceive as an effort to make their deficiencies public and *fix them*."

Confusion over the Meaning of Continuous and Control. The same happens with continuous improvement. Within a learning culture, continuous improvement is a natural by-product of people's commitment and empowerment. Within a controlling culture it is an admission of deficiency. "Why must I improve, unless I'm not good enough now?" From such a viewpoint, continuous improvement is about becoming less deficient. It is not about learning. This is why it is so deeply resisted by workers in many US companies.

In response to this resistance, managers with good intentions resort to exhortation and to driving *highly mechanized* quality programs through their organizations. This creates a vicious cycle of increasing exhortation and increasing resistance. What is needed is understanding and changing the source of the resistance, which stems from bringing tools for learning into a managerial system based on controlling.

We Still Believe Controlling People Is More Important Than Creating a Learning Environment

The second realization is that there is nothing in the American bag of quality tools today that will cause the shift to a learning orientation. And causing such a shift is exactly what is needed in most American corporations. Without a shift of mind from controlling to learning, or as Kim puts it, from "protect and defend" to "create and learn," we "get the tools for quality management without the substance."

Learning Cannot Be Switched On. Creating such a shift is an organic process, not a mechanical one. It demands penetrating to deep levels of the corporate psyche and unearthing and examining deep fears. What will it take to change? To put it bluntly, the shift will not occur if it is not within us. It cannot be faked. It cannot be achieved by public declarations. If at some basic level, we do not genuinely value and truly desire to live life as learners, it will not happen.

My experience is that it can only be caused by small groups of thoughtful leaders who truly desire to build an organization where people are committed to a larger purpose and to thinking for themselves. Such thoughtful groups then must be willing to become models of continually learning, with all the vulnerability and uncertainty that implies. They become lead users of new learning tools and approaches.

Public and Organizational Learning/Education Are Linked

The last, and potentially most important, realization is that the transformation in corporate and public education may be linked. "Humans are the learning organism par excellence" according to anthropologist Edward T. Hall. "The drive to learn is as strong as the sexual drive—it begins earlier and lasts longer."

If the drive to learn is so strong, why is it so weak in our corporations? What happened to our "intrinsic joy in learning?" as Dr. Deming puts it. The answer according to Deming, Hall, and many educators lies, surprisingly, as much in the classroom as on the factory floor. "The forces of destruction begin with toddlers," says Deming,". . . a prize for the best Halloween costume, grades in school, gold stars—and on up through the university."

Performing versus Learning. The young child in school quickly learns that the name of the game is not learning it is *performing*. Mistakes are punished, correct answers rewarded. If you don't have the right answer, keep your mouth shut. If we had operated under that system as two-year olds, none of us would have ever learned to walk. Is it any wonder the manager or worker shows little intrinsic motivation to learn—that is, to experiment and discover new insights from mistakes, outcomes that don't turn out according to plan.

If the conditioning toward performing for others rather than learning is so deeply established in schools, it may not be possible to reverse it on the job. If knowledge is always something somebody else has and I don't, then learning becomes embedded in deep instincts of self-protection not free experimentation.

If the identification of *boss* with *teacher*, the authority figure who has the answers and is the arbiter of our performance is so firmly anchored, we may never be able to roll up our sleeves and all become learners together.

Today, there is no lack of corporate concern for the erosion in our public education. But, there is a lack of vision as to what is truly needed. It is not enough to go back to the 3R's. We must revolutionize the school experience so that it nurtures and deepens our love of learning, develops new skills of integrative or systemic thinking, and helps us learn how to learn, especially together.

FINAL THOUGHTS

I recently asked Dr. Deming if he thought it was possible to fully implement his philosophy of management without radical reform in our schools, as well as in our corporations. "No," was his answer. However, if we come to a deeper understanding of the linkage between school and work in the twenty-first century, we may be able to generate a wholly new vision and commitment to the vital task of rethinking both. This may be the real promise of the learning organization.

17. Quality Improvement: A Patient's Perspective

Charles E. Silberman

INTRODUCTION

To quote Heather Palmer, "Quality is defined as meeting the needs and expectations of customers."[1] There are many customers, of course—some internal, some external—but the ultimate customer is the patient; if this enormous health care enterprise is about anything, it is about meeting the needs and expectations of patients.

My purpose for the conference and for this paper is to speak to you as a patient—a far more frequent patient than I might have wished—and from that vantage point to tell you how we are doing and what we need to do.

We are doing poorly. The health care system fails the Palmer test: it does not meet the needs and expectations of patients; it does not create satisfied customers, which Peter Drucker calls the only valid business purpose.[2] The health care system fails to do so because under the prevailing system of doctor-patient relations, patient preferences play only a minor role; the demand for medical care is largely physician-induced. True, patients initiate most medical encounters, but they have little to say about what happens thereafter; doctors, not patients, decide whether patients will be hospitalized and whether they will undergo surgery, chemotherapy, or some other treatment or procedure. Physicians make these decisions with the best of intentions; they genuinely seek to meet the needs of their patients. But physicians—not patients—define those needs. Physicians usually do so, moreover, without asking patients what they want or think they need and without otherwise taking patients' preferences and values into account.

Source: Reprinted with permission of the Agency for Health Care Policy and Research, Rockville, MD, Pub. No. 93–0034, 1993.

Physicians make these decisions unilaterally, not because they crave power but because, until recently, everybody took it for granted that "doctor knows best." That assumption, in turn, rested on four other assumptions, namely:

1. Physicians know the scientifically correct way to practice medicine.
2. They know the values and preferences of their patients.
3. Physicians are disinterested and objective scientists without preferences or biases of their own.
4. They therefore routinely choose for their patients what those patients would choose for themselves if they had the same knowledge.

None of these assumptions can withstand scrutiny. As Jack Wennberg, Robert Brook, David Eddy, and others have shown,[3-14] physicians frequently do not know the scientifically correct way to practice medicine—not because of personal ignorance or indifference, but because nobody knows; medical science has enjoyed spectacular success in developing new diagnostic tests and treatments but has failed to evaluate the usefulness of those tests and the outcomes of those treatments. That, after all, is why the Agency for Health Care Policy and Research was brought into being. Like other human beings, moreover, physicians have biases and preferences of their own; they usually do not know, and indeed, often misjudge their patients' values and preferences.

These misjudgments are rooted in an enormous gulf between the way physicians think about disease and the way physicians experience it—a gulf physicians often discover when they become seriously ill themselves. "I practiced medicine for 50 years before I became a patient," Edward E. Rosenbaum, M.D.,[15] former chief of rheumatology at Oregon Health Sciences University, wrote in the book on which the film, *The Doctor*, was based. "It wasn't until then that I learned that the physician and patient are not on the same track. The view is entirely different when you are standing at the side of the bed from when you are lying in it."

PERCEPTIONS OF ILLNESS AND DISEASE

To the seriously ill patient, disease is an assault on identity and sense of self, an assault involving disorientation and loss of meaning, erosion of autonomy and control, fear, and dependency. Sickness also is a transforming experience. The transformation is most evident when sickness is chronic or progressive or leaves us with a permanent disability. But even if we "recover," we do not return to our pre-sickness state; we must adjust to a new way of seeing and relating to the world. To the patient, disease always is an existential process.

To the physician, on the other hand, disease is a pathophysiological process—one that is abstracted from the patient and his or her suffering. To a neurologist, for example, multiple sclerosis (MS) is a "slowly progressive central nervous system disease characterized by disseminated patches of demyelination in the brain and spinal cord, resulting in multiple and varied neurologic symptoms and signs, usually with remissions and exacerbations."

That is not how MS patients experience the disease. "What I experience every day is not the demyelination in the white matter of the nervous system," philosopher Kay Toombs[16,17] explains, but the "ongoing and seemingly relentless diminishment of physical abilities which is gradually but surely eroding my independence. For me, multiple sclerosis is the constant effort to overcome my body's resistance so that I can carry out the most mundane activities; it is the frustration of not being able to do the simplest of things. It is the anguished uncertainty of a perilous future."

I know what Dr. Toombs means. For me, a brain stem infarct—in laymen's terms, a stroke—was not "an intra- or extracranial interruption in arterial blood flow," as the Merck Manual describes it.[18] It was the infantilizing inability to stand without collapsing to my left and the unimaginable terror that what already had happened to my hospital roommates would soon happen to me—that I would lose the ability to speak, think, write, or feed myself.

For patients, disease never is just a pathophysiologic process. "What happens when my body breaks down happens not just to that body but also to my life, which is lived in that body," explains Arthur Frank, a medical sociologist who had a massive coronary followed by testicular cancer.[19] "When the body breaks down, so does the life." Fixing the body "doesn't always put the life back together again," Frank adds, because serious illness "leaves no aspect of life untouched . . . your relationships, your work, your sense of who you are and who you might become, your sense of what life is and ought to be—these all change, and the change is terrifying."

Terrifying, as I can attest, because sickness plunges us into an abyss of meaninglessness; we know what our symptoms are but not what they mean. Sickness also is disorienting, for it shatters the web of assumptions on which our lives are based. We take it for granted, for example, that our arms, legs, fingers, feet, and other organs will respond to our usually unconscious commands. It is only when that does not happen—when we cannot stand without falling, as happened to me after my stroke, or when bringing a cup of coffee to our lips without spilling it requires all the concentration we can muster—that we discover the degree to which our sense of self had depended on those assumptions and how disoriented we become when our body turns into an enemy rather than an ally.

No wonder patients and doctors have such difficulty communicating with one another. "In discussing my illness with physicians," Kay Toombs reports, "it has often seemed to me that we have been talking at cross-purposes, discussing different things, never quite reaching one another."[20] For the most part, Dr. Toombs adds, "this inability to communicate does not result from inattentiveness or insensitivity but from a fundamental disagreement about the nature of illness. Rather than representing a shared reality between us, illness represents two quite different realities, the meaning of one being significantly . . . different from the meaning of the other."

IMPROVING THE QUALITY OF HEALTH CARE

We cannot improve the quality of medical care unless both realities are incorporated into clinical practice. Because doctors and patients understand disease so differently, they have radically different expectations of medical care and, therefore, radically different ways of assessing its quality. The assumption that disease is physiological leads doctors to set physiological goals and to measure the quality of care through "intermediate outcomes"—changes in physiological measures such as blood pressure, blood sugar levels, tumor size, or patency of blood vessels.

These are important outcomes, but they are incomplete, at best, and often tell the doctor little about how patients feel and function, the outcomes that interest patients most. In a host of chronic illnesses—conditions such as ulcers, angina, arrhythmia, diabetes, spinal stenosis and disk herniation, and benign enlargement of the prostate, among others—there is remarkably little correlation between the severity of the organic disorder and the amount of pain or disability patients experience; the same pathophysiology is associated with widely different symptoms in different patients. By concentrating on physiological measures, a rheumatologist observes, physicians "may all too easily spend years writing 'doing well' in the notes of a patient who has become progressively more crippled before their eyes."[21,22]

That is not how patients define "doing well." By and large, patients judge the effectiveness of a drug or procedure by its impact on their lives. They want to know whether the treatment will relieve pain or alleviate anxiety; whether it will preserve or restore their ability to see, hear, walk, climb stairs, or dress and feed themselves, and whether it will change their appearance, sexuality, or mood.

In short, patients judge the quality of care by its impact on the quality of their lives—an outcome physicians and hospital administrators rarely measure. Clinicians collect information about the functioning of almost every bodily organ but not about the functioning of patients as a whole. "We appraise the palliative treatment of patients with cancer by measuring. . . tumor size and other paraclinical indexes," Alvan R. Feinstein points out.[23] "We do not regularly measure whether the patient is comfortable or miserable, functional or bedridden, vegetating or vibrant. We compare medical and surgical treatment for coronary heart disease by measuring. . .patency of vessels, changes in electro-cardiograms, and treadmill exercise tests. We do not regularly perform scientif-ically credible measurements of whether the angina pectoris is still severe, whether the patient was truly made able to return to work, and whether the quality of life has otherwise improved for the patient and his family."

These failures are due not to insensitivity or lack of concern but to the prevailing mind-set about the kind of information physicians should seek and study. By and large, physicians are taught that what cannot be readily quantified is unimportant; information about what patients think and how they feel or function has been considered "soft" or "subjective" and therefore less worthy of scientific attention than "hard" or "objective" data, such as the images, numbers, and tracings produced by diagnostic testing equipment. By making this invidious distinction, Feinstein notes, physicians ignore "all the distinctively human reactions—love, hate, joy, sorrow, distress, gratification—that differentiate people from animals or molecules."[24]

Ignoring or slighting the human dimensions of medical care is scientifically untenable; it grows out of an obsolete view of the nature of science. It also is unnecessary. Physicians and hospital administrators now have at their disposal a number of easily used, as well as valid and reliable, instruments for assessing patients' symptoms, functional status, and sense of well being. As Sheldon Greenfield points out, some of these measures are actually "harder"—that is, more valid and reliable—than many of the physiologic measures in common use.[25] The availability of these measures makes it scientifically as well as ethically intolerable for providers to fail to be as concerned with their patients' functional status and well being as they are with their patients' physiologic status.

Physicians and hospital administrators no longer have a choice. Consumerism is rampant; *BusinessWeek* has called the 1990s "the decade of the customer."[26] As Thomas Moloney and Barbara Paul point out, members of the so-called "baby boom" generation want far more information than their elders about the services they buy, including medical care.[27] Indeed, the Picker-Commonwealth survey that Paul Cleary and colleagues describe found that Americans are eager to use survey data to help them decide where to seek medical and hospital care.[28]

Thus, periodic surveys of patient attitudes and experiences must be incorpo-rated into any quality improvement effort; and assessments of patients' function-al status and well being must become a routine part of medical and hospital care. But surveys and assessments are not enough. Patients are demanding more than information; they want to play an active role in decisions about their own care.

That demand must be met; collaboration between patient and physician is a scientific, ethical, and economic imperative. An ethical imperative because there is more than one medically appropriate treatment for almost every illness or condition, and because each treatment poses a different set of risks and benefits whose probabilities often are not known. Because patients differ widely in the degree to which they are bothered by a particular symptom, moreover, they attach widely different values to its relief. Patients also differ widely in their willingness to assume the risks of treatment. Much of the time, therefore, there is no medically "right" or "wrong" decision; what is "appropriate" for one patient may be wholly inappropriate for another. Choice of treatment must involve collaboration between doctors and patients.

Collaboration between doctor and patient should not be limited to the choice of treatment; it must start when the patient first seeks medical help and continue throughout the clinical encounter. If quality is defined as meeting the needs of the customer, the physician must find out what those needs are. Something has happened, after all, to make that patient seek medical help. Without knowing what that something is—what caused the patient to come and see the doctor (and patients are not always aware of the real reason themselves)—the physician may identify and treat the wrong problem.

The risk of treating the wrong problem is increased by the staccato, close-ended style of questioning most physicians favor, a style that makes it hard for patients to reveal what is on their minds. In analyzing doctor-patient interactions, Beckman and Frankel found that, on average, physicians interrupted patients 18 seconds after the patient began to speak; patients were able to complete their opening statements in only one visit in four.[29] Time is not the problem; when patients were permitted to complete their statements, they took only 60 seconds longer.

Indeed, interrupting the patient may lengthen the visit rather than shorten it. Witness the familiar situation in which, just as the physician thinks the office visit is over, the patient asks, "Oh, by the way doctor, I have been having this heavy feeling in my chest. Do you think it might be important?" Most of the time patients are not being perverse; rather, they have not been able to get the question out when the doctor takes their history, or the doctor may not put them at sufficient ease to enable them to ask an embarrassing question or one they are afraid to ask because its answer may be frightening.

The only way patients can tell physicians why they are seeking medical help is through genuine dialog; and genuine dialog cannot occur unless physicians establish comfortable relationships with patients. "To be humane and empathic is not merely a prescription for compassion," George Engel explains. "It is a prerequisite for scientific work in the clinical realm."[30]

Paying "proper attention to the full needs and feelings of patients" (the formulation is that of Oliver Sacks) is not an impossible task.[31] Thomas Delbanco of Beth Israel Hospital describes one way of doing that.[32] In their encounters with patients, Delbanco suggests, doctors should conduct a "patient review" comparable to the organ-specific review of physiologic symptoms that is part of every physician's routine. Delbanco describes seven dimensions of care that need to be reviewed and suggests questions the physician might ask in each dimension. "Incorporating the patient's review into my interactions with patients encourages me to address the nontechnical aspects of care in a systematic way," he writes.

CONCLUSION

To sum up, quality improvement involves more than measurement; it requires a broadening of the goals of clinical practice and a transformation of the patient-doctor relationship. The best physicians have always understood this. As Francis Weld Peabody told his Harvard Medical School students 65 years ago, "One of the essential qualities of the clinician is interest in humanity, for the secret of the care of the patient is in caring for the patient." It may not have been entirely coincidental that when he delivered his classic lecture on "The Care of the Patient," Dr. Peabody was himself a patient, under treatment for the cancer that killed him later that year.

NOTES

1. H. Palmer, Quality Improvement/Quality Assurance Taxonomy: A Framework, in *Putting Research to Work in Quality Improvement and Quality Assurance*, eds. M. Grady, J. Berstein, and S. Robinson (Washington, D.C.: US Department of Health and Human Services, Public Health Service, Agency for Health Care Policy and Research, 1993), 13–37.

2. T.W. Moloney and B. Paul, The Consumer Movement Takes Hold for Medical Care, *Health Affairs* 10, no. 4 (1991): 269.

3. J.E. Wennberg, Dealing With Medical Practice Variations: A Proposal for Action, *Health Affairs* 3, no. 2 (1984): 6–32.

4. J.E. Wennberg, The Paradox of Appropriate Care [editorial], *Journal of the American Medical Association* 258, no. 18 (1987): 2568–2569.

5. J.E. Wennberg, Improving the Medical Decision-Making Process, *Health Affairs* 7, no. 1 (1988): 99–106.

6. J.E. Wennberg, J.L. Freeman, and W.J. Culp, Are Hospital Services Rationed in New Haven or Overutilized in Boston?, *Lancet* (1987): 1185–1189.

7. R.H. Brook, Quality of Care: Do We Care? *Annals of Internal Medicine* 15, no. 6 (1991): 486–490.

8. R.H. Brook and E.A. McGlynn, Maintaining Quality of Care, in *Health Services Research*, ed. E. Ginzberg (Cambridge, MA: Harvard University Press, 1991).

9. C.M. Winslow, D.H. Solomon, M.R. Chassin, and others, The Appropriateness of Carotid Endarterectomy, *New England Journal of Medicine* 318, no. 12 (1988): 721–727.

10. D.M. Eddy, Clinical Policies and the Quality of Medical Evidence, *New England Journal of Medicine* 307 (1982): 343–347.

11. D.M. Eddy, Variations in Physician Practice: The Role of Uncertainty, *Health Affairs* 3, no. 2 (Summer 1984): 74–89.

12. D.M. Eddy, Anatomy of a Decision, *Journal of the American Medical Association* 263, no. 3 (1990): 441–443.

13. D.M. Eddy, The Challenge, *Journal of the American Medical Association* 263, no. 2 (1990): 287–290.

14. D.M. Eddy and J. Billings, The Quality of Medical Evidence: Implications for Quality of Care, *Health Affairs* 7, no. 1 (Spring, 1988): 19–32.

15. E.E. Rosenbaum, *A Taste of My Own Medicine* (New York: Random House, 1988), viii.

16. S.K. Toombs, *The Meaning of Illness* (Boston: Elsevier, 1992).

17. S.K. Toombs, review of *Patient Encounters*, by J.H. Buchanan, *New Physician* (October 1989).

18. R. Berkow and A.J. Fletcher, eds., *The Merck Manual* (Rahway, NJ: Merck, Sharp & Dohme Research Laboratories, 1987).

19. A. Frank, *At the Will of the Body* (Boston: Houghton-Mifflin, 1991).

20. S.K. Toombs, The Meaning of Illness: A Phenomenological Approach to the Physician-Patient Relationship, *Journal of Medicine and Philosophy* 12 (1987): 219–240.

21. R.A. Deyo, The Quality of Life, Research, and Care [editorial], *Annals of Internal Medicine* 114 (1991): 695–697.

22. T. Smith, Questions on Clinical Trials [editorial], *British Medical Journal* 287 (1983): 569.

23. A.R. Feinstein, An Additional Basis for Clinical Medicine: IV. The Development of Clinimetrics, *Annals of Internal Medicine* 99 (1983): 843–848.

24. A.R. Feinstein, The Intellectual Crisis in Clinical Science: Medaled Models and Muddled Mettle, *Perspectives in Biology and Medicine* 30 (1987): 215–230.

25. S. Greenfield, A Perspective on Quality Assurance Research, in *Putting Research to Work in Quality Improvement and Quality Assurance*, eds. M. Grady, J. Berstein, and S. Robinson (Washington, D.C.: U.S. Department of Health and Human Services, Agency for Health Care Policy and Research, 1993) 9–12.

26. King Customer, *Business Week* (12 March 1990).

27. Moloney and Paul, The Consumer Movement.

28. P.D. Cleary, S. Edgman-Levitan, and M. Roberts, Patients Evaluate Their Hospital Care: A National Survey, *Health Affairs* 10, no. 4 (1991): 254–267.

29. H.B. Beckman and R.M. Frankel, The Effect of Physician Behavior on the Collection of Data, *Annals of Internal Medicine* 101 (1984): 692–696.

30. G.L. Engel, How Much Longer Must Medicine's Science Be Bound by a Seventeenth-Century World View? in *The Task of Medicine*, ed., K.L. White (Menlo Park, CA: Kaiser Family Foundation, 1988), 113–136.

31. O. Sacks, *Awakening* (New York: Summit Books, 1987).

32. T.L. Delbanco, Enhancing the Doctor-Patient Relationship by Inviting the Patient's Perspective, *Annals of Internal Medicine* 116, no. 5 (1992): 414–418.

18. Changing Physicians' Practices

Peter J. Greco and John M. Eisenberg

What causes physicians to change the way they practice? This question is especially important today because physicians' decisions influence not only the health of their patients but also the cost of their care. Thus, the ability to change physicians' practices could improve the quality of health care while controlling expenditures.

Changes in practice are sometimes rapid and dramatic. For example, laparoscopic cholecystectomy has virtually replaced the traditional procedure in the past several years.[1] At other times physicians are reluctant to change their practices even when randomized trials demonstrate the effectiveness of a new treatment.[2] In this article we review the recent literature on efforts to change physicians' practices, emphasizing controlled trials, and we offer a framework that may be of use in the planning, design, and evaluation of future efforts to change physicians' practices. Our review concentrates on studies published in the past seven years.

Six general methods of changing physicians' practices have been described: education, feedback, participation by physicians in efforts to bring about change, administrative rules, financial incentives, and financial penalties.[3] Although each method has shown some success on its own, interventions that rely on more than one method appear to be the most successful. In this analysis we categorize such multifaceted interventions according to what we consider the primary type of intervention.

Source: Reprinted from *New England Journal of Medicine*, Vol. 329, No. 17, pp. 1271–1274, with permission of the Massachusetts Medical Society, © 1993.

EDUCATION

A number of randomized trials have examined whether the education of practicing physicians (generally referred to as continuing medical education) improves patient care. The most stringent test of continuing medical education is whether the patients of physicians enrolled in such programs have better health outcomes; a less stringent test is whether such physicians change their practices. Most studies of traditional forms of continuing medical education (such as lectures or written materials) either have not looked for changes in patient outcomes or have not found that the programs succeeded in improving patient outcomes.[4] Changes in practice can occur with continuing medical education, however, especially when the curriculum is designed to change specific types of behaviors.[5]

Clinical practice guidelines, another form of education, have gained popularity as a means of influencing physicians' practices.[6] Such guidelines are primarily educational, in that they attempt to inform practitioners abut optimal strategies for diagnosis and management. Most studies of the effect of practice guidelines have examined changes in physicians' practices, not changes in patient outcomes. Even by this measure, clinical practice guidelines have been remarkably unsuccessful in influencing physicians.[7,8]

Why are most physicians not influenced by practice guidelines? Several explanations have been offered. First, some guidelines are not written for practicing physicians, but focus instead on the current state of scientific knowledge.[9] Physicians may have difficulty applying guidelines of this type to specific patients. Second, physicians may disagree with or distrust guidelines written by so-called national experts. Interviews with practicing physicians indicate that many rely primarily on their own experience or colleagues' recommendations in deciding whether to adopt new techniques or interventions.[10] Finally, physicians may choose to ignore guidelines because of nonclinical factors, such as financial incentives or the fear of malpractice litigation. Thus, despite the current enthusiasm, guidelines by themselves appear to have a limited role in influencing physicians' practices.

Although guidelines themselves may not change practice, providing such guidelines to "opinion leaders" (men and women named by their peers as trusted sources of clinical information) appears to offer great promise in altering physicians' practices. In one study, the rate of Caesarian section was dramatically reduced when opinion leaders were recruited, trained, and returned to their communities to educate their colleagues.[11] In another study, dramatic changes in the perioperative use of antibiotics were seen when department leaders were given literature-based practice guidelines and asked to disseminate them to their colleagues.[12] The changes in practice that followed this intervention persisted for at least two years.

Dissemination of guidelines through opinion leaders is probably more efficient than targeting individual physicians for education (a process referred to as "academic detailing").[13] However, academic detailing has been effective in virtually every study in which it has been used.[14-17] Moreover, this method can specifically target the physicians who most need to change their practices. Unfortunately, both academic detailing and training of opinion leaders are labor-intensive and expensive. Moreover, it is not clear whether these techniques can succeed outside the research setting. If so, they may be important ways of using education to change practice.

FEEDBACK

Feedback involves giving physicians information about how their practices or patient outcomes compare with those of other physicians or with an external standard (such as a practice guideline). It is not yet known whether feedback can affect patient outcomes. Previous research has generally found feedback to be an effective means of altering practices, however.[18] Recent studies of feedback have demonstrated reductions in the length of the hospital stay,[19,20] reductions in the number of medications prescribed to outpatients,[21,22] reductions in the number of outpatient tests ordered,[23] and increased compliance with cancer-screening guidelines.[24] In two studies, however, feedback was found to be less effective than reminders provided at the time of the patient's visit.[25,26]

In other studies, feedback had little or no effect on physicians' practices.[27-31] These failures are useful in delineating the conditions that must exist for feedback to succeed. First, physicians must recognize that their current practices need improvement. In one program that failed to change patterns of drug prescription for outpatients, physicians apparently did not believe that the less costly medications were just as effective as those they were currently using.[32] Second, the person receiving feedback must be able to act on it. In a study that failed to alter prescribing patterns for inpatients, feedback was provided to attending physicians rather than to the house officers who were probably choosing the antibiotic agents.[33] Finally, physicians may not respond to feedback if they are unable to do so immediately. This may explain why prospective reminders are more effective than retrospective feedback.[34,35]

PARTICIPATION BY PHYSICIANS IN THE EFFORT TO CHANGE

Many efforts to change physicians' behavior are imposed by outsiders who may not share physicians' personal and professional concerns. Theories of change[36] and common sense suggest that physicians will oppose changes they perceive as threatening to their livelihood, self-esteem, sense of competence, or autonomy. Thus, interventions that decrease physicians' decision-making authority, reduce their income, challenge their professional judgments, or appear to compromise patient care are more likely to fail. According to these notions, involving physicians in the effort to effect change should make change less threatening. It seems especially important that physicians perceive the proposed changes as beneficial to patients (or at least not harmful). Meeting this goal is particularly challenging at a time when the nation is seeking to limit expenditures for health care.

One way to involve physicians in changing their own practices is to give them a role in setting the standards against which their practices will be judged. Published evaluations of such efforts[37,38] have not been very promising, but they are difficult to interpret because of methodologic problems. Efforts to apply techniques of industrial quality management to health care[39-41] represent another way to involve physicians in the process of change. Several important features of these continuous "quality-improvement" efforts may make them attractive to physicians. First, the focus of many such efforts is on improving the quality of care (rather than controlling costs). Second, there is no presupposition that physicians' practices must be changed in order to improve patient care. Rather, the focus is on improving the efficiency of the complex processes by which care is provided.

Uncontrolled evaluations[42] suggest that these methods can improve the process of care, but no study has shown improvements in patient outcomes. Randomized trials comparing quality-improvement methods with traditional programs of quality assurance are currently underway (Cebul RD: personal communication).

ADMINISTRATIVE INTERVENTIONS

When other efforts fail, changes in behavior can be sought by means of administrative interventions. At one extreme, changes in behavior can simply be encouraged either by creating barriers to undesired practices (for example, requiring the approval of a specialist for certain tests or medications) or by reducing barriers to desired practices (for example, by simplifying order forms). At the other extreme, changes in behavior can be required by laws, regulations, or institutional policies.

Interventions that force physicians to alter their practices are in widespread use. Do they work? Programs in which pharmacists and physicians review prescriptions of antibiotics for inpatients have been successful in reducing expenditures on drugs.[43] However, such programs require new personnel (or assign additional responsibilities to existing personnel) and must be maintained indefinitely in order to achieve results. Simpler administrative interventions, such as altering order forms to reflect the preferred dosing intervals for antibiotics[44] or eliminating certain diagnostic tests from order forms,[45] have been successful. Some administrative interventions are either ineffective or of un-proved benefit. Programs that require a second opinion before surgery have not been the subject of randomized trials; their effect on overall costs and patient outcomes is unknown.[46] Utilization review, though successful in reducing the amount of resources used in inpatient care, has not had a clearly beneficial effect on overall utilization or costs.[47]

Perhaps the most dangerous aspect of administrative interventions is that it is possible to achieve the desired changes in practice but to harm patients nonetheless. For example, a Medicaid program limiting reimbursement for prescription drugs reduced the number of drugs prescribed but was associated with increased rates of admission to nursing homes.[48] Such adverse effects may go unrecognized if the program evaluation does not examine important patient outcomes. Another potential adverse effect of administrative interventions is their contribution to the "hassle factor" that increasingly burdens practicing physicians.

FINANCIAL INCENTIVES AND PENALTIES

There have been very few randomized trials of different methods of payment to physicians. In one, pediatric house officers who received fee-for-service payments for outpatient visits saw more patients than residents who received a fixed salary.[49] Observational studies suggest that differing methods of reimbursing physicians do result in different styles of practice. In one study, physicians in health maintenance organizations were less likely to hospitalize their patients if they were paid by salary or capitation fee, or if they were at personal financial risk for their treatment decisions.[50] Observational studies also suggest that physicians respond to financial incentives directed at hospitals. Since the introduction of the Medicare prospective payment system based on diagnosis-related groups, the average length of stay for certain diagnoses has failed by 24 percent.[51]

FUTURE DIRECTIONS

No particular type of intervention is inherently effective, particularly when it is used in isolation. Whether an intervention succeeds depends on the circum-stances in which it is used. In general, combinations of methods are superior to single methods of intervention.

We suggest that future investigators pose several questions when designing and implementing programs to change physicians' practices.

First, is the chosen intervention appropriate for the desired change in practice? For example, education is appropriate when current practices are due to a lack of knowledge, but it is unlikely to alter practices that are the result of financial incentives, patients' preferences, or the lack of necessary equipment. Thus, success may require an understanding of the motivations underlying current practice.

Second, do physicians support the proposed change in their practice? Investigators and administrators cannot assume that physicians share their enthusiasm for the proposed changes, especially when programs are initiated primarily for financial reasons. When cost reduction is the primary goal, physicians are likely to respond more favorably to evidence that the proposed changes improve patient outcomes, or at least that patient outcomes are not worsened. When data on patient outcomes are not available, physicians may be justified in not wanting to change their practices; in such cases, investigators may wish to pay careful attention to physicians' attitudes toward the specific changes in behavior that are sought. Such information may be useful in analyzing retrospectively why an intervention failed.

Third, how will the intervention itself be perceived? For example, will feedback be viewed as a "hassle" or a threat, or will it be seen as an opportunity for improvement? Many physicians are already dissatisfied with the practice of medicine because of the increasing number of external constraints on their decision making. However minor, the additional requirements of some interventions may be perceived as onerous. Better cooperation and collaboration between physicians and those who would change their practices may substantially reduce physicians' fears and suspicions about proposed interventions. Ultimately, such collaboration may enhance the chances for success.

NOTES

1. NIH Consensus Development Panel on Gallstones and Laparoscopic Cholecystectomy, Gallstones and Laparoscopic Cholecystectomy, *JAMA* 269 (1993): 1018–24.

2. H.V. Fineberg, Clinical Evaluation: How Does It Influence Medical Practice? *Bull Cancer (Paris)* 74 (1987): 333–46.

3. J.M. Eisenberg, *Doctors' Decisions and the Cost of Medical Care* (Ann Arbor, Mich.: Health Administration Press, 1986).

4. D.A. Davis, M.A. Thomson, A.D. Oxman, and R.B. Haynes, Evidence for the Effectiveness of CME: A Review of 50 Randomized Controlled Trials, *JAMA* 268 (1992): 1111–7.

5. C.W. White, M.A. Albanese, D.D. Brown, and R.M. Caplan, The Effectiveness of Continuing Medical Education in Changing the Behavior of Physicians Caring for Patients with Acute Myocardial Infarction: A Controlled Randomized Trial, *Ann Intern Med* 102 (1985): 686–92.

6. A.M. Audet, S. Greenfield, M. Field, Medical Practice Guidelines: Current Activities and Future Directions, *Ann Intern Med* 113 (1990): 709–14.

7. J. Kosecoff, D.E. Kanouse, W.H. Rogers, L. McCloskey, C.M. Winslow, and R.H. Brook, Effects of the National Institutes of Health Consensus Development Program on Physician Practice, *JAMA* 258 (1987): 2708–13.

8. J. Lomas, G.M. Anderson, K. Domnick-Pierre, E. Vayda, M.W. Enkin, W.J. Hannah, Do Practice Guidelines Guide Practice? The Effect of a Consensus Statement on the Practice of Physicians, *N Engl J Med* 321 (1989): 1306–11.

9. J. Lomas, Words Without Action? The Production, Dissemination, and Impact of Consensus Recommendations, *Annu Rev Public Health* 12 (1991): 41–65.

10. A.L. Greer, The State of the Art versus the State of the Science: The Diffusion of New Medical Technologies Into Practice, *Int J Technol Assess Health Care* 4 (1988): 5–26.

11. J. Lomas, M. Enkin, G.M. Anderson, W.J. Hannah, E. Vayda, and J. Singer, Opinion Leaders vs Audit and Feedback to Implement Practice Guidelines: Delivery After Previous Cesarean Section, *JAMA* 265 (1991): 2202–7.

12. D.E. Everitt, S.B. Soumerai, J. Avorn, H. Klapholz, M. Wessels, Changing Surgical Antimicrobial Prophylaxis Practices Through Education Targeted at Senior Department Leaders, *Infect Control Hosp Epidemiol* 11 (1990): 578–83.

13. S.B. Soumerai, J. Avorn, Principles of Educational Outreach ('Academic Detailing') to Improve Clinical Decision Making, *JAMA* 263 (1990): 549–56.

14. J. Avorn, S.B. Soumerai, A New Approach to Reducing Suboptimal Drug Use, *JAMA* 250 (1983): 1752–3.

15. W. Schaffner, W.A. Ray, C.F. Federspiel, W.O. Miller, Improving Antibiotic Prescribing in Office Practice: A Controlled Trial of Three Educational Methods, *JAMA* 250 (1983): 1728–32.

16. W.A. Ray, W. Schaffner, C.F. Federspiel, Persistence of improvement in Antibiotic Prescribing in Office Practice, *JAMA* 253 (1985): 1774–6.

17. W.A. Ray, D.G. Blazer, II, W. Schaffner, C.F. Federspiel, R. Fink, Reducing Long-Term Diazepam Prescribing in Office Practice: A Controlled Trial of Educational Visits, *JAMA* 256 (1986): 2536–9.

18. Eisenberg, *Doctors Decisions*.

19. J.E. Billi, L. Duran-Arenas, C.G. Wise, A.M. Bernard, M. McQuillan, J.K. Stross, The Effects of a Low-Cost Intervention Program on Hospital Costs, *J Gen Intern Med* 7 (1992): 411–7.

20. L.M. Manheim, J. Feinglass, R. Hughes, G.J. Martin, K. Conrad, E.F. Hughes, Training House Officers To Be Cost Conscious: Effects of An Educational Intervention on Charges and Length of Stay, *Med Care* 28 (1990): 29–42.

21. K. Kroenke, E.M. Pinholt, Reducing Polypharmacy in the Elderly: A Controlled Trial of Physician Feedback, *J Am Geriatr Soc* 38 (1990): 31–6.

22. L.M. Frazier, J.T. Brown, G.W. Divine, et al., Can Physician Education Lower the Cost of Prescription Drugs? A Prospective, Controlled Trial, *Ann Intern Med* 115 (1991): 116–21.

23. D.M. Berwick, K.L. Coltin, Feedback Reduces Test Use in a Health Maintenance Organization, *JAMA* 255 (1986): 1450–4.

24. S.J. McPhee, J.A. Bird, C.N. Jenkins, D. Fordham, Promoting Cancer Screening: A Randomized, Controlled Trial of Three Interventions, *Arch Intern Med* 149 (1989): 1866–72.

25. McPhee, et al., Promoting Cancer Screening.

26. W.M. Tierney, S.L. Hui, C.J. McDonald, Delayed Feedback of Physician Performance versus Immediate Reminders to Perform Preventive Care: Effects on Physician Compliance, *Med Care* 24 (1986): 659–66.

27. Lomas, et al., Opinion Leaders.

28. C.O. Hershey, H.I. Goldberg, D.I. Cohen, The Effect of Computerized Feedback Coupled With a Newsletter Upon Outpatient Prescribing Charges: A Randomized Controlled Trial, *Med Care*, 26 (1988): 88–93.

29. T.J. Meyer, D. Van Kooten, S. Marsh, A.V. Prochazka, Reduction of Polypharmacy by Feedback to Clinicians, *J Gen Intern Med* 6 (1991): 133–6.

30. T.A. Parrino, The Nonvalue of Retrospective Peer Comparison Feedback in Containing Hospital Antibiotic Costs, *Am J Med* 86 (1989): 442–8.

31. L.A. Headrick, T. Speroff, H.I. Pelecanos, R.D. Cebul, Efforts to Improve Compliance With the National Cholesterol Education Program Guidelines: Results of a Randomized Controlled Trial, *Arch Intern Med* 152 (1992): 2490–6.

32. Hershey, et al., The Effect of Computerized Feedback.

33. Parrino, The Nonvalue of Retrospective Peer Comparison.

34. McPhee, et al., Promoting Cancer Screening.

35. Tierney, et al., Delayed Feedback.

36. D. Klein, Some Notes on the Dynamics of Resistance to Change: The Defender Role, in *The Planning of Change*, 3rd ed., eds. W.G. Bennis, K.D. Benne, R. Chin, K.E. Corey (New York: Holt, Rinehart & Winston, 1976), 117–24.

37. J.S. Spiegel, M.F. Shapiro, B. Berman, S. Greenfield, Changing Physician Test Ordering in a University Hospital: An Intervention of Physician Participation, Explicit Criteria, and Feedback, *Arch Intern Med* 149 (1989): 549–53.

38. T.J. Wachtel, P. O'Sullivan, Practice Guidelines to Reduce Testing in the Hospital, *J Gen Intern Med* 5 (1990): 335–41.

39. G. Laffel, D. Blumenthal, The Case for Using Industrial Quality Management Science in Health Care Organizations, *JAMA* 262 (1989): 2869–73.

40. D.M. Berwick, Continuous Improvement As an Ideal in Health Care, *N Engl J Med* 320 (1989): 53–6.

41. J.E. McEachern, P.K. Makens, E.D. Buchanan, L. Schiff, Quality Improvement: An Imperative for Medical Care, *J Occup Med* 33 (1991): 364–71.

42. D.M. Berwick, A.B. Godfrey, J. Roessner, *Curing Health Care: New Strategies for Quality Improvement* (San Francisco: Jossey-Bass, 1990).

43. R.W. Coleman, L.C. Rodondi, S. Kaubisch, N.B. Granzella, P.D. O'Hanley, Cost-Effectiveness of Prospective and Continuous Parenteral Antibiotic Control: Experience at the Palo Alto Veterans Affairs Medical Center from 1987 to 1989, *Am J Med* 90 (1991): 439–44.

44. J. Avorn, S.B. Soumerai, W. Taylor, M.R. Wessels, J. Janousek, M. Weiner, Reduction of Incorrect Antibiotic Dosing Through a Structured Educational Order Form, *Arch Intern Med* 148 (1988): 1720–4.

45. J.O. Zaat, J.T. Van Eijk, H.A. Bonte, Laboratory Test Form Design Influences Test Ordering by General Practitioners in the Netherlands, *Med Care* 30 (1992): 189–98.

46. P.A. Lindsey, J.P. Newhouse, The Cost and Value of Second Surgical Opinion Programs: A Critical Review of the Literature, *J Health Polit Policy Law* 15 (1990): 543–70.

47. B.H. Gray, M.J. Field, eds., *Controlling Costs and Changing Patient Care? The Role of Utilization Management* (Washington, D.C.: National Academy Press, 1989).

48. S.B. Soumerai, D. Ross-Degnan, J. Avorn, T.J. McLaughlin, I. Choodnovskiy, Effects of Medicaid Drug-Payment Limits on Admission to Hospitals and Nursing Homes, *N Engl J Med* 325 (1991): 1072–7.

49. G.B. Hickson, W.A. Altemeier, J.M. Perrin, Physician Reimbursement By Salary or Fee-for-Service: Effect on Physician Practice Behavior in a Randomized Prospective Study, *Pediatrics* 80 (1987): 344–50.

50. A.L. Hillman, M.V. Pauly, J.J. Kerstein, How Do Financial Incentives Affect Physicians' Clinical Decisions and the Financial Performance of Health Maintenance Organizations?, *N Engl J Med* 32 (1989): 86–92.

51. K.L. Kahn, E.B. Keeler, M.J. Sherwood, et al., Comparing Outcomes of Care Before and After Implementation of the DRG-Based Prospective Payment System, *JAMA* 264 (1990): 1984–8.

19. Overcoming the Barriers to Implementation of TQM/CQI in Hospitals: Myths and Realities

Douglas S. Wakefield and Bonnie J. Wakefield

Total Quality Management (TQM) and Continuous Quality Improvement (CQI) have captured the attention, and in a growing number of health care organizations, the resource commitments of administrators and quality management practitioners. At its simplest, TQM espouses creating an organizational culture emphasizing employee empowerment in order to move problem identification, analysis, and resolution as far down the organizational hierarchy as possible. Complementing this philosophy, CQI emphasizes that organizations need to continually seek opportunities to enhance the quality of their products or services and that application of statistical analysis and control techniques commonly found in industry will facilitate the assessment and enhancement processes. Expectations are that both the quality and efficiency of care processes will be enhanced with the adoption of TQM and CQI.

To fully integrate TQM and CQI in health care organizations requires a fundamental shift in current understanding and thinking about quality improvement. The existing attitude of "if it ain't broke, it don't need fixing," must be replaced by the attitude of "when it ain't broke may be the only time you can fix it."[1] Organizationally speaking, to do a better job we must expand the focus of quality assessment and enhancement activities to include both processes that are "broken" and processes that are not yet at a crisis stage. TQM provides such a mechanism for organizational preventive maintenance.

Unfortunately, health care organizations, in particular hospitals, face many challenges to successful implementation and integration of TQM and CQI. Recognizing these challenges and associated myths and developing strategies to

Source: Reprinted from *Quality Review Bulletin*, Vol. 19, No. 3, pp. 83–88, with permission of Mosby-Year Book, Inc., © 1993.

address these challenges are essential for making progress toward high quality and toward more effective and efficient health care organizations. This article discusses six such challenges, identifies some of the myths associated with each, and offers strategies for addressing these challenges.

CHALLENGES TO IMPLEMENTATION AND INTEGRATION OF TQM AND CQI IN HOSPITALS

A literature review[2-4] of the use of TQM and CQI in the manufacturing sector is required to prepare for implementing these concepts. Industry-specific differences exist in how customer relationships are formed and defined, in how production processes are developed, and in the ability of the ultimate customers to evaluate the quality of what they have purchased or received. Despite advances in health care technology, the fundamental patient care process is driven by the knowledge base and experience of individual physicians, nurses, and allied health care workers. Therefore, evaluating and redesigning manufacturing production processes built around "batch productions" dependent on machines, relatively consistent raw material supply and quality, and decisions of managers are infinitely easier than evaluating and redesigning "production processes" in the health care industry, which are oriented to the unique needs of individual patients and to the skills and knowledge of the 50–60 health care workers directly involved in their care.

It is precisely because of the high level of individualized physician and employee input into the patient care process that hospitals implementing TQM and CQI face challenges not encountered in the manufacturing setting, including the following:

- Not all the critical players in the hospital's production core are employees;
- Many hospitals have experienced long-standing, profession-driven turf battles involving conflict over responsibility and authority for specific direct care and support services;
- The traditional department-based vertical hierarchy of reporting relationships has been commonly used to manage interprofessional conflicts;
- Traditional employee evaluation and reward systems, which emphasize individual technical competence rather than the overall quality of team performance and productivity, have created a cadre of tunnel-visioned front-line supervisors, middle managers, and in some cases senior executives concerned only about the activities and subordinates under their immediate control with little interest or influence over broader organizationwide quality and productivity;

- Department-level managers and first-line supervisors frequently have well-developed technical skills but lack training in and understanding of basic management, supervisory, and problem-solving skills; and
- Incorporation of industrial statistical quality control methods and processes is frequently viewed as incompatible with the highly individualized nature of patient needs, hospital services, and delivery mechanisms.

Each of these challenges is discussed in the following sections.

PHYSICIANS: THE NONEMPLOYEE CRITICAL PLAYERS

Regardless of the organizational setting, successful efforts to introduce and integrate TQM and CQI require involvement and commitment of employees throughout the organization. This includes everyone, from the senior executive to the nurse at the bedside, the unit clerk, and the housekeeper. This presents a problem, however, because hospitals, unlike other organizations, often do not directly employ some of the most important players, the physicians.

The typical hospital-physician relationship represents a unique constraint to TQM and CQI implementation. First, patients can only be admitted by physicians, thereby tying hospital revenues directly to physician admission decisions. Second, only a minority of most physicians' time is spent in the hospital as opposed to the office setting. This makes it difficult to obtain interest in and commitment to new ways of doing things. Third, the role of the physician in the inpatient setting is essentially one of product designer or project manager—determining the types and timing of various inputs or services for each patient. However, frequently no mechanism exists for directly rewarding or sanctioning a physician's design performance. Finally, whereas physicians are prized by hospital administrators for the business they bring to the hospital, physicians frequently maintain admitting privileges in several competing facilities to maximize their own independence and productivity. For these reasons, it may be difficult to obtain physician support and commitment for management approaches or practices emphasizing the use of employee empowerment, interdisciplinary teams, and consensus decision making. The hospital administration truism—"Change whatever you want as long as you do not disrupt the physician"—underscores this fact.

Related Myths

There is at least one myth about physician-hospital relationships that, if believed and acted upon, makes implementation and integration of TQM and CQI in the hospital difficult.

Myth. Physicians are a relatively homogeneous group and in general do not care about improving the hospital's effectiveness or efficiency.

Reality. Although it is true that physicians share similar knowledge, education, and values, it is not true that the reason it is difficult to involve physicians in TQM and CQI initiatives is because they do not care about improving the hospital's performance. Closer to the truth is that physicians are not interested in making changes that they perceive as being performed primarily to enhance the hospital's bottom line or to give managers greater control over the delivery of patient care. As a group, physicians are interested in helping their patients. When TQM and CQI activities center on monitoring and improving the clinical quality of patient care, physicians become readily involved.

Physician-Related Strategies

The following strategies may help to increase physician involvement in hospital TQM and CQI initiatives:

Involve Physicians in Activities That Are of Direct Clinical Relevance to Patients. Physicians usually view as irrelevant and a waste of time TQM and CQI activities that lack direct clinical significance. Similarly, it is futile to interest physicians in project teams addressing hospital service quality issues. In general, the higher the clinical relevance (for example, reducing the time between emergency Caesarean decision and incision), the easier it is to involve physicians.

Build on Strengths, Not Weaknesses, of the Medical Staff. It is not necessary to include every physician in all TQM/CQI initiatives. Rather, a targeted approach may be more productive, in which the first physician involvement is from physicians who are both respected by their colleagues and clinically knowledgeable about the patient care area selected for improvement. However, to encourage input from all physicians and maintain the credibility of those directly involved, the general medical staff must be kept informed about the initiatives.

Present Data to Physicians in a Form That They Can Appreciate; That Is, Present "Hard" Evidence about Existing Practice, Not "Opinions" of Nonphysicians and Nonscientists. Because physicians are directly responsible for and to their patients and because they want to provide the best care possible, it is important to recognize what the most influential sources of information are and how best to present this information. In practice, physicians base their patient care decisions on a combination of data presented in the professional literature, findings from clinical trials, recommendations from professional societies, product information from pharmaceutical and other health care product suppliers, practices or protocols learned while in residency training, and firsthand experience. In order to change physician behavior, hard data and information about variations in existing practices must be presented in the most meaningful way (tabular or graphic). Likewise, valid and substantively meaningful data depicting current practice patterns may help to reeducate individual physicians (for example, those in private practice), many of whom are simply not aware of the nature and extent to which their practices differ from those of other similar providers.

Such data should not single out individual physicians for poor or questionable performance, but should be presented in such a way as to allow individual physicians to compare their practices with those of other physicians and collectively discuss, debate, and come to consensus as to appropriate practice patterns. Finally, sufficient time should be allowed for physicians to evaluate, challenge, and integrate new information. The goal is not to change all aspects of a physician's behavior, but to stimulate focused changes that are internally driven, not externally mandated. Being patient with the change process may help the quality enhancement professional avoid becoming a "Patient"!

INTERPROFESSIONAL BOUNDARY CONFLICT AND CONTROL

Health care workers have highly technical and extensive educational backgrounds, yet relatively limited scopes of practice as defined by their professional association's self-interests and state licensure laws. Health care workers sometimes display a greater allegiance to a profession's body of knowledge and behavior codes than to the values and goals of the organization they work for, and consequently health care workers move easily among health care organizations. This has led to the development of longstanding interprofessional turf boundary conflicts over areas of patient care responsibility, authority, and ultimately resource control. This orientation to professional over organizational boundaries may cause barriers to the integration of interdisciplinary communication, compromise, and problem-solving techniques and processes into the dominant organizational culture. The mindset of "us versus them" may limit the use of systems-oriented TQM/CQI collaborative initiatives, even when a common focus on improving patient outcomes is agreed on. Hence, successful integration of TQM and CQI in the health care work force requires that time and resources be invested in lowering interprofessional boundaries in the hospital.

Related Myths

There are two primary myths concerning the role of TQM/CQI and the management of interprofessional conflicts.

Myth. Professional groups are homogeneous.

Reality. Professional groups are often very heterogeneous. For example, in the case of nursing, the presence of multiple career entry levels or points (ADN, diploma, BSN) and specialized areas of practice (intensive care unit, emergency room, pediatrics, general medicine) automatically create major subgroups with different experiences and expectations. The same potential for intraprofessional heterogeneity exists in medicine and other health professions. Likewise, interprofessional conflict does not automatically occur among all nurses as a group and members of some other profession (such as physical therapy, social work, medical technologists). On the contrary, interprofessional conflicts most often arise among individual subgroups within each profession. Therefore, TQM/CQI implementation approaches that attempt to address interprofessional conflict based on the assumption that "a nurse is a nurse is a nurse" will be ineffective.

Myth. TQM represents a new way of managing interprofessional conflict because it emphasizes solving intraorganizational problems closer to the level at which they occur.

Reality. Many of the principles embodied by TQM/CQI have been articulated in part by other management theories and practiced at least to a limited extent by most hospitals. Belief in this myth also supports the notion that commonly accepted practice has been to manage interprofessional conflict by getting the respective department chiefs together to "work things out." In reality, most hospitals have always had a high level of interprofessional communication and done informal deal making at the individual staff level. What is true is that supervisors, department heads, and vice-presidents who fear a loss of power or control have established bureaucratic structures and mechanisms that actively discourage problem identification and conflict resolution at the lowest level. Therefore, educational initiatives that present TQM/CQI as a totally new and innovative way of managing interprofessional conflict significantly overstate its newness and insult the very people to whom it is being marketed, as well as ignore the fact that hospital hierarchies have a vested interest in limiting decision-making power of those at the lower levels of the organization.

Strategies for Managing Interprofessional Conflict

Following are several strategies to consider when managing a TQM implementation and interprofessional conflict:

- Because the root causes of interprofessional conflict are often related to organization-specific resource constraints rather than true interprofessional conflicts, make sure that TQM/CQI implementation addresses internal resource allocation issues.

- Present TQM not as something totally new, but as a continuation and an expansion of collaborative processes that have already been used successfully in the organization. That is, TQM establishes, through empowerment of individuals, a mechanism for developing better group problem-solving skills and reformalization of more effective policies.

- Build on existing interprofessional communication and cooperation strengths. In forming interdisciplinary quality improvement teams consider not only the knowledge and skills of the participants but also the existing nature and extent of cooperation among team members.

- Make sure that the facts of interprofessional conflicts are understood equally by all parties. To do this, identify areas of overlap and areas of unique knowledge and skill. Recognize and address the inherent bias of organizations to maintain the status quo by making certain that implementation teams represent all factions of the hospital bureaucracy.

USE OF VERTICAL HIERARCHIES TO MANAGE INTERPROFESSIONAL RELATIONSHIPS

In response to changes in the financing and regulation of health care, hospitals have tended to develop multiple levels of management hierarchy (first-line supervisors, department managers, assorted vice-presidents, group senior vice-presidents, chief operating officers, chief executive officer). As these managers have focused on a portion of the hierarchy, a "vertical" rather than a "horizontal" approach to issues (communication, coordination, and control of interdepartmental production problems; patient care quality assessment and enhancement issues; and conflict resolution) has developed.

The modern hospital has evolved as a collection of organizational subunits linked by the reliance on the traditional vertical hierarchy of reporting relationships—not the "seamless" organization proposed within the TQM framework. Frequently problems that could be best addressed at the immediate patient care delivery level are pushed up through the hospital's bureaucratic structures. Many hospitals must now face the challenge of reducing both the number of management levels within the hierarchy while providing mechanisms and incentives for horizontal collaboration among a multitude of departments and units.

Related Myths

Two related myths about the existing vertical hierarchy challenge any TQM implementation efforts.

Myth. Hospitals should be organized and supported by a vertical hierarchy that emphasizes the quality and efficiency of discipline-specific service provision.

Reality. The truth is that hospitals should be organized and supported by a vertical hierarchy that emphasizes the quality and efficiency of the patient care processes. A focus on the production of discipline-specific services results in complex and fragmented organizational structures that do little to maximize the continuity and comprehensiveness of patient care.

Myth. Staff in a given direct patient care or support department can only be supervised and managed by someone with training and experience in providing those services.

Reality. The result of belief in this myth is a proliferation of organizational entities within the hospitals, each with its own administrative structure and overhead. The link between these departments usually occurs at the director level—far removed from those providing the direct patient care. The combined results of reliance on these two myths can best be seen in the modern hospital's organizational chart. The resultant key quality and cost problems facing hospitals is how to manage the "white space" among the "boxes."

Strategies for Dealing with Existing Hierarchies

For hospitals to implement TQM successfully and improve patient care requires a willingness to do the following things:

- Decide that meeting patient care needs rather than providing services to patients is the primary basis for determining the appropriate structure and reporting relationships in the hospital; and
- Redraw the organizational chart to improve the ways in which patient care needs are met rather than the efficiency with which a specific department can provide its services. To date, many TQM initiatives in hospitals have dealt with superficial issues (for example, improving business office and support service activities)—efforts that have not addressed the appropriateness or effectiveness of the existing organizational structure and reporting relationships. Fortunately, the emergence of the "patient-focused care" concept[5-7] has pointed out a missing key ingredient.

EMPHASIS ON INDIVIDUAL RATHER THAN GROUP PERFORMANCE

Departments and individuals in hospitals have worked hard to define and develop quality control processes and measures specific to the services they provide or over which they have direct control. High degrees of professionalism, strong desires to enhance patient health status and functioning, and external forces such as the traditional review process of the Joint Commission on Accreditation of Healthcare Organizations (Oakbrook Terrace, Ill.) have acted together to reinforce this individualized service or department focus. Unfortunately, the result of this narrow focus is a fragmented and non-systems-oriented approach to quality assessment and enhancement. The vertical rather than horizontal approach to patient care problem identification, analysis, and resolution has limited progress in improving the overall patient care process. Because most patient care requires a combination of knowledge and technical expertise from several different disciplines, fragmenting quality assessment and enhancement initiatives among departments has only led to limited gains.

Related Myths

There is one primary related myth.

Myth. Existing human resource management activities are consistent with successful implementation of TQM.

Reality. The goal of implementing TQM and creating interdisciplinary teams to address opportunities for improving quality often centers on changing the ways individuals and small groups of people relate to each other and the patients. Because patient care processes are controlled by providers, changes in the process require changes that affect how people interact. There is no literature on the role of the hospital human resources department in supporting the implementation of TQM. There appears to be an oversight as to how the hospital's existing recruitment, selection, orientation, training, development, evaluation, compensation, credentialing and privileging, and labor relations activities may either facilitate or hinder TQM implementation efforts. If TQM does in fact involve fundamental changes in the way individuals and groups relate to each other, then the question is, "How do the existing human resources management strategies and policies help with this effort?"

Strategies for Shifting the Priority to Group Performance

Align the organization's human resources department activities in support with the TQM initiative. To begin with, consider whether the methods and processes used to evaluate and reward health care managers and workers need an overhaul. Existing evaluation and reward systems generally focus exclusively on individual and departmental performance rather than on the entire patient care team. Driven by incentives that reinforce a focus on their own areas while ignoring the organization's "big picture," existing evaluation and reward systems encourage the development of individually focused employees and managers. Unless explicitly identified as a performance requirement and sanctioned through the incentive system, behaviors that facilitate interdepartmental team building, problem solving, and cooperation cannot automatically be expected as outcomes.

At issue is the need to develop valid measures of team performance along with incentive systems reinforcing both individual and team performances. With few exceptions, the quality of any organization's products or services is more a reflection of how well the component parts of the production process work together than the strength of individual performances. Therefore, aligning the employees' and managers' evaluation and reward systems to support the underlying tenets of TQM/CQI is one of the most important organizational infrastructure changes that senior management can make.

In a similar vein, the criteria used to select and retain employees may need to be modified. If change in the nature, extent, and effectiveness of interdepartmental or interprofessional cooperation is critical to enhancing the quality of care, then it would seem reasonable to adjust recruitment and retention policies accordingly. Likewise, employee education and development programs should have a focus and purpose consistent with the TQM approach.

Finally, because TQM can be threatening to both union and nonunion employees, actively incorporate effective labor-relations practices into the TQM initiatives. In a unionized setting, involve representatives from the union early on and throughout the TQM implementation; this is not only necessary but highly consistent with TQM philosophy. Likewise, in nonunionized settings, minimize the "fear factor" through frequent, repetitive, open communications processes that keep everyone informed about the focus and potential benefits of implementing TQM.

CLINICAL KNOWLEDGE AND SKILLS ARE NOT SUBSTITUTES FOR MANAGEMENT KNOWLEDGE AND SKILLS

At the same time that the combined responsibilities of increasing productivity and decreasing costs enhance the effectiveness and quality of services, they represent primary challenges facing health care managers at all levels. Traditionally, many managers in health care have been promoted for their technical expertise and ability to closely manage and control service production in their departments. Unlike other industries, little opportunity exists for many of these managers to gain either service, production, or managerial experience by working in other departments or divisions. Ironically, the management style and skills that have hastened their advancement (that is, relatively narrow technical expertise emphasizing the value and knowledge biases of their profession and productivity of their department) may not have prepared them to be effective collaborators.

Related Myths

There are two related myths concerning managers in health care settings which may influence the success of the TQM implementation.

Myth. The best clinicians make the best managers.

Myth. The transition from clinician to manager is relatively natural and does not represent a major developmental process requiring extensive formal education.

Reality. The truth is that being a master clinician requires a different knowledge and skill base than that required for a master manager. The best clinicians enter the managerial ranks for higher salaries. Traditionally, most hospitals have provided little if any formal education to support this change in role and responsibility. Management knowledge, skills, and insights are frequently developed and acquired by observing peers who have undergone similar career transformations. The question is whether those most important to the success of TQM implementation are qualified outside the technical knowledge of their field.

Strategies To Address Limited Management Knowledge Levels

There is one overarching strategy to address the limited management knowledge level of key hospital employees: Senior management must invest in educating its manager cadre in both TQM and basic management skills. Many departmental managers and front-line supervisors need time and opportunity to develop an understanding of and appreciation for the potential benefits of the new system and to develop better management skills. Ways to do this include creating a manager apprenticeship whereby inexperienced managers spend time with experienced managers from other parts of the same organization and providing tuition support or bringing in-house management training in the areas of leadership, motivation, organizational design, finance, strategic planning, communications, decision making, and organization culture. To some extent, the TQM implementation process can become the basis for an internal management development program. If successful, a management "farm team" can be developed in which there is a deliberate rather than haphazard employee development strategy. In any case, senior management must be willing to invest heavily in time and resources to create these opportunities.

RESISTANCE TO USING STATISTICAL QUALITY CONTROL METHODS

For patients and health care providers alike, the provision of health care services is a highly individualized, personal, and sometimes uncomfortable process. Further, the outcome of a given health care provider's intervention may not be related to the quality of the service as much as to the health status and combination of underlying diseases unique to each patient or the appropriateness and effectiveness of the services provided by some other provider. Because of the highly individualized nature of health care services and the somewhat tenuous link between patient outcome and quality of care, many health care professionals feel a natural skepticism toward the applicability of traditional industrial quality control processes in the health care setting.

Related Myths

There are two related myths to consider regarding the use of statistical control tools.

Myth. Most patient care is not highly routinized and hence does not lend itself to the use of statistical control tools.

Myth. The use of statistical control techniques will result in "cookbook medicine" that does not focus on the needs of the individual, and this will result in poor quality care.

Reality. All categories of direct care providers (physicians, nurses, therapists) generally abhor the notion of cookbook medicine. The implication is that little consistency exists in the ways clinicians approach and address similar types of patient conditions or problems. The reality is that in fact clinicians do develop to some degree a consistent "internal protocol" for how they go about the patient care process. The basis for this process is determined in large part by where they were educated and what their peers in the local practice setting deem appropriate. The abundant small-area practice variation literature provides ample documentation of the presence of "de facto cookbooks."[8]

Strategies To Overcome Resistance to the Use of Statistical Control Processes

Use a targeted rather than indiscreet approach to applying statistical control process. These processes should be useful tools, not pervasive time-consuming exercises focusing on data for data's sake. Managers and clinicians must understand what statistical control processes can and cannot do. Statistical control processes do not determine what should be done; rather, they can be used to monitor how consistently providers comply with basic care processes and how often outcomes differ from desirable limits. The goal of statistical control processes is to reduce variation and increase the reliability in priority areas of patient care which are considered routine and well accepted for the standard of care as well as for a few critical outcomes. Finally, clinicians must understand that the roots of statistical control processes are derived directly from traditional statistics, and that manufacturing was the first production area to apply these tools to reduce undesirable variation.

Successful integration and use of statistical quality control methods in health care settings require that all of the following conditions be met:

- Recognition of the uniqueness of the health care setting in providing highly individualized packages or combinations of services that are relatively routine and well accepted;
- Investment in education and information systems support to facilitate use of specific tools and control processes; and
- Creativity in adapting, rather than forcing, a fit between traditional industrial quality control processes and the hospital setting.

In the end, statistical quality control methods imported from industry will be used effectively only to the extent that employees can recognize some of the benefits through better patient outcomes and more efficient and satisfying work processes.

NOTES

1. P. Crosby, *Quality Is Free: The Art of Making Quality Certain* (New York: McGraw-Hill, 1979).

2. M. Walton, *The Deming Management Method* (New York: Putnam Publishing Group, 1986).

3. A. Garvin, *Managing Quality: The Strategic and Competitive Edge* (New York: The Free Press, 1988).

4. A. Zalenznik, Managers and Leaders: Are They Different?, *Harvard Business Review* (Mar-Apr 1992): 126–135.

5. S. Allawi, D. Bellarie, L. David, Are You Ready for Structural Change?, *Healthcare Forum Journal* 4 (1991): 39–42.

6. F. Gomberg, K. Miller, Decentralization, Crosstraining, and Care Paths Define 'World Class Healthcare' at Florida's Lee Memorial, *Strategies for Healthcare Excellence* 5, no. 3 (1992): 1–7.

7. C. Curran, C. Smeltzer, Operations Improvement: Efficiencies and Quality, *Journal of Nursing Quality Assurance* 5, no. 4 (1991): 1–6.

8. N.P. Roos, L.L. Roos, Small Area Variations, Practice Style, and Quality of Care, in *Assessing Quality Health Care: Perspectives for Clinicians*, ed., P.R. Wenzel (Baltimore: Williams & Wilkins, 1992).

PART III.

TOMORROW

Contemplation of the future is not a discretionary matter.
—*Stuart Davidson*

Looking at the research that is ongoing today, we get a glimpse of the future of medical science. Geneticists worldwide are currently cooperating on the Human Genome Project, an ambitious effort to map and sequence the human genome. The implications of the Human Genome Project alone, are staggering. "Predicting your future health and the likelihood of a chronic illness may sound more like science fiction than science fact . . . But physicians of the early twenty-first century *may* routinely make such determinations based on a patient's genetic makeup, current health, and family history."[1]

HEALTH CARE IN THE FUTURE

In the future, genes will be the new sites of care. Think of the advantages of knowing a patient's genetic makeup. The potential is so enormous it is hard to fathom. "Health risks will be analyzed using a data base of a patient's genetic information. In the future, scientists see the promise of reversing genetic damage chemically by replacing damaged or defective genes by infusing genetically altered cells into the body."[2] In Chapter 20, Jeff Goldsmith focuses on the promise and implications that genetic research holds for the future. Combine strides in genetics with the use of *expert information technology* that acts as an interactive electronic assistant to physicians and caregivers, and imagine the emergence of so-called "predictive" or "anticipatory" medicine. Health care will move from its current *diagnosis and treatment* approach to *prediction and management*. This will enable clinicians "to intervene well before problems become acute or chronic and therefore difficult and expensive to manage care."[3]

Whether brought on by this new knowledge and technology or by the "graying of America," trends shaping the future labor force will also have a profound affect on health care. As caregivers' jobs change in response to new requirements, we will see:

- the crosstraining of multiskilled workers who will do everything it doesn't require a license to do[4]
- the emergence of health information specialists who will guide patients through the continuum of care as providers shift their focus from treating sickness to maintaining health
- the increase in alternative health care providers (nutritionists, exercise physiologists, acupuncturists, massage therapists, chiropractors, and aromatherapists) involved in mind/body medicine and non-Western healing techniques[5]
- the decline in the number of RNs and corresponding increase in the number of advanced practice nurses who will manage global use of resources and patient placement
- tighter credentialing of physicians who will practice under guidelines tied to reimbursement, creating a decrease in the variation now common in medical care

Health care—as well as the technology and employees used to deliver that care—is changing at such an accelerated pace that it is difficult to identify the issues that might affect hospitals within the next decade, much less the next century. Looking ahead, health futurist Clement Bezold, explores the possibilities in Chapter 21. This chapter identifies five potential scenarios that, "provoke imagination, raise fundamental questions, and stretch world views."[6]

THE FUTURE OF HEALTH CARE ORGANIZATIONS

As the role of medical science shifts from *diagnosis and treatment* to *prediction and management* of illness, the way in which health care institutions are organized must also evolve.

Perhaps the best way to look at the next hundred years is to look back at the last hundred years. One can draw a striking parallel between the railroads of the 1890s and the hospitals of the 1990s. In the 1890s, railroads flourished. But as transportation advanced and regulations increased, the railroads that were once a central institution in American life were replaced by quicker, more efficient forms of transportation. In the 1990s, hospitals are a central institution in American life and key players in the economy.[7] But, like the railroads, they could soon be replaced by other, more efficient and cost-effective forms of providing health care to the consumer. "Hospitals are to health care as railroads were to transportation 100 years ago."[8]

Does this mean that hospitals are destined to decline like the railroads of the past? No, but to survive, hospitals need to learn new ways of doing business. Hospital facilities and services will continue to exist, but not under one roof. The traditional large hospital with a tightly centralized bureaucracy is incapable of meeting the needs of the future. "Like the railroads before them, hospitals need to reposition themselves."[9] New organizational designs will be needed to save hospitals from being replaced by smaller, more efficient forms of service. When organizations grow, their size usually becomes a barrier to flexibility. As we look at the changes predicted for the future, flexibility appears to be a central ingredient in organizational design.

To ensure flexibility, we must step out of the organizational boxes we have drawn around ourselves and look toward decentralization. What could be an organizational model for twenty-first century health care management? Perhaps we can think of the spider plant, *Chlorophytum comosum*, as the organizational design of the next century. If one is managing in a tight centralized bureaucracy, the image of the spider plant may have little relevancy. If, on the other hand, one is working in health care with alliances, integrations, and trying to launch new initiatives in a more decentralized style, the metaphor resonates with much more validity. The message of the spider plant is that you can grow larger while staying small. Better to create an offshoot of one's business than to grow too large to

remain effective. The offshoot then becomes a semi-autonomous unit and the health care facility decentralizes its organization in order to remain responsive to the needs of its clientele. Effective management of the offshoot now becomes imperative. The purpose of this metaphor of the spider plant is "to illustrate some basic elements of a process that can help us reshape old thinking and old organization designs in new ways. Organizations never change by changing structure. They're changed by changing thinking."[10]

From railroads to spider plants, that is where the future will take us. From rigid chain-of-command organizational designs to more flexible, less cumbersome, decentralized structures. Navigating through the deluge of changes in the field of health care over the next century will require new thinking and the foresight to put those thoughts into practice.

QUESTIONS FOR THOUGHT, DISCUSSION, AND RESEARCH

1. How do you assure quality and improve processes when quality crosses institutions?
2. How reliable and valid are the outcomes measures?
3. Can CQI help foster integrated models of community health?
4. How do you maintain confidentiality of data?
5. Can CQI affect the continuum of health care to the same extent that it can affect episodes of illness?
6. How do you change societal values?
7. What ethical, quality, and economic issues will need to be addressed with the advances in gene therapy?
8. How do you measure provider effectiveness in improving health status and decreasing health risk?
9. What effect do guidelines have on quality, cost, and patient outcome?
10. What will be the future role of TQM in restructuring the U.S. health care system?
11. What will be the effects of the rapidly changing global financial marketplace on the quality of care?
12. How do you manage the rate of change?
13. What will be the role of the hospital?
14. Will there be a more rigorous approach to collecting, analyzing, and using data from patient satisfaction surveys?
15. What have been the measurable effects of QI on the cost, quality, and effectiveness of the health care provided by organizations or networks using QI?
16. How will the emerging capacity of biotechnology to predict and manage health care risk affect the delivery system and the quality of care?

17. What are the societal, ethical, legal, economic, and quality issues related to the predicted quantum leaps in health care research?
18. How do patients and purchasers of health care use data on the quality and effectiveness of health care?

NOTES

1. P.L. Bergman, Quantum Leaps, *Hospital and Health Network* 67 (1993): 28.

2. Ibid, 31.

3. Ibid, 28.

4. Ibid, 30.

5. Ibid, 31.

6. C. Bezold, Five Futures, *Healthcare Forum Journal* (May/June 1992), 29–42.

7. J.L. Morrison, Railways of the Nineties, *Healthcare Forum Journal* (March/April, 1993), 30–40.

8. Ibid., 30–34.

9. Ibid, 34.

10. G. Morgan, *Imaginization* (Newbury Park, Calif.: Sage Publications, Inc., 1993), 88–89.

20. The Reshaping of Health Care

Jeff C. Goldsmith

For most of this century, the American health care system has been organized around the acute illness: a life-threatening Act of God. The role of the health care system was to rescue us from the illness and to take custody of us until we were well again.

We have used a casualty model of health insurance to finance health care, attempting to spread the cost of intervention across as broad a pool of "risk" as possible. We have built a vast and costly apparatus around this acute-care model, premised on the fundamental unpredictability of disease.

As chronic illnesses—degenerative diseases correlated closely to the aging process—replaced the acute infection as our most significant health problem, the "fit" between our health care needs and the health services framework worsened significantly. The acute-care framework was shaken during the past 15 years by rapid advances in diagnostic and therapeutic technologies that enabled caregivers to intervene earlier in chronic disease processes like heart disease and cancer, and to manage more patients on an ambulatory basis (prior to an episode of acute need) without hospitalization.

Changes in the next 15 years will demolish what remains of the acute-care paradigm and force our health insurance system and society to confront the increased predictability of disease risk. Unlike the "revolution" in health care delivery during the eighties, which arose from the imaging and surgical suites, the impending revolution will originate in the pharmacy and clinical laboratory. Parallel advances in predictive genetics and immunology will converge during the next 15 years, making it possible to predict chronic disease risk in many persons before symptoms emerge.

Source: Reprinted from *Healthcare Forum Journal*, May/June 1994, pp. 19–25, with permission of The Healthcare Forum, © 1994.

The paradigm of diagnosis and treatment [Figure 20–1] will be replaced by one of prediction and early-stage management of illness, rendering much of our current armada of diagnostic and curative technologies obsolete [Figure 20–2]. "Acts of man" will be increasingly implicated in our health status, rendering the casualty model of health insurance fundamentally untenable.

UNRAVELING THE GENETIC ROOTS OF ILLNESS

Most acute infections are visited upon us by foreign agents like bacteria, viruses, or other parasites. By comparison, most chronic diseases originate within our genome—our complex genetic programming. Each cell in the human body contains about nine feet of DNA, containing the genetic recipe for a human being.

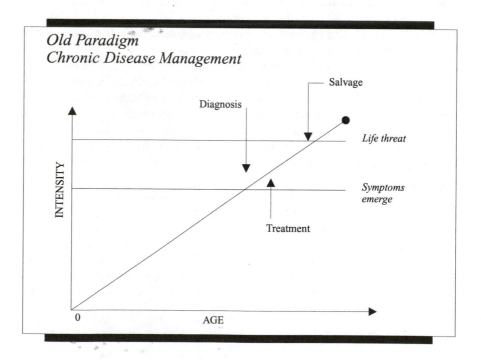

Figure 20–1 Old Paradigm. *Source:* Health Futures.

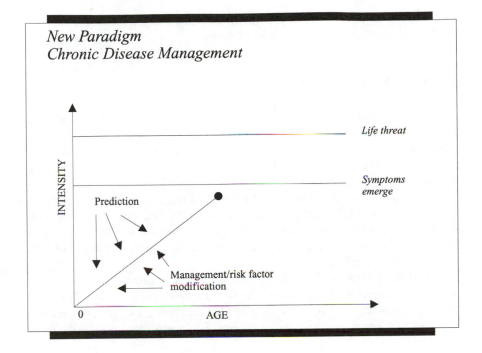

Figure 20–2 New Paradigm. *Source:* Health Futures.

Some 3,000–4,000 human diseases can be traced to defects in a single gene, and many other major diseases, such as diabetes and cancer, are probably the result of multiple, interacting genetic flaws, triggered by environmental or behavioral events. Evidence of these genetic links was uncovered by studying patterns of inheritance of diseases in multiple generations of the same family through population genetics.

During the mid-eighties, a confluence of events in human genetics enabled scientists, for the first time, not only to locate (or map) within a specific chromosome the genetic flaws linked to major illnesses such as cystic fibrosis, but to decode (or sequence) the specific gene at issue and identify the protein product of that gene.

Wedded to the powerful new diagnostic technologies such as the genetic probe, identification of specific genetic roots of disease is leading to rapid development of predictive tests that can tell prospective parents if their child-to-be has inherited defective genes that will predispose him or her to a specific illness later in life. While disease risk is obviously mediated by both environment and behavior, comprehensive risk assessment based upon the genetic makeup of an individual will be possible within 15 years.

HUMAN GENOME PROJECT

During the next 15 years, geneticists around the world will be conducting a massive cooperative research effort called the Human Genome Project. Its goal is to completely map and at least partially sequence the entire human genome. Scientists do not even know how many genes a human possesses (the best estimate is 50,000–100,000).

By the conclusion of this project, the form and function of most of our genes will have been established—and a new dimension of medicine will have emerged. Instead of "diagnosing" disease late in disease processes, we will be predicting disease risk based upon our genetic inheritance, and attempting to manage that risk before symptoms emerge.

The Human Genome Project has been called a biological version of the Manhattan Project, which produced the world's first atomic device. This is an apt analogy, since the information yielded by the Human Genome Project will detonate like a nuclear device in our society. Few institutions will be the same afterward.

The genome project will destroy the population-based actuarial framework on which our health and life insurance industries rest, and it will touch off a violent struggle over the control of genetic testing information and our privacy rights.

The genome project will lead to a capacity to provide prospective parents detailed information on the physical character, personality, intelligence, and life chances of their future child as early as six cell divisions after conception. It will even be possible for a woman to sort through her "inventory" of eggs to find the most "desirable" or heartiest egg for future conception.

It will provide parents of young children with potentially devastating information on the risks they have passed on to them. Genetic screening technologies will probably be inexpensive enough to be applicable to broad populations, enabling us to locate those with the highest prospective disease risk in order to focus our preventive resources on them.

These exciting genetic breakthroughs raise a major question: How will we manage this information and its impact on our thus "empowered" lives?

THE END OF INSURANCE?

The premise of illness as an unpredictable casualty or Act of God will be invalidated by genetic screening. Some such illnesses or occurrences like trauma or viral infection will still remain, but they will be a small portion of our total burden of illness. And though understanding our genetic inheritance will not predict with perfect certainty the likelihood of disease occurrence or premature death, it will dramatically narrow the uncertainty.

For health and life insurers, who have made underwriting decisions based upon actuarial estimates of group risk or life expectancy, genetic prediction represents a cataclysm. If individuals knew, even with 40 percent certainty, that they would contract an expensive or life-shortening illness, they could purchase life or health insurance at a much lower price than their actual risk would suggest. If a significant population did so, insurers would be bankrupted. Because of adverse selection, they would pay out in claims far more than they collected in premiums.

Yet would it be socially responsible to pay out claims for avoidable or manageable illnesses that individuals, having known the risks, did nothing to ameliorate? Could we continue to pretend that illnesses that are predictable or likely consequences of identified genetic flaws are simply "Acts of God" and pay for care for them as if they were accidents?

Under present rules (or lack of them), insurers could demand genetic screening information and use it to exclude individuals from coverage, or mandate that specific actions be taken as a condition of insurance. Parents whose unborn child was found to have a high likelihood of expensive illness could be mandated to abort the child as a condition of continuing to receive family coverage. Or specific therapy could be mandated to ameliorate the identified risk.

Americans are likely to rebel against the use of genetic screening information to restrict their freedom. But who will negotiate the "treaty" between individual rights and the insurance industry? How will publicly financed health insurance programs like Medicare or Medicaid, or their successors, manage genetic information on their covered populations? What is the appropriate balance between individual and societal responsibility for the resultant cost of care? Will life and health insurance underwriting be socially viable in the biotechnological future?

DO-IT-YOURSELF EUGENICS

Even if these problems are resolved satisfactorily, how individuals will behave in response to this information may be even more problematical. The decision to abort a fetus that carries the genes for Huntington's disease may be a morally and socially responsible decision, but what about the decision to abort a fetus with only a 30 percent risk of say, colon cancer, which might not even occur until age 70? American society has a high intolerance of risk of any kind, so why should genetic risk be any different?

What is to prevent parents from aborting if their future child is not going to be tall, blond, and intelligent, or if it carries the genes for a "difficult personality"? Unimpeded by societal restrictions, tides of fashion could sweep through our gene pool, eliminating diversity for those with sufficient resources to afford the intervention, and potentially heightening existing social class or racial differences or life chances. In a way, it is fortunate that such an intense debate is taking place about how we feel about abortion, because the new information prospective parents will acquire will only make the decisions and societal consequences that much more difficult to manage.

It does not take a Rhodes scholar to predict a critical scarcity of human geneticists and genetics counselors by the end of this decade, or the birth of a multi-billion-dollar new industry of genetics testing and counseling. Nor does it take a crystal ball to predict a worsening of societal conflict over abortion and reproductive rights and access to prenatal and postnatal care as well as to the costly, emerging therapies to correct genetic abnormalities.

Genetic therapy may trail definitive predictive genetics by as much as a generation, providing a lengthy period of anxiety and perhaps overreaction to genetic screening information. American society is appallingly unprepared to face these issues.

OPPORTUNITIES TO REDUCE ILLNESS

The eerie gap between the advent of genetic screening and the availability of genetic therapy does, nevertheless, present significant opportunities to reduce needless illness. Broad-based screening of large populations will enable the health care system to focus its efforts on those with the highest identified health risks. Genetic screening will lead to regular, disease-specific prospective monitoring based upon inexpensive diagnostic tests and custom tailored to the genetic risks for individuals.

For many diseases, periodic screening for protein "markers" in the blood or urine of "at risk" children or adults will provide clues to the early onset of the actual disease process. Such markers have been discovered for juvenile onset diabetes (specific antibodies circulating free in the blood signal the body's misguided immune response to its own beta islet cells, which, when destroyed, render the patient diabetic). [See Figures 20–3 and 20–4.] Serum markers have also been discovered that signal the beginning of some forms of cancer.

Controlling environmental and behavioral risk factors that accelerate the genetically determined disease risk will be even more important during the next 15 years than it is today. Specifically identified vulnerabilities may increase the saliency of avoiding risky diets and lifestyles. Parents can thus tailor their child-rearing strategies to minimize the impact of inherited risks. Obviously, dietary

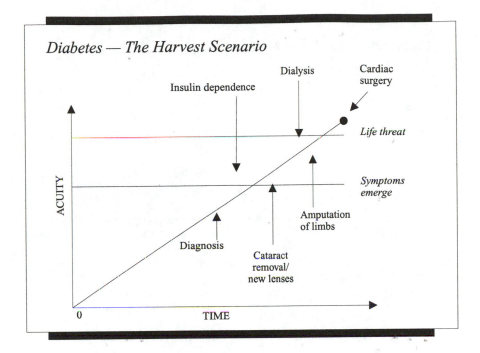

Figure 20–3 Diabetes—The Harvest Scenario. *Source:* Health Futures.

and behavioral risk factors that may uncover or trigger disease-specific genetic flaws will get much attention.

THE "LIQUID NERVOUS SYSTEM"

By far the most complex organ in the body is its immune system, a "liquid nervous system" capable of recognizing and defending against literally a trillion foreign substances the body has never seen before. For more than a generation, scientists have dreamed of enhancing the body's remarkable defense mechanisms as a tool in fighting disease.

Instead of introducing foreign substances into the body, immunotherapy's goal is to selectively stimulate or suppress the immune response to specific events such as viral infection, trauma, or organ transplantation. Given the complexity of the immune system, progress in development of immunotherapy has been slow, and it will be incremental, rather than "revolutionary," in nature.

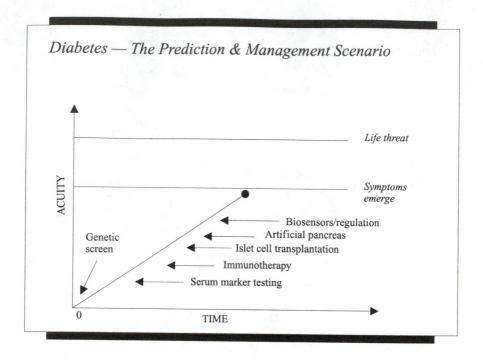

Figure 20–4 Diabetes—the Prediction and Management Scenario. *Source:* Health Futures.

A major goal of immunotherapy is controlling the function of strategic substances that shape the immune response. These substances, called cytokines, are the chemical messengers that not only activate the immune system but heal the body's wounds and guide the growth and repair of its organs and tissues. These cytokines include epidermal and nerve growth factors, blood cell growth factors like EPO and G-CSF, and the interferones and interleukins—an increasingly familiar set of human substances at center stage in biotechnology.

Until the advent of genetic engineering, scientists were reduced to bizarre schemes in their attempts to extract from vast quantities of human blood or urine tiny amounts of these naturally manufactured substances to study their disease-fighting impact. The advent of genetic engineering changed everything.

Now it is possible to take the gene that codes to these complex proteins and splice it into bacteria and grow bathtubs full of them. In ten or 15 years, we will take the same genes and splice them into algae and grow designer proteins in ponds, or splice the genes into cows and harvest their protein products out of the milk. The price will fall as technology improves and the initial high costs of development are paid down.

The explosion of biotechnology stock prices during 1991 was the result of the first wave of genetically engineered cytokines, initially EPO and G-CSF, making their way into pharmacies. These two substances cause, respectively, red and white blood cells to regenerate rapidly. EPO is a substance produced in the kidneys to correct for anemia, which reduces the red blood cell count and oxygen-carrying capacity of the blood. G-CSF causes the white blood cells to regenerate after bone marrow transplantation or whole body radiotherapy for cancer. That is how it restores immune system function, shortening the dangerous period of infection risk after these radical therapies.

These two substances are the first of a wave of new biologicals that will speed the healing process. Epidermal growth factors will speed healing and reduce scarring from burns and major trauma. Nerve growth factors promise to regenerate damaged nerve tissues and restore loss of function from trauma or degenerative diseases like Alzheimer's or Parkinson's disease.

New immunosuppressants will control the body's natural tendency to reject a transplanted organ. Instead of shutting down the entire immune system and exposing the transplant patient to a whole range of infections, the goal in transplantation is to induce organ-specific, donor-specific immune tolerance, leaving the rest of the immune system intact. Pursuit of this prize remains elusive, but significant incremental improvements have been made in immunosuppression with new substances like OKT-3 (a man-made antibody), FK506, and rapamycin.

MAN-MADE ANTIBODIES

There are two types of immune response. One is the production of hunter and killer cells, which scavenge the bloodstream and organs and destroy diseased cells and foreign substances. The other is the production of antibodies, which bind to specific threatening substances, blocking their action against the body and subsequently destroying them. The human body contains almost 10 million different antibodies, which are constantly differentiating in response to new threats.

A major breakthrough in biotechnology was the ability to create man-made antibodies using a mouse as an antibody "factor." In 1975, scientists stimulated a mouse to produce antibodies to a particular foreign substance (called antigen), isolated the antibody by dissecting it from the mouse's spleen, and fused it to mouse cancer cells, which enabled them to grow quantities of that specific ("monoclonal") antibody in a petri dish.

The discovery of this technology has led to widespread anticipation of rapid progress in the fight against cancer. By manufacturing specific antibodies to recognize a particular cancer cell, and fusing it to the antibody substances that could destroy the cell once contact was made, scientists expected major breakthroughs in cancer therapy.

This early optimism has not been borne out. In fact, it took 15 years before the first two major man-made antibodies, neither of which are cancer drugs, made their way through the FDA approval process. These are the immunosuppressant OKT-3 and the antisepsis drug Centoxin.

Using animals as antibody-producing "factories" is time-consuming and expensive. It also yields substances that can trigger immune rejection by the human immune system because they are recognized as foreign and attacked. Advances in genetic engineering may soon make it possible to replicate the entire human antibody library in a colony of bacteria, making possible rapid location and replication of the desired antibodies.

This will markedly reduce the cost of antibody production and enable pharmacists to concoct specific combinations of antibodies for individual patients or for classes of illness. Eventually, scientists hope that hybrid man-made antibodies that both identify and chemically destroy specific cells will be used in a wide range of therapies including treatment of viral illnesses like AIDS and hepatitis, as well as cancer.

CONQUERING AUTOIMMUNE DISEASES

Two of the most widely prevalent chronic diseases—diabetes and arthritis—are believed to be autoimmune diseases. This means that they arise from a malfunction in the immune system that causes the body's natural defenses to attack the body's own cells as if they were foreign. Short-circuiting this inappropriate immune reaction could be the key to preventing these diseases.

There has been sharply rising optimism that these diseases may be prevented by selective immune suppression. In the case of juvenile onset diabetes, it may be possible, by anticipating the body's attack on the insulin-making beta islet cells in the pancreas, to snuff the process with aggressive immunosuppression. [See Figure 20–4.]

The more widely prevalent adult onset version of diabetes, which results from a loss of sensitivity to insulin, may be a more difficult nut to crack.

With arthritis, the very substances that are key to stimulating the immune response—interleukins 1 and 6, and a substance called TNF (tumor necrosis factor)—have been implicated in the destruction of cartilage and bone in arthritis. These substances even play a role in osteoarthritis, which is no longer thought to be a completely mechanical process, but increasingly a chemical or metabolic one. Understanding what releases these substances into the joints and blocking their release or their uptake into the cartilage and bone holds the key to curing arthritis.

This goal, which would liberate tens of millions of arthritis sufferers from increasingly painful disability, appears to be within realization by the end of the decade or the beginning of the next one.

Naturally occurring substances that block inflammation may have wider applicability than merely controlling arthritis. Inflammation is a signal that the body's immune system is actively responding to a threat to our health, but inflammation sometimes flares out of control, as in the gram-negative bacterial infections that bring on septic shock. The body manufactures substances that block inflammation by blocking the inflammatory cytokines, such as the interleukins. Controlling interleukin release and action may be an even more powerful tool for fighting septic shock than the controversial antibody Centoxin.

BEGGED QUESTIONS

Societal readiness to use these powerful new tools is, alas, highly questionable. Some new biologicals are staggeringly expensive (Centoxin will cost $3,700 per dose) and challenge the system to rationalize their use. Others, like the new generation of bioengineered vaccines, may not only cost less but avert massive costs in broad populations by depriving viral agents of a foothold.

Genetic screening and serum marker testing, as well as monitoring devices like biosensors that detect changes in key body chemistries, are likely to be inexpensive enough to be used broadly across society without bankrupting an already strained health care budget. Biotechnology is not synonymous with "costly."

The ability of people to adopt a "life cycle" approach to their disease risk will require marked changes in societal values—lengthening time horizons and encouraging responsible healthy behavior. While the sharp reduction in the number of smokers does suggest that health promoting value and behavioral change is possible, a depressingly large fraction of contemporary illness could be prevented without technological assistance.

Changing societal values is the essential task, and one which requires both public health and political leadership.

Further, the millions who lie outside our present health insurance system do not get access to primary-care physicians or other caregivers who can identify early disease risks and counsel individuals or families on how to avoid them. America is experiencing mini-epidemics of nineteenth-century diseases like measles, tuberculosis, and syphilis, because immunization rates are falling and basic public health measures are not being followed.

If these trends—poor primary-care access and erosion of public heath effort— persist, the new advances will only accentuate the already disgracefully large variation in health status and life chances existing between rich and poor. But if access to primary care or neighborhood-level health care services were improved, the emerging armada of new biological tools could dramatically improve the health of those at the highest risk.

Most important, however, will be devising a new way of thinking about illness. It will be morally and fiscally untenable to continue to think of disease as an inexorable Act of God. Our health insurance system will have to find a new rationale for assessing health care risk and setting premiums.

To the extent that illnesses become predictable and manageable, our passive, reactive approach to financing and delivering care must give way to a proactive approach that implicates the patient, family, and society in appropriate measure in both the avoidance and ultimate financing of care.

Some way must be found of balancing the individual and societal obligation to promote good health with the responsibility for providing needed care for unavoidable or unmanageable conditions. Americans need not be passive victims of disease.

The health care system's new tools will permit it to transfer both power and moral responsibility to families and individuals to manage their own health care effectively.

SUGGESTED READINGS

Bishop, J. and Waldholz, M. *Genome*, Touchstone Books, 1990.

Hood, L. "Biotechnology and Medicine of the Future," *Journal of the American Medical Association*, March 25, 1988.

Biotechnology in Perspective, Industrial Biotechnology Association, Washington, DC, 1990.

Eisenstein, B. "The Polymerase Chain Reaction: A New Method of Using Molecular Genetics for Medical Diagnosis," *New England Journal of Medicine*, January 18, 1990.

Jaret, P. "Our Immune System: The Wars Within," *National Geographic,* June 1986.

Nossal, G. "Immunology: The Basic Components of the Immune System," *New England Journal of Medicine*, May 21, 1987.

"What Science Knows About AIDS," *Scientific American*, October 1988.

21. Five Futures

Clement Bezold

"The future" of society and of health care cannot be predicted with certainty. Major societal events such as the fall of the Berlin Wall and the transformation of the Soviet Union remind us of that. But there are patterns of change that can be anticipated.

We "know" with some certainty, for instance, how many Americans over age 85 there will be in the first decade of the twenty-first century, even if we are not as certain about their health status. Breakthroughs in science and technology can be anticipated in areas such as mapping the human genome and understanding healthy aging. The specific timing of relevant scientific discoveries, their translation into technological applications, and uptake into medical practice are much more difficult to forecast.

Changes in societal values, public policy, and individual behavior are even more uncertain. Yet these changes are often more important. Will we deal with poverty, the single largest correlate to ill health? Will trends toward greater consumer interest in health continue? How will national health care policy and financing evolve?

Scenarios—alternative futures for health care in the twenty-first century—allow us to explore varying answers to these questions. Scenarios are designed to provoke the imagination, raise fundamental questions, and stretch world views.

The five scenarios presented here were developed by the Institute for Alternative Futures as part of a national study that examined the differential between leadership practices today and the organizational demands that health care leaders will face in the next century. The study, "Bridging the Leadership Gap in Healthcare," was conducted in 1991 by The Healthcare Forum Foundation Leadership Center with support from a major grant by the Eastman Kodak

Source: Reprinted from *Healthcare Forum Journal*, May/June 1992, pp. 29–42, with permission of the Healthcare Forum, © 1992.

Company. The scenarios—the most plausible three of which were used in the study—are based on the work of a panel of leading health futurists: Roy Amara, Clement Bezold, Russell Coile, Jeff Goldsmith, Trevor Hancock, and Leland Kaiser.

UNIQUE IMAGES

While each scenario presents a unique image, one revolutionary change—the "predict and manage" paradigm—is common to them all. Advances in our understanding of aging, disease, and genetics will allow us to predict normal declines in health and the course of illness. Better behavioral change techniques and a host of advanced therapies and preventive approaches will allow us to "manage" health, leading to lower morbidity.

These scenarios—set in the early twenty-first century—are thematic images developed as learning tools; as such they simplify a great deal of complexity. The actual future is likely to be some combination of these and other scenarios. Yet these illuminate major plausible futures for health care, posing key choices for health care leadership.

SCENARIO 1: CONTINUED GROWTH/HIGH TECH

National health care reform never did occur, but expensive advancing technology and therapeutics, including function-enhancing bionics, help health care's share of the GNP grow to 17 percent by 2001. Health care providers shift to predicting and then managing illness far earlier and more successfully. Poverty and lack of access to health care for many persist.

The economy continued its long-term upward path. While economic growth was irregular, it was also persistent and the U.S. held its own in global competition. The majority of Americans are better off, though the percent who are poor remain at the levels of the early nineties. Technology advanced on all fronts of society and business. The information revolution provided advanced tools for learning, entertainment, and personal/home management (including health).

In the 1992 and 1996 presidential elections, Democrats tried to make access an issue for poor voters and rising costs an issue for the middle class. It didn't work. National health care reform, which seemed so likely in the early nineties, did not occur. The patchwork of health care coverage persisted.

As the percentage of poor stayed approximately constant, and federal expenditures did not keep pace, most states followed Oregon in consciously setting priorities on what would be available through Medicare and Medicaid for the poor. Malpractice problems went unresolved, and the practice of defensive medicine continued to add to costs.

A Profound Shift

Advances in biomedical knowledge and technology made it possible to predict and increasingly manage an individual's health and illness over his or her life course, profoundly altering health care delivery to the insured. This "predict and manage" paradigm linked the talents of geneticists, clinicians, behavior specialists, and computer-software game developers. They produced very powerful but relatively inexpensive tools that provided the expertise of the best specialists, health forecasts based on each individual's "DNA fingerprint," and entertaining game programs that allowed people to identify and reinforce their own appropriate health promotion strategies.

The result of the shift was profound. No longer do health care providers allow symptoms to grow acute, and then enter late in the game, guns blazing against the symptoms of disease. Major changes in health care after the year 2000, for those who could afford it, were not achieved through policy reform but through implementation of this "predict and manage" paradigm.

High-tech interventions—vaccines for cancers, medications that prevent plaque buildup in the arteries, and the replacement of islet cells for persons prone to diabetes—became common. The affluent and the well insured also have access to organ transplants (both human and transgenic organs), organoids (a new organ or part of an organ grown outside the body and then attached to it), cosmetic surgery, biosensors that augment "closed loop" processes in the body (an oxygen sensor in the kidneys, for example, triggers erythropoietin—EPO—to make more red blood cells), and performance-enhancing bionic implants (for hearing, vision, mobility and athletic performance, and memory/cognition). If a patient has adequate resources or insurance, high-tech medicine can prevent or fix most of his or her health problems.

Health care delivery became more effective and efficient. Multispecialty physician groups direct most care, aided by other health care providers and supported by expert systems. These expert systems constrain physicians' clinical discretion but have improved their outcomes.

Hospitals faced challenging times. As early as the late eighties, approximately half of the capital investment in the hospital arena went to ambulatory care settings. Hospitals were generating strategic alliances with physicians, pursuing more profitable opportunities, and dealing with the decline in inpatient care. This trend continues.

Fewer, Smaller Hospitals

Hospital beds were reduced from more than 900,000 in 1989 to about 750,000 in 2001 and 550,000 by 2010. Hospitals became smaller, and their number declined proportionately as the number of beds fell. Hospitals with a large share of insured or private payers could take advantage of the evolving technology and were able to accelerate their diversification into ambulatory care.

Most consumers who receive consistent care, even the poor on Medicaid, are able to have their major illnesses, including heart disease, cancer, arthritis, and Alzheimer's, predicted, prevented, or cured. The most affluent or fully insured also have access to a broad variety of function-enhancing therapies.

Those with full access to care are satisfied. The number of uninsured among the "working poor" and their families remains at more than 30 million, and while some states provide preventive services to this group, they have benefited least from the revolution in health care.

Most people who receive care are healthier, many are living longer, and the better-insured elderly have fewer hearing, vision, memory, and diabetic problems, thanks to function-enhancing techniques. The "predict and manage" paradigm ultimately lowered lifetime morbidity for most people. Yet the failure to deal with poverty and the limitations on government subsidies kept the poor and near-poor from benefiting as fully.

As the system enhanced its capacities, health care expenditures grew to 17 percent of the GNP by 2001. By 2010 health care's percentage of the GNP declined to 15 percent as the morbidity-reducing effects of the new paradigm and the fully decisive cures in many areas offset the high-tech function-enhancement and life-extension technologies used by many.

Economists in 2010 argue that the percentage of the GNP devoted to health care could be reduced further if the country did not spend so much on life extension and performance enhancement. Politicians, however, recognize that the groups benefiting from the system continue to wield more clout than those who are dissatisfied or benefit little.

Health care leaders are now faced with these questions: *How can organizations more rapidly adapt to the needs of the "predict and manage" paradigm? What strategies are best in the continuing downsizing of inpatient care? Can new options be developed for balancing service for the unfunded, underfunded, and the well insured?*

SCENARIO 2: HARD TIMES/GOVERNMENT LEADERSHIP

Recurrent hard times and a political revolt against health care lead to a frugal Canadian-like national health insurance system. Most states follow Oregon in consciously setting priorities. Heroic measures for terminal patients decline and a more frugal approach to innovation is adopted. Health care's percentage of the GNP is reduced to 11 percent by 2001. Thirty percent of Americans "buy up" to affluent, higher-tech care, and two different systems of health care emerge.

Times were rough for the economy as a whole and for health care. The depression of 1998 was preceded and followed by prolonged recessions. Innovations in health care and throughout society moved far more slowly than had been promised in the early nineties.

More than 40 percent more people were added to the over-65 age group between 1990 and 2010. But those over 85, with the greatest infirmity, increased by more than 70 percent. These people generally are living longer, but many are sicker.

Hard times made it easier for the political liabilities of health care to surface. The relative affluence of physicians irked most consumers. Scandals emerged in the nineties over hospital payments, low-interest capital, and other benefits given to physicians simply for bringing their patients to specific hospitals. The Democrats decided that beating up on physicians made sense.

An effective political coalition of employers, health care reform advocates, and poverty groups made reform a viable issue. The resulting attack was not enough to remove the physician as the captain of the team, but it did lead to much greater regulation of physician business practices, prices, and clinical discretion.

Health care reform created a national reimbursement system in which the federal government, as the single payer, sets prices and keeps them low but gives states discretion over what types of care will be eligible for payment and over the priorities among these.

The "Oregon approach"—consciously choosing which services will be available—was taken, not only for the poor but for the vast bulk of the population.

This new system was like Canada's in that Americans could "buy up" beyond amenities to additional, better, and more costly treatments. Thirty percent of Americans now do this, either through direct payment for services or through supplementary insurance.

The federal government levied a heavy tax on these private health expenditures to help fund public health care. To keep costs down, malpractice reform limited damages that could be awarded, expedited adjudication, and set policies to lower the incidence of malpractice.

Only Bargain Innovations Need Apply

Health care innovation slowed dramatically. To become widely available, an innovation had to have both a low price tag and lead quickly to lower overall costs. Certain cancer vaccines, low-cost bioelectric, and ultrasound diagnostic devices were successful. Other advances, particularly organ transplants, high-cost diagnostic devices, and bionic enhancers, developed more slowly and were available only to those who opted to "buy up." The system favored expenditures with the greatest return on limited funds.

Over time the government encouraged providers to implement the "predict and manage" approach to primary care. Heroic measures to prolong the life of those near death (including extremely premature babies) were dramatically reduced. Rationing in this frugal system also led to greater concern for community health, with some managed care providers and hospitals becoming more active in creating healthy communities.

Affluent consumers, the 30 percent who "buy up," are satisfied (though some grumble about the extra charge they pay). Some members of the middle class still resent their lack of choice, yet most are as satisfied as the Canadian consumer of the early nineties.

The formerly uninsured are better off because of the greater emphasis on services for all. Per capita employment in health care has been reduced, physician incomes have dropped significantly, and nonphysician practitioners provide more services.

With hard times and increased poverty came greater illness, yet this was somewhat offset by the movement toward the "predict and manage" paradigm. The affluent are able to use higher levels of care and technology to significantly improve their health status and functioning.

Health care leaders must grapple with these questions: *What are the community obligations of the health care provider that serves government-funded clients and privately insured clients? How do managers in publicly funded systems prepare their customers to deal with rationing?*

SCENARIO 3: BUYERS' MARKET

Many thought the eighties was the decade of health care's entry into the marketplace—that competition would lead to better, less expensive service. What failed during the eighties worked very well over the next two decades. Markets, including health care, now do a much better job of giving consumers a range of high-quality services, delivered in convenient ways, at relatively low cost over the long term, while maintaining a high degree of innovation. These amazing changes are coupled with better social policies to blunt the inequities and lack of access that accompany the stronger market approach.

The economy rebounded after the recession of the early nineties and grew well, with only minor slowdowns. Technology advanced rapidly on all fronts. While social policy relied more heavily on the market, it did a better job of providing for those left out in the marketplace. The U.S. followed the more progressive European countries in the areas of employment, housing, and welfare policy.

Even more social services were necessary as expert systems and automation, as well as corporate restructuring, reduced more jobs than other sectors of the economy created. New forms of community development, aided by advanced home information systems, gave people left out of the job market meaningful roles.

The dramatic shift toward the market in health policy was prompted by the growing cost and growing dissatisfaction with health care. When the cost of health care reached $1 trillion and 14 percent of the GNP in 1995, a powerful political coalition emerged. Policy makers, employers, and consumer groups became convinced that modest changes would not work: Responsibility for health and health care expenditures should be returned to the consumer. A major philosophical shift took place. First-dollar coverage by third parties was largely removed from the nonindigent.

National health policy was formulated to make all individuals and families who were not poor or "near poor" responsible for their health expenditures up to the equivalent of 8 to 10 percent of their income. Individuals could buy insurance (either indemnity or managed care), though the insurance had to meet certain criteria and the individual was penalized a percentage equivalent to the administrative cost and profit of the insurer. Medicare and Medicaid coverage was adjusted to ensure that all poor and near-poor individuals had basic health care.

Thus the formerly insured portion of the population lost the tax deductions on their benefits but gained a frugal catastrophic care plan (as did the better-off portion of the more than 30 million formerly uninsured population). The poor and near-poor among the formerly uninsured individuals joined those on Medicaid to receive a more nationally consistent, frugal, yet cost-effective set of services. For Medicaid recipients, capitated managed care approaches that take full advantage of the "predict and manage" capacities of health care are required.

Physicians Lose Their Grip

Regulation of the health professions changed as dramatically as health care financing. Consumers and leading politicians concurred in acknowledging that, as a group, physicians had benefited more from physician licensure than had the system as a whole. Several scandals in the early nineties—involving physicians benefiting directly from overutilization of testing procedures, hospital payments to physicians for supplying patients, inexplicable practice pattern variation— lessened physicians' ability to maintain their grip on licensure.

Over the next decade, systems were put in place at the state level that certified health care providers on the basis of their knowledge and competence. They were recertified on the basis of the outcomes of the care they provided. Ineffective physicians and other providers lost their certificates of practice. Local consumers, insurers, and managed care providers reinforced effective care deliverers and shunned poorly performing providers; buyers and markets became smarter.

Once physician control of health care via licensure was pulled back, nurses, other conventional health care providers, and alternative providers quickly sought to practice more independently. Since many buyers paid out of pocket and since the outcomes of all providers could be compared, a diverse and active market for various types of providers and treatments emerged. Even managed care plans began providing both conventional and alternative therapies. Cost-effective innovation was rapid because the resulting outcomes were quickly known.

The individual efficacy of specific treatments and practitioners is consistently evaluated in relation to the longer-term benefits that could be achieved if the individual took full advantage of the "predict and manage" capacities of the system. In-home information systems not only compare the outcome of various health care providers but enable consumers to manage their own diagnosis and treatment for most nonacute conditions. And the capacity to predict and develop better behavioral and medical strategies to prevent or manage disease allows many even greater freedom from health care providers. These home information systems can now decentralize the expertise of the best specialists in any field.

Individuals and families are now rewarded for good health and prudent buying, either by not having to pay out-of-pocket or by yearly rebates from their insurance company or managed care provider. (Government requirements include provision of these rebates.)

Other trends helped make these radical departures work. To maintain a healthier workforce, employers continued to play the role of large buyer for their employees with insurance companies and managed care providers. For those employees who self-manage their expenditures, many employers now ensure that they have the best information available and that a wide range of options among local providers is available.

Some persons still make poor decisions regarding their health and assume the catastrophic coverage will take care of them. However, the bulk of the population learned enough to improve their health conditions and better manage their health care needs. This awareness includes a greater sophistication about which, if any, treatments make sense in the very late stages of life. Combined with greater acceptance of death throughout society, this has lowered expenditure in the days and months before death.

Consumer satisfaction with health care varies. Nearly everyone is aware of how much they pay overall and for specific treatments. Many are bewildered by the array of choices and pay a premium to have someone else decide for them; many are dissatisfied that providers with the best outcomes charge more (the market reinforces this). On the other hand, the use of outcome measurement has improved the effectiveness of even the least successful providers who remain certified to practice.

Health care's portion of the GNP was reduced from its mid-nineties' high of 15 percent to 12 percent by 2000 and 10 percent by 2010 as a result of several factors including better health, better and cheaper diagnostics and therapeutics, and the acceptance of dying. The percentage might have dropped lower, except for the fact that the services of alternative providers such as acupuncturists and various physical therapies are now often sought by consumers on a recurring preventive basis.

Placing responsibility back on the individual for health and for managing his or her health care expenditures has led to better health and to improved and more cost-effective care.

Health care leaders must now deal with these issues: *Given a dramatic shift in the focus of responsibility and first-dollar coverage back to the individual, how should health care institutions adjust their services and communications? Given the broadening of health care providers and the end of the assumption of physician primacy, how should health institutions deal with providers and prepare them to achieve the best, competitive outcomes?*

SCENARIO 4: A NEW CIVILIZATION

Dramatic changes in the paradigms of science, technology, society, and government hasten health care change. Health care broadens its focus from the individual to the community and the environment. National health care reform favors managed care—particularly social HMOs, which are effective at predicting and often preventing various personal and community health problems. High-tech and alternative therapies are common. Health care consumes 12 percent of the GNP by 2001.

The profound turbulence of the nineties proved to have a deep source. Western industrial civilization was changing. Paradigms changed in science, technology, economics, and politics. While values in society became more diverse, there was greater social idealism reflected in the marketplace and public policy.

The materialistic eighties were followed by the ethical and concerned nineties. For many individuals, these shifts also included deeper spiritual development. For most it included greater acceptance of death.

National health reform took place after the 1996 elections. By that time key positive trends, particularly the development of more effective managed care, were visible in health care. Leading HMOs increased their focus on prevention for individuals and their communities. These HMOs also facilitated and sometimes coordinated other community services. While "social HMOs" or SHMOs had been proposed decades before, they began to flourish during the nineties.

National policy established an employer-based insurance program combined with enhanced Medicare and Medicaid for the unemployed. Both private insurance and public programs included incentives and regulations supporting more effective managed care, prevention, and community focus. Greater social acceptance of death was paralleled by significant reductions in heroic lifesaving measures available to the elderly through government and many private insurers.

Outcome Measures

Consumers were empowered by government policies encouraging the development of outcome measures and their application to all providers and therapies. Local health care markets became smarter and were quicker to reward cost-effective innovation.

State laws and regulations changed so that nonphysicians could deliver care directly and be reimbursed. To continue to practice, physicians, nurses, and other clinical care providers are now recertified on the basis of their outcomes, which has reduced ineffective practice.

Malpractice reforms have lowered damage awards. Continuous quality improvement systems are fully operational in most health care systems.

A strong "predict and manage" approach to health evolved, focused on each person's unique biochemical, emotional, and spiritual levels. The twentieth century health care paradigm, prototypical of Western industrial civilization, had split body, mind, and spirit. The rational, empirical approach gave powerful capacities to repair the body, but it ignored the mind. This changed as the role of the mind was rediscovered in health care.

The physician's ability to control the nature and delivery of care was greatly lessened. Local SHMOs offer a variety of alternative therapies, many of which are as effective at preventing or curing as conventional high-tech therapies.

Health Care providers recognized their role in healing their community as well as their patients. They increasingly focused on how to design pathologies, such as drug use or the effects of poverty, out of their community. Social HMOs became a favored vehicle for improving individual and community health, and most of the rapidly downsized hospitals that remained played an active role in sponsoring or allying with these SHMOs.

Health care technology advanced dramatically. Diagnostics, information systems, new drugs, and biotechnology treatments, as well as bionics, are now commonly available to most people. In addition the system is much more focused on enhancing each individual's ability to use his or her mind and spirit for healing.

Social HMOs provide their members with highly sophisticated home health information systems that deal effectively and uniquely with the health needs of each family member. (Their voice input-output chips literally "speak" with each family member in the appropriate voice and dialect to match his or her knowledge and interest level.)

These systems also help all family members play the role they choose in supporting and enhancing the health of their neighbors and the local environment. Most SHMOs have shifted much of their effort to making their communities healthier through environmental and occupational health programs.

The community ambulatory centers of SHMOs can now perform most of the functions of the community hospital of the early nineties. The remnants of twentieth-century hospitals are found in the regional critical care institutions, which also concentrate on transplants and bionic enhancement surgery. The census at these regional institutions is a small fraction of the hospital census of 1990.

While there are gradations in care—the affluent receive more—virtually all consumers are healthier and living longer, including those with low incomes. They are satisfied with the health care system and with its role in the community.

Is "Big Brother" Watching?

Dissatisfaction does appear in some communities where people feel that definitions of community have turned health care into an overly restrictive "Big Brother."

Yet most consumers are satisfied, particularly with the great diversity of conventional and alternative providers available in most communities. Local equivalents of *Consumer Reports* magazine rate competing SHMOs, hospitals, individual providers, and treatments.

In the twentieth century, the Surgeon General had told us that our behavior accounted for roughly 50 percent of the variance in our health over our lifetime. Our genes contributed another 20 percent, environment another 20 percent, and health care the remaining 10 percent.

In the twenty-first century, the health care system, by enhancing its own services, reinforcing positive behaviors, and amplifying the health of the community, is responsible for significantly more variance. This, along with high outcomes for specific practices, is accomplished with a smaller percentage of the GNP than it was during the early nineties.

The benefits of high technology, combined with concern for the individual and community enhancement were also shown in the long-term care area. In the eighties, 5 percent of those over 65 and 20 percent of those over 85 needed to be institutionalized in long-term care settings. By the early twenty-first century, these percentages were cut dramatically.

Disabling morbidity has been compressed to a smaller period late in life because of better nutrition, exercise, social interaction, mental stimulation, and personal or spiritual growth. Where significant degeneration has occurred, bionics, robotics, and smarter homes, and more caring neighborhoods do much to allow the disabled elderly to remain at home.

Health care expenditures declined as a percentage of the GNP after 2000. Greater acceptance of death, far more decisive therapies, the ability to predict and often prevent disease, and more generally cost-effective diagnostics and therapeutics led to dramatic reductions. These were partially offset by the wide range of function-enhancing procedures pursued by many (the phase "to add life to years, rather than years to life," took on new meaning).

Health care leaders are now coping with questions like these: *In very turbulent times how can we create organizations that are platforms for personal growth? How should leaders deal with the absence of physician primacy? How will health care resources be most effectively integrated into community health promotion?*

SCENARIO 5: HEALING AND HEALTH CARE

This scenario shares the fundamental characteristics of the "New Civilization" scenario—the same dramatic changes in the paradigms of science, technology, society, and government—but with a different emphasis. In this scenario the role of the spirit and its integration into health care lead to a greater focus on "healing." Health care providers, particularly those running hospitals, take an early and active role in moving health care toward real personal, community, and environmental health, rather than allowing it to continue to simply cure individuals. Poverty, other social problems, and environmental causes of ill health are dealt with more systematically. Health care structures have changed dramatically, merging with a variety of other community organizations. Healing the planet, particularly the environment for our children, is a dominant issue.

The paradigms of industrial civilization had split body and mind and then focused on the body. Its empirical focus yielded powerful tools, yet ignored the role of the mind in most settings and devalued things spiritual. This has changed. The nineties saw a growing focus on spirituality and on healing the ills not only of our society but of the globe. Poverty, pain, and unnecessary illness remained but were significantly reduced by 2010.

Economic ups and downs occurred, but the overall pattern was one of continuing growth. There was much social ferment and friction in many parts of the country as minorities outgrew the white majority. Social idealism across races and classes was an even more significant factor.

An enhanced consciousness of our personal energy was important throughout society but had particular impacts on organizations; twenty-first-century organizations are both subtly and visibly different from their twentieth-century counterparts. Personal energy and organizational energy are now a conscious part of our operations. Hierarchy is much less important.

Successful organizations are those that have "high-consciousness" people (those able to think in ever-larger rings about the context of the organization) working in an enabling structure (one that encourages the people inside it to grow) and pursuing a shared vision. The resulting energy and contributions of organizations throughout society were a key to hastening the positive effects of the growth of healing in health care.

Access to health care was guaranteed in the mid-nineties through mandated, employer-provided health insurance along with expanded Medicaid and Medicare. This was a major advance, yet overall it was less important than the fact that health policy at the national, state, and local levels became integrated with other key areas of policy. National health policy became far more coherent, recognizing the causes of illness and the contribution to their prevention by various health care approaches, providers, and non-health care components of the budget.

Efforts to develop shared visions of what the health care system should be accelerated change. Effective programs on visions for health became common during the early nineties, and their results energized communities and encouraged a broader focus beyond health care to health, and beyond the community to larger national and global concerns.

Policies at all levels of government focused on the development and use of health care outcome measures, which identified the most effective therapies, providers, and institutions—and allowed direct comparisons between conventional and alternative providers and therapies.

The result over the decade was more cost-effective therapies and greater freedom of health professionals and institutions to use the most appropriate mix of care. Health care providers are now recertified on the basis of their outcomes.

Local health care systems became much more coherent and effective in most communities. Health care integrated four major capacities, so that it is now able to: (1) anticipate and manage each person's evolving health state (the "predict and manage" paradigm); (2) use sophisticated, cost-effective technology to monitor, diagnose, treat, and reinforce positive behavior; (3) focus healing simultaneously on four planes—physical, emotional, mental, and spiritual; and (4) coordinate the various potentially health-enhancing but nonmedical aspects of the community (its environment, housing, and transportation, etc.).

Hospital Without Walls

The enlarged consciousness of many hospital leaders, their perception of their own budget as an ethical document, as well as their focus on outcomes led to an early recognition that the community needed health care providers whose core task was optimizing the health status of all the individuals in the community. Theirs would be a hospital without walls.

National health policy established a variety of insurance mechanisms that favored true health maintenance, allowing expenditures to be made on personal and community prevention. Government and community budgeting evolved to optimize the contribution of housing, transportation, social services, and health care expenditures to build truly healthy communities.

Hospitals in the late twentieth century—the pinnacle of resources for curative medicine in most communities—merged into twenty-first-century health care institutions that became the pinnacle of health design for their communities. In the process, hospitals began to channel their discretionary funds into areas where they would yield the greatest health gains, usually outside the institutions themselves.

In this setting, management became the task of declaring what ought to be, establishing shared visions, and enhancing the organization's energy. One aspect of the CEO's job became the spiritual, mental, and emotional development of every person in the organization. Another aspect was to establish or enhance the myth or metaphor driving each hospital. Healing, in this context, became the dominant metaphor.

The twentieth-century hospital cured the body; the twenty-first-century hospital cures the body and heals the person. The body repair shop metaphor of the twentieth century has broken down: The hospital no longer just repairs the car; it also works on the driver.

Consumers were encouraged and empowered (through very effective home information systems and supportive health care personnel) to take greater responsibility for their health and to select from a wider range of diagnosis and treatment.

There is a high degree of satisfaction with the reconfiguration of health services, and a recognition of the importance of healing in the ways the health care system operates.

Virtually all classes of society have better outcomes than they had in the past from the care they receive. There has been a significant enhancement in the health status of the poor and those in environmentally damaged areas as these problems received more attention throughout the nineties. Morbidity has been compressed; people are living slightly longer and in better health during their last years of life. Healthier, more caring communities than those in the eighties have allowed the frail elderly greater independence until they reach later stages of life.

Health care expenditures have stayed at about 12 percent of the GNP because of the balancing of key forces: More elderly people, some expensive new therapies, an expanded number of health providers offering healing touch services, and community and environmental health measures by health care providers are weighted against the compression of morbidity, greater acceptance of death, more effective therapies (because of R&D and outcome measurement), and healthier communities.

Health care leaders are now addressing such questions as these: *How can health care institutions become more supportive environments for healing? What changes in policy and institutional procedures are most urgent in order to allow the hospital to take responsibility for the health of its community?*

Appendix 21–A. The New Values and Competencies

Who knows what health care leaders will be doing in the twenty-first century? No one, yet. . . . Everything beyond three years ahead is the "far side" of health care management. Before the Leadership Gap study, health management experts had some ideas, but there was little research on the full spectrum of competencies and values health leaders view as important for managing health care organizations in the year 2001.

The Leadership Gap study is a blend of an extensive literature review, and the contributions of many among the "best and the brightest" health care futurists and management experts. More than 80 leadership attributes were originally identified: 60 were tested in an initial pilot study. The study Advisory Committee and a focus group of health care executives suggested reducing the number of attributes and making the survey shorter. Following are the 36 competencies and values that were evaluated by the study participants. The 18 shown unhighlighted were identified as typical of "current practices." The 18 shaded in grey are the values and competencies the study found will be critical to the new leadership model of 2001.

1. *Business planning:* defines needs, identifies niches, assesses competition, and sets objectives in a 0- to 5-year time frame.

2. *Continuous quality improvement:* supports an organizationwide, ongoing process to improve service and clinical outcomes; never satisfied with the status quo; cultivates environment for continuous learning.

3. *Redefining health care:* focuses work on healing, changing lifestyles, and wholistic mind/body/spirit connections.

4. *Business boundaries:* defines business in terms of set geographic boundaries; defends marketshare from competition.

330

5. ***Building shared vision:*** creates a common picture of the future; builds alignment and a sense of purpose with key stakeholders, using a 5- to 10-year strategic horizon.

6. ***Serving the public/community:*** balances mission and profit margin, heavily factoring community health status, environment, and public service into organizational goals and strategy.

7. ***Utilizing marketing techniques:*** targets key customer segments (patients, physicians, payers) using advertising, sales calls, and public relations; measures success in terms of volume, product-line profitability, and marketshare.

8. ***Minimizing risk:*** pursues conservative strategies for growth and development, limiting down-side risks in new ventures; responds to competitor initiatives; pursures proven approaches, waits for "first generation" costs to fall before adaptation.

9. ***Global approach:*** thinks beyond geographic boundaries; focuses on nimble distribution networks/webs of consumers and competitors; considers global implications of events and decisions.

10. ***Mastering change:*** views change as opportunity, focusing on innovation and up-side potential; supports calculated risk-taking by mid-level; develops anticipatory skills; relies on imagination and experimentation to find new approaches and generate alternatives.

11. ***Maximizing short-term profitability:*** sets 1- to 3-year organizational goals in financial terms; measures success by profitability.

12. ***Repairing body parts:*** applies greatest resources to repair and replace malfunctioning body parts of patients; acute-care orientation.

13. ***Managing customer relationships:*** seeks to enhance value; stresses repeat business and customer loyalty; partnership relationships with customers, insurers, and employees (e.g., physician risk-sharing, supplier joint ventures, HMO/PPO contracts).

14. ***Protecting self-interest:*** operates effectively within legal/malpractice environment; focuses on inspection and quality control.

15. ***Managing a diverse workforce:*** encourages a corporate culture of diversity in people, ideas, and ethnicity.

16. ***Cross-functional structure:*** allocates work, decision making and problem solving on a matrix-style, project basis; continuously modifies assignments and teams to make best use of people across department lines.

17. **"They" approach:** delegates responsibility for issues and problems downward; looks for targets to blame for errors.

18. **Individual learning:** focuses accountability and control on individuals; independent, self-directed learning approach (e.g., "lone ranger" style manager).

19. **"We" approach:** seeks a collective sense of responsibility for issues/problems and for initiative in developing and implementing solutions.

20. **Managing through hierarchy:** assigns fixed responsibilities to organizational subunits and individuals; works through channels; develops extensive policies and procedures.

21. **Incentive-based performance:** advocates a pay-for-performance approach for rewarding high productivity; weeds out inefficient performers who do not meet productivity or cost objectives.

22. **Fostering enrollment:** manages people with guidance, support, participation, and shared expertise; coaching and empowering others in their work.

23. **Shaping homogeneous organizational culture:** fosters an organizational identity or "company image" that consciously reinforces homogeneous cultural norms; hires people who "fit the profile."

24. **Systems thinking:** brings a wholistic, integrative perspective to understanding complex patterns of behavior; identifies key system leverage points; develops circular, structural overviews of problems before managing details; builds learning organizations.

25. **Team learning:** interdependent learning approach; encourages group decision making based on sharing assumptions, open dialogue, and nondefensive behavior.

26. **Linear learning style:** uses a rational decision making style based on best business analysis; breaks down problems into separate parts; focuses on events and a thorough understanding of details.

27. **Technology as a specialized tool:** uses technology in specialized applications for expert diagnosis/treatment and to shorten computation or production time; managing technology "to the numbers."

28. **Building information capacity:** expedites the process of storing, recalling, and updating information to support business strategies; synchronizing systems and human capabilities; imbeds information value into products/services.

29. ***Capital budgeting for technologies:*** department-by-department review of current technologies; identifying unmet needs and available options; developing 1- to 3-year capital budget plans.

30. ***Employing technology specialists:*** tasking experts and subordinates to install and use new technologies; provides training; managers delegate and minimize time spent working with and understanding tools and systems.

31. ***Noninvasive therapies and devices:*** emphasizes use of noninvasive technologies and therapies to prevent, diagnose, and treat disease and disorders at their earliest stages (e.g., external monitors, nanotechnology, genetic testing, and vaccines).

32. ***Maximizing use of existing technologies:*** maintains and expands existing systems and ensures their cost-efficient use.

33. ***User-friendly applications:*** techno-savvy networking (e.g., bedside computers and telemedicine); connecting via portable systems (e.g., cellular and video phones, laptop computers, and smart cards).

34. ***Technology as pathway to faster learning:*** integrates technologies; develops infrastructures for a continuum of care using expert systems; encourages interactive learning and enhances clinical quality outcomes; links the ethical and business implications of decisions.

35. ***Invasive medical technology:*** focuses on invasive, high-tech approaches and procedures (e.g., organ transplants, major surgery) to solve medical problems.

36. ***Strategic technology assessment:*** continuously scans for new technology and biomedical advances with a systemwide 5- to 10-year horizon; a "beta-site" or early adapter of new technology.

Afterword

KALEIDOSCOPE OF ILLUSIONS

The predictions about quality, cost, change, ethics, culture, technology, medical science, and the delivery systems of the future are founded on perceptions and assumptions, all of which we are not totally conscious. Tolstoy in *War and Peace* stated that "chance created the situation, genius utilized it.[1]

Caring is the essential ingredient.

Recapturing hope—that is what it is all about.[2]

NOTES

1. L. Tolstoy, *War and Peace* (New York: Simon and Schuster, 1942) 1257.

2. D.M. Berwick, A.B. Godfrey, and J. Roessner, *Curing Health Care. New Strategies for Quality Improvement* (San Francisco: Josey-Boss, 1990), xvi.

Appendix A. Case Study: TQM in a Community Hospital

Rita DiPippo and Steven Schoener

Total Quality Management (TQM) has been, and is being, introduced to American hospitals in the same way Americans have become involved in most enterprises—with a very high degree of individuality, enthusiasm, and gusto. No two hospitals approach TQM implementation in the same way, because no two hospitals are the same. Management, boards of trustees, middle managers, nurses, clinical professionals, staff employees, and physicians all interact in a special way that is unique to each health care organization.

If you have a problem, the typical American way of resolving it is to throw money at it and hope it will get fixed. This is what hundreds of hospitals have done trying to implement TQM: They invested large sums of money in the hope of saving large sums of money. This ill-conceived and badly planned tossing in of money resulted in more failures than successes. As will be seen, it takes a great deal more than money to make TQM work.

One community hospital in Westchester County, New York, claims both failure and success in its approaches to TQM. Some initial steps were failures, but true successes resulted when the basic principles of TQM were followed. The community in which this hospital is located is home to many well-educated and highly competent corporate executives and other professionals who believe in the hospital's mission, and who donate their time and expertise serving as board members and otherwise offering innovative leadership. For these reasons, this was one of the first hospitals to investigate the TQM approach in providing health care.

The hospital's administrators and board members visited other hospitals and interviewed consultants who offered training programs in this "new" discipline. The hospital hired a well-respected and highly diverse service and product company to help implement TQM, providing offsite training for top management as well as middle managers, selected employees representing major areas, and some physicians. In turn, these "trained" individuals would return to the hospital and preach the good news. An astounding 85% of all employees were given TQM training within a nine-month period. This rapid-fire training, as it turned out, was not the best way to train, teach, or create an atmosphere of learning, cooperation, and quality. Not every employee received the same information. Different instructors emphasized different "key points." Mixed messages abounded and a degree of uncertainty permeated the organization. Institutionalizing TQM was a bigger challenge than anyone could have imagined. In spite of this inauspicious beginning, the hospital today has approximately one dozen cross-functional teams that are working on issues ranging from increasing awareness of patients needs to decreasing the time it takes for laboratory STAT orders to be completed.

As a case in point, the Laboratory and Department of Emergency Medicine (LAB-DEM) team is an excellent example of all that can go right—and wrong—with a team. Even before the hospital received its formal preliminary TQM training, it decided to explore improvements in the Department of Emergency Medicine (DEM) and the Laboratory (LAB) that would decrease the time needed for a patient specimen to be sent to the LAB for analysis and for results to be returned to the DEM. A speedier turnaround time for LAB results would enhance the services provided to patients (see Figure A-1). The hospital vice presidents responsible for both areas were well versed in TQM and instinctively realized the advantages to be gained by implementing this philosophy. They were anxious to have the hospital reap the wondrous benefits of TQM—eliminating inefficiencies and getting departments to work cooperatively together.

The vice presidents invited the LAB and DEM managers to explore these issues. They held a series of brainstorming meetings to identify possible solutions to the problem, such as adding more unit clerks, an intercom system, a better image, more space, and so on. Other management personnel were invited to join in the discussion and they expanded the list of what was wrong with the system. With little effort, this group concluded that the transporters needed to prioritize their responses and that the LAB needed more instrumentation. More unit clerks were hired for the DEM and a pneumatic tube connecting the DEM and the LAB was installed. The tube would eliminate the transporter problem, thereby making the system more efficient and decreasing turnaround time.

What was wrong with this picture? Many of the team members knew "exactly how the problem could be solved," *before* they knew the root causes of the delays. Unfortunately, the tube and the additional staff did *not* decrease turnaround time. *Management* was trying to improve a *whole system*, instead of letting hands-on staff concentrate on the specific process of turnaround time.

Fortunately, at this time formal TQM training had begun. The philosophy was starting to sink in but something was still missing. Although the theory was understood, no practical skills were being taught until several groups of employees were organized to receive instruction in team building. These students were then armed with some basic tools for implementing quality

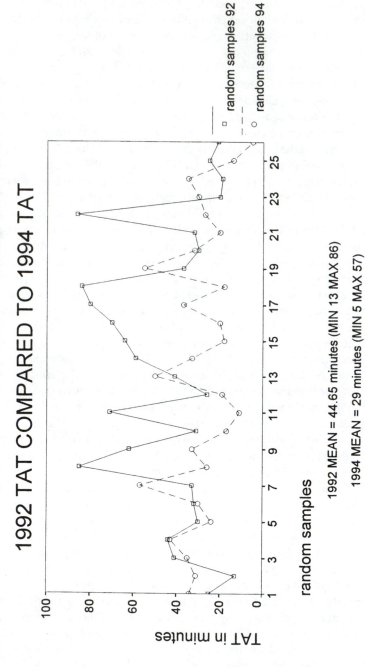

Figure A–1 Community Hospital DEM/LAB Turnaround Time. 1992 TAT Compared to 1994 TAT.

improvement. Whereas the formal training sessions focused on vision and culture and the intangible philosophy behind TQM, the team-building approach was a nuts and bolts method for rooting out the cause of problems. This training, coupled with instruction in the use of Statistical Process Control (SPC) tools, began to play a significant role in the team's progress.

Now, staff employees from the LAB and DEM were organized to form a new team. This time, the employees chosen to participate were those who had hands-on involvement in the process, not just management. From the onset, the team leader was responsible for calling meetings, setting agendas, and suggesting tools to use to discover the root causes of the problem the team was trying to solve. A quality advisor was assigned to the team to keep it focused, moving, and motivated. Minutes were taken at each meeting. Data were collected, reviewed, and studied. After several months, the team made recommendations based on its

Table A–1 Using TQM Approach to Decrease Turnaround Time for Laboratory STAT Orders

Sources of delay identified by LAB-DEM team:	Solutions recommended by LAB-DEM team to improve turnaround time (TAT):
Unit clerks entered orders in computer, but needed RN verification.	Unit clerks empowered to enter orders in computer without RN verification.
Printed computer requisitions required several steps to be retrieved and used.	Bar code label printer installed in DEM to eliminate requisition slips and the manual labeling of each specimen.
Specimens sent in batches to LAB by messenger or pneumatic tube.	Upon collection and labeling, each patient's specimens sent immediately to LAB via pneumatic tube.
Once in LAB, DEM specimens difficult to distinguish from routine specimens.	Special color-coded labels initiated to distinguish DEM specimen from others and to assign them top priority.
Routine testing interrupted to perform STAT testing.	Workstations in LAB reorganized to accommodate STAT testing, with no interruption of routine testing.
Test results called to DEM by phone.	A printer with a direct link to the LAB Information System installed in DEM to provide immediate hard copy reports, eliminating telephone delays.

findings, which are detailed in Table A–1. The suggested changes, based on the team's data collection decreased turnaround time for LAB STAT orders by 36 percent. But the greatest success of this team was the way it helped to erase departmental barriers and encourage people to work cooperatively together.

Change is never easy. People are generally cautious when approaching new things. Getting to the core of issues by applying the team approach using TQM statistical tools and other methods, is the challenge this community hospital met. All that was needed was the right combination of training methodologies to set the process in motion.

SUGGESTED READINGS

Amsden, D., Butler, H., and Amsden, R. *SPC Simplified for Service: Practical Tools for Continuous Quality Improvement.* White Plains, N.Y.: Quality Resources, 1991.

Brassard, M. *The Memory Jogger Plus.* Methuen, Mass: Goal/QPC, 1989.

Melum, M.M. and Sinioris, M.R. *Total Quality Management: The Health Care Pioneers.* Chicago, Ill: American Hospital Publishing, 1992.

Scholtes, P.R. *The Team Handbook,* Madison, WI: Joiner Associates, Inc., 1988.

Appendix B. The Health Care Quality Improvement Initiative: A New Approach to Quality Assurance in Medicare

Stephen F. Jencks and Gail R. Wilensky

This article describes how the Health Care Financing Administration (HCFA) is reshaping its approach to improving care for Medicare beneficiaries. The goal of the Health Care Quality Improvement Initiative (HCQII) is to move from dealing with individual clinical errors to helping providers to improve the mainstream of care. Such a reform implies profound changes.

First, the processes and criteria for review change: Instead of having clinicians use essentially intuitive local criteria to find problems in individual cases, Peer Review Organizations (PROs) will use explicit, more nationally uniform criteria to examine patterns of care and patterns of outcomes. Second, the immediate objective changes: PROs will focus primarily on persistent differences between the observed and the achievable in both care and outcomes and less on occasional, unusual deficiencies in care. Third, the ultimate method changes: PROs will help providers identify problems and their solutions by monitoring patterns of care and outcomes and allowing providers to conduct the more intrusive and detailed study of who, when, and why.

This article explains the reasons for the HCQII and describes the new data and analytic systems that HCFA is putting in place to support it. It then summarizes HCFA's strategy for working with PROs, physicians, and hospitals and some specific activities that PROs will undertake under the new contracts that will support HCQII. Finally, it describes how HCFA will monitor the HCQII itself.

Source: Reprinted from *Journal of the American Medical Association*, Vol. 268, No. 7, pp. 900–903, American Medical Association, 1992.

THE BACKGROUND OF HCQII

Four important forces drive the HCQII.

Variations Research

In the last decade, research has shown that patterns and outcomes of care vary from area to area and from hospital to hospital in ways that we cannot explain from known variations in patient sickness. In particular, Wennberg and Gittelsohn,[1] Chassin, et al.,[2] HCFA,[3] and others have shown large variations in rates of performing important procedures across small and large geographic units. HCFA[4] has shown wide variation in hospital-related mortality for a variety of conditions, and Hannan, et al.,[5] O'Connor, et al.,[6] and Williams, et al.,[7] have shown substantial variations for one condition—coronary artery bypass grafting. Accumulating evidence indicates that variations in risk-adjusted outcomes reflect variations in appropriateness of care.[8–11]

Studies of Peer Review

A growing body of research shows that physician review of hospital medical records to determine quality of care has only modest reliability,[12,13] even in research settings. Actions by PROs based primarily on such reviews tend to lead to acrimonious disagreements that diminish the chance that physicians will accept or learn from them. Measuring the impact of actions based on case-by-case review is almost impossible.

New Models for Quality Improvement

New approaches to quality improvement are entering health care from other industries.[14] These models[15,16] focus on improving the processes of producing typical care rather than using inspection to correct unusual errors. They argue that substandard care generally results from poor process design, inadequate information, and poor training rather than from stupidity, indifference, or greed.

These quality management models suggest that we should inspect care in order to identify patterns of errors, not to correct individual errors.[17,18] This is obvious on one level because we conduct most medical review long after any possible damage is done, but we do not usually think of medical review as a sampling process designed to describe care. Nevertheless, the HCQII will limit review to a sample of cases, not only for economy but also because a sample suffices to give us a good statistical picture of what errors are common; from this picture we can set priorities and design condition-specific projects.

Although the HCQII draws heavily on quality management methods, it does not assume that hospitals or physicians should adopt any particular strategy or orthodoxy of quality improvement. The precise application of many of these models to health care remains somewhat experimental and controversial.[19]

The Guidelines Movement

The federal government and professional groups have started an expanding process of developing and publishing practice guidelines, which provide a potential focus for quality improvement efforts.

NEW DATA SYSTEMS

Modern quality management methods are statistically oriented and data-intensive; explaining HCQII therefore requires a brief description of the two new data systems that make the HCQII possible: the National Claims History (NCH) file and the Uniform Clinical Data Set (UCDS).

The NCH is a system of bill-payment records comprising all claims paid by Medicare, whether physician, hospital, home health, or outpatient. The NCH is both more complete and more current than traditional HCFA claims files, but it is also large and complex—containing more than 1 billion line items a year.

The UCDS will provide detailed clinical information on a 10% sample of discharged patients (about 1 million a year). The UCDS data dictionary defines more than 1800 elements that describe the patients' demographic characteristics, history, findings, and treatment, and the UCDS captures 200 to 350 elements from a typical record. The primary current use of the UCDS is to allow the Patient Care Algorithm System (PCAS) to select cases for physician review in a more uniform and reliable way than traditional nurse review and to allow HCFA to refine case selection criteria rapidly. In the next year, however, the UCDS will become more important as a data base for monitoring care and for risk-adjusting outcomes. HCFA is developing a centralized UCDS data base, which PROs will be able to use as a baseline for comparisons. Six PROs are now using UCDS to screen cases for physician review, and all PROs will be using UCDS, at least for selected projects, by 1994. Abstraction is still relatively slow: The average time varies among PROs from 67 to 115 minutes per discharge; such variation suggests that consistent methods may improve efficiency. Nevertheless, efficient, reliable abstraction remains challenging and will require major refinements of both methods and data-set definitions.

As PROs examine clinical practices, the UCDS and the NCH have complementary roles. The UCDS has the depth to describe inpatient practices in detail and to improve our interpretation of clinical events, but the sample is too small to profile most individual physicians or management of individual conditions in most hospitals, and there are no outpatient data. The NCH provides continuity over time and has data for all patients and settings, but lacks clinical depth. If we study management of breast cancer, for example, the clinical depth of UCDS reveals the patient's clinical condition and hospital course, but only the NCH will show whether the patient had been receiving mammograms before admission or whether she died after discharge.

MONITORING CARE AND OUTCOMES

Monitoring care and monitoring outcomes are complementary. Focusing exclusively on outcomes does not tell providers what is wrong; focusing exclusively on care ignores the clinical bottom line. In both cases, attention to patterns is an important tool for avoiding excessive attention to aberrant events or clinically unusual cases.

Examining Care

The UCDS collects information on the patient's condition and on what treatments were provided. The PCAS applies about 1000 decision rules to identify possible deviations from standard care. These algorithms have two purposes: (1) to screen individual cases for physician review and (2) to describe how well care conforms to published guidelines to profile care for systematic quality improvement.

The original PCAS algorithms were developed by an internal HCFA process that was assisted and reviewed by clinical consultants. An American Medical Association work group is reviewing these algorithms for clinical validity. The PROs are reviewing them for operational validity by examining false positives and false negatives identified by physician reviewers. In 1991, parallel screening of cases for physician review by the PCAS and by nurse screeners showed that the two methods resulted in roughly equal numbers of confirmed quality and utilization problems but that the PCAS referred more cases for review. Comparative performance varied widely among PROs; the PCAS has been significantly refined since that study, but more recent data are not yet available.

Although the PCAS is only a screening tool and all final decisions are made by local physicians, the algorithms are closely related to practice guidelines or parameters. Current algorithms for quality screening are largely adaptations of

Medicare's generic quality screens, while those for admission appropriateness are more specific to diseases or procedures. HCFA contractors are now incorporating published guidelines into the admission appropriateness algorithms for six elective surgical procedures, and other algorithms will increasingly rest on guidelines as the PCAS evolves. Developing algorithms from guidelines is not simple because guidelines often lack the specificity needed in a computer algorithm. Condition-specific algorithms often require additional condition-specific data items, and desired information is often not in the medical record. HCFA intends to adopt published guidelines developed both by professional groups and by the Agency for Health Care Policy and Research and to work closely with those organizations on translation into algorithms. HCFA will be primarily a user of guidelines produced by others, not a developer of guidelines.

Examining Outcomes

An important step in comparing outcome rates among institutions is adjusting for differences in patient illness or risk of those outcomes. Clinical information from the UCDS allows more precise adjustment than is possible in analyses based on claims data such as the Medicare Hospital Information (MHI).[20] Mortality analyses based on claims data alone are strongly correlated with those based on clinical data,[21] but clinically adjusted data will be more accurate, persuasive, and useful.

The information on process of care from UCDS and claims data provides clues to deviations from best practices that may explain poor outcomes. Thus, providers will have information not only on the existence of problems but also on some possible causes. Obviously, however, many problems in technique of care are inaccessible to even sophisticated abstraction of medical records.

ORIENTING THE PARTICIPANTS

The data on care and outcomes that emerge from analysis of UCDS and NCH will be unfamiliar to many physicians, hospitals, and even PRO and HCFA staff. Analyzing the NCH and the UCDS requires some sophistication, and, under new contracts, PROs will acquire both epidemiologic and computer capabilities. The PROs will also have access to other data such as the enrollment file, provider files, and area resource files for analysis.

HCFA will be developing new skills in PROs through pilot projects and a formal curriculum, including a series of national projects in which all PROs will carry out the same analyses. In the first project each PRO will analyze data summarized in the MHI[22] publication. PROs will first duplicate the analyses that

HCFA has carried out and then develop further analyses based on more immediate local knowledge of hospitals and hospital peer groups. The PROs will work with hospital and medical groups and with individual hospitals and medical staffs to develop better understanding of the data. The Connecticut and Wisconsin PROs are conducting a pilot of this project.

Concurrently, PROs will develop local projects to involve hospitals and their medical staffs in pattern analysis. These projects, which may include developing physician study groups or hospital-based collaborative studies, are intended both to pursue issues of local importance and to get physicians and hospitals involved in pattern analysis. PROs will devote about as much effort to local projects that build on their experience and expertise as to national projects. The skills necessary to work with these issues are much like those required by the new accreditation standards for hospitals outlined by the Joint Commission on Accreditation of Healthcare Organizations,[23] so some synergy appears logical.

The design for the second national project gives a clearer picture of what the HCQII is intended to achieve. The Cooperative Cardiovascular Project will study and seek to improve patterns of care and outcomes for acute myocardial infarction, coronary artery bypass grafting, and coronary angioplasty. This project will have a preparatory phase, in which data are analyzed and educational approaches designed, and an implementation phase.

The preparatory phase involves six parallel activities:

1. Abstract almost all discharges for the target conditions using UCDS (in contrast to surveillance samples, which can be quite small, a sample near 100% is necessary to study treatment of a particular condition on a hospital-by-hospital basis).
2. Develop UCDS-based risk-adjustment methods for mortality, complications, readmissions, and other outcomes (HCFA is working on collection of functional status outcomes, but they will not be available for this project). Measure "benchmark" performance (tentatively defined as the consistent performance of the top decile of hospitals) for each outcome. Compare the performance of all hospitals to the benchmarks, to national average performance, and to other standards.
3. Convert patient-care guidelines (e.g., the American College of Cardiology guideline on thrombolysis in myocardial infarction) into PCAS algorithms. These algorithms will be used to profile care rather than to refer individual cases for medical review.
4. Confirm the applicability of the guidelines by analyzing the relationship between patterns of care profiled by the PCAS algorithms (e.g., appropriate thrombolytic use) and risk-adjusted outcomes.

5. Work with national and local physician, hospital, and other organizations, as well as individual hospitals and hospital staff, to develop understanding of the guidelines and interest in and ability to interpret the data that the PROs will provide.
6. Develop, in cooperation with physician and hospital groups, model intervention strategies for hospitals whose performance is below the benchmarks.

In the implementation phase, PROs will do the following:

1. Provide hospital-specific information to each hospital and its medical staff both on patterns of care (e.g., the percentage of eligible myocardial infarction patients receiving thrombolytic agents and on risk-adjusted outcomes (e.g., the difference between the hospital's risk-adjusted complication rate for angioplasty and the benchmark).
2. Meet with hospitals and medical staffs to identify and further analyze areas in which there may be opportunities for improvement (e.g., more appropriate discharge medications). The PROs will provide further data analysis and other analytic assistance to hospitals and staffs.
3. Negotiate a program of change with the hospital and its staff. An acceptable program is likely to include both changing hospital rules and systems and educating individuals and groups.
4. Use the same data sources that identified problems to inform providers of their progress toward guideline practices and benchmark performance.

The cardiovascular project differs from current PRO activities in that it monitors risk-adjusted outcomes, profiles care against guidelines to identify repetitive patterns that might not merit action in any one case, and seeks to move average care toward best practices rather than just detecting gross errors. In early 1993, two or three PROs will begin pilot projects that will run for about 2 years; other PROs will start later in 1993.

The first two national projects emphasize communication with the hospital and its medical staff rather than the individual physician because: (1) hospitals are more likely than individual physicians to have enough patients for meaningful pattern analysis, (2) many problems within hospitals reflect hospital-level processes rather than failures of individual physicians, and (3) accreditation standards[24] require that hospitals have an infrastructure that can respond to the kind of data PROs will deliver. In future projects (possibly, for example, an effort to improve preventive services), PROs may work directly with physicians.

EXTENDING THE MODEL

There are a number of ways to extend this model.

Example 1

A forthcoming guideline on management of prostatic hypertrophy may say that intravenous pyelography (IVP) is not routinely necessary before transurethral resection of the prostrate. Transurethral resection of the prostate is an extremely common procedure for the Medicare population, IVPs are very commonly done, and there are appreciable risks and costs associated with unnecessary IVPs. Neither denying coverage for "routine" IVPs nor preauthorizing every IVP appears practical. The more feasible option is to promulgate the guidelines, translate them into the PCAS, and have PROs analyze the NCH and the UCDS data to identify regions, states, localities, hospitals, and physicians with high rates of IVP prior to routine transurethral resection of the prostate. This strategy would be followed by increasingly energetic education and corrective action at the appropriate levels. Comparing outcomes for patients in areas with high and low rates of IVPs could test whether patients in areas with low rates did at least as well as those in areas with high rates. Such information would be helpful to providers who are asked to change their clinical practices.

Example 2

Carotid endarterectomy rates vary widely, many of these procedures are thought to be unnecessary, and unnecessary procedures are both expensive and dangerous to patients. HCFA could implement preauthorization using criteria from expert panels, but there is considerable uncertainty regarding a number of important indications for endarterectomy, and the literature indicates that small-group consensus panels have difficulty reaching unanimity.[25]

HCFA could also use surveillance of rates and "jawbone" groups with high rates, using averages as norms (this is the approach of the successful Maine Medical Assessment Foundation[26]). This approach does not, however, give physicians any clear theory of which procedures are appropriate. Given these problems, the conservative approach might be to develop PCAS algorithms to identify those indications that are generally agreed to be inappropriate as well as indications that are agreed to be doubtful. Follow-up would emphasize feedback regarding indications that are not well supported and targeted education and continued monitoring regarding indications that are inappropriate.

CHANGING ATTITUDES

Although HCQII presents daunting technical problems, the greatest challenge is overcoming years of distrust between PROs and physicians. The HCQII can only reach its potential if HCFA, the PROs, and the hospital and medical communities work together, because fear and adversarial relations will cripple quality improvement efforts. One of the basic themes of HCQII is to use practice guidelines to define a set of objectives around which HCFA, PROs, hospitals, and physicians can work together. Successes achieved in working together will be much more persuasive than good words in overcoming distrust and in establishing collaboration based on a real community of interest.

HCFA has taken some steps to support collaboration by (1) resting HCQII increasingly on published guidelines rather than on internal decision making; (2) working with physician, hospital, consumer, and other groups to refine methods, as illustrated by work with the American Medical Association and the PROs on PCAS refinement; (3) making the process more open by, for example, making the UCDS/PCAS software freely available to interested parties even though it is still developmental; (4) planning the cardiovascular project in close consultation with the health care community; (5) using pattern analysis in the cardiovascular project without subjecting individual cases to routine physician review; and (6) addressing major historical irritants such as the Quality Intervention Plan, review of specialists by nonspecialists, and appeals for quality decisions in the new PRO contracts.

We have some evidence on effective strategies for changing medical practice. Exhortation and publishing consensus documents appear to achieve little[27]; changing payment policy is quite effective[28]; face-to-face contacts with professionals and opinion leaders appear to occupy a middle ground.[29] However, in every case, change is easier when concepts are backed up with specific information on how an individual's practices and outcomes conform to those in the community. There is strong reason to believe that many physicians will become interested participants in HCQII if PROs can give them reliable, useful data about their practices. This requirement for reliable data will strongly influence the pace at which the HCQII can go forward.

There are other obstacles. Projects in which physician groups have persuaded a community of colleagues to examine and change their practices remain the exception rather than the rule, despite impressive exceptions.[30-35] Pattern analysis will initially be less confrontational than analyzing individual cases, but in the long run, providers may not be happier to be told that their clinical practices need systematic change than that they are sometimes wrong.

The HCQII has a much stronger educational and collaborative emphasis than traditional case review, but HCFA will still be responsible for imposing sanctions if education fails. In addition, there will be tensions because traditional case review will continue in parallel with the new initiative for some years and because many physicians will fear that HCFA's only real goals are to save money and get publicity. Finally, there will be stress over the unresolved issue of how information is made public.

CONTINUED DEVELOPMENT

The topic conditions for the cardiovascular project were selected using five rules intended to maximize the likelihood of improving care for Medicare beneficiaries: (1) the conditions are frequent in the Medicare population; (2) guidelines for care are well defined and widely accepted; (3) methods are available to measure outcomes and risk factors; (4) conforming with guidelines does not require unavailable skills or resources; and (5) there is a substantial, clinically important difference between guidelines and actual practice, and there is substantial variation in outcomes.

These same criteria will be used, in close consultation with the health care community, to design future national projects.

Although the implementation of HCQII may seem very rapid at times, full implementation will take years. In the next four years, PROs will devote comparable resources to the HCQII and to case review. The HCQII is a new project that is still evolving rapidly, and matching the pace of implementation to the development of infrastructure is essential. Regular checkpoints and pilot projects are part of the implementation plan to assure, for example, that UCDS abstraction is reliable and efficient and that PCAS algorithms are sensitive and specific. Use of UCDS will be phased in as criteria are met at each checkpoint.

If HCFA's commitment to quality management is to be convincing, we must also continuously evaluate and refine the HCQII. Ongoing evaluation will take three forms:

1. HCFA will monitor reliability of PCAS abstraction and the sensitivity and specificity of the PCAS in selecting cases for physician review. HCFA will also track how well monitoring patient care and outcomes identifies significant remediable problems.
2. The monitoring tools that are an integral part of the HCQII will permit HCFA to measure the extent to which practice patterns move closer to the guidelines that HCQII adopts.
3. In a more traditional epidemiologic analysis, we can determine whether changes in mortality, morbidity, and cost are associated with HCQII interventions or with the changes in processes of care.

The HCQII is an ambitious effort to make the PRO program a more effective force in improving care. Success will depend on our ability to solve technical problems, our ability to implement a complex reform neither too quickly nor too slowly, and, most of all, the ability of HCFA, PROs, physicians, and hospitals to work together to improve care.

NOTES

1. J. Wennberg and A. Gittelsohn, Variations in Medical Care Among Small Areas, *Sci Am* 246 (1982): 120–135.

2. M.R. Chassin, R.H. Brook, R.E. Park, et al. Variations in the Use of Medical and Surgical Services by the Medicare Population, *N Engl J Med* 314 (1986): 285–290.

3. Office of Research and Demonstrations, Health Care Financing Administration, *Health Care Financing Special Report: Hospital Data by Geographic Area for Aged Medicare Beneficiaries: Selected Procedures, 1986* (Washington, DC: Health Care Financing Administration, U.S. Dept of Health and Human Services, 1990).

4. US Dept of Health and Human Services, *Medicare Hospital Information 1992* (Washington, DC: US Dept of Health and Human Services; 1992).

5. E.L. Hannan, H. Kilburn, Jr, J.F. O'Donnell, et al., Adult Open Heart Surgery in New York State: An Analysis of Risk Factors and Hospital Mortality Rates, *JAMA* 264 (1990): 2768–2774.

6. G.T. O'Connor, S.K. Plume, E.M. Olmstead, et al., A Regional Prospective Study of In-Hospital Mortality Associated with Coronary Artery Bypass Grafting, *JAMA* 266 (1991): 803–809.

7. S.V. Williams, D.B. Nash, N. Goldfarb, Differences in Mortality from Coronary Artery Bypass Graft Surgery at Five Teaching Hospitals, *JAMA* 266 (1991): 810–815.

8. Hannan, et al., Adult Open Heart Surgery.

9. R.W. DuBois, W.H. Rogers, J.H. Moxley, D. Draper, R.H. Brook, Hospital Inpatient Mortality: Is It a Predictor of Quality?, *N Engl J Med* 317 (1987): 1674–1679.

10. K.L. Kahn, W.H. Rogers, L.V. Rubenstein, et al., Measuring Quality of Care with Explicit Process Criteria Before and After Implementation of the DRG-Based Prospective Payment System, *JAMA* 264 (1990): 1969–1973.

11. L.V. Rubenstein, K.L. Kahn, E.J. Reinisch, et al., Changes in Quality of Care for Five Diseases Measured by Implicit Review, 1981 to 1986, *JAMA* 264 (1990): 1974–1979.

12. R.L. Goldman, The Reliability of Peer Assessments of Quality of Care, *JAMA* 267 (1992): 958–960.

13. H.R. Rubin, W.H. Rogers, K.L. Kahn L.V. Rubenstein, R.H. Brook, Watching the Doctor-Watchers: How Well Do Peer Review Organization Methods Detect Hospital Care Quality Problems, *JAMA* 267 (1992): 2349–2354.

14. Institute of Medicine, Division of Health Care Services, *Medicare: A Strategy for Quality Assurance* (Washington, DC: National Academy Press, 1990).

15. J.M. Juran, *Juran on Planning for Quality* (New York, NY: The Free Press, 1988).

16. E. Deming, *Out of the Crisis* (Cambridge, Mass: Massachusetts Institute of Technology Center for Advanced Engineering Study, 1982).

17. G. Laffel and D. Blumenthal, The Case for Using Industrial Quality Management Science in Health Care Organizations, *JAMA* 262 (1989): 2869–2873.

18. D.M. Berwick, Continuous Improvement As an Ideal in Health Care, *N Engl J Med* 320 (1989): 53–56.

19. S.B. Kritchevsky and B.P. Simmons, Continuous Quality Improvement: Concepts and Applications for Physician Care, *JAMA* 266 (1991): 1817–1823.

20. U.S. Dept of Health and Human Services, *Medicare Hospital Information*.

21. H. Krakauer, R.C. Bailey, K.J. Skellan, et al., Evaluation of the Model Used by the Health Care Financing Administration for the Analysis of Mortality Following Hospitalization, *Health Serv Res* (In Press).

22. U.S. Department of Health and Human Services, *Medicare Hospital Information*.

23. Joint Commission on Accreditation of Healthcare Organizations, *AMH: Accreditation Manual for Hospitals* (Oakbrook Terrace, Ill: Joint Commission on Accreditation of Healthcare Organizations, 1992).

24. Joint Commission, *Accreditation Manual*.

25. R.E. Park, A. Fink, R.H. Brook, et al., Physician Ratings of Appropriate Indications for Six Medical and Surgical Procedures, *Am J Public Health* 76 (1986): 766–772.

26. R.B. Keller, D.N. Soule, J.E. Wennberg, D.F. Hanley, Dealing with Geographic Variations in the Use of Hospitals: The Experience of the Maine Medical Assessment Foundation Orthopaedic Surgery Study Group, *J Bone Joint Surg Am* 72 (1990): 1286–1293.

27. J. Kosecoff, D.E. Kanouse, W.H. Rogers, L. McCloskey, C.M. Winslow, R.H. Brook, Effects of the National Institutes of Health Consensus Development Program on Physician Practice, *JAMA* 258 (1987): 2708–2713.

28. Office of Research and Demonstrations, Health Care Financing Administration, *Report to Congress: Impact of the Medicare Hospital Prospective Payment System: 1986 Annual Report*, Health Care Financing Administration Publication 03281 (Washington, DC: US Dept of Health and Human Services, 1988).

29. A.L. Greer, The Two Cultures of Biomedicine: Can There Be Consensus? *JAMA* 258 (1987): 2739–2740.

30. O'Connor, et al., A Regional Prospective Study.

31. Williams, et al., Differences in Mortality.

32. Berwick, Continuous Improvement.

33. Keller, et al., Dealing with Geographic Variations.

34. S.E. Kellie and J.T. Kelly, Medicare Peer Review Organization Preprocedure Review Criteria: An Analysis of Criteria for Three Procedures, *JAMA* 265 (1991): 1265–1270.

35. D.M. Berwick, A.B. Blanton, J. Roessner, *Curing Health Care: New Strategies for Quality Improvement* (San Francisco, Calif: Jossey-Bass, 1990).

Appendix C. Clinical Performance Standards

DEFINITIONS OF DIMENSIONS OF PERFORMANCE

I. Doing the Right Thing

The **efficacy** of the procedure or treatment in relation to the patient's condition
> The degree to which the care/intervention for the patient has been shown to accomplish the desired/projected outcome(s)

The **appropriateness** of a specific test, procedure, or service to meet the patient's needs
> The degree to which the care/intervention provided is relevant to the patient's clinical needs, given the current state of knowledge

II. Doing the Right Thing Well

The **availability** of a needed test, procedure, treatment, or service to the patient who needs it
> The degree to which appropriate care/intervention is available to meet the patient's needs

Source: Copyright 1993 by the Joint Commission on Accreditation of Healthcare Organizations, Oakbrook Terrace, IL. Reprinted with permission from the 1994 *Accreditation Manual for Hospitals*.

The **timeliness** with which a needed test, procedure, treatment, or service is provided to the patient

> The degree to which the care/intervention is provided to the patient at the most beneficial or necessary time

The **effectiveness** with which tests, procedures, treatments, and services are provided

> The degree to which the care/intervention is provided in the correct manner, given the current state of knowledge, in order to achieve the desired/projected outcome for the patient

The **continuity** of the services provided to the patient with respect to other services, practitioners, and providers, and over time

> The degree to which the care/intervention for the patient is coordinated among practitioners, among organizations, and over time

The **safety** of the patient (and others) to whom the services are provided

> The degree to which the risk of an intervention and the risk in the care environment are reduced for the patient and others, including the health care provider

The **efficiency** with which services are provided

> The relationship between the outcomes (results of care) and the resources used to deliver patient care

The **respect and caring** with which services are provided

> The degree to which the patient or a designee is involved in his/her own care decisions and to which those providing services do so with sensitivity and respect for the patient's needs, expectations, and individual differences

Appendix D. Glossary of Terms

Agency for Health Care Policy and Research (AHCPR): eighth agency of the Public Health Service whose purpose is to conduct and support research with respect to the outcomes, effectiveness and appropriateness of health care services and procedures in order to identify the manner in which diseases, disorders and other health conditions can most effectively be prevented, diagnosed, treated, and managed clinically. (Omnibus Budget Reconciliation Act of 1989.)

Capitation: a set amount of money received or paid out, based on membership rather than on service delivered, usually expressed in units or per member per month (PMPM).

Cause and Effect Diagram (Fishbone, Ishikawa): is used to depict causes of a problem and to group them according to categories, i.e.—method, manpower, material, and machinery.

Continuous Quality Improvement (CQI): approach to quality management that builds upon traditional quality assurance methods by emphasizing the organization and systems; focuses on "process" rather than the individual; recognizes both internal and external "customers"; promotes the need for objective data to analyze and improve processes.

Control Charts: are run charts with statistically determined upper and lower limits.

Cost of Quality: the cost of quality is the expense of not doing the right things right the first time.

Critical Path: defines the optimal sequence and timing of intervention by health care practitioners for a particular diagnosis or process.

Customer: anyone who gets the results of another person's work.

Diagnosis-Related Groups (DRGs): a system of classifying an inpatient stay into groups for purposes of payment. DRGs may be primary or secondary and an outlier classification also exists. This is the form of reimbursement that HCFA uses to pay hospitals for Medicare recipients. Also used by a few states for all payors and by some private health plans for contracting purposes.

Effectiveness: concerns the level of benefit when services are rendered under ordinary circumstance by average practitioners for typical patients.

Efficacy: reflects the level of benefit expected when health care services are applied under ideal circumstance.

Efficiency: cost of resources—money, effort, and waste—used to attain specified objectives.

Empowerment: employee involvement and motivation; the assignment of "ownership" of a process to an employee; enabling employees to assume authority over their practice.

Flow Charts: are visual representations of the steps in a process.

FOCUS-PDCA®: strategy that helps build knowledge of process, customer, and small-scale improvement, using the scientific method. Acronym meaning: Find a process to improve, Organize a team that knows the process, Clarify current knowledge of the process, Understand sources of process variation, Select the process improvement, Plan the improvement, Do the improvement, collect data, and analyze data, Check and study the results, Act to hold the gain and to improve the process.

Generic Screen: review of display of medical records that utilizes criteria that apply to all patients, regardless of source or persons responsible for care ordered or given.

Health Maintenance Organization (HMO): prepaid organization that provides health care in return for a preset amount of money on a per-member-per-month basis.

Histograms: are used to measure the frequency with which something occurs.

Independent Practice Association (IPA): an organization under contract with a managed care plan to deliver services. The IPA in turn contracts with individual providers to provide the services, either on a capitation basis or on a fee-for-services basis.

Managed Care: the provision of comprehensive integrated services, usually by a single entity, coordinated by a primary care provider, and paid for with capitated funds.

Monitoring: the planned, systematic, and ongoing collection, compilation, and organization of data about an indicator of the quality and/or appropriateness of an important aspect of care, and the comparison of those data to a prescheduled level of performance (threshold for evaluation) to determine the need for evaluation (Joint Commission definition).

Outcomes Management: a national program in which clinical standards and guidelines are systematically based on patient outcomes.[1]

Pareto Charts: are simple bar charts used after data collection to rank causes so that priorities can be assigned. Their use gives rise to the 80-20 rule that 80 percent of the problems stem from 20 percent of the causes.

Point-of-Service Plan: a plan where members do not have to choose how to receive services until they need them. A common example is a simple PPO, where members receive greater coverage if they use preferred providers than if they choose not to do so.

Practice Guidelines: systematically developed statements to assist practitioner and patient decisions about appropriate care for specific clinical circumstances.

Preferred Provider Organization (PPO): a plan that contracts with independent providers at a discount for services. The panel is limited in size and usually has some type of utilization review system associated with it. A PPO may be risk-bearing, like an insurance company, or may be no-risk-bearing, like a physician-sponsored PPO that markets itself to insurance companies or self-insured companies via an access fee.

Process: all the tasks directed at accomplishing one particular outcome grouped in sequence.

Quality Assessment: the measurement of the level of quality at some point in time with no effort to change or improve the level of care.

Quality Assurance: the measurement of the level of care provided (assessment) and, when necessary, mechanisms to improve it.

Reliability: reproducibility of the findings.

Run (trend) Charts: show the results of a process chart over a period of time.

Scattergrams: illustrate the relationship between two variables, such as height and weight.

Severity of Illness: a term used to describe the acuity of a patient's condition from clinical evaluation and evidence.

Statistical Process Control (SPC): statistical techniques that monitor and help control the quality of process characteristics.

Supplier: individual or entity that furnishes input to a process (i.e., person, department, organization, educational institution, etc.).

System: a group of related processes.

Team Building: act of bringing together a cross section of individuals who are related to the process in question; occurs in four stages: (1) *forming*, initial phase of becoming comfortable with team members; (2) *storming*, determining actions to take; (3) *norming*, beginning support stage; no more competition; significant time and energy spent on project at hand; and (4) *performing*, group becomes cohesive; there is unity of purpose; group works effectively to accomplish task.

Team, Quality Improvement: individuals (cross-department/functions/services) knowledgeable about a particular aspect of care or service and commissioned to improve a *process* that has been identified as requiring attention.

Threshold: a pre-established level, attainment of which triggers an intensified review of a specific component of care.

Trending: the evaluation of data collected over a period of time for the purpose of identifying patterns or changes.

Validity: ability to measure what is purported to be measured; a measure of the extent to which an observed situation reflects the real situation.

Variation: anything that causes a process to deviate from acceptable standards. Sources of variation in a patient care process include materials, machines, methods, manpower, and management. Two types of variation: (1) special cause variation, assignable to specific cause(s) and arises because of special circumstances, and (2) common cause variation, due to the process or system and produced by interactions of variables of that process.

NOTES

1. P. Ellwood, Outcomes Management: A Technology of Patient Experience, *New England Journal of Medicine* 318 (1988): 1551.

Index

3